A
Desert
Gardener's
Companion

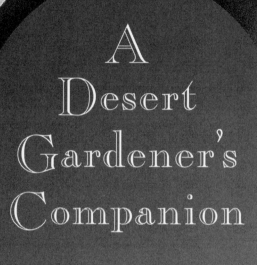

A Desert Gardener's Companion

Kim Nelson

RIO NUEVO PUBLISHERS
Tucson, Arizona

With thanks to
Dorothy McLaughlin and Barbro Huth
for inspiration

Rio Nuevo Publishers
an imprint of
Treasure Chest Books
P.O. Box 5250
Tucson, AZ 85703-0250
(520) 623-9558

First edition

ISBN 1-887896-20-1

Editor: Ronald J. Foreman
Cover and Book Design: Paul Mirocha
Production: William Benoit, Simpson & Convent

Printed in Canada

10 9 8 7 6 5 4 3 2

Contents

January

CHECKLIST 2

Week 1

MAIL ORDER CATALOGS 3

KEEPING A GARDEN JOURNAL 4

PRUNING TREES AND SHRUBS 5

PRUNING DECIDUOUS TREES 7

WATER: HOW MUCH AND HOW OFTEN? 10

Week 2

CHRISTMAS TREES 12

POINSETTIAS 13

HOUSEPLANT CARE 14

HOUSEPLANT PESTS 16

FICKLE, UNPREDICTABLE
JANUARY WEATHER 17

Week 3

SELECTING AND PLANTING DECIDUOUS
FRUIT TREES 18

BARE-ROOT ROSES 20

Week 4

CREATING ANNUAL FLOWER AND
VEGETABLE BEDS 24

FERTILIZING FLOWER AND VEGETABLE
GARDENS 26

PRUNING GRAPES 27

SELECTION AND CARE OF GARDEN TOOLS 29

Week 5

BUMPER CROPS FROM WINTER VEGETABLE
BEDS 31

THE BEAUTY OF ASPARAGUS
IN THE GARDEN 32

YOUR GARDEN'S GENERAL CHECKUP 34

AUTOMATIC IRRIGATION SYSTEMS 36

February

CHECKLIST 38

Week 6

STARTING FROM SEED
FOR SPRING PLANTING 39

WINTER CARE OF ROSES 42

CITRUS INSPECTION 43

Week 7

PLANTING NEW GRAPEVINES 46

FERTILIZING DECIDUOUS FRUIT TREES 47

ONION SETS 48

SPEAKING OF BULBS 49

Week 8

A BASIL PRIMER 50

XERISCAPING 51

Week 9

HARDSCAPE IDEAS 56

FERTILIZATION AND IRRIGATION:
ROSES, LAWNS, GRAPES 57

A QUICK BIT OF ANNUAL COLOR 59

PLANNING FUTURE LANDSCAPE PROJECTS 60

March

CHECKLIST 62

Week 10

A JUMP-START ON THE VEGETABLE BED 63

A CITRUS SYNOPSIS 64

Week 11

A SUNFLOWER HOUSE 72

SIMPLE YET SOPHISTICATED
COMMON SUNFLOWER 74

THE LUXURIANT SPLENDOR OF
TEXAS MOUNTAIN LAUREL 75

CARING FOR PECAN TREES 77

Week 12

THINNING FRUIT TREES 80

PROPAGATING CACTI AND SUCCULENTS 81

FABULOUS FIGS 85

Week 13

INSECTS IN THE GARDEN 86

BENEFICIAL INSECTS 87

COMMON PESTS 89

April
CHECKLIST   92
Week 14
FINALLY FROST FREE   93
THE ANTS RETURN   94
INTENSIVE PLANTING OF WARM-SEASON
   VEGETABLES   95
READY TO FERTILIZE   98
MANURE: IS IT SAFE IN THE GARDEN?   99
Week 15
ANNUALS FLOWERS FROM SEED   99
BY THE LIGHT OF THE SILVERY MOON   104
Week 16
THE DESERT COTTAGE GARDEN   106
GROWING GOURDS   111
Week 17
CREATING A STANDARD TOPIARY   113
THE DROUGHT-TOLERANT TREASURE
   CALLED PENSTEMON   115

May
CHECKLIST   118
Week 18
MUCH TO DO IN MAY   119
THE SAGE GARDEN   121
Week 19
TOMATO TROUBLES   123
CHILE PEPPERS   125
Week 20
THE SOUTHWEST HERB GARDEN   126
Week 21
JERUSALEM SAGE   135
SOIL MIXES   136
PESTS AND MORE PESTS   137
Week 22
CONTAINER GARDENING   139

June
CHECKLIST   144
Week 23
ACCENT PLANTS IN THE GARDEN   145
HOT! HOT! HOT!   147

Week 24
CREATING A DESERT OASIS WITH PALMS   150
THE STATELY SAGUARO   153
WATER: A CONSTANT DESERT ISSUE   154
Week 25
MELONS AND BEANS   155
PERSISTENT PESTS   155
Week 26
A SUMMER PLANTING FRENZY   158
EUPHORBIAS   161

July
CHECKLIST   164
Week 27
A NATIVE AMERICAN VEGETABLE GARDEN   165
Week 28
YOUR GARDEN DURING MONSOON   168
PROTECTING PLANTS FROM
   THE SUMMER SUN   171
SUMMER PESTS AND PARASITES   172
Week 29
WATER HARVESTING   174
TEXAS ROOT ROT AND OTHER FUNGI   176
DETHATCHING BERMUDA GRASS   179
Week 30
AN INDOOR VEGETABLE GARDEN   180
GROWING SPROUTS   182
GENERAL JULY CHORES   184

August
CHECKLIST 186
Week 31
AN INDOOR HERB GARDEN   187
COMPOSTING: MAKING YOUR OWN
   BLACK GOLD   190
TENDING THE VEGETABLE AND HERB BEDS 193
Week 32
THE BUTTERFLY GARDEN   194
CREOSOTE   197
Week 33
IRIS   198
SWARMING ANTS AND TERMITES   203

Week 34
   Palo verde trees   203
   Late August activities   206

September
   Checklist   208
Week 35
   Beautiful bulbs for the desert   209
   Rose rejuvenation   213
Week 36
   Winter vegetable beds   215
   Revisiting the herb garden   217
   Back to landscaping   219
   Poolside plantings   220
Week 37
   Edible landscape plants   222
   Poisonous plants   225
Week 38
   Wildlife in the garden   227
   The Hummingbird garden   232
Week 39
   Mesquite   235
   Sennas and jojobas   237
   Still more pests   240

October
   Checklist   242
Week 40
   'Dig-less' vegetable gardening   243
   Those black nursery pots   245
   Fall and winter color   246
Week 41
   What to plant in October   250
   Preparations for cooler weather   253
   A green winter lawn   254
Week 42
   Erosion control   256
   Pomegranate   259
Week 43
   Wildflowers   263
   Ripening citrus   267
   Eucalyptus   268
   Pruning palm trees   271

November
   Checklist   272
Week 44
   Amaryllis   273
   Forcing bulbs   276
Week 45
   Pressing flowers and foliage   279
Week 46
   Preparing for first frost   280
   Problem-solving in the vegetable
      garden   283
Week 47
   Sharing the bounty   285
   Sweet potato houseplants   285
   Bird feeders and bat houses   287
Week 48
   Harvesting pecans   288
   The asparagus bed   289
   Botanical wreaths   289

December
   Checklist   294
Week 49
   Gifts for the gardener   295
   Indoor holiday plant care   297
   Catalogs for January perusal   299
Week 50
   Gifts from your garden   300
   December flowerbeds   305
   Winter lawn care   306
Week 51
   Winter weed control   307
   Cold frames, hot beds,
      and greenhouses   308
Week 52
   Pines in the desert landscape   310
   Interplanting the rose bed   313
   Cleaning up for the New Year   316

Botanical Nomenclature   318

Plant Index   320

Subject Index   326

A Desert Gardener's Companion

January

- Cover citrus, succulents, and landscape plants in p.m.
- Recycle Christmas tree
- Plant living Christmas tree
- Harvest ripe citrus
- Fertilize overseeded Bermuda lawn
- Plant and prune roses
- Prune landscape trees and shrubs
- Prune grapes and deciduous fruit trees
- Rejuvenate houseplants
- Study seed catalogs
- Watch for gray aphids
- Control winter weeds

January

Mail order catalogs

Catalogs brimming with plants and seeds should be the first order of business on the January calendar of an avid gardener. Although there are many well-stocked nurseries in my southern Arizona community, I'm often unable to locate all the varieties to suit my fancy. Mail order companies fill this void, and perusing their wish books is a delicious ritual. Settling into a comfortable chair with a cup of tea and a generous stack is a lovely way to spend a chilly January afternoon. I take notes, dog-ear pages, and dream of my garden in springtime.

High Country Gardens, Plants of the Southwest, and Native Seeds/SEARCH are three notable catalog companies that offer an abundance of desert-adapted annuals, perennials, flowers, and vegetables. With these references, a notebook, and a set of colored pencils, I can create a paper rendition of what the garden could look like in a few months. It is a good idea to plot and plan this way. Sketch your vision of the garden in full bloom, verifying that you have selected the correct colors, sizes, and combinations. Using the printed plant descriptions, you can design a cutting garden, a perennial bed, a potager, or an entire desert landscape without setting foot outdoors.

Desert gardeners must remember to look at catalogs, and other reference sources with a discerning eye because many of the gorgeously photographed annuals, perennials, fruits, and vegetables will languish in a harsh desert environment. Gardening in the desert is challenging enough without adding inappropriate varieties to the mix, so avoid seeds and plants that are not recommended for your local hardiness zone. Check zone maps and guidelines in each catalog. Pay close attention to the high and low temperatures individual plants can tolerate and make sure that everything you order is suitable for your specific zone. If not, cross it off the list and choose something else. Look for replacements with similar texture, color, or shape that will thrive in these challenging conditions. Take advantage of the experts' recommendations and buy or propagate only what you know will grow in your climate zone.

KEEPING A GARDEN JOURNAL

Katharine S. White, a long-time columnist for the New York Times, was an avid gardener who wrote extensively about her horticultural successes and failures. After her death, her husband, E. B. White, collected some of her unpublished writings and combined them in *Onward and Upward in the Garden*. For the desert gardener, these well-written musings provide inspirational entertainment but not practical instruction, as our conditions vary greatly from Ms. White's. That's precisely why it is important to keep notes on your own forays into the horticultural world. There is nothing more helpful for planning future gardens than documentation of past successes and failures.

A garden journal should be as individual and unique as the person who writes it and the land it describes. Some gardeners write paragraphs and stories, some make charts and graphs, and others make lists and checklists. Any of these methods works as long as the pertinent information is recorded. Note planting dates, specific variety names, and maturation time. Sketch out new beds in your journal and assure the correct selections and placement by drawing mature sizes to scale. I tend to overestimate the space available, but my journal sketches bring me back to reality.

I keep track of soil amendments and fertilizers as well as general watering information. I have learned a great deal about sources for plant material by recording the name of the company or garden center where I made my purchases. After going through several years of my garden journal, I realized that many of my failed plants had come from the same highly recommended nursery. Based on my own research and documentation, I learned a valuable lesson and I no longer frequent that establishment.

My journal is an eight and a half by eleven inch, faux-leather, stitched volume that will stand up to rain, misfired sprinklers, and my own negligence. I include sketches of each part of my garden, with common and botanical names identifying the location of each plant. When I replant annuals and vegetables, I make a dated sketch listing the seed and plant varieties I used so I can comment on their performance at harvest time. I note discrepancies between suggested maturation rates and those realized in my garden, as well as mature size and yield.

I compile running lists of plants I cannot live without as well as those I've purchased and planted. I carry the book into the garden each time I undertake a new project, and refer back to it whenever I purchase new seeds or plants. I take it to lectures and conferences, and even pull it out while watching television programs to write down something new. I jot down recipes that call for ingredients I grow and make pen and ink sketches of future possibilities.

My gardening journal is a rich historical synopsis of the evolution of my garden and of me. Through its pages I can recall not only the physical activity in the garden, but also the thoughts and emotions that led to that activity.

Pruning trees and shrubs

Thanks to the cold winter temperatures, deciduous trees and shrubs have lost their leaves and are dormant, which means that they are alive but not actively growing. Occasionally, in the lower elevations of the Southwest, winters can be so mild that plants don't go completely dormant. But whether they are entirely leafless or still have some fall-like foliage, this is the best time to prune.

Pruning allows you to create specific shapes and directly affects the quality and quantity of the flowers and fruits your trees and shrubs produce. It's also an important factor in maintaining general plant health and restricts plant growth. Most shade and accent trees, if properly selected for their sites, require minimal pruning. By keeping in mind natural characteristics, including height and spreading habits when making tree selections, shaping will entail nothing more than raising the bottom of the canopy, or ceiling, and removing crossed or wayward branches.

In order to remove branches, it is important to know a little bit about the tree's anatomy. The branch collar is a hardwood section between a branch and the trunk. It has a distinctly different appearance, often wrinkly or crackled, and contains a chemical that deters decay. The branch collar performs the vital function of preventing the progression of disease into the main body of the tree. The collar inhibits the spread of decay while the tree is in the process of shedding the branch. When pruning, it is important to cut flush with the outside of the branch collar and leave this natural protective device intact.

Use scissor-style, not anvil-cut, hand pruners for branches up to a half-inch in diameter. Anvil-cut tools are sharp on only one side and tend to crush plant tissue rather than make the clean cut associated with scissor-style tools. To remove crossing branches or those growing into the center of the tree, cut flush with the outside of the branch collar. If you are raising the height of the tree's ceiling, start with the lowest branches and work upward, removing no more than one third of the tree at one time. If you remove too many branches in a single pruning, the tree may become weakened and distressed. Lopping shears work best on thicker branches. If branches are several inches thick, a curved pruning saw, which cuts on the backward stroke, is the best tool. By removing no more than one third of the branches with each pruning it may take several years to raise the ceiling of the tree, but it will be healthy and longer-lived because of your care.

The most common type of pruning for deciduous shrubs is thinning out. When thinning out a shrub, remove no more than one third of the branches at the point where they meet the main stem or at the base of the plant. Thin out the oldest and tallest branches to stimulate fullness and new growth and to lower the plant's height. Never shear the entire plant to one height. This stimulates bushy new growth at the top of the plant, compounding the existing problem in the future and eventually leading to a woody base with new growth only on the tips of the branches. If properly thinned out, shrubs will keep full, natural shapes for many years.

To rejuvenate an old, overgrown or improperly pruned shrub, remove one third of its branches at the base of the plant. Begin with the tallest branches; making selections that will leave the shrub nicely shaped during the process. Next year at this time remove another third. Do the same the following year. By the end of the third year, the shrub will have a healthy, more appealing form that can be maintained by thinning out only a few branches every year thereafter.

PRUNING DECIDUOUS FRUIT TREES

Deciduous fruit trees require the most precise pruning of all landscape plants. Pruning stimulates shoot growth and maintains manageable height for easier harvest. It also improves structure and prevents unbalanced overgrowth that can become too weighty and lead to breakage. Removing overgrowth also effectively thins the crop and encourages larger fruit size.

In the desert Southwest, with its low humidity and intense sunlight, creating an open center is the best approach for pruning fruit trees. An open center provides better air circulation and allows you to easily determine height and shape. It also creates a beautifully shaped shade tree, as well as a food crop. Always keep the form and shape of the tree in mind. Your final result should be something that is pleasing to the eye, and an attractive accent to your garden.

Growing a tree is much like raising a child. To develop positive, life-long habits you must guide and train from the beginning. Immediately after tucking your tree into the ground, cut it back. If it is a single trunk with no branches, cut the top off so that it is only thirty inches from the ground. I know from personal experience how drastic this sounds. Some years ago, my husband left for work with five newly planted fruit trees swaying gracefully in the breeze, only to come home to bare sticks poking two and one half feet out of the ground. He was certain I'd killed the trees, and no amount of explanation could change his mind. He didn't renew his faith in my gardening until weeks later when several branches emerged just below the cut points and grew rapidly into attractively shaped trees.

If your sapling already has branches, select three or four that fit the following criteria: Each must form an angle greater than 45° from the trunk, they must be spaced 4–6 inches apart on the trunk, and they must be arranged on different sides of the trunk. Occasionally only two branches will fit these requirements. That's fine, go with those two. It's better to start out with fewer appropriately placed branches than to have branches too close together or coming out from the trunk at too close an angle. Once you have selected the best branches, prune them back to one-fourth their original length. Completely remove all other branches, cutting back to the branch collar. Last, prune the main trunk just above the base of the top branch. You're done. Pruning for year one is complete.

For older or mature fruit trees, the following simple guidelines will ensure success:

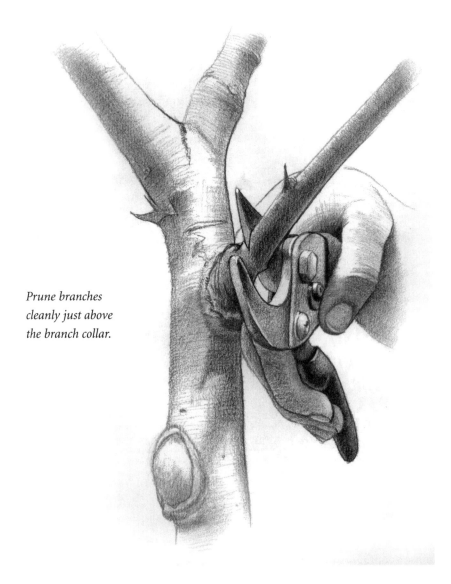

*Prune branches
cleanly just above
the branch collar.*

1. Prune annually. You will only make next year's job more difficult if you skip it this year. It is much easier to determine what must be removed when you are dealing with only one year's growth.

2. Remove broken limbs and dead, dying, or diseased wood. When removing infected or diseased wood, it is important to make the cut in healthy wood—beyond the point of infection—and to clean the tool blades with a ten-percent bleach solution after each cut to prevent the spread of disease.

3. Limbs should never touch one another. Remove one whenever this occurs, leaving the more desirably positioned branch.

4. If two limbs are parallel, the top limb will shade the lower one. Visually inspect each branch from the point at which it emerges from the trunk to its tip and consider whether it will eventually grow into an undesirable location. Taking future growth into consideration, remove the least desirable branch.

5. Remove any branches that grow into the center of the tree. If left, they will ultimately rub and damage other branches.

6. Trim the tips off last year's growth to a height that suits your needs. Consider appearance and harvesting ease. Remember: This will stimulate new shoot growth on those tips.

7. Water sprouts are shoots that grow straight up from older branches. Clean them out whenever they appear. If you catch them early enough, you can firmly grasp them in your gloved hand and pull sharply to remove. When they're too large for this treatment, cut them with hand pruners.

8. Remove suckers coming up from the rootstock as soon as you notice them. They take energy and nutrients from the tree, reducing the supply to fruiting branches. If allowed to grow uncontrolled, hardy root stock suckers can overtake the tree.

9. When pruning large, overgrown trees, remove no more than one third of the branches in a given year. Begin by pruning out the most delinquent branches: those that cross, rub, or have grown much too tall. Once they are gone, look at the tree from a distance to assess its current shape and form, and then imagine what it would look like with the removal of each remaining branch. This will help you to determine what to leave and what to prune away. Take out those branches that do not contribute to the desired

shape. Once this is done, remove any remaining suckers and water sprouts and prune several inches from the tips of the remaining fruiting branches.

Gardening advisors in years past often recommended the use of pruning paint. However, many university studies have proven that this practice is not beneficial. It may actually be detrimental to the plant's health by locking in potential pathogens and providing a dark, moist environment in which they can flourish. I recommend leaving the pruned site exposed to the dry desert air to heal on its own.

WATER: HOW MUCH AND HOW OFTEN?

How much to irrigate at this time of year depends on the timing and amount of winter rainfall your region has had. The Sonoran desert normally receives about half of its annual precipitation during the winter months, and the other half in summer. The Chihuahuan and Mojave deserts receive an even greater portion of their annual rainfall now, and correspondingly less in the summer. Normal is difficult to rely on in the desert, and some years will be wetter than others. During a wet winter, turn your irrigation system off and save precious water. Keep a watchful eye on your plants, looking for dull color and slight wilt. If these water-stress symptoms appear, turn your sprinkling system back on. When enduring a dry winter, leave your irrigation system on, but reduce watering frequency to accommodate for the season's lower temperatures.

Every gardener has a different landscape plan and a varying selection of plants in different types of soils. Every irrigation system must be unique to its location, components, and installation, making it impossible to suggest a single, precise watering schedule. There are overall irrigation guidelines that you should follow, however.

Lawns, color beds, herbs, and vegetables need water once or twice in a seven-day period. These plants have shallow root systems and will wilt and take on a gray cast if not irrigated enough. Watch for these signs and irrigate more frequently if necessary. If rain adequately soaks the ground within an irrigation cycle, you need not water.

Citrus and other evergreens, as well as palm trees and other hardy exotics, need a deep irrigation once every three or four weeks. Like the smaller plants in your garden, their color will dull and they will lose their naturally glossy sheen when in need of water. Be careful not to wait too long. You don't want leaves to curl, turn brown, and dry out or drop off. Even dormant plants in your landscape, though they are not supporting foliage, need water about once a month to keep their roots moist. Desert-adapted plants and natives usually do not need additional irrigation in the winter, although in the case of drought, one or two deep irrigations over the remainder of the winter would be beneficial.

A proper irrigation provides water to a depth of 3 feet for trees and 1½–2 feet for shrubs. A thorough watering for annuals, herbs, vegetables, and ground covers will reach a depth of twelve inches. Lawns require water to a depth of 8–10 inches. Check the depth of your irrigation beneath the canopies of shrubs and trees by forcing a soil probe into the ground following a regular watering cycle. A soil probe can be a product developed especially for this purpose. I use a piece of three-quarter-inch rebar. It is just as effective and much less expensive. I have also used a wooden dowel, although these tend to decay when exposed to the elements. The probe will go down fairly easily through moist soil and stop when you hit dry ground. If your irrigation has not provided water to the required depth, increase the length of time for each irrigation, but do not water more frequently. It is more beneficial for the plant to receive infrequent, deep irrigations rather than more frequent, shallow irrigations.

Succulents are an exception to the winter irrigation routine. When watered, succulents take up and store moisture in their fleshy leaves as insurance against future dry times. If the leaves are plump with water at the time of a freeze, this water expands and the walls of individual cells rupture, causing cellular death and damage to the plant. To protect succulents from this kind of damage, hold off on the water when below-freezing temperatures are forecasted.

Citrus trees also may need some extra attention if temperatures are predicted to drop below 28° for more than one hour. If the trees are young, they are more susceptible to serious frost damage because they have so little foliage to spare. When a freeze is expected, cover your citrus with an old sheet or similar fabric—not plastic. If at all possible, prop the sheeting so that it does not actually touch the leaves. Three or four PVC pipes or tree stakes pounded into the ground around the tree will support fabric above the foliage quite well. Additionally, a 40-watt bulb hung in the center of the tree, or a string of heat-producing Christmas lights draped within the branches, will provide warmth through the cold winter night. After sunrise, remove the cover and turn the lights off. Let the plant and surrounding soil soak up the day's heat in order to prepare for another cold night ahead.

CHRISTMAS TREES

WEEK 2

By the middle of January, those of us who celebrate Christmas are ready to take down holiday decorations and get our homes back to normal. If you have enjoyed a living tree this holiday season, it's time to get it out of the house and into the ground. An evergreen will survive the low-humidity warmth of our winter homes for a week or two, but beyond that length of time its health can be seriously impaired. Once you carry your tree out into the yard, hose it down from top to bottom with a hard jet of water. Reach into the interior of the tree and remove all of the loose, brown needles. As the pot drains, decide on the best place to plant your evergreen. Keep the tree's ultimate size in mind and choose a site that will allow it to grow to its full potential. You want to avoid future pruning that will affect the tree's natural form and beauty.

When you have selected a site, dig a hole only as deep as the root ball and about five times as wide. Gently remove the tree from the container, taking care not to disturb the root ball. If the roots are tightly packed or wrapped around the edges, cut through them four or five times with a sharp knife or razor. Place the tree in the hole and stand back. Look carefully to make sure its position and location are pleasing. When you're certain you have it in the right place, backfill the hole with the soil you originally removed. Do not add any amendments or fertilizer. Use only the native soil. Stomp the dirt to firm it up and build a doughnut shaped rim around the tree to create a watering well. Fill the well with water. When the water soaks in completely, add dirt to the obvious low spots. Tamp them down with a shovel or your shoe. Remember that the soil should be at the same level as it was in the can. Fill the well with water again and allow it to soak in thoroughly.

Keep the roots damp for the first couple of weeks. You may need to water every two or three days. Gradually increase the number of days between watering, with 10–14 days as your goal. Irrigate twice a month for the remainder of the first year. After that, your tree will require deep irrigation every three or four weeks and annual springtime fertilization.

If you had a cut evergreen for your Christmas, look for opportunities to recycle. If you have access to a chipper/shredder, pine makes excellent mulch around the base of landscape plants. Many cities and counties have recycling programs that chip the trees and use them as mulch on public lands. If these options are not available to you, cut your tree into manageable sizes and dispose of it properly. Do *not* burn your Christmas tree in a barbecue, fire pit, or fireplace. Pine trees contain volatile oils and are highly flammable.

POINSETTIAS

The poinsettias that graced holiday tables, entryways, and hearths are hybrids of evergreen perennials native to Mexico. With minimal care, they thrive indoors or outside in frost-free areas. To keep poinsettias indoors it's usually necessary to transplant them into a slightly larger container with good potting soil. The medium in which they were initially potted is usually low in nutrients and often without soil.

To transplant, water the plant thoroughly and remove it from its original container. Gently rough up the roots with your hands to encourage them to grow into the new soil. Place the plant in a pot with its drainage hole partially covered and a layer of fertile, new potting soil in the bottom. Fill the space surrounding the plant's root ball with additional potting soil and water well with a high-acid, water-soluble fertilizer such as Miracid. Some leaves may fall as the plant adjusts to its new container, but others will replace them if the plant is watered once a week with a weak solution of Miracid water and kept in a room with bright, indirect light. Don't let water sit in the pot's saucer and avoid sudden temperature changes as this, too, will cause the leaves to fall off. In late winter or early spring, cut the stems back to two buds and reduce watering.

For most of the year the plant will produce green leaves or bracts. To encourage the traditional red bracts for the next holiday season, you must simulate long nights beginning in early fall. Write a note on the calendar to put the plant in a dark closet every night for fourteen hours starting the first week of October. Move it back into the light each morning for ten hours.

13

Continue to water and fertilize weekly. By the middle of December, your poinsettia will wear the traditional bright red bracts for the holidays.

If you have a frost-free location in your garden that offers bright, indirect sunlight, your poinsettia will do well outdoors. These requirements usually relegate it to a corner on the patio, but it can be planted in a pot in other parts of the garden. Because it prefers more acidic conditions than our native desert soils offer, it rarely does well when planted directly in the ground. Follow the same guidelines as those for indoor plants and it could reach a height of ten feet by next winter.

Houseplant care

Because we live in close quarters with our houseplants and they are not exposed to outdoor elements, we often disregard their needs. Midwinter is a good time to give them an annual checkup to keep them looking their best. Examine the leaves and stems. Brown, dry leaf margins and dying lower leaves are signs of mineral buildup in the pot. Another warning is a white, powdery, alkaline residue building on the soil-line and pot edges. Thoroughly rinsing the soil will solve this problem. Put the plant, pot and all, in a bathtub or on the patio and run a gentle but steady stream of water through the soil. Allow the water to run for a minute or two so that it comes out the bottom of the pot, then set it out of direct sunlight to drain. When the water no longer drips through the drainage hole, return the pot to its proper place and fertilize the plant with a water-soluble fertilizer. Because our water is both hard and highly alkaline, it is wise to repeat this procedure every six months. Mark your calendar and check for the telltale signs and symptoms again in early June.

If your indoor plant has not grown in many months or appears lackluster, it may be time to pot up, i.e. transplant into a larger container. Immediately after watering your potted plant, gently pull it from the container and examine the root system. If thin, threadlike roots are emerging on the outside of the root ball or planting medium but few large roots are obvious, the plant can remain in the current container. If the roots are a solid mass, winding around the interior of the pot, growing out of the drainage hole, or over the soil line, it is time for a bigger pot. Most indoor plants are happiest moving up only one or two pot sizes. When choosing a new vessel select one that has a diameter no more than 2–3 inches larger than the original container. Depth is not as critical.

Put a pottery shard over the drain hole of the new pot and fill the bottom of the pot with enough fresh potting soil to allow you to place the root ball in the pot and maintain the existing soil line. After gently removing the plant from its original container, rough up the roots with your fingers or score the root ball three or four times with a sharp knife, cutting about one-quarter inch deep. Place it in the new pot and fill around the edges with additional potting soil. The plant should not sit higher or lower than it did in the original pot. When firmly planted, irrigate with a water-soluble fertilizer mixed according to product directions. Add more soil to the edges as it dries out and settles down.

If plants have outgrown their space in your home, you can judiciously prune them down to size. The rule of thumb is to remove no more than one third of the plant. Do not simply "top," or remove the upper section of the plant. This weakens it and destroys the natural form. Instead, look at the plant with an artist's eye and decide which branches or sections can be removed down to the soil line or trunk while maintaining an attractive shape. Make the cuts at the base or trunk with sharp, clean pruners. Wipe the blades with a ten-percent bleach solution after each cut to avoid transmitting disease.

While some experts recommend pruning the root ball, too, I find this unnecessary and sometimes detrimental. It is possible to damage roots that correspond to sections of the plant that you have left intact, which could result in dieback of the remaining plant. I recommend gently pulling large, winding roots away from the outside of the root ball and trimming them back by several inches. Following this sprucing up, repot your plant in its original or slightly larger container, adding new soil as needed. Give it a dose of complete fertilizer and it's set for another couple of years.

Now that your houseplants are potted up and pruned back, they are ready for a bath. Using clear water and a soft cloth, wipe the leaf surfaces of each plant. This will remove dust and small insects that hamper the plant's ability to transpire. Transpiration is the process whereby the plant transports nutrients from the soil through its stems and leaves, cools itself through evaporation, moves sugars and plant chemicals, and maintains turgor in its tissues.

Commercial "leaf shine" products are available, but can actually cause poor transpiration by clogging the small openings in the leaves, called stomata. If you keep a healthy plant clean and dust-free, it will shine on its own.

HOUSEPLANT PESTS

As you wipe down leaves, look for spider webbing, white flying insects, or other indications of pests. If you see any such evidence, spray tops and undersides with insecticidal soap, available at most garden centers. You also can make a safe, effective insecticide by combining one tablespoon of dishwashing liquid with a gallon of water and pouring the mixture into a spray bottle. Dawn brand liquid provides the best results, but others can be used as long as they are not lemon-scented. Occasionally, an infestation of white flies or spider mites will be so acute that insecticidal soap is ineffective. In this case any commercial product containing the organic, chrysanthemum-derived poison pyrethrum works well. A word of caution—even though these products are organic, they are still poisonous and require careful handling.

Another frequent problem in potted plants is the fungus gnat. This obnoxious little pest and his companions make their presence obvious by buzzing around your home much like fruit flies. They live and lay eggs in soil, feeding on the fungus that naturally grows there. Soap solutions and pyrethrum have little or no effect on fungus gnats, so the most efficient eradication is two or three consecutive waterings laced with rotenone. These organic pesticides come in liquid and powdered forms that you add to regular irrigation water. Carefully follow package instructions so that you dilute the concentrated poison to proper strength.

To ensure that clean, healthy, properly potted plants continue to do well for many years, fertilize regularly. I recommend one of three approaches to provide your houseplants with the nourishment they need to keep them healthy. 1) Mark your calendar to remind you to fertilize every other Saturday using the recommended strength of a water-soluble plant food. 2) Use one fourth of the recommended dilution every time you water. 3) Mix a time-released fertilizer, such as Osmocote, into the soil every 3–4 months.

January is a most variable month in the desert. It is not unheard of for daytime highs to climb into the 80s, nor is it impossible for nighttime temperatures to fall into the low 10s. While these two extremes don't usually take place in the same January, they do occur from year to year and your perennials will eventually be exposed to both. In addition to variable and extreme temperatures, moisture is unreliable and unpredictable.

January frequently is the wettest month of the winter rainy season. Many Januarys have experienced several inches of precipitation during the history of weather record keeping. This can be a month of flooding, running washes, and local emergencies. It also can be a month of deep irrigation and high water bills for gardeners whose plots of land receive nary a drop of rain. Who knows what to expect? During an El Niño season, the desert dweller can anticipate wetter than normal conditions. This means that an excess of six inches of rain will fall during the winter with much of it in January. Frequently, La Niña follows El Niño by a year. This nearly opposite weather phenomenon characteristically includes higher than normal winter temperatures and minimal winter rain. A thin blanket of January snow is not unusual in the desert Southwest. Although it quickly melts, snow adds additional stress to plants unsuited to harsh weather. Conversely, on those rare occasions when temperatures fail to climb and the snow sticks around for a while, it provides a layer of protection from the frigid air.

January's unpredictability persuades desert gardeners to continue to do what they always do—pay attention to the nightly news and the daily conditions. If temperatures below 28° are predicted, take precautions and cover frost-tender plants. If winter rains fail to develop, reconcile yourself to watering to supply the necessary moisture.

In addition to capricious temperatures and rainfall, January winds often wreak havoc on the desert Southwest. This is the most challenging element for me. My patience wears thin, like the leaf margins on my evergreens, if we have too many windy days in a row. Wind dehydrates everything outdoors. Potted plants need more frequent irrigation and the landscape requires additional water. A vegetable garden can become quite tattered if winds are strong and prolonged, and if combined with uncharacteristically high temperatures, the negative effects are doubled.

Wind. Rain. Sun. They are all part of the natural wonder of things. Sometimes their unpredictability becomes part of the challenge, part of the fun. In many ways, gardening is a game, a competition between the gardener and the elements. We have the advantage of learning the needs and requirements of the material we put in the ground, and we can make life easier on ourselves by choosing plants that will roll with the punches and survive the extremes. We can go a long way in stacking the lineup in our favor, but fickle, unpredictable January weather may still throw us a curve.

SELECTING AND PLANTING DECIDUOUS FRUIT TREES

WEEK 3 I've never lived without a garden that harbors at least two or three fruit trees. For me, few of life's pleasures compare with plucking fruit so ripe its burnished skin barely contains its color, juice, and flavor. Or sinking your teeth into the soft flesh, and enjoying the warmth of juice running down your arm and dripping off your elbow.

If you, too, harbor memories or fantasies like these, then it's time to invest in a crop-producing fruit tree of your own. Wandering the grounds of your favorite nursery or the aisles of the nearest discount store, you may be overwhelmed by the variety and availability of bare-root fruit trees. These are not citrus, but rather the pome and stone fruits—apples, pears, quince, apricots, peaches, and plums. Since these trees are deciduous, they are sold in winter with neither container nor soil.

Nurseries and garden centers usually carry many fruit tree varieties, each with specific characteristics and requirements. Base your selections on those requirements and the conditions that exist in your garden. Some varieties will not do well in the desert, but you can find them alongside the more suitable varieties in many stores. The most significant issue is the chill factor, defined as the number of hours below 45°, which prompt the opening of blossoms and sprouting of leaves. Many require more chilling hours than your garden receives in the average winter. Some areas in our region receive adequate nighttime lows for nearly all varieties. But in most of the desert Southwest, trees requiring more than four hundred chilling hours do not do well. Since this information is often absent from nursery labels, I am including the names of varieties that have attainable chilling requirements for most of our garden microclimates and are self-fruitful, meaning they don't require another tree for pollination. The varieties that do best in the desert Southwest are:

Apple: Anna, Ein Shemer, Golden Dorsett
Apricot: Castlebrite, Gold Kist, Katy
Fig: Black Mission, Kadota, White Mission
Peach: August Pride, Babcock, Desert Gold, Earligrande, Flordaprince,
    Midpride, Royal Gold, Tropic Snow or Sweet Ventura
Pear: Early Season (does only moderately well)
Plum: Santa Rosa, Satsuma
Pomegranate: Wonderful
Quince: Orange, Pineapple, Smyrna

As you choose fruit trees, remember that each one will need 15–20 feet of growing room and consider this in your landscape plan. If you don't have this much space, it is possible to keep them smaller with careful pruning; so anticipate annual pruning and how much you are willing to do. You must be faithful for the life of the tree, which is about fifteen years in the desert.

Planting a bare-root tree is simple. Dig a hole about two feet deep and two feet wide. Carefully remove the roots from their wrapping and spread them out. With clean, sharp pruners, cut away any evidence of infection, decay, or damage. Using the native soil, build a cone-shaped mound in the center of the hole and set the tree atop the cone, spreading the roots around the mound. Return the remaining soil to the hole, firming it as you go. Do not use any amendments or fertilizers. Make sure that the bud union, which is the slightly bulging point where the trunk is grafted onto rootstock, is above the ground. Prune the tree as suggested for year one. (See Week 2 pruning advice.) Water the tree thoroughly with a slow hose or bubbler. You must moisten the roots and all of the surrounding soil.

Water every 5–7 days until it is fully leafed out. You can then decrease watering to once every 7–10 days through spring and summer. Your ultimate goal is one deep irrigation every three or four weeks for the life of the tree. Becoming familiar with your tree's foliage and its appearance, both when well irrigated and when water stressed, is key to keeping it healthy. Learn the visual clues to its health and act when these clues are obvious. By closely observing the leaves on your tree on a regular basis, you'll soon recognize changes and their causes.

In addition to pruning and adequate irrigation, your tree will benefit from an annual application of dormant spray while completely dormant. Dormant sprays are horticultural oils that smother insects while they are spending the winter on the tree. Application is simple. Using a garden sprayer, drench the bark of the tree, avoiding the foliage of nearby plants. If you do hit other foliage, promptly wash it with a strong jet of water. Experts agree that this is the most important time of year to apply dormant oil, and some also suggest an application after the leaves fall in autumn.

20

BARE-ROOT ROSES

Roses are beautiful in the landscape as well as in the vase, but they are not the ideal plant for the desert. The most significant drawback in our hot, dry climate is the frequent deep irrigation they require to perform well. If you're not willing to do this, don't plant them. There is nothing more disheartening than a potentially beautiful garden stymied by insufficient water. Like fruit trees, roses require annual pruning. If they are to do well, you must learn how to prune and then do it. Roses also are susceptible to fungal disease, including powdery mildew, and infestations of aphids, and thrips. Watch for and treat each of these problems before they do too much damage. Roses need regular fertilization. They will either refuse to bloom or produce puny blossoms if unfertilized. I fertilize my rose garden every two weeks beginning in early March and continuing through October. If the months of July and August are particularly dry, I stop fertilizing until September, when I resume the twice-monthly cycle until the end of October.

While shopping for bare-root trees, you will undoubtedly see similarly packaged roses. For the same dormancy reasons, the bushes are ready for purchase and planting at this time of year. Roses abound in a profusion of colors and types. The labels alone will be your guides, since each bush currently looks like a tightly wrapped bundle of thorny sticks. There will be climbing roses, floribundas, grandifloras, hybrid perpetuals, hybrid teas, miniature roses, polyanthas, and shrub roses. While all types, if not all varieties, can be grown in the desert, floribundas and hybrid teas are the most successful. An exception to this rule is the Lady Banks rose, the cultivar type of the legendary Tombstone Rose. It thrives when planted in native soil, just like a desert-adapted plant. This variety is rarely available in bare-root form, and can be planted nearly any time of year. The other rose types require more special care.

Floribundas are vigorous growers that produce numerous medium-to-large blooms. These hardy plants blossom continuously from mid-April through October, slowing only in the peak of the heat. The aromatic blooms grow in clusters of several flowers per branch rather than single blossoms on a long stem. Flower size is directly related to soil fertility.

Hybrid teas are the most popular type of rose grown in the desert Southwest. They provide excellent cut flowers and add beautiful color to the landscape. Performing well in spring and fall, they commonly stop producing flowers during the hottest months. Like floribundas, they bloom best when fertilized on a regular schedule. Both floribundas and hybrid teas are available in a vast array of colors. I have suggested particular varieties within color categories, which have proven themselves sustainable in the desert.

Floribunda

White or white blend: Class Act, French Lace, Iceberg
Apricot or apricot blend: Amber Queen, Apricot Nectar, Cathedral
Yellow: Sunbright, Sun Flare
Yellow Blend: Circus, Judy Garland, Redgold, Summer Fashion
Orange blend or orange-red: Gingersnap, Impatient, Marina,
    Orangeade, Playtime
Red, dark red, or red blend: Europeana, Priscilla Burton, Showbiz
Pink or pink blends: Cherish, Gene Boerner, Neon Lights, Origami,
    Pleasure, Simplicity
Mauve: Angel Face, Deep Purple, Intrigue

Hybrid Tea

White or white blend: Fountain Square, Garden Party, Honor, Pristine,
    Sheer Bliss
Yellow: Celebrity, Gold Medal, Lanvin, Oregold
Yellow blend: Broadway, Peace
Apricot or apricot blend: Brandy, Just Joey, Lucille Ball, Summer Dream
Orange blend: Cary Grant, Veldfire

Orange-pink or orange-red: Ain't She Sweet, Fragrant Cloud, Touch
of Class
Light pink: Bride's Dream, Dainty Bess, Royal Highness
Dark pink: Elizabeth Taylor, Friendship, Miss All-American Beauty,
Perfume Delight
Pink blend: Chicago Pace, Color Magic, First Prize, Keepsake, Secret,
Sheer Elegance, Vision
Medium or dark red: Chrysler Imperial, Mister Lincoln, Olympiad
Red blend: Double Delight, Mikado, Milestone, Perfect Moment
Mauve or mauve blend: Paradise, Plum Crazy, Silverado

Preparing a rose bed is a major undertaking, but when properly done it will guarantee healthy bushes with rewarding bloom. While roses will grow in a wide range of soils, they do best in a loamy, organically rich environment. In our intensely hot summers, they also benefit from afternoon shade, so locate your rose garden on the east side of larger plants or structures. Avoid planting roses on steep slopes where water runs off before soaking in.

Begin your preparations by spreading a 6–8 inch layer of composted material over the entire planting area. On top of this, sprinkle both soil sulfur and a balanced fertilizer at two pounds each per hundred square feet. This means a ten foot by ten foot rose bed will require two pounds of soil sulfur and two pounds of balanced fertilizer. A balanced fertilizer will have three numbers, such as 5–10–5, on the label. With a rototiller or spade, till the soil to a depth of eighteen inches. Double digging is also an efficient method of tilling.

To double dig, visually divide your bed into parallel trenches. Remove the soil from the top 8–10 inches of the first trench and put it in a wheelbarrow or at the far end of the bed. Loosen the remaining soil in this trench to a depth of twelve inches. Moving to the next trench, dig out the upper 8–10 inches and throw it on top of the trench you just filled. Next, turn the lower twelve inches of the second trench. Continue double digging in this manner until you have progressed across the entire bed. Shovel the soil that you originally set aside into the last trench.

Now that the bed is completely tilled and organics are worked into the soil, smooth and level it with a tined rake and water it thoroughly. Keep it damp until planting time.

If you encounter caliche, hardpan, or heavy clay while preparing your bed, remove it completely. These gardening nuisances impede drainage and limit root development. In caliche-laden areas, knock drain holes through the cement-like material to allow excess water to escape. A caliche bar, sold at most home improvement and hardware stores, is the most effective tool for this job. I find it an invaluable tool when digging planting areas and tree holes, or tilling new beds. Thus far, it has been my wisest gardening investment.

Once the rose bed is completely prepared, you are ready to select bare-root plants. Look for moist, pliable roots and sturdy, disease-free canes. No part of the plant should be dark, shriveled, or dry. Nor should it be slimy or mushy. If you discover unhealthy roots after your purchase, return it immediately. In our harsh climate, you want only vigorous plant material. This also is why you should buy only No. 1 or No. 1½ field-grown plants. Anything else will be substantially weaker, lacking the vigor to quickly adapt and grow. When considering how many bushes to plant, plan to set them six feet apart, allowing three feet in all directions from the center of each plant. This is called planting on three-foot centers. Your bushes will fill that space nicely over a couple of seasons without crowding one another and contributing to powdery mildew problems.

After purchasing the appropriate number of plants from the recommended list, remove the plants from their packaging and moisten the roots. Dig a 12–15-inch hole for each plant and sprinkle a cup of phosphorous fertilizer, such as ammonium phosphate or bone meal, into the bottom of each hole. Refill with the original dirt so that the hole is just deep enough to accommodate the roots of the bush. Create a mounded soil cone in the center of the hole and spread the clean roots around the sloping sides. Make sure that the crown or graft point is at least two inches above the final soil line, after you have firmly filled the hole with the remaining soil.

After planting, build a well around the base of each plant. Slowly and carefully fill with water, making sure not to erode the sides of the wells. If the soil settles too much and a root section emerges, add more soil and pack it down. If the crown settles into the soil, gently lift the plant and fill in around it with additional soil. Keep the bed moist for two or three weeks until the roots are well established, watering every other day if necessary. Your bushes should exhibit growing buds within four or five weeks, indicating the beginning of the long and lovely desert rose season.

CREATING ANNUAL FLOWER AND VEGETABLE BEDS

WEEK 4 — When I speak of gardening, I include an entire range of plants and landscape elements, as well as their combinations and possibilities. If it grows on my plot of land, I consider it part of my garden. My garden is not a yard. A yard is a place for storing tools or junk or construction materials. Contractors have yards. Rental companies have yards. Dogs have yards. People have gardens.

A garden is one's own bit of land, a place to create a sense of home in the out-of-doors. Eden. Gardening requires labor, but it is never "just plain work." It is an act of creation—the creation of something wonderful. It is nurture and development, growth and encouragement. I realize that most people have a more simplified view of a garden. To many, it is just a fertile section of soil in which to grow vegetables, some flowers for cutting, and maybe a few herbs. Even for that view of a garden, I have a deep and long-lived respect, rooted in the knowledge that in the desert Southwest, this type of garden requires the greatest amount of care and preparation.

I have grown vegetables and flowers in many different ways. I have amended the native soil and planted right down in the earth, grown them in pots and boxes, and planted them on hills, in troughs, and in raised beds. All of these methods work. I find raised beds to be the most convenient and preferable method. The elevation of the bed keeps hungry desert critters out of my crops. At a raised height, the beds are easier to plant and harvest, an issue that is more relevant to me the older I get. I also like raised beds because they are attractive and add structure to the landscape. You can use almost anything for construction material. I have had beds made from scrap lumber, pressure treated boards, railroad ties, river rocks, concrete block, and stucco-covered block and mortar. I have even made beds out of discarded industrial metal shelving. Anything that will contain soil and water will work.

The height of a raised bed is an important and personal consideration. I prefer 16–24 inches in height, but a six-foot-tall friend wanted her beds built thirty-six inches high. It's a good idea to look around and experiment with height to determine what is best for you. Equally important is the width of the bed. It should be wide enough to hold a decent crop, yet not so wide as to limit access to any section. You want to be able to reach every plant without kneeling on or stepping into the bed, which leads to soil compaction and damaged plant material.

Regardless of what type bed you have, its location is most important. Vegetables and flowers like lots of sunshine. When selecting the place for your bed, make sure that the plot will get at least 6–8 hours of direct sunlight. It is also helpful to provide afternoon shade on scorching summer days. Beds on the east side of a wall or to the east of a deciduous tree are good. Some Native Americans planted their vegetables to the east of mesquite trees so that they were shaded on summer afternoons. When the mesquites dropped their leaves in the winter, the beds got a full day of sunshine. Those dropped leaves also added organic material to the soil.

After location, increased fertility is the most important element to success. You need to add organic material; aged manure, homemade compost, or commercial soil amendments are all good choices. To get started, spread a 4–6-inch layer of organic material over the entire planting area. Till it in using a rototiller or the double digging method described in Week 3. After tilling, sprinkle soil sulfur over the bed. You will need two to three pounds for every hundred square feet. You will also need to add a phosphorous fertilizer. The second number on fertilizer packaging indicates phosphorous content. Ammonium phosphate, bone meal, and a balanced, general-purpose fertilizer are all good sources of phosphorous. Follow label directions regarding the amount to use.

Once the soil sulfur and phosphorous have been applied, till the soil again to a depth of 8–10 inches. It is important to till thoroughly because phosphorous is immobile in the soil. It only serves as a nutrient to the roots that are in its direct vicinity. By tilling it into the soil, you are putting the fertilizer where your new plants will set down roots. This advance preparation guarantees their nourishment. After tilling, rake and smooth out the bed and water it deeply. Let your plot rest for a day or two.

After letting the garden bed settle, go back and re-rake it. Make sure that it is level and smooth so that your irrigation will be efficient. You don't want water to drain off or puddle in low spots. A level bed will ensure irrigation to all of the plants you grow. Soaker hoses, bubblers, or small sprays attached to a drip irrigation system work best. Individual drip emitters are not effective in this type of garden because all of the soil must receive moisture, not just a few circles throughout the bed. Test your irrigation method to make certain the entire bed receives adequate coverage. To do this, run the system for 10–15 minutes and then check the soil in several spots to assure that it is evenly moist. Wait for a week to plant your seeds and seedlings. Water every two or three days and correct high and low spots after each irrigation. Also check for and remove any weeds that pop up.

Fertilizing flower and vegetable gardens

Although many gardeners are just now planting flower and vegetable beds, others are reaping the rewards of seeds sown last season. Radishes, beets, turnips, lettuces, and other greens spent the last several weeks maturing and consuming available nutrients. Rapidly growing plants quickly deplete the soil and probably need a good fertilization. There are lots of options for providing nutrients to a vegetable or flowerbed to encourage consistent, abundant production.

Water soluble, complete fertilizers are always a good choice. These can safely be applied to annuals as often as every two weeks. Another option is to side dress the plants with aged manure, compost, a complete fertilizer, or ammonium phosphate every four weeks. You can also use a combination of blood meal and bone meal, but be very careful not to overdo it, since too much can burn the roots. Sprinkle the fertilizer on the soil surrounding your plants and gently till it in with a hand-held spade or fork. This is also a good time to remove weeds that compete for water and food, but be careful not to disturb the tender roots of your vegetables and flowers. After mixing the fertilizer into the soil surrounding the plants, water well.

Another wise gardening practice is mulching. In my garden, mulch is a layer of chipped or shredded bark surrounding the plants in the garden bed. A 2–4-inch layer spread evenly over the entire bed but kept 2–3 inches away from the plant stems will protect plant roots from temperature extremes, help retain moisture, and inhibit weed growth. I usually apply mulch two times a year, in October and May. But it also can be applied now and your plants will benefit. You will find that the mulch dresses up your garden and makes very attractive planting areas. As it decomposes, the soil becomes richer and healthier. Over several years, the practice of mulching can dramatically alter and improve soil quality, save water, and improve crop production.

PRUNING GRAPES

If you have established grapevines in your garden, you are lucky. Grapes are one of the most beautiful and useful plants in the Southwest repertoire. The large leaves are green and lush, and the fruit clusters are beautiful as well as delicious. When trained on a trellis, grapevines provide a gorgeous, dense screen. Planted on the west side of vegetable beds, grapes make an excellent backdrop, providing shade during the hottest months yet allowing the sun to shine through during winter dormancy. This is also a good reason to plant grapevines in front of west-facing windows. When grown on an overhead arbor, the romantic, shady area beneath them is without comparison.

If you are training vines on a trellis, you should have the plant situated between two posts set 12–15 feet apart. Two wire supports should stretch between the posts at two and one half and five feet above the ground, respectively. Make certain they are heavy duty, because over time grapevines can become quite heavy. Proper pruning is key to maintaining healthy grapevines anywhere in your garden. For the novice, it's difficult to remove the large amount of growth necessary each year, but doing so will improve the health and productivity of the vine. The goal of pruning is to leave an arm stretching along each wire, one to the left and one to the right at both levels, allowing four arms from each plant.

One at a time, select four canes that originated at the base of last year's renewal spurs. Look for the thickest, sturdiest canes. Cut each one back to a length that includes only 10–12 buds. The upcoming season's growth and fruit will stem from these buds. After you have chosen and cut four canes for new growth, you must choose four more canes that will serve as renewal spurs. They should be emerging near the trunk. Again, look for thick, strong, healthy wood. Cut those four canes back to only two buds. These will grow rampantly over the next several months and will be the source of next year's fruiting canes. Now you have cut eight arms on each plant—four with 10–12 buds and four with two buds. Completely remove all other growth. You must ruthlessly remove this huge amount of vine in order to allow the plant to energetically grow this year.

For an arbor, you prune nearly the same way, except that your guide wires will all be at ceiling height, 7–8 feet above and parallel to the ground. You can use an overhead structure made of wood or other building materials to support the weight of the vines. Some home gardeners dispense with aggressive pruning once the vine has grown up and over its structure. Should you decide to allow unrestrained growth, be aware that the weight will become substantial and your structure must be sturdy enough to support it.

Unlike many gardening tasks, pruning grapevines need not create waste material. The vines are beautiful when wound into wreaths and swags, and make unusual custom shapes as bases for wall hangings. I have friends who earn their living making decorative items from grapevines, dried pods and flowers, and other botanical material. With a little practice, you can create your own masterpieces from things that have grown in your own garden.

Properly pruned grapevines promote fruit production.

The difficulty of landscape and gardening activities directly relates to the appropriateness and quality of the tools being used. When we installed our first irrigation system, we had to deal with compacted soil left by heavy machinery. Working long and hard, I made slow progress with a square shovel I had chosen because it was the correct width for the job. I thought I would save time by using it as a guide. When my husband joined me on the task, he immediately turned on the hose and dampened the soil. Next, he grabbed a pointed spade and loosened the dirt to spade depth by putting his entire weight on the shovel each time he plunged it into the earth. Then he used the square-ended shovel to remove the dirt. What a difference his approach made. He was able to dig a much greater length of trench in an equivalent amount of time. Some of his quick progress was surely due to sheer strength, but the proper use of the right tools for the job was the most significant factor.

29

It's important to properly choose and care for your tools so they last a lifetime, and so you can add to, rather than constantly replace, your collection. The first step is to buy good quality. I always look for tools with handles secured to the head by a bolt or other sturdy hardware. Handles that are slipped into the head and then clamped on do not last long. Here in the desert, I try to buy tools with fiberglass handles that stand up to hard use and weather, but I still have many wooden-handled tools from earlier years that are too good to discard. Wooden-handled tools can last for decades when properly cared for. Never leave them exposed to the weather, since after a relatively short time outdoors, wood handles splinter and split.

If your wooden-handled tools do start to deteriorate, repair them. Sand the handle with a heavy grain sandpaper to remove the roughest damage, and then switch to a fine-grain sandpaper to smooth out the wood. Then wipe the wood with a soft cloth and apply a coat of paint or varnish to the entire handle. Dry it thoroughly and apply two more coats, allowing them to dry between applications. The refurbished tool will hold up for many more years.

Sharp tools are safe and efficient tools. Dull blades make you overcompensate and exert too much force to get the job done, which is detrimental not only to our muscles but also to the tool. Repeated force will stress, bend, or break the tool's hardware, so sharpen the blades when you notice yourself exerting more energy than usual on a typical job.

I keep a small whetstone handy and, with water, regularly sharpen the blades of hand pruners, loppers, garden shears, shovels, and hoes. This task requires a little practice, but is quick and easy once learned. I leave sharpening the blades on my lawnmower to professionals. Since the lawn is growing slowly and demands less attention in January, this is a good time for a tune-up and sharpening. Since everybody else waits until late spring or early summer to take his or her tools in, turn-around time is short. I usually can take the mower in on Monday and have it back before the weekend. Not a bad deal.

This is also a good time to check the working order of other tools. Electric or gas-powered trimmers, chainsaws, rototillers, blowers, and edgers require an annual inspection. Follow guides provided in the owner's manuals, or take the tools to a reputable professional. Repair or replace damaged cords or plugs and fill all fluids, changing them if they are dirty. If the tool is complicated enough to require a tune-up, do that now, too. Preventative maintenance is faster and more reasonably priced than repairs.

Keep your tools in good working order by cleaning them after each use and properly storing them at the end of a gardening day. Wipe away all dirt and mud before storing shovels, rakes, and hoes. Before hanging digging tools on their rack, I wipe them with an old cloth and plunge them into a bucket filled with sand and a quart of oil. This mixture clears away any remaining soil and lubricates the metal, preventing rust. The action also has a sharpening effect, keeping the blades true and sharp for a longer period of time. In my garden the bucket sits in a corner of the potting shed, out of the way, yet convenient to use.

It's especially important to have adequate tool storage and to always put each tool away when not in use. A section of the garage fitted with shelves and hanging racks is the most common storage solution. Wood and aluminum sheds are watertight and protect their contents from damaging sun, rodents, birds, and other wildlife. Pesticides, herbicides, fertilizers, and other gardening necessities also can be locked in sheds to keep them out of reach of children and pets.

Bumper crops from winter vegetable beds

WEEK 5

Either you've prepared your vegetable bed recently, or you've just fertilized the plots that you planted last fall. In either case, you can take advantage of the next few weeks of moderate winter weather and plant a bumper crop. When started from seed, beans, beets, carrots, lettuce, peas, spinach, and turnips will mature and ripen before it gets too hot. Most of these seeds are still available in garden centers, sometimes at clearance prices. Order hard-to-find varieties from a reliable seed source by phone or over the Internet to ensure quick delivery. Seeds ordered by mail won't arrive in time for planting and maturation before high temperatures set in.

I also use this bumper crop planting time to try new varieties. It is fun to try things like black or French breakfast radishes that grow up to eight inches in length. It is a good time to expand on beet selections and plant golden varieties. They have a distinctly different flavor and look beautiful when prepared and served with the more traditional crimson sort. I get great pleasure out of growing "sunshine yellow" and scarlet carrots. Their lacy foliage decorates the garden as beautifully as the roots embellish a crudite plate, making them excellent choices for interplanting with flowers and potted plants. As long as pots are at least twelve inches deep, most vegetables adjust well to container culture when given proper sunlight, irrigation, and nutrients.

Lettuces are always a great boon to the desert kitchen garden. For decades, commercial farmers have successfully grown head lettuce as a winter crop, a success you can replicate in your garden. Even more successful, however, are the easily propagated, non-demanding leaf lettuces. Seed companies have ventured into the increasingly popular exotic lettuce market by offering scores of choices, from the simplest romaine to the most unusual and spicy European and Asian greens.

My favorite lettuces include mesclun mixes, which include several types of leafy greens in one packet. My family enjoys sweet and spicy mixed greens all winter and spring from one small bed that I plant intensively, harvest regularly, and partially reseed every 2–3 weeks. We produce far more than I normally would buy in the supermarket during this time of year and enjoy the additional benefits of organic, pesticide-free salads. With such mixes frequently costing $4–7 a pound in grocery stores, our little bed is a real bargain.

31

In addition to the lettuce mixes of which I'm so fond, my kitchen garden would not be complete without a steady crop of arugula and roquette. These greens have been grown and served by French, Italian, and Greek cooks for centuries. In a fertile bed they grow exceedingly well and are quite versatile. They are tasty when quickly sautéed in olive oil with a little garlic, and are delicious and spicy when part of a green salad. I also like to add them, raw or lightly cooked, to pasta and include them frequently in stir-fry meals. Packed with vitamins and minerals, they complement almost any dinner menu. When I run out of original ideas, I substitute arugula and roquette in recipes calling for spinach with excellent results.

I like to grow cruciferous vegetables—the cancer-fighting wonder foods that include broccoli, brussels sprouts, and cabbages—in gaps and spaces in my garden. Generally, they are a little bit difficult to grow in the home garden and can be less productive and of lower quality than some of the crops I've already mentioned. Don't be discouraged. It's worth experimenting to discover which ones do well in your plot. Brocolli-rabe, or rapini, has done very well in my Tucson garden. If I hadn't been willing to risk failure, I never would have discovered this.

Rely on the good judgment of local nurserymen who start their vegetables and annual flowers from seed and carry the plants throughout the season. After many seasons of experimentation, they know which specific varieties do well in your climate zone. If you are unsure about the viability of a new vegetable or flower, experiment with pony packs or small pots started at the nursery. If they perform well in the garden, propagate from seed next season.

THE BEAUTY OF ASPARAGUS IN THE GARDEN

Asparagus is a gorgeous plant, billowy and feather-like. The brilliant green foliage provides a lovely accent to cut flower bouquets and annual flowerbeds. In summer and fall, bright red seedpods make a striking visual contrast. Because asparagus requires fertile soil and moderate water, plant it close to the house so you can enjoy it. A raised planter is an excellent home for the asparagus bed. Start now, at the end of January or beginning of February, and enjoy the attractive plants through the spring, summer, and early fall. In just over a year, you'll harvest the first tasty green spears. In three or four years your plants will produce a full crop, an experience that, with proper care, will repeat itself for many years.

Like annuals and other vegetables in the desert, asparagus needs highly amended soil. Once established, a five-by-five plot of twenty-five plants will provide your family with a reasonably sized crop. Several bare-root varieties are available from garden centers and mail-order companies, including the traditional Mary Washington, European Purple Passion, all-male Jersey Giant, and UC 157, developed by the University of California for mild winter gardens. Any of these will grow in the Southwest if the plants are healthy and free of damage or decay before being planted. Till the bed to a depth of eighteen inches and remove any rocks. Spread and incorporate into the soil a six-inch layer of composted steer manure, two pounds of soil sulfur, and a half pound of ammonium phosphate into the soil, then smooth the bed with a tined rake. Create five 6–8-inch trenches and set five plants in each, spacing them evenly. Your bed should look like a grid pattern when you are done. Cover the roots with a thin layer of soil, water very gently, and wait for new green shoots.

When the young shoots begin to appear, add enough soil to barely cover them. Continue this as the shoots grow until the trenches are level with the rest of the bed. This may take up to a month. Once the bed is level, sprinkle it with a half pound of ammonium sulfate and water well. Fertilize in this manner every 4–6 weeks and irrigate regularly. Take care to keep the beds watered during the summer months. When summer wanes, the plants will grow more slowly. As the cold temperatures arrive, they will die back and become brown and brittle. Stop all irrigation and fertilization, giving the bed a monthly drink only if there are no winter rains. When the plants have been in the ground for an entire year, clear out the dry material and cut everything back to the ground. Spread the bed with a 2–3-inch layer of composted manure and water well. The new green sprouts will emerge in a short time.

When the plants re-emerge, begin watering and fertilize every 4–6 weeks. You also can start harvesting the first few spears, using a sharp blade and cutting each spear at an angle below the soil line. Always harvest the spears before the buds on the top begin to unfurl. Take only those that are thicker than one-quarter inch, leaving some stalks so the plants continue to grow and rejuvenate.

Every morning, I give my garden a thorough checkup, keeping my eyes open for potential problems. Just like our own health, a garden's well-being relies on prevention and early detection. During my early morning and evening surveys through the garden, I notice signs of water stress and excess moisture, both of which would indicate irrigation malfunction. I prowl for evidence of disease, including powdery mildew; insects, such as gray aphids; and weeds that would rob my plants of water and nutrients.

Powdery mildew is a common fungal disease in the desert Southwest. It often becomes active on sennas, crape myrtle, elm, euonymus, grapes, hibiscus, honeysuckle, ivy, magnolia, Mexican palo verde, oak, penstemons, roses, and zinnias. The disease affects many other species and can do a great deal of damage if left unchecked. Powdery mildew is aptly named. It appears on leaves, stems, and sometimes bark as a whitish, black-flecked, powdery substance. It causes the plant to brown out and curl up, leading to general decline. Powdery mildew is usually the result of overwatering and overcrowding, both of which create a prime environment for the fungal spores to become active and multiply. When you find it, assess your gardening practices and the plant's immediate environment and correct them if possible.

Although powdery mildew thrives in damp conditions, it cannot survive in free-flowing water. Spraying water on the affected foliage early in the morning can actually kill the disease. A word of caution—this is only effective if the general area will dry out quickly. If the plants and soil remain damp, you'll contribute to the problem by adding more moisture. Effective chemical treatments to control powdery mildew include sulfur spray, travertine, thiophanate methyl, Bayleton (systemic), or triflumizole, all of which are commercially available. Read the labels for application instructions and environmental risks, strictly adhering to suggestions regarding plants on which the products can be safely used.

In addition to powdery mildew, gray aphids are a common winter problem. We usually think of aphids as spring and summer pests, but gray aphids—aptly named for their characteristic gray, black, or brown coloration—are very active in the desert during cooler months. They love tender new growth and often congregate in flower and vegetable beds, although they will infest anything with new foliage or buds. They frequently congregate on the leaves of the brassica or cruciferous family—broccoli, brussels sprouts, cabbage, cauliflower, radish, stock, sweet alyssum, and turnips. When I see clusters of these pesky little insects (the adult form looks like a small black gnat with relatively large wings), I get out the insecticidal soap.

If you don't have insecticidal soap, mix 1–2 tablespoons of Dawn brand dishwashing liquid in a gallon of water and then saturate the plants using a spray bottle. Allow the solution to run into the folds, creases, and leaves. The soap solution works by coating and disabling the insect's breathing apertures and leaves behind no toxic residue. I usually apply once, early in the morning, and then again two hours later. On food or flower crops, I wash the residue off with a heavy spray of water several minutes after the second application.

There are times when an infestation is so severe insecticidal soap will not be successful. The following chemical products, listed from least to most toxic, are useful in extreme cases: pyrethrum, rotenone, Malathion, and Orthene. For non-edibles, the systemic pesticide Dysiston can be used. A systemic product enters the plant's system and remains effective for a longer period of time so that insects that probe, suck, or chew on the plant are poisoned. Systemics are more effective because they kill not only the current pests, but also those that arrive in the near future, providing longer-term protection.

Winter weeds, encouraged by winter rains, are the last major garden nuisances at this time of year. In a normal year, southern Arizona receives nearly half of its annual rainfall in the winter and the desert areas of Nevada, southern California, southern New Mexico, and west Texas get most of their precipitation now. It is not unusual for a crop of weeds to appear 7–14 days after a rainstorm. They are easy to remove from damp earth but difficult once the soil has dried. If you are lucky enough to get another storm after the young weeds appear, pull them right away.

Round-up is a good weed-killing product. It is absorbed through the foliage and stimulates excessive growth, which the plant cannot support. The plant dies within two weeks. Round-up is safe for animals and will not run off into the soil like many other herbicides. Once dry, it stays where you've sprayed it. Another product, marketed under the commercial name Finale, is similar to Round-up, but works within 4–7 days. The biggest problem with these products is overspray. Any sprayed plant will be affected. If the wind is blowing or you have a careless hand, you will damage or destroy other plants. Never spray

Round-up or Finale if there is even a slight breeze, always be cautious around other plants, and follow dilution instructions precisely. A regular schedule of herbicide application efficiently controls weeds with minimal chemical use, eliminating the development of large-scale weed problems. Keep an eye open for newly sprouting weeds and never allow them to mature to the seed-setting stage. Weed growth can be a sign of water waste. If you find a healthy clump of weeds, you may have an irrigation leak or overspray problem.

Automatic irrigation systems

Desert dwellers must irrigate in order to landscape and garden. Even transplanted natives require regular irrigation for the first two years. To reduce labor and waste, consider installing an automatic irrigation system. Most cooperative extension offices and water companies give workshops that cover every facet of irrigation, from layout to schedules. Hardware and home improvement stores carry many types of systems with varying methods of installation. Retailers often give free seminars and offer literature on irrigation to homeowners. Professionally installed systems are more expensive, but will be in and running in a matter of days, with no labor on your part. Take advantage of what you can and get a system in as soon as possible.

Trees, shrubs, ground covers, flowerbeds, kitchen gardens, and lawns all have different water needs that require separate irrigation stations. This is a key point to keep in mind when designing your irrigation system, although it's often overlooked by landscapers and other irrigation professionals since they are not always aware of the details of varying plant needs.

When planning your system, water plants with similar requirements with the same station or line. Determine how many stations you will need based on the types and number of plants in your landscape. In my garden, all of the desert-adapted and native trees are on one station. Deciduous fruit trees are on another. The lawn has two separate stations to ensure adequate pressure, and the annual flowerbeds have a station all their own, as do my herbs and vegetable beds. Drought-tolerant shrubs and ground covers have a separate irrigation line as well. I water my citrus trees by hand, as I described earlier. By designating irrigation lines based on need, I never overwater some plants in order to attain minimum requirements of others.

This less-demanding season is a good time to turn on each station and inspect for leaks, breaks, and clogs—problems easily identified if you take the time to look at each outlet and plant during and after the cycle. Leaks will be apparent as water puddles or runs in undesirable areas. The juncture between irrigation pipes or tubing and risers is the most common location. Tighten these connections and replace any components that are no longer watertight.

Breaks generally cause obvious water loss and flooding. They are easy to locate if aboveground, more difficult if underground and hidden from view with only a damp spot or excessive nearby plant growth to indicate a problem. Investigate by digging down to buried components of the irrigation system and inspecting those parts too. Since saving water is a priority for every desert gardener, find irrigation problems and fix them.

If you run your irrigation system and water does not emerge where expected, the system may have a clog. Beginning where the water should emerge, remove and clean the parts one at a time. Check the system after cleaning or repairing each component to see if the problem has been solved. Most of the time, pebbles that have found their way into the pipes, residue from repairs, or new system components may be the source of the problem. If you suspect an obstruction in your sprinkler, remove the sprinkler or tip and allow the water to run unregulated so the pressure blows out any debris before replacing broken components.

A change in water pressure often causes inadequate water delivery and can completely alter the effectiveness of an entire irrigation system. Check the water pressure at the regular irrigation time and make sure it is correct. Pressure varies at different times of day and also can change when more outlets are added to a line. Most valves have a pressure regulator that can be adjusted if your water pressure has changed since your last inspection. Water pressure problems can occur as more homes are built in your neighborhood.

If the pressure is too high, your components can blow off or break and you will spend a lot of time repairing and replacing parts of the system. If the water pressure is too low, the force needed to push the water through the entire line will be inadequate. Make sure your irrigation system is in prime condition when the heat hits—your plants are relying on it for survival.

37

February

- Plant onions and other bulbs
- Plant new grape vines
- Plant desert marigold, evening primrose, penstemon, and sage
- Plant a tree for Arbor Day
- Start spring vegetable seeds indoors
- Fertilize citrus
- Fertilize roses, lawns, and grapes
- Fertilize deciduous fruit trees
- Plant annual color plants

February

STARTING FROM SEED FOR SPRING PLANTING

WEEK 6 Now is the time to consider what to do with winter vegetable or flower garden spaces, which will soon be available for the upcoming season. Review the plants that caught your fancy as you perused catalogs and seed racks last month and buy them now, choosing varieties that mature quickly and can be picked before the hottest part of the summer. It is difficult to contemplate hot weather while enjoying winter's cool temperatures, but your anticipation and preparation will pay off when it's time to plant and harvest your garden.

The number of freezing nights and the last frost date vary by region, but the possibility of below-freezing temperatures exists through the end of March. Don't be deceived by the heat wave that frequently moves through the Southwest in February, because frost warnings inevitably follow. If you intend to plant tender varieties, wait until April. But get seeds growing in containers now so you'll have sturdy little seedlings to put into the ground when the last frost date has passed. This is an excellent practice in the hottest desert areas, where the growing season is short due to rapidly rising summer temperatures. Because little sprouts struggle with the heat, a slightly older plant copes better.

Growing plants from seed in containers is a 6–8 week commitment. If you are not able to do this, wait and buy your seedlings from the nursery. Another word of warning: you cannot start seedlings on the kitchen windowsill. The indirect light source forces the plants to stretch to the sun, making them leggy and weak. You must build outdoor cold frames, carry your plants in and out of the sun each day, or dedicate space in your home or garage to mini-beds under lights.

You can purchase "grow" lights or use a combination of warm and cool fluorescent bulbs that will provide the full spectrum of light rays. The location must be draft-free, with a fairly stable temperature, and the lights should be close enough to the plants to provide warmth, leaving several inches for growth. Keep the soil evenly moist and the lights on at all times. This sounds like a huge electricity expense, but it works out to only pennies a day. For most people, the difficulty is in dedicating the space for two months. If your outdoor space is more abundant than your indoor space, you may want to consider building cold frames.

A cold frame can be as simple as a cinderblock bed covered with Plexiglas or an old window, or as fancy as a sturdily built garden box with a hinged, wood-framed Plexiglas lid. As long as it blocks out cold winds, accumulates heat during the day, and provides enough depth for the seedlings to grow straight and sturdy, it will be effective. Locate the cold frame in full sun, facing south, to catch the sun's rays. Some people turn their cold frame into a hot bed by laying a heating cable in the bottom to maintain the temperature at or above 70°. I have not found this to be necessary. On the coldest nights, a heavy blanket over the cold frame will hold the day's heat. On unusually warm days, vent off some of this heat by propping open the lid a few inches, then close it tightly before sunset.

Carrying the seedlings in and out of doors daily is the least technical. Keep your plants in a wooden box, on a large cookie sheet, or in a heavy cardboard flat. Tightly cover the container with plastic wrap and place it in the sun every morning. Make sure they remain in full sun all day. At the end of the day, carefully carry them back into the house. This method demands that you get those young plants into the sun every day or you will permanently weaken them. Plus you must raise the plastic wrap above and away from the container tops as the plants grow. If the new leaves touch the plastic, they will get too hot or too moist and usually rot. In addition to keeping the plastic elevated during the entire process, be meticulous about maintaining moisture in the soil. Even slight drying damages seedlings.

No matter which method you use, planting the seeds will be the same. Fill either purchased seed-starting flats or simple Styrofoam cups with a sterile seed-sprouting medium. If you make the medium at home, use equal parts sand, peat moss, vermiculite, and perlite. Add a small amount of water while mixing for an even consistency. This medium provides a balance between water-holding capabilities, good drainage, and oxygen flow to encourage strong, healthy roots, and the absence of both fertilizer and soil eliminates the introduction of soil-borne pathogens that lead to disease.

Once the soil is in the containers, tamp it down and spritz or squirt it with a little water to settle the soil before planting. Plant one or two seeds in each compartment or cup at a depth two or three times the size of the seed. Scatter very small seeds on the soil's surface with only a sprinkling of additional soil on top, and then water gently. Check daily to make sure that the soil is always damp, but never wet. Put them in your designated area and be prepared to baby-sit them for the next 6–8 weeks.

Fertilize your seedlings when they have 4–6 leaves. An easy way is to add a teaspoon of a complete water-soluble fertilizer to a gallon of water and use this each time you water the plants. I use a watering can with a fine, gentle sprinkle that does not damage tender young stems and leaves. I have also used a squirt bottle with an adjustable misting spray. Check and irrigate every day if necessary. When it is nearly time to set the plants out into the garden, you will need to "harden them off." About two weeks before you intend to plant your beds, expose the new plants to the real world a few hours at a time. Put them out into the garden for a few hours each day, making sure they are moist enough to withstand the exposure, and then put them back into their safe growing space before the day's temperatures start to drop. Gradually increase the time they are out until they are ready for their permanent place in the garden.

By the end of March, your plants will be healthy and sturdy and the danger of frost will have passed. Prepare the bed as instructed in Week 4. Add some organic material and a phosphorous source, as well as some soil sulfur. Till and smooth the bed, and water well. Now you're ready to transplant. Do it in the evening so that the young plants have the nighttime temperatures to help them adjust to their new surroundings. Grab the seedlings by their strongest set of leaves to remove them from the container. Do not grab the stem, as it is fragile and easily bruised.

Working quickly so the tender roots do not dry out, plant the seedlings at the same soil level to which they are accustomed and water gently. If the days are hot, provide some afternoon shade until they are tough enough to withstand the heat. You might also want to provide some shelter from wind, although I find that planting intensively greatly reduces this need. Water the plants daily until they are established.

WINTER CARE OF ROSES

Even though they are labor-intensive, requiring regular pruning, deadheading, fertilizing, and pest patrol, I still have a dozen delightful rosebushes nestled in the perfect spot in my garden. I enjoy the lovely blooms and don't mind the necessary care. A major component of that care is the annual pruning to ensure lush growth and large, healthy April blossoms. If you disregard annual pruning, plants deteriorate, become more susceptible to diseases and pests, and produce smaller blossoms.

I usually begin this process by sharpening and disinfecting my tools. Using a very small whetstone, I make sure both blades on my pruners and loppers are straight and sharp. I used to have my tools professionally sharpened until I realized how simple the process is. Most sharpening stones come with reliable directions. A little practice and you'll wonder why you ever paid someone

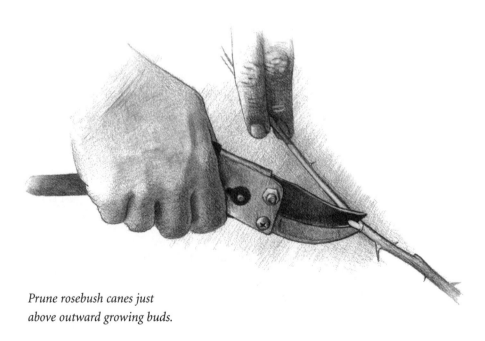

*Prune rosebush canes just
above outward growing buds.*

to do this simple task. Once they are sharp, wipe the blades with a ten-percent bleach solution and you're ready to cut.

The first step in any pruning job is the removal of dead, damaged, or diseased wood. Cut below the damage, at least one inch into the healthy wood, and consider taking those canes all the way down to the crown of the plant if necessary. Wipe your tools with the bleach solution after every cut to prevent the spread of disease. Next, remove any canes that are thin, weak, growing inward, crossing, or interfering with other branches. Your goal is to have about five sturdy, healthy canes. If more are still on the plant, remove the least desirable. If removing the necessary branches leaves you with only three or four canes, don't worry. It's better to have fewer, healthy canes than to leave questionable plant material. Cut the remaining canes back to a height of eighteen inches.

When finished pruning, put a dot of Elmer's All Purpose Glue on the end of each cane to protect the open end from insect and pathogen invasion. Water the plants thoroughly, fertilize them with an all-purpose fertilizer, and water again. Don't water again until the leaves begin to unfurl with the bright green shoots of new growth.

Citrus inspection

One of the wonderful things about having citrus trees in the desert is the lush green color they provide all winter long. If you have mature citrus, you've been harvesting oranges and tangerines for weeks now. By mid-February, navel oranges begin to deteriorate if left on the trees. Fortunately, grapefruits are ripening and getting sweeter by the week. I love having a grapefruit tree because it provides fresh fruit for a long period of time. We begin to enjoy them in January, harvesting only for our immediate needs and we continue through the end of May. By June, I pick the last of the fruit and bring it indoors, where it remains fresh and usable for a couple more weeks. Considering the beauty of the plant and the quality of the fruit, I can't think of a better producer for a desert garden.

The birds in our area agree. They flock to the orange and yellow globes hanging amidst the green foliage. Flickers, cactus wrens, and thrashers puncture that brilliantly colored skin and use their sharp beaks as straws, enjoying a long, cool drink of fresh fruit juice. Initially, you may not notice they've been imbibing. A day or two later, however, it will become obvious when ants, flies, and gnats swarm to the exposed nectar. Some even lay eggs in and around the fruit, beginning a cycle of heavy infestation. You may be tempted to use insecticide to solve the problem, but I strongly caution against such action. The problem is the birds, not the bugs. If the buzzing of the bugs is bothersome, remove pierced and fallen fruit each morning. As for controlling the birds, some deterrents, such as metallic ribbons or the tops of juice cans hung in the branches, are mildly successful. Generally, you must resign yourself to the fact that you will share a portion of your harvest with the wildlife whose territory you inhabit. After their first few years, citrus trees produce enough fruit to share.

44
∾

Another problem with citrus fruit becomes apparent about now. The outside of the fruit looks brightly colored and ripe. The size of the fruit may or may not be suitable. When cut open, the inside is dry, shriveled, and not very appetizing. The most common cause of this is inadequate watering. If your citrus tree is shallowly watered, even if frequently, it may not have developed a root system large enough to support active foliage growth and fruit development, which can lead to small, dry fruit. To avoid these and other problems, irrigate citrus once every 2–3 weeks to a depth of three feet. Every irrigation should cover the area under and just beyond the canopy of the tree. I usually lay a slow hose under my trees and let it run for many hours to achieve the necessary depth.

Frost damage also can be the culprit when fruit is dry and pithy. This usually occurs on the outer sections of the tree, where the fruit is directly exposed to cold. Although your citrus trees may be the greenest things in your garden right now, they are probably showing signs of weather-related stress. If overnight temperatures sink below 28° for any length of time, individual cell walls deteriorate, and leaves become visibly damaged. Frost-damaged foliage and smaller twigs will be dry, brittle, and grayish-brown. Many people decide to prune unsightly foliage and branches. *Don't!* It will stimulate new growth, which will be tender and more susceptible to freezing in subsequent weeks.

Additionally, those outer, affected areas can actually insulate and protect the underlying foliage. Be patient. Don't do any cutting on your citrus until the beginning of April. The last frost date will have passed and you will see areas of new growth to which you can cut back.

Another common symptom during cool months is yellowing and dropping leaves, which is natural. Unless your tree completely defoliates or loses very large sections of leaves, don't be concerned. You also need to check for the iron deficiency called iron chlorosis, indicated by yellow leaves with bright green veins. Large quantities of calcium carbonate in our desert soils capture, or chemically "bind up," non-chelated iron and prevent its use by plant roots. Treat iron chlorosis with an application of chelated iron. Non-chelated iron products may be wonderful for amended soils such as rose beds, potted planters, raised beds, and kitchen gardens, but they won't work for citrus trees in native desert soils.

To keep your citrus strong, healthy, and disease-free, water deeply every three weeks and fertilize three times a year. February is the ideal time for the first fertilization. Unlike deciduous fruit trees that require pruning and the development of new wood to produce fruit, citrus trees bear fruit based on the amount of their foliage, so use a fertilizer that will encourage abundant leaf growth. Nitrogen, which stimulates leaf development, is the most important nutrient to supply. Ammonium sulfate and blood meal—both high in nitrogen—are good choices. Fertilizers that have been developed especially for citrus trees also are excellent nitrogen sources. Whichever product you choose, follow package directions to determine the correct amount to use.

It is important to water the tree thoroughly, apply the fertilizer, and follow with a second watering so that the nitrogen goes to the roots immediately. Never apply fertilizer to dry soil and let it sit. Two things will happen: the roots will suffer nitrogen burn damage and the fertilizer will lose much of its potency to the atmosphere.

There are certain instances where you should not fertilize your citrus tree at this time. One is if your last crop produced fruits that were somewhat teardrop in shape, elongated on the stem end. This phenomenon is referred to as "sheep-nose." It is most common in grapefruit, but can also occur in other citrus. It's a clear indication of overfertilization, revealing that you gave your tree a bit too much last August. Don't worry, but do skip the February application. Another clue that fertilization is unnecessary is excessive, rich, green

45
∾

foliage over the entire tree, with no signs of winter stress or depleted energy. If your tree has no yellow leaves, no leaf drop, and no reduction in leaf size, and continues to produce leaves, wait until May to apply fertilizer.

PLANTING NEW GRAPEVINES

WEEK 7

By February grapes are available in nurseries in both bare-root and container forms. Those in containers are probably a year older than their bare-root counterparts and will produce fruit a year sooner. Container-grown plants should be purchased and planted as soon as the gray and lifeless plants begin to leaf out. Waiting until the grapes are actively growing assures you that they are healthy and viable.

I prefer to plant bare-root grapevines because the plants are much less expensive and I can check for root development and health. They also require a smaller hole and less digging. There are many varieties suitable to the desert Southwest. The three I most heartily recommend for the home gardener are Black Manukka, Flame Seedless, and Thompson Seedless. All three are seedless table grapes (not wine grapes) that yield large crops when mature and are available in most good nurseries.

Before you plant your grapes, develop a plan for supporting the large vines. Either a trellis or arbor system provides adequate support and creates a beautiful focal point in the garden. Select a sight where the vines will receive full sun. The soil should drain well and be free of clay or caliche. Plant the vines between two posts set 12–15 feet apart. If you are planning to keep the vines low, place only one plant between each set of posts. If you will train some vines high and some low, you can put two plants between each set of posts, separating them by at least six feet. To begin planting, loosen a two-foot wide section of soil between the posts 12–18 inches deep. In that loosened area, dig 18–24-inch planting holes.

Using the soil you removed, build a conical mound in the center of each hole on which to rest the plant and drape the roots. Inspect the roots and remove any that are dead or damaged. Place the vine atop the soil mound and drape the roots around it. Return the original soil to the hole, tamping it down firmly. Build a berm around the vine to create a watering well. Fill the well with water, let it soak in, and then fill it again. You must keep the roots damp

A DESERT GARDENER'S COMPANION

until they are established and you see signs of spring growth. I recommend adding a thick layer of mulch to retain moisture.

When the first leaves appear, fertilize with a nitrogen source at half the recommended amount and water in thoroughly. You can now reduce the watering schedule, irrigating once every 5–7 days. Using a soil probe, make certain the water reaches a depth of two feet with each irrigation. If the leaves droop or lose their glossy sheen, water more frequently. Pay attention to the plants and they will show you what they need.

FERTILIZING DECIDUOUS FRUIT TREES

Last month you should have pruned and sprayed your dormant deciduous fruit trees, and now it's time to prepare for bud break. Even though it is still winter and we can expect below-freezing temperatures through next month, desert weather prompts early blooming. Before long, the sweet perfume of apple blossoms will float on the desert breeze. If you are from a northern or eastern climate, the growth and change during a desert February will amaze you.

Pome (*Malus* or apple family) and stone fruit trees require fertilization now to ensure full leaf and fruit development. As with citrus, the most important nutrient these fruit trees require is nitrogen, but they also need magnesium and zinc. So use a complete fertilizer developed especially for fruit crops. Different from citrus food, it may be a product developed specifically for fruit trees or for vegetables, fruits, and berries. Follow the label directions for application amounts.

A good rule of thumb is to supply a half pound of actual nitrogen to each tree. If the product is ten percent nitrogen and the package weighs twenty pounds, then it contains two pounds of actual nitrogen. In this case, apply five pounds, or one-fourth of the package, to each tree.

Following a deep irrigation, evenly broadcast the fertilizer under the entire tree. Immediately water again to spread the fertilizer throughout the root zone. An adequate irrigation will supply water to a depth of three feet beneath, and slightly beyond, the canopy of the tree. Use a soil probe to verify that the water has reached the necessary depth. You will need to irrigate in this manner every three weeks until the tree loses its leaves in the fall. Don't fertilize again until that final irrigation, just as the leaves drop. As a reminder, I go through my

47

calendar and write "water fruit trees" on every third week. This guarantees that I won't lose track of time. If it has rained heavily near the time of a scheduled irrigation, I skip it.

Onion Sets

If you are growing onions from seed, you planted in September or October. If you didn't get those in the ground, don't fret. Onion sets, or bulbs, take hold and grow beautifully in the desert. Unless I have a really special packet of seed, I save time and water by planting sets. Many companies sell onion sets in stores and through catalogs. Look for the short day type that grows well during the shorter days of winter and spring.

Two different kinds of onions do well here. The first is bunching onions, which spread and multiply out from the original bulb. I recommend four specific varieties of bunching onions: 'Beltsville Bunching', 'White Sweet Spanish', 'Crystal Wax', and 'Papago Bunching'. The Tohono O'odham of southern Arizona cultivated this latter variety. Once established, bunching onions can be harvested at any time. You will have a perpetual crop of scallion-sized and larger onions if you harvest carefully and always leave some to multiply and grow larger. The dry bulb onion is the other sort that does well here, producing one large onion from each bulb, or set. Two specific varieties that have done well for many years in the desert Southwest are 'Granex' and 'Grano'. They are ready to harvest in late June or July.

Onions are a great food crop to consider because they grow in meager soil. I have loosened lean, rocky, native soil, added ammonium phosphate, watered well, and planted 'Papago Bunching' onion sets. Given nothing more than a weekly 6–8-inch irrigation, they provided a perpetual harvest for more than a year. They only stopped when I finally pulled the last few from the ground. While not demanding the highly amended soil other food crops require, the adaptable onion also will grow nicely in your kitchen garden or vegetable bed. Taking advantage of another facet of onion versatility, I like to plant a few sets in my vegetable garden and allow them to bloom. Late in the season, I am rewarded with a bold floral display. Since they have gone to seed, these onions are no longer edible, but the beautiful globe-shaped allium blossoms are worth the sacrifice.

Flower-producing bulbs are more common in the garden than onions, and fall is generally the time to plant most of those bulbs. There are just a few that provide a colorful summer display and go into the ground now. Two bulbs that do their best when planted now are tiger flower and canna. They both require rich, fertile, well-drained soil, and will rot if allowed to sit in wet dirt. Also susceptible to sunburn, they do better in afternoon shade, so plant them where they get some protection from sun. From the time the leaves begin to emerge, fertilize every two weeks with a water-soluble, all-purpose fertilizer to encourage profuse, repeated flowering.

Tiger flower (*Tigrida*), sometimes called Mexican shell flower, resembles an iris in form, and grows from an elongated bulb planted four inches deep. When first sprouting, it looks like a weed—so don't pull it. Allow the narrow, sword-like leaves to grow and they will reach a height of one and a half feet here in the desert. In more temperate climates, they actually grow twice that tall. Tiger flower produces 3–6-inch flowers for several weeks in July and August. Each blossom, lasting only a day, has three large segments forming a triangle, joined with three smaller sections in the center. The blossoms can be orange, pink, red, or yellow, with darker, spotted centers.

Cannas are native to the tropics and subtropics. They have large, green, banana-like leaves that are sometimes streaked with deep bronze. I like to use the leaves as a decorative base on platters of fruit or grilled fish, adding a tropical feel to the table. The brightly-colored flowers, resembling ginger lilies, come in white, ivory, yellow, orange, pink, apricot, coral, salmon, red, and bi-color varieties. They look fabulous in the garden but do not keep well when cut. Resign yourself to enjoying them outdoors.

'Grand Opera', 'Pfitzer's Dwarf', and 'Seven Dwarfs' are low-growing strains that reach only two feet. Most other varieties grow 3–6 feet tall. Plant the tubers five inches deep and ten inches apart. They look best when planted in masses and work well in borders, near pools, in large pots, and around patios or ramadas. Cut off individual blooms as they fade and entire stalks when they stop blooming. Expect them to freeze back in the winter. Leave all of the brown foliage until February or March, then cut back, fertilize, and irrigate deeply. Like an annual gift, the cycle will begin again. You can expect to divide the

49

clumps every two or three years, so look forward to creating more beds or sharing with friends.

A BASIL PRIMER

WEEK
8

Fresh herbs are one of the great pleasures of the active gardener. When moist and green, herbs add texture, color, and flavor to dishes. Dried, they bring a bit of spring and summer into the cool-season kitchen. There was a time when the only herbs a cook used were those grown in the kitchen garden, but mass production in agriculture and convenience foods changed the way Americans live, shop, and eat.

Fortunately, appreciation for the fresh flavors of recently harvested herbs has never completely died out. A few farmers and gardeners have always maintained herb gardens, and the better restaurants have continued to use fresh herbs in their signature dishes. As is usually the case with cultural and lifestyle trends, the pendulum has begun to swing back.

Basil (*Ocimum*) is the herb that most gardeners grow and most home-gourmets want. It's a tender annual and cannot be set out until after the last frost date. Even though that is several weeks away, I start basil seeds by late February in a protected area to have a jump on cultivation in the spring. Basil seeds germinate quickly and easily, especially if grown under a fluorescent light system. Because they are both ornamental and utilitarian, I try several different types of basil every year so I'll have enough plants for use in the flowerbed and the pasta sauce, as well as in salads, sandwiches, and teas.

I start seeds every two weeks so that I have plants at different levels of maturity and always have seedlings to share with other gardeners. (This sharing has led to some of my most treasured friendships.) I begin harvesting leaves in about eight weeks—the same time I start putting seedlings into the garden bed—and enjoy continuous crops, augmented by a second planting in August, until late November. I usually buy my favorite basil seeds from Burpee or Shepherd's Garden Seeds. I plant several "standards" every year and experiment with new and different varieties.

I cannot imagine a spring and summer—or a fall and winter for that matter—without fino verde basil. It is a petite, little-leaf Italian variety that packs a lot of flavor into those perfectly sized leaves and performs well in the ground or a large pot. The best thing about fino verde is that the leaves don't have to be chopped. They are the right size for most recipes. I have had this variety year-round for several years now. I propagate from cuttings at the end of the warm season for an abundant cool-weather supply.

I also won't be without lettuce leaf basil. It is at the other end of the leaf-size spectrum, with leaves that grow up to six inches long and have a firm, crisp texture. They hold up to warm sauces and vinegar dressings, and are perfect garnishes and table decorations. 'Green Ruffles' basil is nearly as good and nearly as large, but not a perfect substitute. Its heavily textured leaves nicely garnish large platters of grilled meats or sliced tomatoes, and the stout plants are attractive in the garden.

For reliability and durability, you can't beat sweet basil. This traditionally grown plant, along with lemon basil, withstands weather changes better than any others. It takes the heat and hangs on longer in the cold. Sweet basil leaves are mildly flavored, giving them universal appeal. Lemon basil, with its small and sometimes hairy leaves, is delicious in risotto, rice, or fish dishes and makes a comforting tea.

In addition to those favorites, a full basil collection should include 'Cinnamon', 'Purple Ruffles', 'Genovese and Napoletano', 'Dark Opal', and 'Siam Queen'. They are beautiful in the garden, alone, in groups, or mixed with annual flowers. They are the first things I put out after the threat of frost has passed and the last plants I protect as frost returns.

XERISCAPING

While the rest of the country faces several more weeks of winter weather, here in the desert we are installing landscapes. Although early fall is the best time to plant landscape material, this is second best. Even though we still have several more weeks of possible freezing nights, the desert-adapted landscape plants have little trouble with low temperatures.

When choosing species, consider the needs of the plants, the gardener, and the available resources, the most significant of which is water. By definition the desert is a place of environmental extremes, most notably a lack of water, so available water must be used thoughtfully and purposefully. Xeriscaping is the most practical and ethical way to landscape.

I do not oppose growing plants with high water needs. If they provide useful crops or products, I am happy to give them the water they need. I have a lot of herbs, vegetables, fruits, and flowers in my garden, but I cluster them near the house so that their transpiration actually cools my home and they visually soothe on a hot day. When plants are grouped by need, no water is wasted.

The xeriscape concept actually has seven hallmark practices:

1. Good landscape planning and design
2. Appropriate turf areas
3. Efficient irrigation
4. Soil improvements/Water harvesting
5. Use of mulches
6. Incorporation of low-water-use plants in the landscape
7. Appropriate maintenance of plants and irrigation systems

Good landscape planning is significant because it allows the gardener to know what the final picture will look like and how to get there. If you don't plan well, you will waste time, water, and money as you make mistakes and correct them.

Following the xeriscape concept, your garden should include three general zones. Plant the most water-thirsty species nearest your house, where you receive the greatest benefit. They can be enjoyed from inside as well as outside and will help cool your house as they transpire. This well-irrigated area is the mini oasis. Just beyond the mini oasis, xeriscaping calls for a transitional zone, which requires supplemental irrigation, but not as much as that needed by the lush growth in the mini oasis. These plants generally require infrequent irrigation once established. Beyond the transitional zone is the arid zone. Plants in the arid zone will survive on annual rainfall alone, once established. All of these plants should be native varieties or desert-adapted plants. After the first two years of increasingly infrequent irrigation, they will make it on their own.

Lawns are appropriate in the oasis zone or between it and the transitional zone. When developing the landscape plan, be aware that grass requires a huge amount of water. Turf is not for everyone. If you have no children or pets and play no lawn sports, you may not understand why anyone wants turf in the desert. Yet many people need a small lawn for a variety of reasons. An appropriate turf area is one that provides the homeowner with just enough lawn to serve the family's needs. Anything larger is excessive and expensive.

Efficient irrigation is a recurrent topic in these pages. Irrigation accounts for a majority of the water used in the desert. With efficient procedures, we can save thousands of gallons every year. It requires us to do several things. Observe your landscape plants and water them only when necessary. For established desert-adapted plants, this can range from weekly to monthly. There are many native varieties that require no supplemental irrigation after the first year or two and do just fine on rainfall. Other desert-adapted varieties require irrigation indefinitely.

Awareness of plant needs now will save time and water later. Irrigate plants of similar need with one station. Once you know how often the plants get thirsty, set your automatic system to that frequency. Changes are only necessary when dictated by weather, so increase irrigation frequency as temperatures rise and reduce it when temperatures decline. In addition to knowing when to water, you need to know how much. Based on studies of root development, shrubs require irrigation to a depth of two feet. Trees require irrigation to a depth of three feet.

Use a soil probe to check the depth of moisture after running the system for fifteen minutes. Continue adding irrigation time and probing after each increment. When you've run the system long enough to reach the desired depth, you will know the length of time. After this test run, your system will take care of the amount. Even when the weather changes and you need to apply water more frequently, don't increase the duration since watering beyond the recommended depth only wastes water.

Incorporating low-water-use plants in your landscape is the most significant thing you can do to save water, effort, and disappointment. When properly combined, drought-tolerant plants are lush and inviting, and create a distinctive Southwest look. Many species have proven to be reliable and pleasing in our landscapes here. Begin with trees, since they are the largest and most significant element of the garden. Think of them as the walls and ceiling of your outdoor rooms.

Trees:
Acacia
chaste tree (*Vitex agnus-castus*)
desert ironwood (*Olneya tesota*)
desert willow (*Chilopsis linearis*)
Eucalyptus
evergreen elm (*Ulmus parviolia* 'Sempervirens')
feather bush (*Lysiloma microphylla thornberri*)
chilean mesquite (*Prosopis chilensis*)
honey mesquite (*P. glandulosa*)
screwbean mesquite (*P. pubescens*)
Arizona or velvet mesquite (*P. velutina*)
palms (see Week 24)
blue palo verde (*Cercidium floridium*)
foothill palo verde (*C. microphyllum*)
Mexican palo verde (*Parkinsonia aculeate*)
Sonoran palo verde (*C. praecox*)
Texas ebony (*Pithecellobium flexicaule*)
western hackberry or palo blanco (*Celtis reticulata*)

Shrubs:
birds of paradise (*Caesalpinia gilliesii* and *C. mexicana*)
chuparosa (*Justicia californica*)
Cordia
creosote (*Larrea*)
Dalea (such as *Dalea greggii*)
fairy duster (*Calliandra eriophylla*)
hop bush (*Dodonaea viscosa*)
jojoba (*Simmondsia chinensis*)
Mt. Lemmon marigold (*Tagetes lemmonii*)
ocotillo (*Fouquieria splendens*)
Ruellia
sages (*Salvia ssp.*)
senna (*Cassia*)
sugar bush (*Rhus ovata*)

Texas mountain laurel (*Sophora secundiflora*)
Texas ranger or Texas sage (*Leucophyllum*)
yellow or coral bells (*Tecoma stans var.*)

Ground covers:
blackfoot daisy (*Melampodium leucanthum*)
Dalea
desert marigold (*Baileya multiradiata*)
evening primroses (*Oenothera ssp.*)
Gazania
germander (*Teucrium*)
golden fleece (*Thymophylla [Dyssodia] tenuiloba*)
hummingbird flower (*Zauschneria californica*)
Lantana
Myoporum
prairie zinnia (*Zinnia grandiflora*)
rosemary (*Rosemarinus officinalis*)
Texas betony (*Stachys coccinea*)
thyme (*Thymus vulgaris*)
verbena (*Glandularia*)

Vines:
bougainvillea (*Bougainvillea spectabilis*)
Carolina jessamine (*Gelsemium sempervirens*)
cat's claw (*Macfadyena unguis-cati*)
common trumpet creeper (*Campsis radicans*)
coral vine (*Antigonon leptopus*)
Lady Bank's rose (*Rosa banksiae*)
orchid vine (*Mascagnia*)
passionflower (*Passiflora incarnata*)
pink trumpet vine (*Podranea ricasoliana*)
Pyracantha
star jasmine (*Trachelospermum jasminoides*)
yellow morning glory (*Merremia tuberosa*)

Soil improvement is necessary if you are planting annuals, vegetables, herbs, exotics, or non-native perennials, which all require a soil type quite different from those of the desert. Generally, these plants belong in the mini oasis or special planters. If they survive in our native soil, they will always appear to be lacking something, tempting you to give them more water. Planting them in amended soil from the beginning promises greater success.

Trees reside in all three zones, and like natives and desert-adapted plants, require no soil amendments. They grow well in native soil as long as it was loosened at planting time. Most of the plants requiring amended soil are fairly small, and have correspondingly small root systems. Trees and shrubs have root systems that are 4–5 times the diameter of the top of the plants. You couldn't possibly supplement the soil to accommodate an area that size. This is one of the main reasons that a desert landscape should include primarily desert-adapted and native plants.

Apply mulch twice a year and your plants will be happy. As mulch degrades, some nutrients leach into the soil. While it sits atop the soil, it inhibits evaporation and helps maintain an appropriate soil temperature. It looks good, does its job well, and is relatively inexpensive when purchased in bulk. If you cannot locate a bulk source, buy materials in large bags from a nearby hardware or home improvement store.

Hardscape ideas

WEEK 9 As a great lover of plants, I'm fascinated by their quirks, needs, and potential. I love to mix varieties, textures, colors, and heights. Planning, choosing, preparing, planting, nurturing, and observing are constant pleasures for me. Season to season and year to year, the landscape changes and evolves to present an ever-changing palette of possibilities. Yet within this dynamic setting there must be some constants to bring stability to the scene. Thus, the hardscape: the ramada, the arbor, the raised beds, and the paths. These are the sturdy, permanent structures against which all the green things are highlighted. I even have a potting shed in which to propagate and create more horticultural delights. These structures anchor my garden and provide the backdrop for all that is wonderful. They afford the eye something solid and reliable on which to focus, while the flashy and fascinating fills the in-between spaces.

A ramada is utterly "Southwest," offering a space to sit, relax, and enjoy. As a multi-functional garden space, a ramada becomes an outdoor dining room as well as a place to congregate and play. It offers covered protection from the heat of the day, although the cover need not be solid. If it is slatted, heat can rise and dissipate, making it cooler than a solidly covered structure.

To create a quiet, reflective garden space, consider an arbor. As a structure on which vines and climbing plants grow, an arbor affords privacy and seclusion. Rustic or formal, it provides height in the landscape and a focal point when viewed from a distance. You can build one from wood, metal, or PVC pipe. Once constructed, it can be hidden under foliage or left unadorned.

Many other constructed elements provide structure and "bones" to your garden. Birdhouses and feeders elevated on poles of varying heights are both decorative and functional. Raised beds hold richer soil and add levels of visual interest. Wrought iron hooks holding candles or lanterns provide nighttime path illumination and visual contrast.

Wrought iron is a terrific choice for small fences and garden gates, delineating the perimeters of potagers, herb gardens, iris beds, or play spaces. I also like wrought iron accessories, including baker's racks, tables, chairs, and trellises. The use of wrought iron in several projects throughout the garden provides a unifying effect.

FERTILIZATION AND IRRIGATION: ROSES, LAWNS, AND GRAPES

In the desert, rosebushes display their grandest blossoms only four weeks from now, during the first part of April. You should now see signs of growth, including buds and leaf development, signaling the need for deep irrigation and the first fertilization of the season. Old rose growers are superstitious about the components of that first fertilization, and happily share their recipe. The following suggestion is one upon which my rose aficionado friends agreed.

Rose fertilizer
1/2 cup ammonium phosphate
1/2 cup gypsum
1/2 cup soil sulfur
1/2 cup magnesium sulfate (Epsom salts)
1 tablespoon chelated iron

Thoroughly mix all ingredients and sprinkle around the base of one rose bush. Water in.

Although I'm certain that the above recipe produces exceptional results, I take a much simpler approach. I sprinkle a handful of Epsom salts and a handful of commercial rose food around the base of each bush, and water them in. Every two weeks through May, I fertilize again with the rose food only and believe that the roses appreciate any fertilizer and will produce bigger, more profuse blossoms upon receiving it. They aren't too fussy, so neither am I.

Once they are actively growing, "deadhead" the roses every day. By consistently removing the blossoms, you stimulate new growth and flower production, increasing the yield and extending the season. Roses need water every 5–7 days to a depth of eighteen inches. Maintain this schedule until the average daily high is above 90°, at which time increase the irrigation schedule to every two or three days throughout the summer.

Take a similar approach with grapevines. When you see signs of new growth, irrigate and apply a cup of ammonium sulfate around the base of each plant, then water again to wash the fertilizer into the root zone. For an organic approach, use blood meal according to package directions. I notice a quicker response with ammonium sulfate, but the plants seem to react similarly in the long run. Fertilize grapevines once a month through summer and fall.

A friend of mine who is developing a vineyard with the goal of opening a winery fertilizes more frequently. His vines grow vigorously and the vineyard is a beautiful sight to behold—which proves that an increased application of fertilizer leads to more growth. My friend also waters a lot more than I do to support the additional growth. But I'm happy with the growth rate of my vines and comfortable with the amount of water dedicated to them.

If you overseeded your hybrid Bermuda lawn with perennial rye, apply a commercial lawn fertilizer according to package directions, or you can use four pounds of ammonium sulfate to every thousand square feet of turf. As always, water before and after the application.

Turf experts often recommend using a preemergent for broadleaf weed control in February. You may never have to do this since a healthy, well-groomed lawn doesn't allow weeds to compete. However, if you did not overseed, or had trouble with fungus, use a preemergent, since the resulting thin or bare spots are susceptible to weeds.

"Weed and feed" products conveniently include fertilizer, herbicides to kill weeds, and a pesticide to control turf insects and the resulting damage. Read and compare product labels to determine which ingredients address the problems in your lawn and apply the one that contains only the necessary products. Avoid excessive chemical use by applying products that treat the specific needs of your lawn.

A QUICK BIT OF ANNUAL COLOR

As winter plods on and I become restless, I need a quick floral fix—something new, fresh, and colorful. Pots or open spots look desolate as they await new plants, and entire beds lay empty. It's on these spaces that I focus my energy when compelled to plant now. Driven by the need to get my hands in the soil, I take a trip to the local nursery. It is easy to know what to plant now, as nothing else will be on the shelves. Tucked safely away in the greenhouse, tender annuals won't be pulled from their protective domain for several weeks, and I don't step inside those warm environs for fear of silly temptation. I only allow myself to look at the material sitting out in the open. It always includes more pansies and petunias, as well as pink, foxglove, flowering kale, larkspur, primrose, poppy, stock, and violas.

To fill a small bed or section, begin in the back and move forward. Larkspurs (*Delphinium scaposum*), tall and beautifully foliated, make terrific back-row plants. Their flowers grow on stalks that stand above the rest of the plants in the bed and make a bold background statement. Stepping down in height to the middle of the bed, stock (*Matthiola incana*) is a good choice, its gray-green foliage contrasting nicely with the bright green stems and leaves behind it. The pink, purple, and white blooms boldly accent the middle of the bed as a sweet fragrance (stock's best feature) naturally perfumes the air.

If stock is not to your liking, fill the center of the bed with poppies (*Papaver*). When planted close together, the fragile stems and petals support one another against wind and create extra protection from winter storms. In addition to adding color and contrast to a mixed bed, poppies are exceptional when crowded together with nothing else to detract from their bright, crepe paper beauty.

Once you have filled that middle ground, consider planting a row or two of primrose (*Primula*) or violas. Each comes in a wide range of colors, including blues, lavenders, purples and whites. Choose shades that complement the colors of those plants already in the plan, and then scatter a section of sweet alyssum right up front to cascade down the planting area, filling nooks and crannies. Another option for this spot is thyme (*Thymus vulgaris*). Although any type is appropriate, the golden variety is especially attractive, and lemon thyme offers a refreshing scent when you brush over it.

While at the nursery buying your plants, look at color and texture as you line the pots up in the same arrangement they will assume in the garden. A full wagon will give you the same impression you want to create in your flowerbed. Use this as a test-run and experiment with different plants to create a pleasing combination. If the plants are not in bloom, ask for assistance or read descriptive labels to determine what the blossom colors will be.

Create a color scheme for the entire bed, using no more than three basic colors. Check labels for mature height and width, making sure that what is destined for the back row will actually be the tallest plants when fully grown. Buy enough plants to touch their neighbors when they've reached full size without crowding one another or competing for nutrients and sunlight. The idea is to build a bed of solid plant material so that no dirt shows through once the plants mature.

White stands out against green foliage during the day and reflects the moonlight at night, making it an excellent color choice near living spaces. Blossoms of white accentuate cool and relaxing blues, greens, and violets, and create a particularly comforting scene in warm weather. Beautiful together, these shades lend themselves to a contemplative environment. Warm, vibrant colors, including red, orange, and yellow energize both the garden and people in it. This color combination offers visual stimulation during the winter months. Another eye-popping color combination is purple and yellow, often observed in nature. By considering height, texture, color, and their various combinations you can create a variety of planter and garden possibilities that perfectly suit the spots you need to fill now.

Planning future landscape projects

February is an excellent time to plant native or desert-adapted plants. Hardy enough to withstand the remaining cold nights, these plants benefit from extra time in the ground to establish roots before the heat arrives. If you have a landscape plan, whether on paper or in your mind, you already know where you want trees, shrubs, and ground covers. If you don't have a firm plan, now is the time to create one.

To develop the best plan for your particular needs, consider what your garden activities are and where you want shade, height, color, and contrast. Do you need to create a visual screen? Are there places in your garden that beg for a strong accent plant such as agave or euphorbia? Does your current landscape have water-wasting plants that you want to replace with drought-tolerant species? Answer these questions and determine what you need to add, remove, or accent. Make your sketches, and then use your ideas to begin preparations.

When adding new plants to your property, mark the planting areas, with the mature size of the plant in mind, before you begin digging. Based on several university studies conducted throughout the United States, guidelines for landscaping have changed and no longer require huge planting holes. Additional university studies, conducted over the last twenty years, proved that amending the soil for new plantings does not benefit the plants. Actually, just the opposite is true.

When you take a plant from a container and put it in the ground, the roots grow beyond the container's soil. If you create a wonderfully rich place in the ground, the roots rapidly grow into the medium, which is similar to the original potting soil. When the growing roots reach the native soil, however, they rebel. In the majority of researched cases, the roots chose to grow around and around in the amended soil rather than extend into the native soil, leading to root-bound plants. Conversely, when the plants were placed directly into the native soil and irrigated properly, the water encouraged the roots to grow into the challenging native soil. It took them longer, but ultimately they were healthier and better adapted to their environment, developing root systems at the normal width of 4–5 times that of the plant.

Look at your piece of land and decide what it really ought to be and then make arrangements with yourself to get it to that point. This time-consuming process is a labor of love. Each of my last three gardens took nearly five years to complete, working one season at a time and creating what I had the resources to create. Be patient; do what you can. There will be another season, another year, a little more time to complete the picture. The key is to have that picture in your mind and to visualize what you're working toward.

March

- Thin deciduous fruit
- Propagate cactus from cuttings
- Divide perennials
- Plant perennials, shrubs, and trees
- Prune oleanders
- Clean up herb beds and ornamental grasses
- Plant herbs
- Plant late spring and summer vegetables
- Plant warm-season annual flowers
- Fertilize grapes and roses
- Fertilize overseeded Bermuda lawns
- Control weeds
- Spray 'Olive Stop' to prevent blossoming on mulberries, olives, and others
- Mulch under and around plants to conserve water and cool soil

March

GETTING A JUMP-START ON THE VEGETABLE BED

WEEK 10

In the desert, hot temperatures quickly follow the last frost date, creating a short spring and summer vegetable season. Temperatures above 95° cause many fruits and vegetables to shut down production until cooler temperatures return. In particularly warm years, this leaves only a few weeks of prime vegetable weather. Anticipating this possibility, many gardeners risk late frosts and put their seedlings out early.

Beans, cucumbers, melons, peppers, squash, and tomato plants can go into the vegetable garden now. As the daytime temperatures increase, their roots spread through the moderately warm soil and the plants acclimate to their new surroundings. Frequently, we have no freezing weather during the month of March and plants benefit from an early, uninterrupted beginning. But the last frost date is the end of March, so if you put your plants out early you must protect them from potential freezing temperatures. Protect young plants from freeze by covering each seedling with a glass cloche or large, overturned glass jar. Cardboard boxes with some sort of weight on them also provide protection when placed over the plants without touching the leaves.

If daytime temperatures aren't too high, leave the glass covers, like miniature greenhouses, over the plants, but remove the boxes in the morning for full sun exposure. Plastic row covers or old sheets work too, but must be elevated above the plants to avoid damage when they touch the leaves. Any system that allows full exposure to the sun and protection from the frost will work. If you fail to listen to the evening weather report and leave your young plants exposed to a freeze you will have to start over since they tolerate no frost. It takes an attentive gardener to set out early and enjoy the rewards of a longer vegetable season.

A CITRUS SYNOPSIS

The versatile citrus fruits are paradisiacal gifts borne on trees that stand out as specimen plants or solid screens in the garden. Delicious when peeled and eaten fresh, they liven up salads and sauces, and make tangy-sweet preserves. For centuries, the ruling classes coveted and grew dozens of citrus varieties whose presence in the garden indicated stature and wealth. Continuing their rich history, these stately evergreen trees add color, flavor, and interest to the desert garden.

Although some areas of the Southwest get too cold in the winter, most desert dwellers can create a microclimate conducive to citrus. If the temperature never drops below 28°, your garden is perfectly suited to all types of citrus. Likewise, if native ironwood trees proliferate in your locale, citrus trees will thrive. Beyond these obvious indicators, close observation of your garden will help you to determine if citrus trees will survive, and where they should be planted. Some basic weather information will help you accurately assess your particular property.

Warm air rises, while cold air settles into pockets and flows downhill, usually following waterways and washes. Hence gardens adjacent to riverbeds and natural washes are most susceptible to frost damage. Similarly, as cold air passes through your neighborhood it drops into low spots, settles in, and hangs around for a while, much like the puddling of water. As the cold air sits in these locations for long periods of time, the potential for frost damage increases.

Other significant contributors to microclimate temperatures are structures—buildings, block walls, fencing, paving, and even large trees or hedges. Like a dam, upright concrete or block structures hold back cold air and prevent it from seeping out of low spots, but they also absorb and reflect sunlight. This reflected heat can raise the microclimate temperature as much as 10° during the day. Those same structures hold heat at night, reflecting it back to warm the immediate area.

A questionably cool location can be acceptable for citrus if it benefits from radiant heat from an adjacent western or southern exposure. Because the sun rises in the east and sets in the west, western exposure means that a wall is to the east of the garden area and the sun shines on it in the afternoon. Southern exposure means that the wall faces the south, thus receiving sunlight much of the day in the desert Southwest. For many plants, a western exposure provides too much heat in the desert, but this location is perfect for citrus. They thrive on heat as long as they receive ample water.

Ample water supplied by the thoughtful gardener must saturate the soil to a depth of three feet and drain well, too. Drainage is often a big problem in the desert. Some of our very sandy soils (especially those along riverbeds and washes) drain too rapidly. If this is true in your garden, your citrus will need more frequent irrigation, but you will also escape the potential problems associated with the heavy clay or caliche-laden soils often found in our region.

If your garden soil contains lots of clay and caliche, a few simple guidelines will help you to properly prepare it before you plant your citrus tree. Dig a hole that is 2–5 times the width of the root ball, and only as deep. Fill the hole with water and allow it to drain. If after twenty-four hours water remains in the hole, you must correct the drainage problem. To effectively provide drainage, dig a "chimney," or tunnel, through the clay or caliche, off to the side of center. This positioning of the chimney allows excess water to drain away from the root ball and prevents the roots from growing directly into the drain sight. Dig the chimney deep enough to break through the caliche or clay layer and then fill it with organic material mixed with the native soil. (Do not use gravel.) Test again for drainage, filling it with water and making certain it drains within twenty-four hours. If a problem still exists, repeat the procedure on the opposite side of the planting hole. This should create a properly draining site in even the most challenging soils.

In addition to microclimate temperatures, airflow, structural exposure, and soil requirements, choice of variety plays a major role in a citrus grower's success. Some varieties are more cold tolerant than others. They rank in the following order, from most frost-sensitive to most tolerant: Mexican lime (28°), Tahiti or 'Bears' lime, lemon, grapefruit, pummelo, tangelo, limequat, sweet orange (26°), navel orange, 'Valencia' orange, tangerine or mandarin orange, 'Improved Meyer' lemon (24°), kumquat, and calamondin (20°).

When selecting citrus trees, patronize a reputable nursery that identifies not only the tree variety, but also the rootstock on which it is grafted. Sour orange rootstock is most advisable in the desert Southwest, since it is tolerant of colder temperatures, alkaline soils, and pathogens. Careso and Troyer are the two preferred rootstock varieties based on vigor, disease resistance, and soil preference. If you prefer a dwarf tree, Flying Dragon rootstock naturally controls ultimate tree size and is well adapted to our desert soils. You may also find citrus trees grafted onto rough lemon rootstock. While adapted to our soils, it is hardy to only 28°, making it unacceptable if temperatures typically fall below that in your area.

Mexican lime (*Citrus aurantiifolia*), often referred to as Key lime, frequently graces the produce section of your local grocery store. Small and green to yellow-green, the tangy fruit grows on upright, twiggy trees whose mature height is 12–15 feet. Unable to tolerate temperatures below 28°, Mexican limes are unsuitable for most Southwest landscapes, but do well in easily moved and protected pots and planters. The lime's glossy, evergreen leaves and year-round production make it an excellent botanical decoration for patios, ramadas, decks, and poolsides.

'Bears' lime is the best cultivar for the desert Southwest, usually doing well where oranges grow. It is more frost tolerant than Mexican lime, but still requires frost protection. A hybrid between a small lime and a citron, 'Bears' lime is a thorny tree that is angular when young, but rounds out at maturity. The tree drops many leaves during winter, leaving it more exposed to cold temperatures. Fruit ripens August through January. For guaranteed success, plant 'Bears' lime in a pot at least eighteen inches wide, and move it to a pro-tected area by mid-November. Move it back into a full-sun location the first week in April.

Among the lemons (*C. limon*), the rough-surfaced 'Eureka' found in super-market bins ripens continuously on twenty-foot trees with large, dark green leaves, dense canopies, and few thorns. Lisbon lemons taste almost identical to 'Eureka', and have a more prominent pointed blossom end than other lemons. These smoother-skinned fruits grow on slightly larger, thornier trees and are only a little less frost-tolerant. Ponderosa, a beautiful ornamental, is most likely a hybrid of lemon and citron. Each thick-skinned, mildly flavored fruit weighs up to two pounds, but is inferior to 'Eureka' or 'Lisbon'. The ponderosa tree itself is often chosen for its ornamental value as an attractive composition-in-contrast between huge, year-round yellow fruits, and dark, glossy leaves.

The most popular home garden citrus choice is the grapefruit (*C. paradisi*), the easiest citrus to grow. Grapefruits adjust to transplanting more quickly than other citrus trees and grow rapidly. Our high summer heat increases sugar content in the fruit, ranking them among the finest. Desert-grown grapefruit, the sweetest you'll ever taste, are ready to eat in December but grow sweeter with increased time on the tree. Fruit left through the month of May will be incomparably sweet. Since mature grapefruit trees reach 12–20 feet in height, with a spread of up to twenty-four feet, select a location to accommodate that size.

Seedless 'Marsh' is the most frequently planted white grapefruit in both commercial and home situations, with seeded 'Duncan' a distant second. Since these requires high heat to reach peak sugar levels, the desert is an ideal environment. The pink grapefruits commonly grown in the desert are, from lightest to darkest pink, 'Flame', 'Redblush', and 'Texas Star Ruby'. They require desert heat to color up nicely. 'Oroblanco' and 'Melogold', (grapefruit-pummelo hybrids) are larger and smoother-skinned than standard grapefruit, have a higher sugar content, and require less heat to "sugar up."

All of the grapefruits are most flavorful when eaten shortly after harvest, but will keep for about two weeks at room temperature. Because the coolness of a refrigerator causes loss of sweetness and flavor, it is best to harvest as needed, beginning in December and continuing through May. If I still have fruit on the tree by the first week in June, I harvest it all and juice it. Usually, however, my family manages to eat them along the way and very little goes to waste.

The tangelo (*C. paradisi x C. reticulata*) is a cross between grapefruit and tangerine, or mandarin orange. 'Minneola', which produces large orange-red fruit, is the most commonly planted. These easy-to-peel, juicy fruits usually have 7–12 seeds. Less vigorous than 'Minneola', but more cold tolerant, 'Orlando' is the second successful desert grower. It ripens from November to mid-January and is an exceptional juicing fruit, while 'Minneola' matures from January through February and is best eaten out-of-hand.

The compact, shrubby limequats (*Fortunella margarita x Citrus aurantifolia*), hybrids of kumquats and 'Mexican' limes, make excellent container plants. The fruits ripen from early November through mid-March and resemble large, light yellow olives. Because they tolerate slightly colder temperatures, lime-quats are a good lime substitute for many gardeners. The most successful variety in the desert Southwest is 'Tavares'.

Arizona sweet oranges (*C. sinensis*) good for juicing and fresh consumption, may soon be the most frequently planted orange in the desert. Three varieties that perform reliably are: 'Hamlin', an early ripener that bears frequently seedless, medium fruit; 'Marrs', a smaller tree bearing medium to large, lightly-seeded fruit; and 'Trovita', an excellent full-size tree bearing medium to large fruit. One variety I caution gardeners against is 'Pineapple' sweet orange, so named because the fruit has a mild pineapple aroma. Each orange has from 20–25 seeds, making them a nuisance for fresh eating and this variety is neither as juicy nor flavorful as the 'Valencia'.

Navel oranges, grown for their delicious fresh fruit, are the most frost sensitive of the sweet oranges. Juice them immediately before serving the juice because a naturally occurring compound called limonin causes bitterness when stored. Among the navels, 'Parent Washington' grows most extensively in the desert Southwest. It produces large, juicy fruits that are ripe by Thanksgiving. Other varieties of similar quality are 'Robertson', 'Newhall', and 'Thompson' improved. 'Fukumoto' is an earlier repining variety often ready for harvest by the end of October, but because of its early maturation the skin sometimes remains green tinged. This confuses gardeners as to ripeness and is the major reason this variety does well commercially but not in the home garden. Lane Late, an Australian cultivar, ripens later and is the last of the traditional navels recommended for the desert. Several newer varieties promising potential in the desert, include 'Autumn Gold', 'Barnsfield', 'Chislett', 'Powell', and 'Summer Gold'.

'Valencia', prized for its juice quality and high sugar content, is very ornamental when bearing the deep orange-red fruits that ripen in March. It is suitable for only the warmest desert regions or microclimates, because fruit must winter on the tree and becomes unpalatable in colder areas. I recommend it for the city gardener who has warmer winter temperatures from high levels of reflected and accumulated heat. Two favorite varieties are 'Campbell' and 'Olinda', and two promising new varieties are 'Delta' and 'Midnight'.

My favorite homegrown oranges are the pigmented or blood oranges. Three varieties that do best in the desert are 'Moro', 'Sallustiana', and 'Sanquinella', all vigorous, open trees that produce medium to large fruit with few seeds and develop a deep red pigmentation in the flesh and skin. Sweet, delicious, and beautiful when sliced or segmented, they make a memorable addition to green salads and an attractive presentation when alternated with traditional oranges. Blood oranges ripen in late winter or early spring and develop greater amounts of red pigment when exposed to more hours of winter cold. The cooler the winter, the redder the fruit.

The names tangerine and mandarin orange refer to the same plant (*Citrus reticulata*). These 12–15-foot trees produce small, tasty fruit that ripens from November through January, but it stores poorly and is best eaten soon after harvest. Since they are loose-skinned, clip them from the tree rather than plucking to prevent "plugging" the fruit away from the stem end, which leaves a hole in the skin. The popular varieties ripen at different times, with 'Clementine' and 'Fairchild' ready to harvest in November, 'Daisy' and 'Dancy' in December, and 'Kinnow' in January. They all store best on the tree, but for only a few weeks. A common tangerine trait is the tendency to be alternate bearing, meaning that a large harvest is generally followed by a small harvest the next year.

Next on the hardiness scale is the 'Meyer' lemon (*Citrus sinensis x Citrus limon*) called valley lemon in regions of Texas. A hybrid of sweet orange and lemon, round in shape, smooth-skinned, and less acidic than traditional lemons, 'Meyer' lemons peel easily and get quite large, while the tree remains fairly small. Unfortunately, this, my favorite citrus, is not universally available. It silently harbors the devastating disease, Citrus Tristeza virus (CTV), also known as citrus quick decline. Because of the threat to all citrus trees, 'Meyer' is illegal in many areas, including the state of Arizona. The University of California at Riverside developed 'Improved Meyer' lemon, which some areas have approved. They attain a maximum height of 12–15 feet and are excellent for pot culture. If legal in your area, look into this exceptional plant.

Kumquats (*Fortunella margarita*) are frost-tolerant close cousins to the citrus and bear fruit from October to March. With tart flesh and sweet skin, the fruit makes excellent marmalade and pickles. The trees grow slowly to a height of 6–25 feet, living for decades if properly cared for. 'Fukush', 'Melwa', and 'Nagami' are the most common kumquats grown in the desert. 'Melwa', the sweetest of the three, is preferred for fresh eating. They make interesting container plants and are beautiful when planted around pools and patios.

Calamondin (x *Citrofortunella mitis*) an evergreen and columnar cousin to the citrus, attains a maximum height of ten feet with an eight-foot canopy. The two-inch-round, sweet and sour fruit ripens from March through December and is a base for marmalade or pickle. I have a friend from Spain who thinks calamondin makes marmalade most similar to her native 'Seville' orange. The highly ornamental calamondin adds character to courtyards and planters, and its attractive shape and size predestine it to patios and outdoor dining areas. It makes an excellent base planting on the south or west side of a building, looks fabulous in large terra cotta containers, and is lovely when grouped 4–5 feet apart and clipped as a hedge. Whether viewed up close or from a distance, calamondin is an attractive landscape plant.

After determining the best location and variety of citrus for your garden, dig and test the hole for drainage, then carefully remove the tree from its container and settle it into the damp hole. Citrus roots are extremely sensitive to disturbance, so use extra care when removing your tree from its original container. Cut the bottom off the can and slit the sides so it slips off easily. Gently position the tree and re-fill the hole with the same soil you removed (minus any caliche or solid clay). Firm the soil into the hole, making sure the tree sits slightly above the level it did in the container and that the bud union is above ground. The trunk must be above the irrigation level so that it never sits in water for any length of time.

Build a watering well with about a two-foot radius from the base of the tree and immediately fill it with water. Citrus is susceptible to a fungus disease called gummosis or foot rot, which is caused by a soil-borne fungus that attacks the trunk material. To prevent gummosis, plant the tree at the correct level and never let the trunk sit in water. If your tree does develop gummosis, examine the tree's planting depth, check your watering practices, and make any necessary adjustments. Then remove the diseased bark and paint the affected area with a copper-based fungicide or Bordeaux mixture.

When given proper care, citrus trees remain relatively trouble free. Aphids sometimes colonize lush new growth, but a strong jet of water or insecticidal soap easily controls them. Thrips also infest citrus trees, causing deformed or curly leaves. But I don't recommend a treatment for these benign pests since their damage is purely aesthetic and insignificant to tree and fruit health. Other pests include the swallowtail butterfly, which lays its eggs on the leaves of citrus trees. When the young caterpillars emerge, cleverly camouflaged to look like bird droppings, they begin to eat. On a mature tree their presence is inconsequential, but they can cause a lot of damage to a young tree, sometimes completely defoliating it within days.

Keep your eye open for swallowtail butterflies and disappearing leaves; when you notice them, remove the caterpillars immediately. When you know what to look for, they are easy to locate and remove. If you don't want to touch the little creatures, Bacillus thuriengensis (Bt) is an effective, organic pesticide that affects only caterpillars.

Do not fertilize your citrus tree for the first year. Water it regularly and work toward extending your irrigation frequency to a 2–3 week schedule. Don't worry about seeing very little growth, because citrus trees are slow to adapt to a new environment. You can't see that the tree is developing a root structure that will support the eventual top-growth. It's not unusual for citrus trees to take 3–4 years to really start growing, but once they do, they quickly develop into full-sized fruit producers.

Next February, begin the regular cycle of fertilization, following package directions. Repeat the treatment in May and again in August, continuing the thrice-yearly practice every year. These specific times provide nutrients to the trees at high-growth periods while avoiding weather extremes. Occasionally, citrus trees become chlorotic and need an iron treatment. Always use chelated iron as directed by the manufacturer. Aside from the removal of frost damage, crossing branches, or dead wood, you should not prune your citrus trees. They need their foliage and long, skirt-like branches to protect the trunk from cold temperatures and the sun's blistering rays.

If you plan to grow several varieties of citrus trees, I heartily recommend the book *Citrus: Complete Guide to Selecting & Growing More Than 100 Varieties For California, Arizona, Texas, The Gulf Coast, Florida*, by Lance Walheim. Nearly all of the information in this specific, yet comprehensive book applies to citrus in the desert. It is an excellent resource if you have more than the occasional concern.

Provide your citrus tree with minimal, consistent care, and you'll enjoy years, maybe even decades, of pleasure and production. With few trees more attractive, citrus must certainly have grown in abundance in Eden. They are so exquisite, how could they not?

WEEK 11 We worked like pioneers that first spring in our current home. There were so many projects on the list and a limited number of weekend and after-work hours—we had ditches to dig, irrigation lines to lay, shrubs to plant, and river rock to collect and set. For the most part, these tasks were heavy work, requiring the strength and abilities of an adult. My husband and I spent hours in the sun and felt a pleasant sense of accomplishment, and I wanted my kids to feel a sense of success and contribution, too. One section of the backyard was as yet unplanned. We had thoughts of a potting bench or a picnic table, maybe even a small pond or fountain, but until we made up our minds, it was a full-sun plot of barren land waiting to be used. This is how we decided to grow a sunflower house, whose enticing pictures I'd seen in a magazine.

Common sunflower
(Helianthus annus)

Russian mammoth sunflowers and moonflowers, a type of morning glory, were our seeds of choice. This was the plan: The sunflowers would grow to a height of 8–10 feet in just over two months, while the moonflower vines would take a little longer to germinate and grow and then weave up and around the sunflower stalks. When they reached the flower heads, we would lace twine between the blooms to construct a beam structure for them to cling to, creating the "roof." It sounded like a great spring and summer activity.

We drew an outline of the exterior walls on the ground with a stick, leaving a gap for a door. We tilled the marked sections to a depth and width of about eight inches, blended in an all-purpose fertilizer, smoothed it out, and began to plant. Our youngest daughter, only five at the time, was assigned the task of irrigation. She did an excellent job of filling the furrows we constructed around the "walls," taking care not to disturb the mulch spread along the planting sights. With her daily attention, it took only a couple of weeks for the sunflower seedlings to emerge.

Then we discovered that gardening in an unenclosed section of the desert is truly a battle between man and nature. One day we had lovely 2–3-inch, evenly spaced seedlings around the perimeter of the "house." The next day we discovered a series of one-inch holes in the ground. The seedlings had disappeared, but where had they gone? We had no clue.

We planted again, determined to be more attentive. Lisa watered meticulously, and after about ten days we began to check the ground several times a day, knowing sprouts would soon emerge. Sure enough, they came up. We watched the plot like hawks and discovered that bunnies were very fond of sunflower seedlings. Now we knew what we were up against and we planted again. For our third attempt, we put up barricades to discourage the rabbits and faithfully watered the seeds, expecting sprouts in 10–14 days. Like clockwork, they emerged. We were so proud! A month behind schedule, we could still envision tea parties and picnics within the walls of our rapidly developing structure.

And then they were gone…again. I walked into the backyard one day and a thrasher greeted me with a seedling hanging from his curved bill. Most irritating was that the thrashers didn't eat the seedlings, but seemed to pull them up for sport. I hate to admit this, but we gave up. After four attempts, we were beaten. The desert and her native creatures won each round, and we didn't have the grit to go another.

Since then I have planted hundreds of sunflower seeds, the bulk of them reaching maturity. We've used them as border plants and screens, in the backs of flowerbeds, and tucked into nooks and crannies. But we have not yet grown that sunflower house. I still dream of doing it and have told many others how. I even gave simple instructions, replete with precautionary advice, to a class I taught. I just haven't developed the courage to try again; but if I do, I know several sunflower varieties that will make great walls.

SIMPLE YET SOPHISTICATED COMMON SUNFLOWER

Helianthus annuus is the Latin name for the most American of flowers—the common sunflower. A versatile plant, the sunflower's beauty and utility have made it a favorite for generations. It's no wonder we enjoy them in today's gardens as much the ancient peoples of North and South America enjoyed them hundreds of years ago.

Every part of the sunflower is usable. Seeds are cultivated for birdseed and snacks. Pioneers used stalk fibers to create a coarse, linen-like fabric. Livestock consume the stems and leaves, and the petals are the source of a murky yellow dye. The oil from the pressed heads, often used in cooking, is low in saturated fat. Kernels ground into coarse flour in eastern Europe, and added to bread and cereal recipes. These full sun plants even entertain as the faces of the maturing flowers follow the sun across the summer sky.

Sunflowers aren't particular about soil. Slight amendment produces larger, healthier plants and flower heads, but I've grown lovely specimens in caliche- and stone-laden soils. Plant the large seeds an inch underground and cover with soil. Water them in and keep them damp. To prevent thrashers and others from stealing your crop, secure bird netting over the planting site until the seedlings are several inches tall. Once they have emerged, irrigate every three days, adjusting for your soil type and temperatures. As temperatures increase, you may need to water more frequently, although the mature plants become somewhat drought tolerant. Test their limits by waiting for the wilt point between irrigations, but be careful not to push the limits too far, since there is such a thing as permanent wilt. When they need water, the leaves of the small plants wilt dramatically. Irrigate when you notice this symptom and then use that time period as your schedule base.

If you are growing sunflowers for large, heavy heads with lots of seeds, choose 'Mammoth Russian', 'Super Snack', or 'Aztec Gold' varieties. These grow on thick, sturdy stalks and produce blossoms that are ten inches in diameter and packed with seeds. Cure them on the stalk, or cut them off and lay them out in a warm, dry location when the petals begin to drop. I plant as many of these varieties as my garden will hold, saving the dry heads for cardinals and orioles that visit our birdhouse throughout the year. Salted and roasted, these same seeds make tasty, portable snacks.

For florist quality sunflower arrangements and bouquets, choose 'Del Sol', 'Sunbeam', 'Sunrich Lemon', 'Sunspot', and 'Tangina', all of which develop 5–7 flowers on sturdy stalks. Cut them when the petals are mature and put them in a vase containing an equal blend of lemon-lime soda and tap water. To avoid decomposition and stagnation, remove all foliage below the water line and change the water every day. If kept out of direct sunlight, the cut sunflowers will stay fresh for at least five days.

For small clusters, try 'Sundrops' or 'Valentine', which are fine for cutting and look more like their wild counterparts when left in the garden. For very tight spaces, consider some of the hybrids that remain very small. 'Sundance Kid' is one such variety, reaching a mature height of only fifteen inches. 'Elf' is another dwarf whose short stalks support four-inch blossoms. These and many others are available through mail-order catalogs and on local seed racks.

If you cannot find particular varieties, read specific package descriptions to learn the characteristics of each available type. Make your selection based on the garden space you have allotted and the intended uses of the blossoms. I enjoy looking at the many types that are available every year and always plant new varieties along with the old reliables.

THE LUXURIANT SPLENDOR OF TEXAS MOUNTAIN LAUREL

If pressed to identify my favorite landscape plant, Texas mountain laurel (*Sophora secundiflora*) might be it. Often called mescal bean, it is admirable in almost every way. It's a slow-growing native of Texas, New Mexico, and northern Mexico, taking nearly a decade to attain a height of about twenty feet, eventually reaching thirty feet at maturity. Texas mountain laurel tolerates extreme heat, cold, wind, drought, and poor soil. While consuming very little water, it graces the garden with year-round beauty and seasonal splendor, dazzling with its bright green 4–6 inch leaves, divided into glossy, oval leaflets. The sculptural branches bearing these verdant leaves are generally upright and silvery-gray in color, and remain unchanged in appearance despite extreme heat and cold.

Adding to the beauty of Texas mountain laurel foliage is its spectacular floral display. Even very young plants put on the sweet-smelling show. From February through April, this amazing tree bears wisteria-like clusters of pea-shaped, eye-catching, violet-blue flowers that are some of the most fragrant blooms in the garden. From early morning through evening the luscious scent of sweet grape soda saturates the air. Developing as the flowers fade, cream-colored pods dry to look like strands of giant pearls. If left on the tree, the pods eventually open to expose bright red seeds, which are poisonous but possess an outer coat so hard that they pass through most digestive systems intact. As a precaution, I clip the pods off my trees when they are young.

In addition to removing a potential source of accidental poisoning, this is beneficial in two ways. First, when I trim the pods off, the tree rewards me with another round of flowers. Second, because the weight of the maturing pods pulls branches down, their removal allows the plant to maintain an upright stance. I store the pods in my garden shed until they are completely dry, and then use them in dried floral arrangements.

An excellent specimen plant, Texas mountain laurel can anchor a section of the garden or stand gloriously alone. Planted in clusters of three, they create a pleasing oasis if left unaccompanied or underplanted with yellow flowering groundcover like lantana or evening primrose. I like the look of several Texas mountain laurel shrubs planted 8–10-feet apart as a natural screen or divider in the landscape. I have seen them trimmed as hedges, planted in masses, and espaliered (trained to grow flat against a wall or trellis).

Planting Texas mountain laurel could not be easier. Because they'll grow in the poorest soils, I've used them as "solution plants" in areas of my garden that have either heavy clay soil or caliche-laden ground. Most literature indicates that these hardy plants must have well-drained soil, but this has not been my experience. When planted in tight soil they need water much less frequently. I have never lost one to fungus or root rot, as would be expected if an intolerance for poor drainage were a serious consideration. They thrive in almost anything.

Since Texas mountain laurel is very slow growing, plant from five- or fifteen-gallon containers. Dig the hole only as deep as the root ball, loosening the dirt several feet around the actual planting hole. Gently remove the plant from its can and score the roots several times. Place in the hole and back fill with the original soil, then firmly tamp down the soil and water well. Plan to irrigate every other day for the next two weeks. After that, water every 5–7 days for a month. Begin stretching the time between waterings as you work toward the ultimate irrigation schedule of once every 2–3 weeks. After two years in the ground, Texas mountain laurel survives nicely on annual rainfall alone. In times of drought, however, they benefit from a monthly irrigation.

I fertilize my Texas mountain laurel plants twice a year, in early fall and early spring, with a nitrogen-rich fertilizer. As with all fertilization, I water thoroughly before and after the application. I also keep my eyes on the new growth as it emerges, since it is the preferred food for the larvae of a small blue-gray butterfly. Throughout the spring and summer, whenever I see signs of caterpillars or caterpillar damage, I immediately spray with *Bacillus thuriengensis* (Bt). This prevents the possibility of losing the entire season's new growth to these voracious creatures. Bt is the best solution for caterpillar problems because it's a natural insecticide that affects only caterpillars. Even a bird that eats an infected caterpillar remains unharmed.

The only other maintenance these desirable plants require is occasional light pruning. I remove crossing or rubbing branches and those that impede traffic or drag on the ground. Generally, I let them follow their naturally attractive growth pattern. If you prune heavily, they still look good, but if you hedge them, you run the risk of removing flowering tips.

Caring for pecan trees

Although neither native nor drought tolerant, pecan trees are often planted by thrifty desert gardeners, especially those interested in permaculture. These popular trees grow well in the desert Southwest and provide dense, abundant shade while producing a nutritious, edible crop. This is the only nut tree my grandmother insisted on planting on her half-acre lot, and it has provided both shade and food for many years. If you have the necessary space and water, and will regularly supply nitrogen and zinc, pecan trees may be for you.

Several pecan varieties with varying nut size, kernel percentage, tree shape, and production capacity grow well in the desert Southwest. In most cases, the home gardener has room for a single pecan tree, which will provide abundantly for the needs of one family. 'Apache', a nicely shaped tree, produces consistent crops year after year. 'Burkett', with a willow-like form and attractive leaves, produces a medium-sized, consistent crop. 'Cheyenne' bears beautiful golden nuts at an early age, but is highly susceptible to yellow pecan aphid infestations. If you are looking for a shade source, consider 'Mohawk', whose handsome shape, dense shade, and early production compensate for the fact that it produces nuts only in alternate years. 'Wichita', an attractive, heavy producer, bears at an early age, every other year. 'Western Schley' consistently bears excellent nuts at an early age, making it one of the most frequently planted pecans.

For best results, purchase a five- or fifteen-gallon pecan tree from a reputable nursery between January and March. Choose a planting location that's large enough to accommodate the tree's ultimate fifty-foot size, away from driveways and car parks that could be stained by black honeydew secreted by inevitable aphid infestations. Loosen the soil as deep as the root ball and five times as wide, digging a hole in the middle. If clay is present, remove as much as possible, or choose a different location. In the case of caliche, break through the layer, creating a "chimney" or funnel through which water can drain. Remove the tree from its container, taking care not to disturb the roots, and then set it in the center of the hole. Refill the hole with the native soil and tamp it down to remove any air pockets.

Build a watering well around the tree and fill it. When the water has soaked in, firm up the soil and add additional soil to bring it to the level that existed in the can, then water again. Prune the tree back by about one third and water it every week for the first month, tapering off to reach the desired interval of 3–4 weeks between irrigations.

When planted in the desert Southwest, pecans require additional nitrogen and zinc in order to grow and produce good nut crops. Before bud break each spring, apply a nitrogen fertilizer. Ammonium sulfate is a good source of nitrogen and can be sprinkled under the tree's canopy at a rate of one and one third pounds of ammonium sulfate for every inch of trunk diameter. Zinc can be applied to the soil in the form of zinc sulfate and to the foliage in liquid zinc sulfate (or NZN). Do not use zinc chelates.

When applying the fertilizer, thoroughly water under the canopy of the tree, and then evenly broadcast the granules over the entire area and water again. Follow directions on the container for liquid foliar spray. If the leaves on your pecan tree become stunted or develop in rosettes at the tips of branches, or if your nut crop is black and powdery inside, you probably have a zinc deficiency, which must be treated to avoid similar damage next year. To treat or prevent a zinc deficiency, make a zinc sulfate solution by mixing a half ounce of NZN per gallon of water and saturate the foliage according to the following schedule, as recommended by The University of Arizona Cooperative Extension office:

First spray: when leaves are two inches long
Second spray: one week after first spray
Third spray: two weeks after second spray
Fourth spray: two weeks after third spray
Fifth spray: two weeks after fourth spray

When watering pecan trees, saturate the soil to a depth of 4–5 feet, and repeat every 3–4 weeks from the time leaves begin to emerge until the tree is completely dormant. Soaker hoses coiled in concentric circles around the tree, or sprinklers placed under the canopy, apply water evenly. Use a soil probe to determine the length of time necessary to reach the desired depth.

Pecans don't require annual pruning like peach or apple trees, but broken branches, dead or diseased wood, downward growth, and crossing limbs should be removed on a regular basis. It's not harmful to prune for shape, but don't cut more than a third of the tree in a given year. The only other care pecans require is insect control. Aphids, a common problem, can be managed with insecticidal soap or Sevin. Stink bugs and leaf-footed plant bugs, which cause black spots in nut kernels, can be controlled with Sevin.

WEEK
12

The blossoms on your fruit-bearing deciduous trees have already burst forth in floral glory, like fireworks on the Fourth of July. They perfumed the air for a couple of weeks and the petals flew around like snow flurries in late spring wind as leaves began to unfurl and fruit began to form. As you look at branches covered by clusters of four or five fingernail-sized fruits, you begin to imagine the crop. Take a few moments to enjoy and appreciate the obvious bounty and then get down to work, because the next task is very challenging for most gardeners. Not physically difficult, but emotionally wrenching and completely necessary, it is time to thin the fruit.

We have such a hard time with thinning. It's hard to believe that in order to fully enjoy the fruits of our labor, we must destroy some of them. Strange as it may sound, it's true. If all of the fruits remain on the tree, they will be small and underdeveloped. Thinning now allows the tree to concentrate available energy on a smaller number of fruits, encouraging them to grow bigger and better.

Apples grow in clusters of 3–7 blossoms. In order to harvest a crop of good-sized fruit, only one or two can remain in each cluster. Look at each group and identify the apple that will have the best position if left on the tree. It should benefit from leaf protection on the west side, and enough space to grow without rubbing branches or other fruit. It is also better to choose the fruits hidden within foliage, and those that are hanging down rather that projecting up, to provide shade and reduce the opportunity for birds to perch and peck. Using your thumb and forefinger, pinch the remaining fruit off where the stem meets the branch. Take your time and do a thorough job, covering every branch on the tree. I usually brew a pot of coffee and thin sections of the tree between hot, milky cups. This approach turns the task into a slow-paced, comfortable ritual to which I actually look forward.

The stone fruits, including apricots, peaches, and plums, are simpler to thin. I used to assign this task to my children, who hoarded the thinned fruit to use later as grenades in their games of "War." A properly thinned stone fruit tree has spaces no smaller than six inches between remaining fruit, which should be on the underside of the branch, away from twigs and woody growth. This ensures adequate nutrients and space for unimpeded growth. Leave fruit beneath foliage whenever possible, protected from sunburn and birds. You'll be glad you considered these factors when you harvest larger quantities of unblemished fruit.

Thinning is the gardener's opportunity to take a creator's role and select the strongest, most viable specimens to continue on to maturity. It is a partnership between tree and steward, with the shared goal of an exceptional crop.

PROPAGATING CACTI AND SUCCULENTS

Cacti and succulents, both natives and those from regions with similar climates and soils, grow abundantly in the desert Southwest, making them attractive to the gardener who wants to grow new and interesting plants while conserving water and the integrity of the desert. Fortunately, these plants are easy to propagate using a variety of simple-to-learn methods. They can be grown from seed, harvested and potted as offsets, bulbuls or plantlets, and propagated by cuttings.

Growing cacti and succulents from seed is similar to starting other plants, and the most significant factors in success are good drainage and sterile soil. Good drainage prevents emerging seeds and roots from becoming too wet, which causes oxygen depletion, root rot, and plant death. Sterile soil is free of naturally occurring fungi, viruses, and bacteria that could attack vulnerable young sprouts and cause damping-off or other common diseases.

Choose a growing container that allows excess moisture to drain off. Seed starting trays purchased at discount stores work well, but any container that holds the potting medium and water, yet drains well, is fine. Fill the container with a germination medium of equal parts of perlite and vermiculite and a small amount of Osmocote fertilizer. Once the soil is in the container, saturate it with a fungicide diluted with distilled water. This will eliminate the common problems of fungal growth and damping off. (For more on appropriate soils, see Week 21.)

Aloes, agaves, and yuccas are easily propagated from seed. Sprinkle your seeds on the top of the soil, leaving them exposed to light, and cover with plastic wrap or a tight-fitting lid. Place the container in a cool, well-lit location and in about a week seedlings will begin to emerge. Don't be alarmed if growth does not occur within that time, as it can take as long as four weeks for germination and initial growth. Once the seedlings have emerged, remove the plastic wrap and keep the soil moist. Heavy misting with a squirt bottle is the most effective way to water without damaging the young plants. At this critical point in the process the plants can dry out and die quickly because they have such immature root systems, so be attentive and water the plants several times a day if necessary.

When the young plants have developed a second set of leaves and are large enough to work with, carefully transplant them into small pots filled with cactus potting soil. Long tweezers and a gentle touch are necessary tools for this job. My fine motor skills aren't fine enough and I have to be very careful, working slowly and meticulously to avoid damaging the small plants. If I try to do this kind of work with my fingers, I destroy a large amount of plant material.

Once the plants are in individual pots, water them regularly and fertilize every two weeks with a diluted, water-soluble fertilizer. Pot them up into larger containers when their roots generously fill the pot. Most of these varieties can be added to the landscape when they are fairly small, as long as they have sufficient roots to support them and protection from afternoon sun. They will require regular irrigation until they are established.

Bulbuls, plantlets, offsets, and pups are all terms for baby plants that grow directly from the mother plant. Some agaves and aloes develop plantlets around their bases or from their root systems. Others develop pups along their flowering stalks, which rapidly grow in spring or early summer. This is a generous offering, since the mother plant dies when she has put forth this fabulous display, but small consolation to the gardener who loses the prized five-foot wide, rosette-shaped accent plant.

To propagate these miniature plants, remove them from the mother stalks and root them in pumice or the perlite/vermiculite mix used for seed propagation. They require less attention than seedlings because these tough little pups are fully functioning plants and are not as susceptible to fungal infection and sudden drying. Nevertheless, keep them moist until roots fully form.

Occasionally, agaves will produce their stalks and pups during the cooler months. While they will still develop, the young plants are more difficult to propagate at this time of year. Since they do much better in the heat of late spring and summer, you can simulate that warmth by creating a nursery in a warmer part of your home or garden. Covering an outdoor area with plastic to amplify daytime heat and repel cold night air is helpful. You can also build a small cold frame or utilize a greenhouse. Although these measures aren't vital, they will greatly accelerate the growth of cold-weather pups.

Many other cacti and succulents develop new plants around the base of the mother plant. They spread in a clumping fashion when growing in the ground and develop into large group specimens. These new plants have roots and can be dug up, then planted in potting soil. If they lack developed roots, plant them in a seed-starting mix, then transplant them when roots have developed.

Kalanchoe develops its characteristic clumping, full appearance by forming plantlets on leaf edges in fall and winter. If growing in the ground, the clump continues to spread, putting down new roots wherever the plantlets touch the soil. In a pot, the mother plant displays the same habit, but plantlets have no place to become firmly rooted. Roots will still develop if the plantlets remain on the mother plant long enough. Remove these plantlets from the stem that bore the original leaf and plant them in flats or individual pots to continue growing. Once they develop mature, functioning root systems, pot these little plants into larger containers. Long-lived and easy to maintain, kolanchoes make excellent gifts.

Native agaves are easy to transplant. Just dig up the side-shoots and put them in a small hole dug in an area of the garden that offers some relief from the intense afternoon sun. Then water them in and leave them alone. They take hold and grow slowly at first, then rapidly to a mature 3–6-foot width. Over a period of several years, I planted an entire parkway with pups gleaned and added in this manner.

The last, yet simplest method of propagating cacti and succulents is by cuttings. Propagate prickly pear, cholla, cereus, pincushion, and ice plant from stem cuttings in the spring and summer. Propagate Dutch wings (*Gasteria*), bowstring hemp (*Sansevieria*), kalanchoe and stonecrop (*Sedum*) from leaf cuttings during the fall and winter. Various planting media, including charcoal, pumice or perlite/vermiculite mixes, produce good results when growing these plants from cuttings. Remove the stem or leaf from the mother plant and dip it into a root-developing hormone powder, such as Rootone, then make a small hole in the potting medium with a wooden stick or your finger and gently place the cutting in that hole. Firm the soil around the cutting and gently water. Keep the plant damp, but not wet, and roots will begin to develop in a few weeks.

To propagate columnar cacti, remove the top of an arm or stem using a sharp knife or saw. Allow a callous to form over the wound and prevent infection by propping this cutting upright in an empty container for two weeks after taking it from the mother plant. Some gardeners apply sulfur powder to the wound as extra insurance. I've had good success without doing this. Once the wound is healed, plant the cut end several inches deep in a permanent container filled with a cactus mix. When watered once or twice a week the cactus will slowly develop a root system and begin to grow in a few months.

When propagating euphorbias, exercise great caution, since cut euphorbias exude a poisonous, milky liquid that, in some varieties, is quite caustic. Avoid contact with skin and eyes, and call poison-control immediately if accidental exposure causes burning or irritation. I always wear gloves when working with euphorbias to avoid exposure to this sticky substance. After cutting a stem or branch from the mother plant, seal it off by putting the cut edge in a vase or bucket of water for a few hours. Plant these cuttings directly into a rooting medium and water them twice weekly until roots develop.

Make prickly pear and cholla cuttings by removing sections of the mother plant at a natural joint between two pads or segments. Many gardeners let these cuttings lay in the sun for two weeks to heal over before replanting them. I have done this and I have put them directly into the ground with equal success. Once roots develop on plants grown from cuttings, they can be transplanted into other containers filled with a cactus potting mix.

Of course, native or landscape plants can be put directly into the soil, as long as you remember the needs of the plant when deciding on a location. Most of these drought-tolerant, desert-adapted, or native plants have specific environmental requirements. Plant them on a berm or hillock to allow for adequate drainage. Since some species need protection from intense direct sunlight, plant them under trees or to the east of shrubs or structures that will provide that protection. Other varieties are frost sensitive and require protection from temperature below 28°. Locate these plants under trees or near buildings, or plant them in pots that can be moved during cold weather.

Before you propagate specific plants, do your homework and know their particular needs. Armed with this information, select the best location for the plant you so carefully nurtured.

FABULOUS FIGS

Figs (*ficus carica*) are wide spreading, densely foliated trees that grow on their own rootstock and produce abundant fruits after only two or three years in the ground. They do very well in the desert Southwest, bearing almost continuously through summer and fall by producing two crops a year. The first crop develops in June on last year's wood, and the second from August through November on the current summer's wood. Despite the fact that these self-fruitful trees are susceptible to summer leaf burn and Texas root rot, the rich, abundant fruit crop makes them a worthwhile endeavor.

Figs freeze back hard in areas that commonly have low temperatures. In these locations, the weather naturally maintains tree size and the plant develops and retains a shrubby appearance. In warmer locales, prune fig trees to reduce size or allow them to attain their maximum fifteen- to thirty-foot height. Unless a formal, structured appearance is desired, figs require no pruning beyond the removal of dead or crossing wood, and that which impedes traffic flow.

For a highly managed fig tree, espalier it along a wall or wire, or annually prune it, flat and hard, to create a tabletop-shaped tree that bears its fruit under a low canopy. This method is used to form an attractive, grapevine-like plant, and has also been used to create some of the most unattractive botanical specimens I have ever seen.

Figs are not particular about soil type, growing in almost any well-drained location. Planted in the ground, they require regular irrigation for the first couple of years and then do well with only an occasional deep watering. If planted in a large pot, your tree will always require regular irrigation and protection from freezing temperatures. One application of a balanced fertilizer in early spring is enough to keep fig trees strong and healthy. I usually apply composted steer manure and a thick layer of mulch beneath the canopy of my black mission fig. This treatment maintains large, bright green leaves and encourages fruit development and general growth. Even in winter, when this tropical-looking foliage has dropped, the smooth, gray bark creates an interesting silhouette.

Although there are many kinds of fig trees, only three varieties are recommended for the desert Southwest. 'Black Mission', the best known and most reliable, produces rich, dense fruit with black skin and strawberry colored flesh. A heavy bearer, it provides even more fruit if ripe figs are regularly removed. Mine bears continuously from June through frost, and what I don't harvest the cardinals enjoy. 'Brown Turkey', the preferred variety for gardens at elevations below 2,000 feet, bears less abundantly than 'Black Mission', but makes up for small numbers with larger fruit of excellent quality. The tasty figs are brown-skinned with a rosy-beige interior.

'Canadria' is the best white fig for the desert, producing heavy crops of greenish-yellow figs whose pink, fleshy interiors are moister and sweeter than other white varieties. While not as intensely flavored as dark figs, 'Canadria' requires fewer chilling hours than most fig trees and is less susceptible to sour fruit beetle infestations than the darker varieties. These features make it a popular tree in areas where other types of fig trees fail to perform.

INSECTS IN THE GARDEN

WEEK 13 Following an inaugural warming trend, spring seeps into the desert and announces itself with a burst of new growth that encourages insects to come marching in. A healthy garden usually can fend off the onslaught with minimal human support, but intervention is sometimes necessary. In the interest of maintaining the natural balance, I recommend the use of controls that are the least intrusive and lowest in toxicity. A strong jet of water or insecticidal soap, either homemade or commercially produced, is always my first choice.

Except for insecticidal soaps, the use of pesticides should be strictly limited since they kill beneficial insects as well as garden pests. There is nothing more precarious than an environment whose smallest inhabitants have been completely removed. When natural processes cease to function, ecological balance no longer exists, and diversity is eradicated. A lack of diversity in the insect population is a serious and difficult problem to correct. Sometimes when insect infestation seems unmanageable, the best solution is to allow nature to run its course and begin again when the balance has been re-struck. This is difficult for many of us, because we want things to be just as we have planned. When tempted to intervene, remember that intervention is often a self-perpetuating activity.

Gardens that require large amounts of poison and human intervention are those in which these methods have already be overused. It becomes a vicious cycle. Poisons used to kill pests also kill beneficial insects and destroy the fragile balance. With no natural enemies to keep them in check, new populations of pests rapidly multiply and severely damage the garden. The gardener steps in with more chemicals, often as the beneficial population is beginning to redevelop, and the cycle of destruction begins again. Thoughtful use of insect controls is the only way to guarantee a healthy and diverse garden. As the insects become more noticeable, keep in mind this balance and its fragility.

Beneficial insects

Three insects every gardener loves to see are ladybugs, lacewings, and praying mantises. These are the most visible and easily recognized beneficial insects, which prey on bugs that we consider pests. Ladybugs are rounded beetles that come in many colors and sizes, although they are usually red with black markings. Adult Ladybugs lay their eggs near aphid colonies. When they hatch, small, black and orange, lizard-like larvae emerge and feed on the nearby aphids. They can eat thousands of aphids in just a few days, destroying the current colony.

Ladybugs can be purchased and released near aphid colonies. The mature adults almost immediately lay their eggs. Even though they leave quickly, the eggs they've left behind develop into aphid-eating machines. In a healthy, balanced desert landscape, ladybugs will arrive naturally when a large population of aphids exists. Ladybugs, either purchased or naturally migrating, will help create a biological balance in your garden that requires fewer chemical controls.

Lacewings are delicate green or brown insects with heavily veined, translucent wings. Attracted by light, they often hover around windows and lamps in the evening. Lacewings lay their yellowish eggs at the tip of a hair-like structure along plant stems and on the undersides of leaves. Hatchlings emerge in just a few days and begin to satisfy their monumental hunger by devouring large numbers of aphids and moth eggs. If you disturb mature insects on the tops of your plants, be glad. They're a promising sign that the beneficial ones are present and doing their job—they're good for your garden.

Like lacewings, praying mantises wander along window screens and hover in porches at night. They are fascinating creatures, large enough for us to really observe their habits. They sit and wait until another insect crosses their path and then they pounce. Capable of catching moths in mid-air and eating hundreds of tiny crawling insects during the course of an evening, praying mantis are not only entertaining to watch, but are also quite helpful.

The female praying mantis lays one or two egg cases along twigs or branches in the garden. These glued-on, three-quarter-inch cases house the developing young through the colder months. If you find one while pruning or doing winter cleanup, leave it alone. You'll appreciate the work its occupants perform next spring, summer, and fall. When they hatch, baby praying mantises look like miniature versions of their parents, and their appetites match those of the adults as they immediately begin to hunt. I love to watch for them as they return each year to particular parts of my garden. In many cultures, they are welcomed as a good omen or blessing.

Other beneficial insects:

assassin bugs	syrphid flies
ambush bugs	wasps
damsel bugs	mud-daubers
big-eyed bugs	dragonflies
minute pirate bugs	damselflies
spined soldier bugs	spiders

Each of these predators feeds on the eggs, larvae, or adult forms of insect pests. They live in crops, plants, grasses, and weeds. Many of them are also excellent pollinators, and can be seen hovering around flowers. Only a few of the insects that inhabit our gardens are actually pests; the majority are performing a vital role in the great drama of ecological balance and diversity. The wise gardener welcomes and respects their presence.

With the arrival of mild spring weather, the winter-residing gray aphid welcomes its winged and wingless cousins to the garden. These piercing, sucking insects favor tender new growth and congregate on any herbaceous plant producing it. Born pregnant, aphids colonize and quickly multiply, depleting necessary nutrients in the host plant. If the colony's large numbers are not the first noticeable sign of their presence, mottled, wilted plants will be.

Italian cypress, false cypress, and arborvitae attract the brown arborvitae aphid. Oranges, poppies, chrysanthemums, begonias, spinach, and beets are among the host plants for the cotton or melon aphid. This particular pest moves along to other vegetables as the year progresses. Tender new growth of oleander and desert milkweed is attractive to the bright yellow-orange oleander aphid, which can heavily populate an oleander bush without causing any significant damage.

89

Unopened rosebuds become quite deformed following infestation by green- or pink-colored rose aphids. If left untreated, they will destroy the flower crop. The rusty plum aphid rapidly multiplies to cover entire branches of plum trees. These masses are visible from a distance of several yards. I vividly recall the bright spring morning I looked out my kitchen window and thought my plum tree had become the new home of a migrating swarm of bees. Considering the time of year, I should have known better—it was still too cold. Nonetheless, I slid on my garden clogs and tromped to the back of the lot, prepared to inspect the hive and determine a plan of removal. Imagine my surprise when I discovered a plum aphid colony that covered several branches, their twigs, and foliage. A strong jet of water applied two or three times took care of the problem. The new leaves were only slightly tattered, since rusty plum aphids do far less damage than their appearance would suggest.

Once knocked off the plant and onto the ground, aphids do not return. If the infestation is heavy, water alone may not solve the problem, and a spray with insecticidal soap might be necessary. Insecticidal soap kills pests by inhibiting their ability to breathe and does not harm beneficial insects. It is nearly always effective, especially when repeated every third day until the insects are under control. Occasionally these non-chemical treatments are not effective enough for the fastidious gardener. For tough cases pyrethrum, an insecticide derived from marigolds, is effective. Other chemical controls include rotenone and Malathion.

Leafhoppers are the second most common pest in the spring garden. They are, like aphids, sucking insects that weaken plant tissue by removing fluids and depositing a sticky substance called honeydew. Their presence often precedes the development of sooty molds, which can appear to be the original problem. The honeydew they leave behind is a treat for ants, which flock to plants where leafhoppers have been at work and become prime suspects and targets when gardeners investigate and treat plant damage. Leafhoppers are an eighth of an inch long, winged, and wedge-shaped. They are difficult to control and eradicate because of their ability to fly, rendering most insecticides ineffective. The best defense against them is the use of floating row covers, which are expensive and cost-effective only if a serious problem exists.

Whiteflies are almost as tough to get rid of as leafhoppers. They are very small—less than a sixteenth of an inch long. The pale yellow body of the winged, mature whitefly is covered with a white, waxy material. They flutter around the plant when disturbed, creating a snow-flurry effect. When young, they are wingless, scale-like creatures that reside on the underside of leaves. These sedentary sucking insects converge in large numbers and do serious and obvious damage to the plant whose leaves they attack. The topsides of whitefly-infested leaves become pale and mottled, eventually browning, drying, and dying. Little black dots of fecal matter are left on the leaves' undersides. If enough leaves are damaged, the plant will die. Control whiteflies with the same insecticidal soap recommended for aphids, making certain to spray the underside of the plant. If heavily infested, spray the plant early in the morning, wait two hours, then repeat the treatment. Do this every three days until the insect population is under control.

If the infested plant is in a pot, support the plant and the soil with one hand and, using the other hand, turn the plant upside down and dip it into a sink filled with soapy water solution. Turn the plant right side up and let the foliage dry. Repeat the procedure in two or three hours. This is very effective since it enables the soap to penetrate into hard-to-reach sections of the plant.

If you are unable to eradicate whiteflies with insecticidal soap, the most effective chemical controls include pyrethrum, rotenone, sabadilla, dimethoate,

Malathion, and Orthene. These are listed from least to most toxic; and the first three, although still toxic, are organic.

Spider mites also do a lot of damage in the garden. The smallest of the common garden insects, they are only visible through a hand lens. To check for them, hold a white piece of paper under a section of the infested plant and tap the leaves and branches. Small pinpoint-sized dots in shades of yellow red, brown, or green that move on the paper are spider mites. Much like a spider, they leave a fine webbing on the surface of the leaves they infest. Spider mites suck sap from leaves and fruit, leaving yellow stippling and causing deformation of the leaves. Some mites also cause galls, small cyst-like growths, on plant surfaces. Insecticidal soap is extremely effective on these creatures. It is an unusual case that requires a more aggressive approach such as Kelthane, Di-Syston, or Pentac.

91
∾

April

- Prune freeze damage after last frost
- Add color plants to garden
- Plant melons, squash, cucumber, and corn
- Plant new citrus trees
- Apply chelated iron to deficient plants
- Fertilize established Bermuda grass
- Fertilize palms
- Fertilize roses every two weeks through heavy bloom period
- Remove spent blossoms to promote more bloom
- Watch for clouds of false chinch bugs
- Harvest potatoes
- Remove young pads to maintain overall size of cacti
- Deep water deciduous fruit trees every 10-14 days

April

FINALLY FROST FREE

WEEK 14 As we enter the first week of April we can count on the nighttime temperatures staying above freezing until mid-November, and anticipate many months of active gardening. The first task is the removal of frost damage left behind by winter's cold, pruning out the brown-gray branches in bougainvillea, lantana, sage, citrus, and other tender perennials. It may have been difficult to wait to do the pruning since most of us are fond of a tidy garden. The dull, colorless twigs have been an irritation for weeks, but it's a good thing you waited to remove them. By doing so, you avoided exposing plants to additional freezes that would have threatened their existence.

Most bushes and trees, in response to warmer daytime temperatures, are sprouting new leaves and branches. This emerging greenery is an excellent indicator for the gardener. Prune back to the point at which the plant is sending out this new growth, removing everything beyond that point. Use this approach for shrubby plants and trees alike. Some species will be re-growing from the base or crown of the plant and nowhere else. In this case, carefully prune down to that point using newly sharpened pruners and a steady hand to avoid removing healthy new material. Take the same action with citrus and other evergreens. Look for the new growth and prune back to it.

At this time you can also remove dead or crossing wood. Pick up all the trimmings and dispose of them by chopping them into pieces that are three inches or smaller and adding them to the compost heap to develop next year's soil-boosting mix. While you're at it, rake up leaves and other yard debris and add this to the compost heap, too. Many pests over-winter in this decomposing matter, making its removal beneficial to your garden. After a day of pruning and raking, clearing and cleaning, you'll feel a sense of accomplishment as you survey the dramatic difference in your landscape.

An octogenarian friend of mine insists that she knows when we've had our last frost because the ants re-emerge from the deep soil that has insulated and protected them during winter's cold. After spending the last few springs observing and analyzing, I believe her. Without exception, no frost attacked my garden after the ants began their aboveground work, so I now use them as an indicator to begin my own spring-cleaning.

Among the many types of ants that live in my garden, there are two that remove the leaves from my plants beginning in spring and continuing through summer. One, *Pogonomyrmex rugosus*, is commonly called the harvester or bearded ant, and the other, *Acromyrmex versicolor*, is called a leafcutter, although a distinction between the two is rarely made in gardening circles. While the plant damage they cause appears to be identical, their motivations are quite different.

The black and red harvester ants, varying in length from ¼–½-inch, live in large colonies over a foot beneath the surface of the soil. When the weather is acceptably warm, workers emerge at dawn and dusk to strip foliage from nearby plants to prevent their roots from removing moisture from the humidity-controlled site. Mounds of uniformly sized pebbles, which the ants have removed from their underground home, surround the entrances to the colony. They also guard these entrances aggressively, and the ants are certain to deliver a painful sting to any invader.

The clay-red leafcutter ants are the same size as harvester ants and create similar mounds in the garden as they remove soil particles to create extensive lengths of underground tunnels. Drying leaves stripped from preferred plants surround the main entrances. Rather than stripping the foliage that is nearest their homes, Harvester ants return to plants for which they have a preference, often bypassing others en route. They carry leaves into the nest and use them as a growing medium for the fungus on which they feed. It seems that the cultivated fungus provides a higher nutrient concentration than the original plant material. The little leafcutters are, in actuality, farmers.

In either case, the ant colonies may require control. My preferred method of control is orange peels, blended in a cup or two of water, then poured around, but not in, the entrances to colonies. This seems most effective during hot weather. Insect baits containing a combination of boric acid and avermectin are also effective. Carefully place the insecticide around, but not in, the entrances. Avoid filling the holes with the poison, since this encourages the ants to seal off that tunnel and create another. It's also effective to sprinkle the pesticide along the path they follow as they defoliate, and around the base of the plants they prefer.

I only poison the ants in my garden if they repeatedly and extensively damage specific plants or when their aggression is dangerous to people or pets. I am mindful of the important role ants play in the aeration and health of my soil. I want to live in harmony with them as much as possible.

Intensive planting of warm-season vegetables

Although you had to wait to pass the last frost date at the end of this month before setting out seedlings, it is now time to rework the vegetable bed and plant for the spring and summer harvest. If you have been gardening year-round, some vegetables are not yet ready to harvest. Lettuces and greens are still going strong, and will continue to do so until the temperature rises above 80–85°. I sometimes pull most of the lettuce and have really big salads during this time of year. Other times, I hope for continued mild weather and leave them in, harvesting just enough to add character and depth to store-bought lettuce. I stretch the season of piquant salad stuff as far as I can; regardless of when the last fresh arugula leaf is plucked from the garden, I always mourn their loss.

Determine what you want to leave in the beds and remove everything else. Clear out all the debris and garden waste and put it in your compost bin. Once the soil looks clean, add fertilizer that is high in nitrogen and phosphorous and mix it in well. If the garden soil is mainly native soil, add soil sulfur, too. Turn the irrigation system on and do a quick check-up. If there are leaks or clogs, take care of them now, before you plant anything else in the bed. Level your soil and prepare to plant. In this extreme climate of ours, I always opt for intensive planting of spring/summer vegetables. I plant them as closely as possible so that, at maturity, they shade one another and cover most of the soil surface with foliage and shadow. This inhibits evaporation and decreases the need for irrigation.

Tomato seedlings must be planted now. They need the additional growth in order to produce a crop before the real heat hits. Because most tomatoes will stop setting fruit once the temperature gets above the mid nineties, the goal is to have the fruit ripe and ready before then. This is the precise reason tomatoes are not a particularly good crop for the desert, but we all seem to want homegrown tomatoes anyway. If you didn't start tomatoes from seed several weeks ago, buy young, healthy plants at a reputable nursery. The full-size tomato varieties I recommend are 'Champion', 'Columbia', 'Flomerica', 'Hope No. 1', 'Golden Boy', 'Lemon Boy', and 'Roma'. Although many others are available, these have always produced well in my desert garden.

Small tomatoes always do better in a desert climate. Year after year, the best performers are 'Sweet 100' and 'Yellow Pear'. The new bite-sized orange varieties, and small pearl and pear types are also promising. When planted and harvested together, they create a stunning combination of flavor and color, and make a beautiful and tasty Italian tomato salad. Whichever varieties you choose, an intensive spacing recommendation would leave only 1 1/2–2 feet between plants. They'll grow, sprawl, and fill this space nicely. I sometimes let them grow unsupported and other times I make my own tomato cages from rolled wire fencing that has six-inch spaces. This material provides more support and is easier to harvest through than commercial tomato cages.

Peppers and eggplants can be planted from seed now but, like tomatoes, they do better if you plant seedlings. The sweet pepper varieties I recommend are 'Big Bertha', 'Bell Boy', 'Cubanelle', 'Pimiento', and 'Sweet Banana'. I've tried many exotic and colorful sweet peppers, including black, purple, brown, orange, and bright red. They need more sun protection and stop producing at lower temperatures than the suggested varieties. If you have a space that is cooler, try them. They are lovely in the garden and on the table.

Hot peppers do well here and are much better suited to our climate than bell peppers. The varieties most people have success with are 'Cascabel', 'Jalapeño', 'Pasilla', 'Serrano', 'Takanotsume', and 'Chimayo'. There are many others from which to choose so experiment to find your personal favorites.

The best eggplants for the desert are 'Ichiban', 'Black Prince', 'Black Bell', and 'Dusky'. All of the long Japanese varieties produce well, too. Space these plants a foot and a half apart. They grow upright and require no additional support. If you want to try new varieties, choose plants whose fruit is born underneath foliage or hanging down rather than rising up. The foliage of the plant will protect the ripening fruit from sunburn on the hottest June and July afternoons.

Plant bush beans, lima beans, and soy beans six inches apart, and then thin later. Cantaloupe and other melons require eighteen inches between plants. Some exceptional cantaloupe varieties are 'Ambrosia', 'Sampson', and 'Venus'. 'Klondike', 'Sugar Baby', and 'Yellow Baby' are watermelon varieties that do well. New varieties come out every year. Try one or two and see how they do in your garden.

Plant sweet corn fifteen inches apart, in no fewer than four rows to ensure proper pollination. Good varieties include 'Golden Beauty', 'Honeycomb', 'Silver Queen', and 'Kandy Corn'. Okra requires that same fifteen-inch spacing. I usually try whatever varieties Burpee or Shepherd's is recommending each year. Excellent summer squash varieties are 'Scallopini', 'Kuta Hybrid', 'Aristocrat', 'Gourmet Globe', 'Gold Rush', and classic zucchini. Good winter squashes, which are planted now, but store well for winter use, include acorn, 'Butterboy', butternut, and spaghetti squash. Plant them two feet apart.

Cucumbers and pumpkins, also planted now, do well in the desert with the exception of the hothouse or English varieties, which need more humidity than we typically have. They often require help in pollination, so be prepared to go out in the early morning with a cotton swab and touch the interior of each flower. Move from flower to flower, just like a bee, sharing pollen grains and helping the fruit to set and form.

If your vegetable bed receives no afternoon shade, cover it with a seventy-percent shade cloth by mid-June. This fabric, available in garden centers and home improvement stores, provides enough protection so that the fruit won't be sunburned and also modifies the microclimate so that many plants continue to produce. Since vegetables are annual plants that grow quickly and use a lot of energy to create a crop, you must fertilize them every 2–4 weeks. Read packages carefully and apply fertilizer in the suggested manner. It is also important to water the garden plot both before and after fertilizer applications to avoid damaging plants and roots, and to wash the nutrients into the root zone.

After many months of effort and attention, harvest time arrives. It's exciting to present the bounty of your harvest to family and friends, and to try new things and learn different ways to prepare garden-fresh fruits and vegetables. (My two favorite garden cookbooks are *Recipes From the Kitchen Garden* and *More Recipes From The Kitchen Garden*, both written by Rene Shepherd. These volumes present a selection of simple, healthy recipes for the preparation of fresh fruits, vegetables, and herbs. I also recommend the *Country Garden Cookbook Series* published by Collins Publishers, San Francisco, which devotes a separate volume, each by a different author, to a single fruit or vegetable.)

Ready to fertilize

With the dead stuff out and the debris gone, your landscape is ready for its annual fertilization. If you haven't already done this, now is the time. Not unlike other gardening topics, fertilizer is one that swirls with ideas and controversy. For years, experts counseled us to apply nitrogen for foliage growth and phosphorous and potassium for fruit and flower development. Investigating this theory, The University of California tested a variety of fertilizers. The resulting data indicated that the only fertilizer component significantly effecting plants when added after planting was nitrogen. It seems that in our alkaline soils, the phosphorous and potassium don't move through the soil and affect the plants the way we had always thought. So for the landscape plants in your yard, you need to apply a fertilizer high in nitrogen.

The first number on all fertilizer packages indicates the percentage of nitrogen in that product. Phosphorous is the second number and potassium is the third. Any fertilizer that has a high first number is fine. Follow instructions regarding quantities and be sure you water the fertilizer completely in. For this once-a-year shot-in-the-arm, I often use aged manure or a blend of cotton-seed meal and blood meal. Ammonium sulfate, the cheapest form of nitrogen, is also a fine choice for the gardener not committed to organics.

Manure: Is it safe in the garden?

In the wake of reports of Mad Cow Disease in Britain, many gardeners expressed concerns about supplementing their garden soil with cow or steer manure. These fears are not completely unfounded. Pathogens can be transmitted from animal manure to humans. *Salmonella, Listeria,* and *E. Coli* have all been linked to applications of manure to home garden soils. In addition to pathogens, parasites like roundworms and tapeworms also have been linked to the use of fresh manure. In one documented case, a woman who fertilized with fresh manure from her own cow and calf became ill. The source of her illness was isolated and identified as *E. Coli.* When tested, her cows were free of disease but had elevated antibodies for *E. Coli,* indicating that they previously had been infected. The woman's garden soil was then tested and, sure enough, *E. Coli* was present. Based on this case, and others like it, the use of green or fresh manure can be risky.

A solution is to use only aged manure. Even if your own animals are the source, manure must be aged at least two months before application to garden soils or the compost heap. When using bagged manure, buy it before you need it and allow the bags to sit in the sun and heat up for several weeks. This will kill most pathogens that could still be present.

Cat, dog, and pig manures are unacceptable and should never be used in the garden. Pathogens found in these feces survive in compost or soil and remain infectious for people. As always, gardeners must be certain to thoroughly wash their hands after working in the soil, and wash all home-grown vegetables before consumption. If you adhere to these simple guidelines, manure in the garden should not cause any health problems.

Annual flowers from seed

WEEK
15

There is something wonderful about growing plants from seed, about being involved in the process from its onset. I anticipate this undertaking with great pleasure and enjoy choosing seeds and deciding on colors, sizes, and varieties. The beauty of the activity during this particular reason is the directness of the task. There are no peat pots to deal with, no artificial lighting concerns. I don't have to worry about a seed starting medium or the fungus gnats that love to invade it. I just have to choose the seeds, put them in the ground and wait for them to grow. What a simple and rewarding scheme.

I usually have seeds stored away in my refrigerator, waiting until the threat of frost has passed. Remember those catalogs we all scoured in January? I ordered my seeds way back then, sometimes purchasing with a specific bed or design in mind. Others I order because I know they'll do well in the desert and I want to give them a try. No matter what my rationale, I always manage to find a spot for every packet I order and often run out to the local nursery or garden center to buy more.

I follow the planting instructions printed on the packets, with two exceptions. First, I disregard the recommended planting dates and base my timing on my last frost date and germination times. Second, I always plant my seeds slightly closer than recommended. This allows the plants to shade one another and conserves water when the summer sun blazes and temperatures rise above 100°.

Many beautiful annuals blossom and thrive in our warm springs and hot summers. Every year I plant new and different varieties and combinations. I also plant many old faithfuls that still add as much color and excitement to the garden as they did years ago. Cockscomb, also called Chinese woolflower, provides tropical color to pots and garden beds. It is an attractive addition to cut bouquets and creates a striking effect when arranged alone. There are two kinds of cockscomb, one (*Celosia argentea*) with a plume-like flower and another (*C. cristata*) with a tighter, compact blossom. Both come in tall and short varieties. Its blooms, coming in shades of orange, purple, red, and yellow, hold their color when dried. Requiring moderate to ample water, celosia thrives in an amended bed located near your home or patio.

Coreopsis, a member of the sunflower family, is more drought-tolerant than most other annual color plants, extremely easy to grow from seed, and often reseeds itself. I enjoy these surprising developments and look forward to the results of self-sowing. If I don't like where they've grown, it takes very little effort to dig them up and move them around. Coreopsis requires full sun and slightly amended soil, but will grow in rich soil too. While most are annuals, some are perennials that come up from a crown year after year, spreading in a clumping, mounded fashion.

The perennials are nice because they transplant easily. To keep them continually blooming and looking their best, remove the blossoms regularly. If this task gets ahead of you, shear the entire plant down by ⅓ and it will begin producing more blossom heads in a couple of weeks. Their rangy growth makes coreopsis appropriate in an informal setting or behind plants that are shorter and more compact.

Somewhat similar in growth habit, *Cosmos* is from the same family as coreopsis. It is drought tolerant, is even less picky about soil, and requires full sun even in the desert. Native to Mexico, it produces numerous daisy-like flowers on tall, ferny stems. Because mature heights vary greatly between varieties, check seed packages carefully when planning the flowerbed and buying seeds. Cosmos is an excellent candidate for a single species bed, planted with varieties in several heights and colors. It is reminiscent of a field of wildflowers and something worth trying along the edge of a garden or in a back border. The yellow cosmos, 'Klondike' or 'Sunny' by name, produces hundreds of double flowers in shades of orange and yellow. Other types bloom in hues of crimson, lavender, pink, purple, and rose. Some come in striped variations as well. Look at the pictures on packages and in catalogs to determine what will fit into your color scheme and space limitations.

Gaillardia plants are dense, compact, and produce sturdy, daisy-like flowers in shades of bronze, red, and yellow. They are excellent companions for coreopsis and cosmos, looking their best when planted in front of the medium or taller varieties. They're easy to grow, readily reseed themselves, and look great in cutting beds and borders. Native to the central and western United States, gaillardia varieties reach a mature height of 18–24 inches and have thicker, denser leaves and stems than the other plants mentioned, creating nice textural contrast. Most varieties have petaled blossoms resembling sturdy sunflowers, but some have disk-shaped flowers that look like brightly colored powder puffs. Mix the various types to add interest to the bed.

Globe amaranth (*Gomphrena*) is an everlasting flower that serves the gardener well. Its beautiful variegated bronze and green foliage makes for excellent borders that require infrequent irrigation. These plants produce pink and white blossoms that hold their shape and color for weeks and look nice in fresh bouquets or dried. The dried blooms also remain colorful for many months, a trait that makes them an excellent ingredient in potpourri and useful in dried

Hummingbird moth and sacred datura (Datura wrightii)

wreaths and arrangements. I like to mix the flower heads with lavender flowers for an attractive and aromatic botanical room freshener. Another pleasing mix is pink and red rose petals, globe amaranth blossoms and rosebuds, a nice touch on a guest room dresser or bathroom counter.

Marigolds (*Tagetes spp.*) are tough, trouble-free plants that home gardeners have been growing for generations. Their bright green, lacy foliage and blossoms in colors ranging from bronze and crimson to maroon and orange are easily recognized. The plants themselves give off a strong scent that repels insect pests, which is why marigolds are often interplanted with tomatoes and other vegetable plants. They also once were thought to control nematode infestations in the soil, but this has been proven untrue. Two types of marigolds, African (*T. erecta*) and French (*T. patula*), flourish in the color bed. African marigolds are tall plants with full, double flowers, while French marigolds are shorter with single and double flowers and an interesting bicolor feature. Both flower through summer and continue until November's frost. Excellent when mixed with other flowers or in single-variety, staggered rows, marigolds are beautiful in the vegetable bed, too, where they act as a natural insect repellent.

Other marigolds that grow well in the desert include the perennials Mt. Lemmon marigold (*T. lemmoni*), and Mexican tarragon (*T. lucida*). I have both plants in my garden and love them. Mt. Lemmon marigold requires no irrigation after the first year or two, and blooms almost continually. Its filigree branches are stunning when covered with bright yellow blossoms. Mexican tarragon is a reliable culinary replacement for French tarragon. The plant itself, brilliant green and drought tolerant, dies back to the ground in the winter, but the narrow, uncut leaves re-emerge each spring to take their place in the herb garden. Like their ornamental counterparts, these marigolds grow rather effortlessly and make significant contributions to the garden.

Moss rose (*Portulaca grandiflora*) is a low-growing annual succulent most often used as a border plant. Brilliantly colored paper-like flowers open fully in the sun and close in the late afternoon. The flowers emerge as both singles and doubles along fleshy, trailing, reddish branches. Although it likes occasional water, moss rose is drought tolerant, and frequently is used with great visual effect on dry banks, in parkways, in rock gardens, and as a border plant. It is versatile enough for hanging baskets, cascading over the edges of planters, and planted in shallow containers, and grows well in any soil type, usually reseeding itself in milder areas.

Last on my list of annual summer flowers is the inimitable zinnia. There is nothing like a zinnia bed for splashy color and beautiful foliage. I rarely plant fewer than three varieties and have planted many more in a given season. I taught my children to make zinnia bouquets as soon as they had enough coordination to control a pair of scissors. To them and to me, zinnias are the best. The colorful, round flower heads range in size from less than an inch to huge seven-inch blossoms. They all require full sun and hot weather, making them perfect for the desert. Zinnias prefer amended garden soil and frequent fertilization. Use Miracle Grow, Peter's, or another water-soluble fertilizer every 3–4 weeks. Water plants from beneath, since overhead watering encourages mildew to which zinnias are susceptible. When properly cared for and cut regularly, they bloom profusely through fall, providing flowers from every color of the rainbow.

By the light of the silvery moon

We give so much attention to the sun and its effect on our garden that we nearly forget the moon and its pleasant possibilities. Because many communities in the desert Southwest have nighttime light regulations, the moon plays a significant role in the ambiance of the hours beyond dusk. To take full advantage, consider a silver, or "moonlight," garden. Many of the species in arid regions have silvery foliage that contributes to their drought tolerant nature. You can take advantage of this and create a stunning bed or plot that will reflect the moon's rays and catch the attention of after-dark visitors.

The plants I recommend for a moonlight garden appreciate alkaline soil, lots of sun, good drainage, and moderate water. They are generally perennials, although some of them behave like annuals in colder areas. Create a small theme bed with petite varieties, or an entire landscape with plants of all sizes.

The smallest silver plants are excellent for borders, pots, or as accent plants. Several of the herbs fall into this category. *Santolina*, particularly the variety 'Nana', grows twelve inches tall and twice as wide. It produces minute yellow flowers in the summer, adding to its appeal. Miniature culinary sage reaches a diminutive 8–12 inches and has the distinctive silver-gray foliage and lavender blossoms of its larger counterparts. Thyme, especially silver thyme, will spread through the garden and add its lovely aroma and culinary uses, as will Dittany of Crete, a member of the oregano family.

Also included among the smallest plants are several members of the succulent family. *Echeveria*, which forms fleshy rosettes in shades of gray or light green and has markings in darker colors, frequently is available at discount stores. The best known of this plant type are called hen and chicks. I love to plant them in a pot and plop them down in the company of plants that are growing in the ground. They cascade over the edges and make a bold visual statement in very little space. *Senecio serpens* and *S. mandraliscae* are other low-growing silvery choices that add color and textural interest while requiring little water or attention.

Providing the height of small shrubs, lavender is a must in the moonlight garden. Except for 'Green Dentate', all varieties have gray foliage and interesting texture. Lamb's ears, sage, artemisia, helichrysum, and yarrow, are also excellent choices. Aside from yellow-blooming artemisia, these contribute purple or lavender flowers to the garden in spring and summer. Yarrow comes in many blossom colors and several foliage types, making it of particular interest. An entire bed of yarrow nicely dresses up any desert garden.

Slightly taller, the *Daleas*—hybrids of Sonoran Desert natives—are excellent choices for the extended moonlight garden. Some varieties are more green than gray, but all have a silvery cast, making them perfect candidates for this theme. I particularly recommend 'Monterey Blue' for its blossom color and fragrance. Black dalea, trailing indigo bush, and indigo bush are three others that have proven themselves in the Southwest for many years. They are particularly desirable because they require no supplemental irrigation once established. Also in this size range are the visually interesting *Agaves*—most notably century plant, octopus, and 'Queen Victoria'—which add contrast and texture with their upright, rigid growth habit and sword-shaped leaves.

For fun, throw in a few old man cacti, which are native to Mexico. These wonderful conversation plants are covered in hair-like structures and look very much like bearded old men. While you are looking through the cactus and succulent section of the nursery, watch for more silver or gray plants. You will find many, and may have a hard time limiting your moonlight garden additions to just a few.

If this theme is motivating you to do more, consider adding height. The blue fan palm is an excellent desert landscape plant. This Mexican native is hardy to 15° and grows to a tall twenty-five feet. Growth is slow, however, so it will take many years for that height to develop. It requires no irrigation once established.

Other plants for height in the moonlight garden are the silver-foliated eucalyptus trees, native to Australia. They hold up very well in our climate, are fairly long-lived, and drought tolerant, but be frugal with irrigation since they are susceptible to wind damage if overwatered.

Recommended Eucalyptus varieties:

blue gum (*Eucalyptus globulus*)
dwarf blue gum (*E. g.* 'Compacta')
ghost gum (*E. papuana*)
Kruse's mallee (*E. kruseana*)
large-fruited yellow gum (*E. leucoxylon megalocarpa* 'Rosea')
red-flowered mallee (*E. erythronema*)
silver dollar gum (*E. polyanthemos*)
silver mountain gum (*E. pulverulenta*)
silver-topped gimlet (*E. campaspe*)
white ironbark (*E. leucoxylon*)

THE DESERT COTTAGE GARDEN

WEEK 16 Cottage gardens. You've seen them. They're the spectacular flower and herb beds gracing the pages of nearly every periodical and garden publication on newsstands today. Breathtaking photographs highlight floral displays that rival the greatest gardens in the world. Many of those photographs were taken in the greatest gardens in the world, where the designs showcase every plant as a star. The accompanying text often gives variety suggestions and planting dates, along with descriptions of potential problems and pitfalls. With so many helpful details, how can the gardener fail? The gardener can't—if he or she lives in Britain, the Northeast, or even the Midwest. California residents are likely to find these articles helpful if they live in the more temperate zones. For those of us in the desert, the stories serve as nothing but a source of frustration and failure.

I realized this shortly after moving to the desert and, as a result, canceled subscriptions to several magazines. Initially, it was too depressing to look at those pages, read the text, and know that none of it would work for me. After a time, it seemed wasteful to purchase material that was attractive, but useless beyond the pretty pictures. Still, I yearned for a cottage garden. I wanted to look out my window and see blooming flowers in that enticing variety of heights. I visualized contrasting foliage and complimentary colors and I wanted to see the components of bright springtime bouquets. I craved a bed of blues, purples, pinks, and whites to soothe my eyes in the heat of the summer. I wanted a place to grow herbs and flowers that would contribute fall colors to my autumn dinner table. I wanted it all. And then I realized that, with careful, thorough planning, a re-thinking of the traditional concepts, and a lot of preparation, I could have it all.

Locate your cottage garden in a spot that receives at least six hours of sunlight every day. Since the plants that make a cottage garden so attractive and desirable require a significant amount of water, also consider the source and ease of irrigation. Lastly, plant your cottage garden where it will provide maximum enjoyment, where it can be viewed from indoors as well as from other parts of the landscape. Once you've selected the site, determine which plan or style you intend to follow, and then prepare the soil.

Most of the flowers that make up the traditional cottage garden are perennials, although biennials and annuals also fit into the scheme. Like other flowers and vegetables, they require amended soil. Going back to previous lessons regarding soil development, this means adding composted material to the native soil and tilling it well. Cover the entire bed with a six-inch layer of amendments and an application of a complete fertilizer, and fully incorporate them. Then level the soil to the shape you've planned. If you want the plants in the center to be the focal point, elevate the middle of the bed, gradually sloping the sides outward. By the time you finish, it will look like an eroded hill. If the garden backs up to a wall, fence, or other structure, it can be either completely level or slightly elevated at the back. If you plan to surround your cottage garden with a short fence and a garden gate, amend, till, and level the entire enclosed area.

Not a single plant can go into the ground before the installation of an irrigation system. A cottage garden will always require a fair amount of supplemental water, so a consistent watering method is necessary. Grade the ground to eliminate water running out of the bed. Using a sprinkler is usually out of the question because it allows too much water to evaporate and encourages the development of fungal disease. Drip irrigation restricts irrigation to localized areas, limiting the locations of plants and dictating the overall design. The plants and their characteristics should dictate the design, not the irrigation method. Hence, a soaker hose woven through the entire bed, liberally supplying water to the entire surface area, is the most effective irrigation method.

The concept of a cottage garden differs from a cutting garden in that it is a year-round source of color and visual intrigue and should never be "between seasons" or lying fallow. There should be something worth looking at any time of year. When viewed from a distance, a proper cottage garden beckons and invites a closer look. The foliage is as interesting as the color. The flowers are as enjoyable in the garden as in the vase. This is not to imply that they cannot be cut. They should be cut, since cutting and deadheading stimulates additional blossom production and a continual show of color.

The following plants appear in groups based on ascending order of mature height. The tallest, background plants, will grow furthest from the vantage point, possibly against a wall or fence. Base plants, being the shortest, should grow nearest the path or the front of the bed. Between these two extremes are upper, center, and lower plants, as determined by height. They can be planted in an order different from that listed, so long as one plant doesn't block another from view. All of these plants grow well in the desert Southwest.

BACKGROUND PLANTS

NAME	MATURE HEIGHT	BLOOM COLOR	TYPE
hollyhock (*Alcea rosea*)	5–7 ft.	Rose, Pinks, White	biennial
tall mallow (*Malva sylvestris*)	5 ft.	Magenta, Purple	perennial
matilija poppy (*Romneya coulteri*)	8 ft.	White	perennial
yarrow (*Achillea*)	3–5 ft.	All colors	perennial

UPPER PLANTS

NAME	MATURE HEIGHT	BLOOM COLOR	TYPE
giant hyssop (*Agastache*)	3 ft	All	perennial
Jupiter's beard (*Centranthus ruber*)	3 ft.	Pink, Red	perennial
Gaillardia	2–4 ft.	Orange, Red, Yellow	annual/perennial
gaura (*Gaura lindheimeri*)	2–4 ft.	Pink, White	perennial
bamboo muhly (*Muhlenbergia dumosa*)	3–4 ft.	None	perennial
fountain grass (*Pennisetum setaceum*)	3–4 ft.	Purple foliage	perennial

CENTER PLANTS

NAME	MATURE HEIGHT	BLOOM COLOR	TYPE
lily-of-the-Nile (*Agapanthas*)	2–3 ft.	Blue, White	perennial
belladonna lily (*Amaryllis belladonna*)	2–3 ft.	Pink	perennial
pincushion flower (*Scabiosa caucasica*)	2–3 ft.	Pink, Purple, Rose	perennial
Watsonia	2–3 ft.	Scarlet	perennial

LOWER PLANTS

NAME	MATURE HEIGHT	BLOOM COLOR	TYPE
Artemisia	2 ft.	Silver w/yellow	perennial
blackfoot daisy (*Melampodium*)	2 ft.	White	perennial
Coreopsis	2 ft.	Yellow	perennial
gayfeather (*Liatris spicata* 'Kobold')	2 ft.	Purple, Rose	perennial
Mexican hat (*Ratibida columnifera*)	2 ft.	Orange, Yellow	perennial
Penstemon (var.)	1–3 ft.	Blue, Pink, Purple, Red	perennial
Sage (*Salvia var.*)	1–3 ft.	Purple, Rose	perennial
hummingbird flower (*Zauschneria Californica*)	1–2 ft.	Fuschia, Scarlet	perennial
Zinnia elegans	1–3 ft.	All	annual
Zinnia grandiflora	1–3 ft	All	perennial

BASE PLANTS

NAME	MATURE HEIGHT	BLOOM COLOR	TYPE
creeping zinnia (*Sanvitalia procumbens*)	6 in.	Yellow	annual
desert marigold (*Baileya multiradiata*)	12–18 in.	Yellow	perennial
flax (*Linum var.*)	12–15 in.	Blue, White	annual/perennial
Lobelia laxiflora	4–6 in.	Blue	perennial
thyme (*Thymus vulgaris*)	4–8 in.	Pink, White	perennial
verbena (*Glandularia [Verbena]*)	8–15 in.	Purple, White	perennial

Cool seasons herbs that make excellent filler include clary sage, chives, and bee balm. During warm seasons, dill, cilantro, and fennel do well. Windowsill tomatoes, carrots, kohlrabi, and rainbow Swiss chard are some vegetables that make a strong statement in the cottage garden.

It's also nice to add a few strategically placed containers bursting with color and texture to increase diversity and interest. I am most fond of old wooden crates and galvanized metal tubs and buckets. They add charm and whimsy—exactly what the cottage garden demands.

Naturally, the size of your allotted space will determine the number of plants you can install. If your garden is very large with a lovely fence and old-fashioned gate, you may be able to include everything on the list. If it is only four feet deep, utilize two staggered rows to create a fuller effect and line the edges with selections from the smallest plants. Whatever you choose, make sure that you consider the plants' ultimate sizes and situate them as close to one another as possible. If you're working with a large area, plan a meandering path through the garden and keep the tallest plants at the back of the garden as determined by the path's vantage point.

Plants, like people, are individuals and don't perform exactly as we anticipate when reading charts and making plans on paper. There undoubtedly will be spaces and gaps in the cottage garden. Fill these in with currently available annual plants, herbs, and vegetables. Choose plants whose flowers complement the permanent plants in the bed. These may include, but are not limited to:

African daisy (*Arctotis, Dimorphoteca, or Osteospermum*)
Alyssum
Coreopsis
Cosmos
evening primrose (*Oenothera*)
marigold (*Tagetes*)
nasturtium (*Tropaeolum*)
Nicotiana
pink (*Dianthus*)
purslane (*Portulaca oleracea*)
scented geranium (*Pelargonium sp.*)
Zinnia

Growing Gourds

Sooner or later, most gardeners find the need to screen or camouflage an unsightly view. Fast-growing, drought-tolerant gourds, which produce fruits in interesting shapes and colors, solve the problem. In fact, for the creation of a quick screen, seasonal shade, or a dense green backdrop, gourds are an excellent medium.

There are actually two types of gourds: soft shelled and hard shelled. The soft-shelled gourds include those frequently sold in grocery stores and at farm stands, including turbans and crown of thorns. The soft-shelled varieties produce bold yellow blossoms in the morning, not unlike the squashes. They ripen about three months after the seeds are sown, and are generally not edible. Soft-shelled gourds make attractive seasonal decorations but cannot be dried. Instead, they wither and mold after several weeks, a circumstance that can be delayed by washing them thoroughly in a ten-percent bleach solution. Some decorators and florists also wax soft gourds to extend their usefulness.

The hard-shelled gourds include luffa, bottle, and calabash gourds. They flower at night, their large white blossoms seducing pollinating moths with their rich and heady fragrance. Interestingly, their fruits are tender and edible when young and hard and long-lasting when mature and dried. Harvest the small fruit when they are fully colored and firm, then peel, dice and cook them to create tasty squash-like vegetable dishes. If left to mature on the vine, they develop a thick, tough skin that hardens as the fruit dries. The hollow shells can then be used for a variety of household items including dippers, spoons, and bowls, and in the case of the luffa gourd, natural sponges. They are also the basic raw material for many ethnic artisans.

Gourds are easy to grow. Both the soft- and hard-shelled varieties require full sun, rich, fertile soil, and lots of space in which to sprawl or climb. Plant the seeds in mounds or along the base of a trellis or fence beginning when all danger of frost has passed and up through the end of July. Enrich the soil with lots of organic matter, such as compost or aged manure. Keep the area moist until the seedlings emerge, then reduce water to every four or five days. As temperatures climb and leaves droop and remain limp after sunset, increase watering frequency. Application of a water-soluble fertilizer every month will encourage abundant growth. If allowed to sprawl, gourds make a splendid ground cover, and they climb at an incredible rate, creating a solid green screen.

To harvest soft-shelled gourds, remove them from the vine by cutting them, along with a two-inch section of stem, when they are firm and vividly colored. Wash them in a bleach solution and use them as fall decorations. Hard-shelled gourds should remain on the vine until frost withers the plant. When this occurs, harvest and wash them in the bleach solution, then hang them to dry in a cool, dark place with good air circulation. Not unlike other gardening activities, drying hard-shelled gourds requires a great deal of patience, since they may take six months to a year to dry.

Don't worry if a layer of mold appears on the outside shell. This is a natural part of the process and will rub off when drying is complete. Occasionally, gourds will develop soft spots along with the usual mold or mildew. If this happens, discard the affected gourds and wipe adjacent fruits with a bleach solution to prevent spread of the disease.

Soft-shelled gourd varieties include apple, egg, orange, and pear gourds. They each resemble their respective namesakes and make colorful and attractive table decorations, as well as excellent fillers for the traditional Thanksgiving cornucopia. Ball-shaped, soft-shelled gourds come in several solid and striped varieties, and create a brilliant bowl of balls when grouped together. Crown-of-thorns gourds look like orange, green, or yellow baseballs with a circle of spikes around the shoulders. Turban gourds resemble the traditional headwear for which they are named, and spoon gourds have green and orange fruits that grow to be eight inches long with a handle-like neck and a rounded base.

Hard-shelled gourds include the traditional bottle gourd that produces hourglass-shaped fruits used, when young, in traditional Indian cooking. Mature and dried, they are made into flasks, birdhouses, and musical instruments. Bushel gourds are rare, growing to an incredible twenty inches and up to one hundred pounds. When dried, they make durable bowls and baskets, and historically have served as beer-making bowls in Africa. Calabash gourds are the raw materials for calabash pipes, averaging twelve inches in length, with a five-inch-wide bowl at the base.

Canteen gourds require little description. When dried, they become hollow vessels to which only a cork or fabric stopper must be added to create a container for liquids. Several hard-shelled gourds originated in the Mediterranean region. Corsican and cucuzzi gourds are both grown as vegetables that are baked or stewed in Italian recipes. Other reliable hard-shell gourds include Chinese bottle gourds, long-handled dippers, marankas, marmoratas, siphons, and speckled swans. All of these grow well in the desert Southwest and are available from seed companies including Burpee Seeds and Plants, Native Seeds/SEARCH, Nichols Garden Nursery, and Shepherd's Seed Company.

CREATING A STANDARD TOPIARY

WEEK 17 | As cold weather retreats into memory and the impending heat moves to the forefront of challenges in my garden and in my mind, I reflect back on the last few Decembers when holiday decorating reached its peak, and recall the topiaries that graced tables and store windows. Clear mental pictures of small-scale trees and balls of growing foliage with gilded fruit or dried miniature pomegranates emerge. The problem is, I haven't planted any topiaries and they usually are unavailable in the stores during the winter months. I must create and train my own topiaries at home. If I begin now, with the onset of the desert heat, they'll be mature enough to fulfill my decorating fantasies during next winter's holiday season. Among the many lessons learned through years of gardening, preparation and forethought again rise to the top of the list.

The art of growing and shaping topiaries is a very old one, developed and practiced by ancient Egyptians, then improved upon by early Romans. Like many artistic skills, topiary-making disappeared during medieval times and enjoyed a revival during the Renaissance. Not surprisingly, Italy was the home of the art's rejuvenation and the practice slowly migrated to French and English country estates. There, artistic gardeners created life-sized creatures and elaborate mazes as their craft reached its artistic pinnacle. My goal is not nearly so lofty; I have my sights set on something smaller, more standard.

Small topiaries are versatile and can be moved from windowsill to centerpiece on a whim. They can bask in their required environment during the day and adorn and decorate a table or mantle at night. A single globe, called a standard, is the simplest of the topiaries. Rosemary is my topiary plant of choice, but there are many other possibilities. A good candidate, one with small leaves and a hard, woody stem, should be generally trouble-free and able to survive in the planned environment. Some of the more traditional plants used as topiaries are bay, eugenia, myrtle, santolina, and of course, rosemary. Faster-growing plants that also work, but require more frequent pruning, include coleus, French lavender, and scented geranium.

To begin, choose your plant. A four- or six-inch container specimen is best. Transplant it into a traditional terra cotta pot and get your materials ready. You will need small scissors or pruning shears, a bamboo stake for support, and raffia to tie the plant to the stake.

The first step is to identify the strongest, straightest stem. Remove all other woody stems at the base of the plant. This may be a little intimidating because the plant is so small, but don't worry. Just make a choice and live with it. You will have many months to nurture it into the proper shape. On the remaining stem, leave the three or four uppermost side shoots to supply the plant with nutrients. Remove all other shoots. Gently push the bamboo stake into the soil, close to the stem and trim it to the height you want your topiary to achieve. Train the stem by tying it to the bamboo with water-soaked raffia. Tie it loosely and be gentle to avoid damaging the tender stem. As the plant grows, replace the raffia with looser pieces, soaking them in water first each time. Pinch off any growth that emerges below the shoots you left in the beginning.

After the main stem has reached the desired height, prune the side shoots that you initially left to a height below the topmost growth. Pinch the terminal, or top, bud to stop upward growth and encourage the development of side shoots, which ultimately form the globe. Begin pinching back the side shoots, leaving only two or three pairs of leaves to encourage branching. Then pinch the resulting new branches to encourage fullness. Do this gentle pinching and pruning whenever you see a need. Frequent pinching will lead to earlier shape formation. As the head fills to the shape of a globe, regular pinching and pruning will promote dense, healthy growth and encourage the development and maintenance of the desired form.

Creating a full, finished topiary takes several months. Begin now, and with patience and diligence, you will have a young topiary you can display proudly when December company comes. And as the years progress, you'll enjoy an ongoing work of horticultural art as you "pot-up" your topiary and it grows fuller and more mature, while maintaining the standard shape.

Although numerous penstemons are native to the desert Southwest, many originate in wetter, cooler, or more alpine climates, making them inappropriate for our arid landscapes. These are often not identified as such, and so I've experienced more gardening failures with penstemons than with any other plant type. I push their natural limits, often thinking I have created the right mini-environment for a new species, only to lose it at the change of season. But this doesn't discourage me, since I learn more from my failures than I do from success. If nothing else, I learn what not to do and consider it progress.

All native or desert-adapted penstemons require good drainage and minimal water. They like infrequent, moderate irrigation and dislike crowded conditions. If you don't heed these requirements, the plants will succumb to fungal disease. They are susceptible to root rot, which will kill them, and powdery mildew, which will stunt their growth and render them unattractive. Most gardeners who have poor luck with penstemons are overwatering, easy to do since they require very little. Thanks to my experimentation, I am comfortable recommending specific varieties to grow with ease in our desert climate. I only offer suggestions that I can make without reservation or qualification. If you know the basic needs of the genus, you'll have success with these specific types.

Cardinal penstemon (*Penstemon cardinalis*) is native to the southwestern United States and northern Mexico, where conditions are generally dry, but include summer monsoon moisture. The leafy, matted plants send up tall flower spikes that can reach three feet in height. The small, crimson flowers that boldly line their gracefully leaning spikes attract hummingbirds and create a brilliant contrast between flower and foliage. The floral display lasts a lengthy 5–6 weeks during mid to late spring. Sometimes a second, summer bloom occurs. *P. cardinalis* was my first penstemon and I now have several in my garden. It is an evergreen clumping plant that is easy to separate or divide, then replant in early spring. A lucky gardener can divide and transplant for many years, developing quite a collection.

Scarlet bugler (*P. centranthifolius*) is a succulent-looking plant with leathery gray or bluegreen leaves. This Baja California native bears bright red flowers on three-foot spikes. The broad and unserrated leaves give scarlet bugler a smooth, plastic appearance. More tolerant of moisture than many of its cousins, scarlet bugler will respond to excess water with flopping flower spikes that may even lay flat on the ground. If your plant does this, it is a sure sign that you are over-watering, so reduce the amount of irrigation.

Closely related to Cardinal penstemon, Firecracker penstemon (*P. eatonii*) develops deep scarlet flowers on stalks ranging in height from 1½–3 feet. The flowers perch vertically on arching spikes, resembling the sparks produced by Fourth of July fireworks, from whence the common name firecracker penstemons is derived. This is one of the most persistent growers, surviving in the garden for many years. It can be propagated from seed and cuttings, or by division. It clumps like cardinal penstemon, making divisions easy to transplant. It deals well with extremes in temperature, and aside from the flower spikes, hardly changes appearance during most of the year.

Palmer's penstemon (*P. palmerii*) is most particular about good drainage. If you cannot guarantee it, don't plant it. If you can assure it, you will be glad to have this blue-green plant in your penstemon bed. This large variety is favored among gardeners for several reasons. It grows to a height of six feet and spreads into surrounding bare ground when enticed by only a little moisture. The tall spikes, displaying white or pink flowers, emerge from clumps of serrated leaves. Unlike most other penstemon, the flowers exude a sweet-smelling fragrance that wafts through the garden.

An Arizona native, Parry's penstemon (*P. parryii*) will reseed itself with abandon if the right conditions exist. Its requirements include rocky soil with crevices for the seeds to fall into and germinate. It needs little irrigation, doing very well with average rainfall. Too much water almost always leads to severe powdery mildew, which kills individual plants in a single season. On its own, Parry's penstemon is not spectacular, remaining rather small aside from its flower spikes. But it becomes spectacular when it reseeds and develops into a meadow of blue-green smooth-edged leaves and small, deep pink flowers. Mixed with yellow-blossomed native flowers, the resulting scene is breathtaking. I once attempted to create this meadow-like appearance with only fair initial results. After a couple of years to naturalize, however, the tiny meadow I tried to create came into its own and looked stunning. I should know to expect this—nature is usually the better designer.

If you experience success with these reliable penstemons, I recommend a couple more for the slightly advanced gardener. *P. pinifolious* is a dwarf evergreen species that resembles heather, with its bright green needle-like leaves. Its yellow, pink, red, or orange flowers are so narrow and tubular, only hummingbirds are able to reach the nectar. I like this plant when growing near something with distinct textural contrast, like octopus agave. Together, these two plants create captivating visual interest. If you can be very certain not to over irrigate, try royal beard tongue (*Penstemon spectabilis*). Like Parry's penstemon, this cultivar smells divine. It attains a very respectable three feet in height, and the leaves are not serrated. Abundant pink and purple flowers practically cover the entire plant, blooming in mid-to-late spring and lasting for about a month. This is an ideal specimen plant and an excellent choice for highlighting a focal point in the garden.

P. barbatus is familiar throughout Europe and in North America, from Utah to Mexico. Frequently cultivated, varieties exist in nearly every color of the rainbow. Requiring good drainage and protection from afternoon sun, *P. barbatus* is more finicky that any of the others mentioned, but you usually will see several specimens in local nurseries, making them very tempting. For best results, plant this variety in an amended bed that receives minimal but regular irrigation and afternoon shade. If you baby it along, your reward will be dense, healthy plants with deep green foliage and brilliant blooms.

May

- Increase irrigation
- Mulch, if haven't already done so
- Mist new plants to avoid midday wilt
- Plant melon, pepper, cucumber, squash, and okra
- Plant agave, cacti, citrus, and palms
- Plant basil, marjoram, mint, and oregano to invite pollinators into garden
- Plant annual and perennial flowers
- Fertilize citrus
- Fertilize lawns
- Blast spidermites from evergreens with water or insecticidal soap
- Harvest onions and garlic
- Collect dry seeds from spent flowerheads
- Harvest early-maturing deciduous fruit
- Watch for grape leaf skeletonizers and orange dogs on citrus

May

MUCH TO DO IN MAY

WEEK 18 May Day was a big deal in my childhood home. There were always flowers in the garden and everyone in the neighborhood had a door-knob worthy of decoration. With an excess of energy, and perhaps time, too, that was all we needed. We gathered blooms from our garden and Grandma's, too. We even pilfered blossoms from the gardens of those who would later be the recipients of our floral surprises. Year after year I approached May 1st with a happiness and excitement surpassed only by the major holidays. Perhaps this enthusiasm presaged my horticultural penchant. I don't know. But I do know that when May 1st rolls around each year, I miss making nosegays for my neighbors and the childish thrill I got from elusively ringing the bell and leaving the gift.

Once I get into the garden, the length of my "to do" list quickly increases. First to catch my attention are the fruit trees, heavy-laden with ripening fruit. I am reminded of the year that nearly-ripe peaches hung in great number from the full branches of our shapely tree as a micro-burst of wind hit our little community, causing a great deal of damage. After the dust and debris settled, my garden was a mess, and the peach tree was most severely affected. Every branch broke, either at the collar or midway, leaving little to salvage. I had to take down the tree, but I learned a valuable lesson. I now use two-by-fours to prop up and support the cumbrous branches, alleviating the stress of the weight and preventing another such loss.

Wind, while damaging, doesn't come close to the continual havoc wrought by birds. To conserve some of the harvest, the trees must now be covered with netting, which is available at the local hardware store. There are a couple of important tips to remember when draping this material over trees. First, buy a larger net than you think you'll need and firmly secure it to the trunk of the tree to prevent birds from flying in from below. (Not realizing this possibility the first year I used netting, I unintentionally trapped a bird and had quite a chore releasing it.) Second, remove the netting after harvesting the fruit to prevent malformation of the rapidly growing branches. You also can harvest some fruit early and allow it to ripen in brown bags.

I usually give my fruit trees a heavy irrigation while I'm tending them, and look around the garden for signs of drought stress on other plants. Since temperatures are steadily increasing, non-native plants will need water more frequently. If you haven't already adjusted your watering schedule, do that now. Reduce the time between irrigations by a couple of days and watch to make sure it is enough. You will need to increase the frequency again as summer begins, but this minor adjustment should be adequate for now.

In order to retain as much moisture as possible, I always mulch during the spring. Shredded or chipped bark and desert compost make good mulch. Bagged mulches bought at home improvement stores are great, too. I usually buy mulch by the truckload because it's so much cheaper, and then spread a four-inch layer under all of my landscape plants, in tree wells, and on all beds. The first time I did this, I realized a thirty-percent decrease in my water bill. I'm not sure the results are always so dramatic, but I have no doubt that the money spent on mulch is more than recouped in water savings. The mulch also gives a finished, manicured look to the garden. Even a naturalistic landscape is more attractive when exposed soil is covered with a visually consistent mulch material.

Refrain from spreading mulch beneath citrus trees because citrus is susceptible to foot rot, or gummosis. Keep the soil pulled back from the trunk and never allow organic material or water to sit against it. Instead, fertilize your citrus for the second time this calendar year. Any nitrogen source will do, just as in February. I water the trees thoroughly to moisten roots and flush mineral deposits out of the root zone, then apply fertilizer according to package directions and completely water it in. This fertilization provides nutrients to the trees as they enter their most active growing season and encourages them to produce fuller, more lush foliage.

Sage, or salvia, is one of the most popular indigenous plants in the Southwest. There are hundreds of varieties, many of which do well in our landscapes. Some sages originate from more temperate regions, and some are tender to frost, but most will thrive in our alkaline soils with very little water. These factors make sage one of the best choices for a single species bed or garden—the "china cabinets" of the horticultural world. Each item is on display, to be recognized both as part of a group and as an individual. It is fun to plant an entire bed with many varieties of the same species and then label each one. When you have visitors to the garden, they'll enjoy reading the common and botanical names and comparing the plants. It is wise to write all of this information on the label. Also note blossom color and the year in which you planted the plant. On the backside of the label, put the name and toll-free number or address of the nursery where you bought the plant. This is particularly helpful if you have received plants through a mail order company. Two or three years down the road you may not remember where you got an individual plant, and the information will be right there on the tag. If you don't want to tag every plant in the bed, make a sketch in your garden journal and identify each plant and source.

121

Inspired by other gardener's collections, I now have a substantial sage bed. I added composted manure because the clay-laden site tends to hold water and prevents drainage, and sages regularly die of root rot or fungal disease when planted in poorly drained soil. After I supplemented the soil to insure good drainage, I laid out my plan. There were many sages on my wish list.

Edible:
culinary or common sage (*Salvia officinalis*)
tricolor sage (*S. officinalis* 'Tricolor')
purple sage (*S. officianalis* 'Purpurea')
golden sage (*S. officianalis* 'Aurea')
miniature culinary sage
Berggarten sage (*S. officinalis* 'Berggarten')
pineapple sage (*S. elegans* 'Pineapple Sage')
Holt's mammoth sage (*S. officinalis* 'Holt's Mammoth')
honey rose sage (*S. officinalis* 'Honey Rose')

Decorative:

electric blue sage (*S. chamaedryoides*)
Cleveland sage (*S. clevelandi*)
scarlet or blood sage (*S. coccinea*)
mealy cup sage (*S. farinacea*)
autumn sage (*S. greggii*)
Mexican bush sage (*S. leucantha*)
purple sage (*S. leucophylla*)
little leaf sage (*S. microphylla*)
clary sage (*S. sclarea*)
S. x superba

Many other varieties tempted me, but would freeze and die if the temperature dipped below 25°. Unless I'm planting for annual color, I no longer consider species or varieties that are marginal in our extreme temperatures. I have learned that a successful gardener doesn't make everything grow everywhere. A successful gardener makes wonderful things happen within the natural parameters. Always keep our temperature ranges in mind when looking for plant material.

Once I assembled my plant list, I shopped the local nurseries and was able to find most of what I sought right here in town. Much to my surprise, I found some of the more unusual varieties at the nearby Wal-Mart. I ordered those plants that were not locally available from High Country Gardens. Regardless of the source, all of the plants were healthy when I received them and survived the ordeal of transplantation without a problem. Most of them were in small pots, so I immediately potted them up. In their new eight-inch pots, I babied them along with frequent feedings of a water-soluble fertilizer and filtered afternoon sun.

When the root balls significantly filled the pots, I planted the collection into the prepared bed. I arranged them by height, with the tallest plants at maturity in the back, and by texture, with plants near others that complemented or highlighted unique features. Lastly, I planted them so that the mature plants would just touch their neighbors without crowding. The bed is in scattered sunlight all day long. It is lined by local river rock.

TOMATO TROUBLES

A few weeks back I told you that tomatoes weren't an appropriate desert crop, but if you're a determined gardener like I am, you planted them anyway. I've never had a spring or summer without homegrown tomatoes and I probably never will, although I confess that since living in the desert I haven't been able to grow enough to supply my needs. The challenges inherent to growing tomatoes in the desert Southwest are formidable.

Fungal diseases that can attack and destroy tomato plants include: Anthracnose (sunken gray, tan, or dark spots along rib line of leaves, and on twigs and branches), alternaria leaf spot/early blight (dark-brown or black, yellow-rimmed "bull's eye" spots on lower leaves), fusarium wilt (yellow, dry lower leaves), gray mold fungus (moist, gray lesions on leaves, and concentric circles on fruit), and phytopthera/late blight (white-gray mold followed by dark purple spots on leaves, and gray-green spots on fruit). If you detect any of these problems, pull up the plants immediately and put them in the garbage along with any surrounding garden debris. Don't put this material in a compost heap because reproductive spores will survive in decomposing organic material. Avoid overhead watering and change the location of your tomato plants year-to-year. Remove infected plants immediately and spray soil with a copper-based fungicide.

If nighttime temperatures drop below 55° for more than four nights, or if they rise above 76°, tomato blossoms will drop. If daytime temperatures rise above 90°, blossoms will drop and fruit will not set. Smaller tomatoes tend to be more tolerant and will continue to set bloom slightly beyond these temperature limits. This is the reason I made particular variety suggestions in Week 12. Some gardeners have managed to use mister systems or other methods to create cooler microclimates, which produce larger fruiting varieties for a longer period of time.

Tomatoes often develop a soft, dark circle on their blossom end that continues to grow. The spot can cover half the fruit, becoming brown or black and leathery. This frequently occurring problem is called blossom-end rot and is caused by the plant's inability to utilize calcium. Prevention measures include proper soil preparation prior to planting, regular and adequate irrigation, adding a layer of mulch around the plants to retain moisture, and careful cultivation to avoid root damage. If the soil has a heavy salt content, water deeply to wash the minerals below the root zone.

There are many insect pests that attack tomato plants. Armyworms are actually black, brown, or tan caterpillars with white or yellow stripes. They usually emerge in large numbers from eggs hatched in grasses and other weeds near the garden. When they hatch, they begin to eat the foliage off the vegetable plants. They only feed during the night and on cloudy days, a habit that allows the gardener to identify them. The plants will look fine one evening and be partially defoliated and skeletonized the next morning. Keep grasses and other weeds away from the garden plot. Dig trenches or place boards around the bed as obstacles. If an invasion occurs, either handpick in the very early morning or apply Bt or neem.

Colorado potato beetles have black and white wing covers and black and orange spotted upper bodies. The 1/3-inch-long beetles, their small yellow eggs, and their dark red young usually are found on the same plants. They feed on the foliage and leave black dots of excrement. In a short period of time, a major infestation can completely defoliate an entire bed of tomato plants. Deep tilling before planting reduces adult populations. Because the adults emerge from the soil in the spring, a thick layer of mulch often can prevent them from reaching the plants.

Flea beetles are shiny, 1/10-inch long, brown, black, or bronze beetles that jump like fleas do when disturbed and prefer hot, dry locations. They chew leaves, leaving very small holes that look like miniature buckshot damage. They jump from plant to plant, spreading pathogens; hence they're vectors for many plant diseases and are often the culprits who spread blight and bacterial wilts. Because the adults over-winter in leaves and other plant debris, keeping the garden clean and tidy will inhibit available habitat. Insecticidal soap effectively kills flea beetles if you find them in your garden.

The most recognizable tomato pest is the large, green, striped hornworm. Growing to a length of five inches, larvae of the sphinx moth are rarely noticed before growing quite large. Dark beads of excrement are usually the first indication of its presence. It chews leaves and stems, and then moves on to the ripening fruit. In spring, the moths emerge from brown, shiny two-inch pupae buried in the soil. The moths lay small yellow eggs on the undersides of leaves, which then develop into the hornworms. To prevent infestation, till the soil and remove any cocoon-like pupae that you find. Once the worms are evident on the plants, the most effective method of control is handpicking. Bt is ineffective on all but the smallest hornworms.

Greasy yellow or bronze colored leaves almost always indicate the presence of mites on tomato plants. During hot, dry spells, mites suck juices from the soft tissue of plants, affecting foliage and flowers. The entire plant eventually dries out and turns brown. Webbing may be present on the leaves if the infestation is heavy. Regular irrigation prevents infestations and a strong jet of water applied in the late morning can remove the mites from the plant. Sulfur dust sprinkled on the tops and undersides of the leaves will kill any that remain.

If you see bright green, shield-shaped beetles in your garden, you have stinkbugs. They insert their mouthparts into the plant and suck out the juices. This creates a mottled yellow appearance on the leaves, and affected fruits become malformed and blemished. Because the adults over-winter in the soil, a good tilling and thorough cleaning up of the garden and surrounding area usually prevents stinkbugs from becoming a problem. Keeping weeds out of the garden during the season is another management method. Handpicking and insecticidal soaps are the only recommended controls.

Whiteflies suck plant juices, weakening and stunting growth. Adults lay their tiny eggs on the undersides of leaves, which hatch in only a day or two, and begin to feed. They molt and become immobile, transparent, oval pupae. Winged adults emerge in a couple of days and the cycle begins again. Because of the rapidity of reproduction, a heavy infestation can take place in less than a week. Stippled, yellow foliage, honeydew, and the fluttering of adults when the leaves are rustled indicate a whitefly infestation. Insecticidal soap, if used regularly and repeatedly, is an effective control. Pyrethrum and neem also are recommended for food crops. Be sure to spray the undersides of leaves and follow directions carefully.

Chile peppers

My culinary preferences tend toward spicy, intensely flavored fare. From the time I was very little, I enjoyed the rich flavors of cumin, garlic, ginger, and cracked pepper, and appreciated the charged tingle on my lips and tongue after a session with pickled chile peppers (*Capsicum frutescens*). I love spicy Chinese, Italian, Thai, and Indian cuisine, but my favorite, by far, is Mexican food. And nothing says Mexican food like chiles.

Aside from the famous 'Big Jim' variety, 'Anaheim', 'Jalapeño', 'Red Cherry', and 'Sante Fe Grande' do particularly well in the Southwest. 'Ancho', 'Mulato', and 'Yellow Wax', much milder varieties, also do well in the desert. All are easy to grow, requiring amended garden soil, regular irrigation, and monthly fertilization. If protected from temperatures below 32°, chiles will bloom and bear fruit through two full years. I usually move some plants onto my back patio and never go without fresh chiles.

The southwest herb garden

| WEEK |
| 20 |

Let's hear it for the "useful plants," a customary term for herbs, including anything used for flavor, fragrance, or medicine, and encompassing hundreds of species and varieties. Since many herbs originated in the Mediterranean or Middle East, they grow well in our similar soils and temperatures. The main difference in our climates is low humidity, which excludes a few plants from the Southwest. It is not unusual for herb lovers to have hundreds of these useful plants in their gardens. My herb collection numbers well over a hundred, and I add varieties every season.

Growing herbs in the Southwest makes sense for several reasons. Aside from being useful, they take minimal water and are highly decorative. The perennial herbs are pest resistant, often protecting nearby plants from infestation. They develop a greater concentration of essential oils when the thermometer goes up, making them more fragrant and flavorful when cultivated in the desert. A mainstay in a sensory garden, they contribute diverse textures, colors, and aromas.

Most herbs are quite hardy and provide success for even the least accomplished gardener. They are often drought-tolerant, require good drainage, generally prefer lean soil, and perform exceedingly well in full morning sun with filtered afternoon shade. A few are absolutely bulletproof and will flourish in the middle of the garden, with no protection from the elements. Good air circulation is vital. Herbs quickly succumb to fungal infections if planted in an area that is very close and very still. Given a little space and a little time, herbs are rewarding to every gardener.

Like most other vegetation, herbs fall into two broad groupings: annuals and perennials. Propagate and grow annuals as you would flowers and vegetables. They have roughly the same requirements and needs. Plant them in highly amended native soil, containers, or raised beds. I dedicate a large bedding area to basils, sections of my vegetable beds to other annual herbs, and large pots to invasive perennials and annual herbs mixed with flowers.

Cool-weather annual herbs do best when started in August. They grow and provide harvest through April. Warm-weather annual herbs should be planted now and need at least six hours of sunlight daily. If planted in full sun, they thrive from the end of March until the middle of June, when they require afternoon shade. Come September, they again enjoy full afternoon sun, producing until first frost in November. If protected from that frost, they will yield even longer. The warm-weather annual herbs that I consider necessary are basil, summer savory, and salad burnett.

Basil (*Ocimum*) is at the top of my list. I am not alone in my deep affection for this exceptional plant. In Italy basil represents love, and a pot traditionally was placed on the balcony outside a woman's bedroom sending the message that she is ready to receive her beloved. It is also believed that a woman receiving basil from a man will fall in love and never leave him.

Sweet basil
(Ocimum sp.)

The different varieties of basil, each with unique characteristics, bring diversity to the garden and the kitchen. 'Dark Opal', stunning when planted in the flowerbed and mixed with color or vegetable pots, produces a particularly attractive blossom. I don't clip off 'Dark Opal', but I do keep all other basils deadheaded since flower formation alters flavor and limits leaf development. It's also important to regularly pinch back and harvest leaves to encourage bushy growth.

I most enjoy cooking with 'Fino Verde' and 'Lettuce Leaf' basils, using them liberally in salads, vegetable dishes, and Italian cuisine. Sweet basil, lemon basil (especially 'Sweet Dani'), and 'Lettuce Leaf' make the best pesto. 'Purple' and 'Green Ruffles' are loveliest used as a garnish and for flavor in heavy pasta dishes. For a superb caprese salad use 'Fino Verde', 'Genovese', or 'Napoletano', along with your freshest tomatoes and mozzarella. 'Siam Queen' is actually a perennial that over-winters if protected from frost. It is a great addition to the sage bed, blending well with the purples and greens of these plants. Lemon basil makes a refreshing tea, either alone or combined with other lemon herbs. Based on personal experience, I'm convinced that sweet basil repels both bugs and birds when interplanted with tomatoes.

I avoid making herbal oils because of the possibility of bacterial contamination, but frequently combine the smaller-leafed basils with garlic and chive blossoms in champagne vinegar to make a light, flavorful salad dressing. If I want a more robust taste, I use the purple leafed varieties, including 'Siam Queen', in balsamic or red wine vinegar. This is delicious mixed with olive oil when ready to serve.

Summer savory (*Satureja hortensis*) is historically valuable, having been the world's main savory spice until explorers brought black pepper into European kitchens. It has been used to flavor foods for over two thousand years. I have planted it in my warm-weather vegetable bed with good results. It is a highly aromatic plant, releasing its scent when brushed against, making it a good choice for the front of the bed where the eighteen-inch plants can perfume the garden as you work and wander through. It would also serve well as a foliage plant, displaying its fine, hairy stems in a flowerbed. Summer savory blooms in late summer. The small, pale pink, or white flowers are not terribly showy, but their development doesn't alter the flavor of the plant, so it isn't necessary to deadhead them. In the fall, the leaves turn purple-gray before the plants die back from exposure to frost. Summer savory grows well from seed, or from cuttings made in September.

As its name implies, salad burnett (*Poterium sanguisorba*) is a traditional ingredient in green salads. It also has a long history of medicinal use. When ingested, it was said to protect people from the plague and to quell hemorrhaging. I like it for the cucumber-like taste it imparts to cold foods. It's an excellent addition to salads and adds a nice flavor to sandwiches. Use the leaves fresh, since they don't dry well. You can also mince salad burnett with other herbs to make salad dressings, marinades, or cheese spreads. Although it is a perennial, treat it as an annual in the desert Southwest. I grow it beneath large potted trees on my back patio so that the leaves are easy to get to when putting together a quick salad on a summer evening.

In addition to the three warm-weather annual herbs, perennial herb plants do well when planted now. Either make cuttings or buy small plants, since it takes too long to propagate from seed, and success rates are usually not good. If you purchase plants, start with four-inch pots and transplant them into larger containers until they are sturdy enough to survive in the landscape. If they will remain in containers, increase the pot size as they grow until they are in pots that are twelve inches or larger across. Anything smaller demands too much attention in the summer heat.

Bay laurel (*Laurus nobilis*) does nicely in the desert Southwest. When planted in a microclimate that includes other trees or structures, bay trees usually get enough protection to grow moderately well in the landscape. They suffer sunscald and lose a good deal of new growth when overexposed to the sun, so if you cannot guarantee adequate summer protection, plant your tree in a large pot. Anything larger than eighteen inches will work, and the size of the pot will dictate the tree's growth and ultimate size. When in a pot, the tree can be moved to a more protected location during the summer and back to full sun in the cooler months. Leaf browning and burning indicate the need for more shade. Fresh or dried bay leaves add flavor to soups, stews, sauces, seafood dishes, and meats. In our climate, they take less than two weeks to dry and, if stored in tightly sealed containers, will stay fresh for over a year.

Bee balm (*Monarda*) adds color and texture to the flowerbed, herb garden, or containers. The citrus-scented leaves on this deciduous perennial grow in bold green clusters on square stems, indicating membership in the mint family. The brilliant red, pink, white, salmon, or purple flowers appear in July and August and are excellent for cutting or salads. They also make lovely floating garnishes as they add a pleasant flavor to fruit drinks and wines. A native of North America, bee balm was traditionally used as a medicine. When brewed into a tea, the leaves provide reliable relief from a cough. They also are used to relieve sore throats, nausea, flatulence, and menstrual cramps. Even if the efficacy of these remedies is unproved, the tea does no harm and is quite tasty. The plants themselves require moderate water and well-drained, amended soil. They benefit from afternoon shade and thorough mulching, if exposed to freezing temperatures in winter.

Catnip (*Nepeta cataria*) makes a healthy and refreshing tea that was often consumed by the English prior to the importation of the Chinese teas. It is a hardy herb whose mounding 1–2-foot growth is an excellent underplanting for the rose garden, since it likes highly amended, well-drained soil and frequent springtime fertilization. It serves as an effective insect repellent and provides an interesting textural contrast to the formal and stately rose. I used catnip to deter insect pests from the vegetable beds, and unwittingly lured a neighborhood cat into the garden. Be aware of the strong cat attraction when planting this delicate-looking herb. When you wander through your garden and find the mound crushed and flattened, you need not wonder why.

Members of the *Allium* family, chives and garlic chives add a fresh taste to potatoes, salads, and pasta. Garlic chives add a light garlic flavor to any dish, when added in the last few minutes of cooking or as a tasty garnish. While they prefer well-drained soil, both of these plants will tough it out in native soil with slight amendment. Excellent candidates for pot culture, chives and garlic chives grow easily from seed or divisions and look great on the kitchen counter. If you do not harvest and eat them regularly, you must divide clumps every few years. Your herb-growing friends will love you when you arrive bearing gifts of divided chives or garlic chives for their gardens.

When temperatures dip below freezing, chives die back to the crown, allowing the bulbs to store energy for next year's leaves. Before this happens, remove a section of the clump and pot it up. This will provide enough chives to get a family through the winter. Garlic chives may shrivel some, but don't usually go completely dormant. I have never potted mine up and have always had a steady supply of the slightly piquant leaves. A simple hint when harvesting—cut the long strands at the base of the plant to avoid development of an unsightly clump.

Hyssop (*Hyssopus officinalis*) is a member of the mint family with the characteristic square stems and odor of mint. The blue or purple flowers form in whorls at the tips of tall spikes, increasing the height of the normally diminutive plant to two feet. Hyssop is a good companion plant for vegetables because it repels flea beetles and moths. It attracts hummingbirds and butterflies, and often is planted near commercial beehives to add flavor to the honey. Hyssop historically has been prescribed as a remedy for bronchitis and sore throats, and also is said to speed the healing of bruises and wounds when applied as a poultice. It adds flavor to green salads, chicken dishes, fruit salads, and lamb. Many cooks also add it to poultry stuffing, along with the traditional sage. Hyssop needs little-to-moderate water, occasional pruning, and infrequent fertilization. It does well in slightly amended native soil with some afternoon shade.

Lavender (*Lavandula*) is a bushy, branching shrub that requires good drainage and minimal water. The smell of lavender and the beauty of its flowers are universally recognized. They begin flowering in May and continue through summer. When harvested and dried, the leaves and flowers make aromatic potpourri, sachet, and bath products. Bundles hung in closets or chests repel moths and silverfish. Many herbal enthusiasts use the blossoms in cooking. They make excellent landscape and border plants, but require space and air circulation in the perennial bed. If the soil drains well and they get some winter weather protection, lavender plants spread and clump for many years. If the soil is too tight, they usually die in less than two years.

The varieties I recommend are: 'Goodwin Creek', 'Spanish', 'French', 'Green Dentate', 'Spiked', and 'Dwarf Munstead' lavenders. English lavender is touted as the easiest to grow in the home garden, but in the desert it is more susceptible to fungus than the other suggested varieties.

Lemon balm and lemon grass are two very different plants that impart the same rich, lemony scent and flavor. Lemon balm (*Melissa officinalis*) is a loosely branched, low-growing plant that is native to southern Europe and North Africa. It's beautiful as an ornamental, growing well in the cottage garden, herb bed, or pots. As a member of the mint family, lemon balm likes well-drained soil and some shade in the desert. It also requires protection from winter cold, although it will recover if damaged. It is at its best when harvested regularly after the first year. Other than a susceptibility to powdery mildew, it is problem-free. The leaves make a tasty tea, but are also excellent flavorings for asparagus, beans, broccoli, corn, lamb, and shellfish. Frozen in ice cubes, they are attractive and tasty in lemonade, punch, or iced tea.

Lemon grass (*Cymbopogon citratus*) is an attractive ornamental used in Asian cuisine. It grows to a height of three feet and can become very large as it spreads in a clumping fashion. Delicious when added to the cooking water of aromatic rice, it also makes a flavorful lemon tea. Because of its visual appeal and strong lemon scent, I keep a clump growing near the ramada or patio so I can smell it as the wind rustles the tall leaves. It is one of my favorite garden herbs and I'm always excited to see it sprout after winter dormancy.

Lemon verbena (*Aloysia triphylla*), a deciduous, woody shrub that grows into a small tree in mild climates, imparts the strongest, truest lemon flavor. Even when well protected from cold, it rarely grows above five feet in the desert Southwest. The light green, slender, pointed leaves contain heavy concentrations of lemon-scented essential oil. They make a soothing tea and impart lemon flavor to almost any dish. But as the leaves are rather tough, remove them prior to serving. The oil from this plant contributes the familiar lemon scent to perfumes and other household products. A handful added to a tub of water makes a wonderful, refreshing bath.

In our climate, lemon verbena does best when container-grown in a rich potting soil. It likes regular water, frequent fertilization, and lots of sunshine. In the winter, provide protection from the cold and be prepared for the leaves to drop along with the temperature. They'll sprout out again in the spring. If you have not been harvesting the leaves continually, cut the plant back by half in midsummer. This will keep it compact and full rather than rangy.

Useful, aromatic, and attractive, varieties of mint (*Mentha*) nearly outnumber the basils in my garden. In order to contain their aggressive habits, I grow them in large pots with only a couple of exceptions. The plants I have in the ground grow in caliche-laden areas with little irrigation. These two factors limit their insatiable need for more space. When planted in the ground, mints normally require an underground barrier to a depth of eighteen inches to contain their growth. They spread by way of underground runners that escape anything shallower. Mints like full sun or partial shade, require very little fertilizer, and need a lot of water. They have numerous culinary and medicinal uses. I often use them for teas, fruit drinks, and garnishes. Although some gardeners dry mint, my large supply of fresh leaves makes it unnecessary. Like the basils, I use different varieties for different purposes.

Egyptian mint (*M. Nilaca*) is my favorite aromatic mint, although I do not like to cook with the fuzzy leaves. Orange mint (*M. p. citrata*) has a fresh, clean flavor and bright green leaves whose oval shape is most attractive. Peppermint (*M. piperita*) is unbeatable for settling an upset stomach. Make a warm tea from the leaves or simply chew on two or three. Spearmint (*M. spicata*) is crisper and brighter in flavor, adding a nice element to iced tea. I love the ruffled appearance of grapefruit mint as it mounds up and cascades over the sides of its pot. It's an attractive garnish. My wild New Mexico mint (*M. arvensis*), a gift from a friend's garden, has thinner, more pointed leaves and is resistant to whitefly. Chocolate mint (*M. p.* 'Chocolate') grows best on my kitchen counter, where it gets lots of attention.

Marjoram (*Origanum majorana*) grows like a weed in the corner of one of my flowerbeds, sending up dense clusters of insignificant white flowers through the spring and summer. I sheer it to the ground once it blooms, and it comes right back. I sheer it again and keep all of the cuttings for culinary use. Some years the persistent plant gets cut down several times. It is one of those bulletproof herbs that can take full sun and needs less water. A dry year will concentrate the essential oils in the leaves. Marjoram relieves sinus congestion and hay fever when consumed as a tea, and has antioxidant and antifungal properties. I started my tough specimen from a four-inch transplant that I put directly into the soil. It immediately began growing and never slowed down. To contain its clumping growth, I remove sections and keep runners pulled out.

Oregano (*Origanum vulgare*) is an aromatic, herbaceous perennial that is a favorite flavoring in tomato sauce, pizza, and other Italian dishes. Used even more widely in Greek cuisine, it imparts classic flavor to nearly all savory Greek dishes. Its name in Greek means "joy of the mountain." From the same family as marjoram, oregano requires minimal water and fertilizer, and grows easily in lean soil. It has historically escaped the confines of the kitchen garden and now grows wild in many parts of the United States. This naturalizing habit may cause oregano to move about in your garden, but probably not into the wild since it requires more water than it would receive in the desert.

Rosemary (*Rosemarinus officinalis*) is the culinary herb most frequently used in desert landscaping. Once established, these tough plants survive on rainfall alone and thrive in full sun, in the leanest desert soils with no fertilization. The usually pest-free rosemary is sometimes infested by spider mites. The telltale webbing identifies the problem and should prompt you to use insecticidal soap as a remedy. If left too long, spider mites cause severe drying and dieback, although they rarely kill an established plant. Rosemary comes in many varieties, but 'Tuscan Blue' is the most popular. Root rot is sometimes a problem in heavy clay or poorly drained soils. If your planting site falls into one of these categories, amend the soil and be frugal with water.

Sage (*Salvia*) is another herb whose hymn of praise I've already sung. Look back at Week 9 for a discussion of the many types of sage you can grow in your desert garden. If we are focusing on culinary uses, common sage (*Salvia oficianalis*) does remarkably well in the desert. I also like to cook with 'Berggarten' sage and dwarf sage (*S. pachyphylla*). They are incomparable in flavoring poultry, lamb, pork, and stuffing. Sage grows in well-drained native soil, amended soil, or potting soil. It also likes moderate water and afternoon shade, although it can take a lot of sun.

When used in vegetable dishes, sage imparts a familiarity that makes the meal equally enticing to meat eaters and vegetarians. The flowers from 'Honey Rose' sage and the blossoms and leaves of pineapple sage are flavorful additions to fruit and sweet dishes. Sage leaves have been used to perfume soaps, cosmetics, incense, and homes for hundreds of years. Because sage seeds store poorly, propagate by cutting, layering, or division. The plants are susceptible to wilt and root rot, so good drainage and air circulation are necessary.

Thyme (*Thymus vulgaris*) is the last of the perennial culinary herbs that comprise the basic herb garden. It's another exceedingly tough plant, growing well in full sun and lean soil. Thyme requires good drainage and minimal-to-moderate water and is an excellent choice for the front border of the herb garden, cutting garden, or cottage garden. It is also excellent in rock gardens and as an interplanting between pavers or stepping-stones, since it exudes a rich, spicy odor when tread upon. Many cooks use thyme as the essential flavoring in their cooking, as there are few dishes that don't benefit from the addition of thyme. It also has been used medicinally for centuries.

A native of the Mediterranean, thyme has been propagated all over the world and, like oregano, has naturalized in many parts of the U.S. It is susceptible to root rot and spider mites, although neither problem is very common.

Propagated from cuttings or divisions, thyme blooms with fragrant, pink or white flowers that attract bees and should be cut back to encourage new growth. Tie the harvested branches into bundles and hang to dry for a couple of weeks. Strip the leaves from the branches for most food preparations, or use whole branches and remove them before serving. While drying, the hanging bundles perfume the room and repel insects, making this hardy plant especially beneficial.

JERUSALEM SAGE

| WEEK |
| 21 |

As a desert dweller, I entertain outdoors as much as possible during the incredible month of May. It's the perfect time of year to enjoy clean air, clear skies, and beautiful sunsets when the garden is putting on one of its feature shows. Spectacular colors and interesting blossoms abound for guests to enjoy and appreciate. I welcome the company and look forward to the festivity, sometimes with literally hundreds of people in my garden. The plant prompting the greatest amount of conversation is Jerusalem sage (*Phlomis fruticosa*). In slightly amended clay soil, my Jerusalem sage blooms profusely every year, scenting the air around the courtyard with a fragrance so gentle even I wonder about the enticing aroma.

Jerusalem sage, so dubbed because of its woolly, sage-like foliage, is drought-tolerant and undemanding about soil type. It even grows in poorly drained soil as long as irrigation is slight and the grade allows runoff. In the worst dirt, a perfect solution is planting Jerusalem sage on top of a small berm so that water cannot settle around its crown. It is evergreen in my backyard, where the immediate microclimate falls to the mid-twenties in winter. It grows to a height and width of four feet. The flowers are showstoppers as they cover the plant, with several layers developing on each stem.

Just when I think the plants have exhausted their store of energy producing so many custard-yellow balls skewered on each stem, they surprise me by putting out another set of leaves and blossoms on their tips. They stay on the plant for many days and make excellent cut flowers. When dried, the color deepens to apricot yellow and lasts for a couple of years out of direct sunlight. Or you can allow the petals to fall off in the garden and used the remaining thistle-like pods in dry arrangements. They have a curious shape and texture, adding interest to a display.

Jerusalem sage likes full sun, scattered sunlight, or afternoon shade. It has few pest or disease problems, and will bloom several times during the spring and summer if cut back by one third after each flush of bloom. It's thirstier cousin, *Phlomis russeliana*, is similar in appearance, with larger leaves and a slightly smaller overall size. Unlike the clumping *P. fruticosa, P. russeliana* spreads by runners, making it a good choice for ground cover. I occasionally see *P. fruticosa* in the nurseries, and always find it in mail-order catalogs. It stimulates several senses, making it one of the plants I will never be without.

Soil mixes

When gardeners are not digging holes and planting in the native soil, they are usually propagating in small pots or transplanting into bigger ones. Depending on the type of plant, each of these potting tasks requires attention to the components of the soil going into the pots. There are many packaged soil mixes available in stores, each labeled for a specific purpose. It is less expensive, however, to buy the individual components at nurseries and home improvement stores and mix them at home. This gives you complete control over the ingredients while saving a little money. The trick is to know which specific components to buy.

Different types of plants have different soil requirements, based on the native habitat of the species. Plants whose origins were pine-covered mountains will have different requirements from a plant that originally inhabited the desert. Potting mixtures are blends of different components that mimic the soil conditions most preferred by different species. Some planting mixes actually contain garden soil, while others are completely devoid of soil. They serve different purposes. Those containing soil are generally heavier and provide better support to the stems and roots of plants; they contain some nutrients that the plants can access and more effectively retain moisture. Non-soil mixes drain faster, preventing the development of fungal growth and root rot.

They are sterile and free of pathogens, providing the best environment for cuttings and new roots that are most susceptible to disease. Below are several use-specific recipes.

All purpose mix
1 part peat moss
1 part sand
1 part aged steer manure
1 part perlite or pumice

Seed starting mix
1 part peat moss
1 part perlite or pumice
1 part vermiculite
1 part sand

Cacti and succulent mix
4 parts pumice
2 parts organic potting soil
1 part sand

Bulb-forcing mix
1 part vermiculite
1 part medium-grade charcoal
2 parts peat moss
3 parts sand

Orchid mix
1 part peat moss
1 part fine shredded bark
1 part medium shredded bark
1 part medium-grade charcoal

Pests and more pests

Yes, there are more pests to look for. Each season has its share of interesting creatures and late spring is no exception. I remember the first time I encountered one of the most unusual. I was out front watering some potted plants when I noticed a residue on my Mt. Lemmon marigold (*Tagetes lemmonii*) and annual flowers. On closer inspection, it looked like someone had spit all over the plants. I was disgusted and curious as to who would wander onto my porch and participate in such a vile activity. Thinking more logically, I realized it would have taken a whole classroom of twelve-year-old boys to produce that much spit—a ruckus I most certainly would have heard. It was then I knew it was a pest problem of a different sort. I did a little research and learned about the not-so-famous spittlebug.

Spittlebugs, which appear on the foliage of annuals, perennials, herbs, spring bulbs, and evergreens, are sucking insects that rarely damage their host plants. The nymphs hatch from over-wintered eggs and begin feeding immediately. They reach maturity in a couple weeks and then the spittle phenomenon is over, although there may be two or three outbreaks per year. Wash away the unsightly bubbles with a hard jet of water. No other treatment is required.

The beautiful butterflies and moths we enjoy along with our desert wildflower displays have to develop from something. That something includes several pesky caterpillars. If you have Mexican evening primrose in your garden, you probably have noticed the munching activity of a green and black striped hornworm. This caterpillar develops into the white-lined sphinx moth, or hummingbird moth. It spends its evenings darting about the garden pollinating and collecting nectar from many flowering plants. I like the moths and am usually willing to sacrifice some evening primrose. If you are not of the same mind, spray the infested plants with Bt to eradicate the problem.

Another admired garden visitor is the spectacular yellow and black giant swallowtail butterfly. As mentioned in an earlier section, this beautiful creature develops from the orange dog caterpillar, often found on citrus leaves. The butterfly lays eggs on the foliage, from which emerge caterpillars, which look incredibly like bird droppings. Large trees tolerate an infestation and no control is necessary. The caterpillars will defoliate a small tree if not controlled. Handpick the culprits when you find them, or spray the plant with Bt.

If you have grapevines in your garden, vigilantly check them for signs of western grape leaf skeletonizer. These small yellow and blue-black caterpillars develop from eggs left behind by a small, bluish butterfly. The caterpillars feed first on the underside of leaves, where they hatch. At this stage, the leaf has an opaque appearance. If left to continue eating, the caterpillars eventually eat all of the flesh between the veins of each leaf, leaving behind a skeletal leaf structure that no longer functions. It is not unusual for three generations to exist in a vineyard, destroying your potential for a crop if left unchecked. Inspect the leaves regularly and apply Sevin at the first sign of infestation. Reapply as necessary, following directions on the label.

Spider mites continue to be a problem on evergreens as well as other landscape plants. They are not insects but, along with spiders, members of the arachnid family. They love hot, dry conditions and multiply rapidly during this time of year. Spider mites thrive in gardens where pesticides are used regularly because natural predators, which include predatory mites, lacewings, ladybugs, and damsel bugs no longer exist.

Spider mites have developed a tolerance, if not immunity, to many insecticides. Signs of their presence include white or yellow stippling, tiny yellow or red dots on leaf surfaces, and speckling with excrement and cast off skins on the undersides of leaves. Leaves, flowers, and stems may be covered with fine webbing. The leaves dry out and growth becomes distorted and discolored. Insecticidal soap is the best control. Treat the undersides of leaves, and then re-treat in two hours for maximum effect. If infestation is heavy, spray every 3–5 days for two weeks.

Grasshoppers emerge from eggs over-wintering in grasses and garden debris. They grow rapidly, molting their skin 5–6 times during early spring. In gardens free of debris, grasshoppers are rarely a problem, although the adults sometimes invade in plague-like fashion. If you see large numbers of tiny, soft grasshoppers, squish them or spray with insecticidal soap. They quickly become too hard-bodied for this to have the desired effect, however. If handpicking is not effective, try stronger measures. The product Nosema locustae targets only grasshoppers and is most effective when applied over large areas. It is rather expensive, making it practical in extreme cases only.

In my garden, I am merciless. With clippers or scissors in hand, I stalk and search through the lush green foliage that grasshoppers prefer. When I see one, I chop it in half with lightning speed. It takes a little practice, and it isn't pretty, but it works.

Ants, leafhoppers, and leafcutter bees are doing their work in the spring garden. Orange peel slurry poured around anthills is effective. Control leafhoppers with insecticidal soap. For further discussion about leafcutter bees, see Week 25.

Container gardening

WEEK 22 When I first moved into my home, I looked out my windows at over a half-acre of decimated desert. We built our house on a lot that had been bladed several years earlier; and the construction process destroyed what little re-growth had managed to develop during the intervening years. I moved from a lushly landscaped garden to this bleak setting and felt depression oozing in. My mental health depended on getting a quick botanical fix, so we immediately bought several large terra-cotta pots and plopped color and vegetables right outside my windows. It worked. This buoyed my spirits while we created the landscape we envisioned.

There are many situations in which container gardening is the best alternative. It fills a temporary need to garden when a permanent opportunity is not at hand. Containers allow the gardener to cultivate her hobby in the most concrete-covered environments. As decor, potted plants accent the landscape as well as outdoor rooms. They soften sharp architectural features and highlight focal points. I often use a potted succulent or cactus to fill a hole in my landscape when I don't want to dig anything down into the ground. This approach offers not only instant color and texture, but also the added height of the pot.

If the native soil in a section of the garden is caliche or clay-laden so as to be unsalvageable, then large pots on top of the worthless stuff are an excellent solution. Containers are the answer for a gardener determined to grow a specimen that is not appropriate to the native soil. Azaleas and camellias are perfect examples here in the desert. Pots also contain plants that like our environment a little too well and overtake everything else when planted in the ground. Think mint! Pots allow us to grow and relocate plants that can tolerate one of our seasonal temperature extremes, but not the other. Remember the 'Bears' lime that loves the heat and can't take the cold? In all of these cases, a potted alternative is the best solution to a specific gardening dilemma.

Creating a successful potted garden requires the use of the right materials. Like many gardeners, I favor terra cotta pots. They have a natural, earthy appearance that melds them into the landscape. Terra cotta complements most architectural styles, and is at home on the porch, in the ramada, near the pool, or out in the garden. When coated inside and out with Thompson's Water Seal, fired terra cotta withstands outdoor elements for many years. I specify fired because the inexpensive Mexican clay pots commonly sold in the Southwest are usually oven dried rather than fired. They last fewer than five years before flaking and degrading, leaving piles of red dust at their bases. Their initial economy doesn't compare to the long-term value of their fired counterparts.

I also use the new resin or fiberglass pots that bear an uncanny resemblance to terra cotta. They are much lighter, making them essential for large plants that require seasonal relocation. They haven't been on the market long enough to know how durable they will be, but the outlook is promising. I have several in my garden that show no signs of degradation after four years outside.

I also recommend galvanized metal containers with drain holes drilled in the bottom. Discarded wheelbarrows, buckets, pails, and washtubs are charming. Half whiskey barrels hold up for quite a few years and look especially nice when planted with a combination of color plants and succulents. I water-seal them and enjoy their natural appearance. They're also eye-catching when painted in bright colors that complement the planted material or garden structures.

I do not recommend the long-term use of black plastic nursery containers. They are fine in garden centers when packed closely together and shading one another, but this is not usually the case in a home garden. When exposed to direct summer sun, the pots heat up and retain that heat through the night. This intense heat burns and destroys delicate roots. I use these containers to propagate, but never to landscape. Another reason I don't like them in the landscape is purely aesthetic. They are ugly. The exception is when they contain draping or cascading plants that completely hide the pot from view. I had a huge creeping Charlie (*Pilea nummulariifolia*) in such a container, and it never received direct sunlight when hidden beneath all that foliage. It served its purpose for many years.

Once containers are selected, fill them with an appropriate planting medium. It is important that the mixture retains moisture and drains well. Native soil shoveled into a pot rarely meets these needs, since it's extremely heavy and will often become hard and impermeable. If you want to create your own blend, refer back to Week 21 on potting soils for specific recipes. You can also buy prepared or bulk potting mixes. Add a time-released fertilizer, like Osmocote, to make nutrients available for several weeks. After you transplant container plants, feed them every two weeks with a water-soluble fertilizer. This care and appropriate sunlight will ensure container garden success.

I have many containers with only one or two plants in them. My scented geraniums are lovely when displayed, one or two per pot, on a baker's rack. I also have many potted succulents, euphorbias, and agaves scattered throughout the landscape, filling holes and accenting otherwise insignificant spots. I must admit, however, that I prefer arrangements that include several plants of varying textures and colors. These potted collages look like miniature gardens in and of themselves. A favorite contains windowsill tomatoes, variegated society garlic, and nasturtiums. It is a study in complement and contrast.

Most vegetables and annual flowers thrive in pot culture. This is an excellent alternative to building raised beds if you plan to work on a smaller scale. A potted vegetable garden easily supplements the menu for a family of four. Container selection must allow for maximum plant size and proper air circulation, so be aware of each plant's growth habits and choose wisely. If green beans are on the list for a container garden, choose bush beans rather than pole beans. Peas and tomatoes fall under this guideline as well. Select types that grow upright rather than sprawl.

Miniature roses and hybrid tea roses also flourish in pot culture. Two of my most attractive rose bushes grow in pots set on soil that would be unsuitable for nearly everything.

As accent plants, the cacti and succulent families offer some interesting choices. Agaves, cacti, euphorbias, aloes, and sedums all grow exceptionally well in pots when protected from freeze. Cycads and small palms, including the ponytail palm, also add interest with their distinct and unusual textures and colors. The fact that they require very little water makes them even more attractive for those spots where the gardener wants plant material without extending the irrigation system.

Melons and other vining plants aren't good candidates for pot culture, but many summer and winter squashes develop on compact, upright plants. Eight ball zucchini squash is an example of a plant that will produce a small crop when planted in a large container. Read seed packets and nursery tags to determine if the plant you admire pairs well with the pot you intend to use.

You can plant an entire herb garden in containers if you're so inclined. There isn't an herb that will rebel, given the right size of pot, the right soil, and proper irrigation. In fact, many herb gardeners never deal with native soil, preferring to provide the specific requirements of each herb in pots. Overcoming the common herb-growing problems of poor drainage and tight, heavy soils makes this type of herb garden a sure winner. In my herb garden, over one third of the plants grow in containers. The only challenge with this many containers is irrigation, overcome by adding a drip line to include potted plants. Another helpful irrigation tip is clustering potted plants together so that as they transpire, they create a cooler, moister microclimate.

A DESERT GARDENER'S COMPANION

Pot culture: Ground covers
asparagus fern (*Asparagus setaceus*)
Gazania
ivy (*Hedera*)
Lantana
rain lily (*Zephyranthes atamasco*)
verbena *(Glandularia [Verbena])*

Pot culture: Shrubs
Bougainvillea
  (*Bougainvillea spectabilis*)
Camellia
crape myrtle (*Lagerstroemia indica*)
Gardenia
Hibiscus
Mexican bird of paradise
  (*Caesalpinia mexicana*)
myrtle (*Myrtus*)
Podocarpus
dwarf pomegranate (*Punica
  granatum* 'Chico')
bird of paradise (*Strelitzia reginae*)
Pittosporum
Yucca

Pot culture: Taller plants
bay laurel (*Laurus nobilis*)
calamondin (*Citrofortunella*)
crape myrtle (*Lagerstroemia indicia*)
cypress (*Cupressus*)
Japanese maple (*Acer palmatum*)
kumquat (*Fortunella margarita*)
lemon (*Citrus limon*)
oleander (*Nerium oleander*)
bonanza peach (*Prunus persica*
  'Bonanza')

Pot culture: Perennial flowers
giant hyssop (*Agastache*)
Lantana
autumn sage (*Salvia greggii*)
mealy cup sage
  (*Salvia farinacea*)
Mexican bush sage
  (*Salvia leucantha*)
Russian sage (*Perovskia*)

143
∾

June

- Garden during early morning and late evening
- Watch plants for signs of water stress
- Avoid over-watering
- Water container plants twice daily
- Keep fruit trees well-irrigated to minimize June fruit drop
- Harvest early grapes
- Plant agave, cacti, and palms
- Plant beans, melons, pumpkins, and yard-long beans
- Plant native vegetable crops, indoor vegetables, and herbs
- Protect fruit from birds and insects
- Shade vegetable plots
- Apply pre-emergent weed control prior to monsoon season

June

ACCENT PLANTS IN THE GARDEN

WEEK 23 When all of the basic landscape components are in place, you are ready to add interest and character with accent plants. Accent plants have a unique appearance that allows them to stand alone or in groups and hold the interest of the beholder. They provide variety in color, texture, and shape, and demand attention. In the desert, there are a wide variety of accent plants that will appeal to, and please, garden visitors. Aloes, agaves, desert spoons, and yuccas all have distinctive, spiny shapes, like giant blossoms emerging from the soil. Their varying shades of green and gray create a striking effect when planted singly or in masses. Most of these bristly plants send up towering, spiked shoots on which blossoms form. The blossoms, aside from creating an amazing visual treat, proffer sweet nectar favored by hummingbirds and bats. Their most impressive characteristic is their minimal water requirements, making them even more desirable in the arid garden, since they accent the landscape without increasing irrigation demands.

I like to plant aloes, agaves, desert spoons, and yuccas in the ground as well as in pots, considering their ultimate size so that I'll never have to prune and destroy their unique, natural shape. When I have a bare area in need of pizzazz, I often add these fascinating species, which are terrific planted singly, in rows, or in clusters of three. Remember that when a plant is barbed, prickly, or otherwise armed, its distance from paths, play areas, and seating is an important consideration. These are not the plants with which to line driveways or walking paths. Since their form and characteristics are most notable from a slight distance, setting them back from frequently used areas is good practice.

A discussion of accent plants for the desert landscape would not be complete without the inclusion of the cacti and succulents other than aloes and agaves. Tough, distinctive cacti vary in appearance, but they all share the ability to survive hot dry conditions with little water. Except for the golden variety, which needs protection from extreme cold, barrel cactus will root and survive almost anywhere, require almost no soil preparation, and adjust to whatever environment they land in. I have seen them re-root and re-establish themselves after being toppled on their side for long periods of time.

Prickly pear and cholla cacti, all members of the *Opuntia* family, can live almost anywhere and are difficult to get rid of if you change your mind. I recently saw prickly pear and cholla emerging through soil that had been bladed seven years earlier. They'd lain underground all that time and finally

began to grow again.

Clumping grasses also make excellent accent plants, ranging in size from ten feet in height, down to only several inches. Some of them require regular irrigation. Others need nothing but rainfall once established. They fill empty corners, make great screens, act as accents behind contrasting textures and colors, and hold their own when planted in groups of several varieties.

Many desert gardens benefit from the addition of colorful, textural clumping grasses. There are two significant characteristics of the grasses that concern me, however. First, many are not sterile and will multiply uncontrollably. Avoid these varieties completely. They reseed themselves in every nook and cranny of the garden and develop persistent root systems that are a challenge to remove. When they start reproducing, you won't be able to keep up with them. Several are on noxious weed lists in the Southwest. Your nursery worker will be able to tell you about each variety's reseeding habits and their status as weeds in the desert.

My second concern deals with a characteristic that is, in every sense of the phrase, a double-edged sword: texture. The grasses sway beautifully in the wind and make a delightful sound in a breeze, but their texture is sometimes a surprise. Many of the grasses are smooth and non-threatening, but others are razor sharp. I have seen children covered with bleeding cuts from grasses. If children, animals, or sports equipment are in your life, avoid the sharp grasses. The rapier-like edges are detectable even when the plants are young and the blades are small, and become more menacing as they grow longer and firmer. Use your thumb as you would to check a knife for sharpness, and assess the edges of any clumping grass before you buy it for your garden.

Hot! Hot! Hot!

It's June. It's hot. When working outdoors we drink lots of water and take frequent, short breaks. We avoid the sun between the hours of ten and two and, when in the sun, wear sunscreen and protective clothing. Lightweight cotton clothes and hats are the uniform of the desert gardener, and many of us cover more skin in the summer than at other times of year to prevent sunburn and skin damage. The garden requires the same sort of consideration.

Intense sunlight and high temperatures have serious effects on landscape material. An increased water need is the most noticeable response to increased temperatures and desert gardens require more frequent irrigation beginning in June. That means fewer days between irrigations, not longer irrigations. In the summer, many gardeners water every two or three days. Look at your plants. They'll tell you what they need. The most obvious indicator is prolonged or continued wilt. If your plants noticeably droop in midday and remain limp or bowed after the sun sets, you need to irrigate more frequently. Start by watering the very next morning and then shorten the time between irrigations by one day. Check the plants between irrigations to make sure that the new schedule is adequate, and adjust as needed.

Even plants that love heat may show signs of sunscald, which is a burning of the leaf surface caused by too much direct sunlight. More unsightly than health threatening, sunscald appears as brown, gray, or white patches on foliage most exposed to sun. Plants with larger leaves, such as citrus or photinia, are most susceptible. Desert-adapted plants usually suffer little sunscald and quickly overcome the stress. If too many leaves are burnt, however, photosynthesis decreases and the plant may decline.

Tropical plants, like philodendron, never flourish in direct summer sun in the desert. They often make it through the cooler months and mild spring only to decline in the summer. This is an indication that the microclimate or exposure is not appropriate and that the plant should be moved to a more suitable location when the heat subsides. In the meantime, shade cloth propped over the injured plant provides short-term protection.

Vegetables that are not planted to the east of a structure or tree will also need shade cloth beginning this month. Tomatoes, peppers, cucumbers, and many others benefit from shade cloth that can be purchased at hardware stores and nurseries. Support it with stakes or poles so that the cloth does not touch the plants. This additional protection not only prevents sun-scald, but also lowers the microclimate temperature, and extends blossom set and fruit development.

You will also notice some changes in your fruit trees. Citrus trees often experience June drop, which refers to the loss of leaves and some fruit. This shedding does not indicate poor health. Continue to water regularly—about every two or three weeks. Deciduous fruit trees also go through June drop, a natural thinning of growing fruit that allows the tree to maintain only what it can carry to maturity. Regular watering will keep this to a minimum. If deciduous fruit trees have not received adequate water all spring, it is possible to lose the entire crop at this time—another reason regular irrigation is vital. Consistently good gardening practices, year round, produce plants that are equipped to deal with the environmental challenges of a desert summer.

June's dry heat is not all bad. There are several ways to take advantage of this unique-to-the-desert feature. During the harvest of ripening fruits and vegetables, many gardeners wonder how to deal with an over-abundance of particular crops. Natural drying is an excellent option in the desert. Apples, apricots, figs, peaches, plums, tomatoes, and many others are easy to dry the low-tech way. I've successfully dried all of these, as well as other produce. The process is quite simple: Harvest the fruits when fully ripe, and then carefully wash and inspect them. Using only fruits free of blemishes and bruises, cut them in half and remove pits or seeds. Remove the cores and slice apples into thin rounds. Tomatoes can be dried in either halves or slices.

Lay the prepared fruit on screening lined with cheesecloth. Make sure none of the pieces of fruit are touching one another and leave a half-inch space between the pieces for air to circulate. Cover the fruit with another layer of cheesecloth, tack down the edges, and place the screens in direct sun in an area free of ants. Most other insects can't get through the cheesecloth, but ants can be a problem. I've had success placing the screens atop the slats of a patio cover. Birds are not usually a problem, because the cheesecloth is secured over the fruit, prohibiting access. Check the fruit daily and bring it inside if a storm threatens. Depending on humidity levels, the fruit will be dry, yet still pliable, within several days. Store it in airtight containers.

My grandmother followed a similar practice to make fruit leather. I have done this several times using peaches, plums, and apricots, with tasty results. Once the fruit has been washed, selected, and pitted, run the halves through a food mill, processor, or blender. Combine the pulp with an equal amount of sugar. Add one teaspoon of freshly squeezed lemon juice for each cup of fruit. Pour the mixture on parchment- or plastic-lined screens and cover with cheesecloth. The trick here is to secure the cheesecloth without allowing it to rest on the pulp. Dry in the same fashion, checking daily for the moisture to dehydrate and the leather to firm up. I cut mine with scissors once I removed it from the screen and rolled it in the same parchment it dried on. I try to store the rolls in large airtight jars, but my children ate them so quickly, storage never really became an issue.

In addition to drying food, desert heat is excellent for drying flowers. I cut roses, zinnias, globe amaranth, herb blossoms, and lavender and dry them for future arrangements and potpourris. If I want just flower heads, I cut close to the blossoms, lay them on a paper-covered surface out of direct sun, and leave them until they are completely dry. When they are ready, I spray them with a sunscreen product available at craft stores to prevent the blossoms from losing their color and to discourage insects. Then I let the blooms dry for one more day before storing them in airtight containers. If I want the blossoms to dry on the stem, I clip them with as much stem as possible, tie them with raffia and hang the bundles upside down, out of direct sunlight. Like the flower heads, I spray these with the protective sunscreen.

In addition to drying fruits and flowers, the summer heat can help correct problems in the garden. If there is an area in which you have had weed, fungus, or nematode problems, solarize now. Till the soil to a depth of twelve inches and smooth out the surface. Water thoroughly, then cover the entire area with a clear plastic tarp. Use rocks, boards, or additional soil to hold the edges of the plastic in place and leave the cover on for 6–8 weeks. This treatment superheats the soil, killing weed seeds, fungus, and nematodes. In late summer prepare the area for fall planting.

The heat and constant activity sometimes wear me down in June. Evening is my favorite time, when I most appreciate the comfortable splendor of my garden, when I know all the effort is worthwhile. Relaxing in the ramada with a glass of wine and good company at sunset, I take in the beauty around me and wonder at my good fortune.

CREATING A DESERT OASIS WITH PALMS

The use of palms in the desert landscape creates the impression of other, more exotic lands. Unite those palms with smaller varieties and unique underplantings and the illusion is complete. I have a wood deck leading to my pool, surrounded by several types of palms and other unusual plants. Here, dinner by candlelight transports the diner to another land. It is an intriguing retreat from the norm, a getaway just beyond the back door.

In contrast to most landscape plants, palm trees are best planted during the hottest months. This is the time of year to choose your favorites and get them into the ground. If you plant the right species, palms require minimal effort in planting and maintenance. Like other trees, the planting hole needs to be as deep as the root ball and several times as wide, and the soil should be loosened and not amended. Place the new transplant in the hole at the same level it grew in its container and firmly tamp down the soil to remove air pockets and support the plant. Water thoroughly and irrigate every day for the first two weeks. After two weeks, irrigate every third day for several weeks, and then stretch the cycle out even longer. Your goal is to irrigate once every 2–3 weeks by the end of the first year. If irrigation is sufficiently deep and surrounds the entire area under the palm's canopy, this schedule will sustain the tree for many years.

Unlike other trees and shrubs, palm trees benefit from fertilization during their first year in the garden. Every eight weeks, apply a nitrogen-rich fertilizer to the planting area and water it in. After the first year, apply a fertilizer that is formulated specifically for palm trees. This will provide the unusual balance of micronutrients that they require. Apply this fertilizer every March and July for the life of the tree.

There are two types of palm trees worth considering for the desert landscape. The first type is the feather palm, whose long fronds with pinnate leaves look like giant feathers. The most commonly planted feather palms are the Canary Island date palm (*Phoenix canariensis*) and the date palm (*P. dactylifera*). These wide-spreading varieties grow to be sixty feet tall, making them excellent choices near commercial property or large, multi-level homes, but oversized and inappropriate for the average home garden. Instead, I recommend two smaller feather palms: the queen palm and the pindo palm.

The queen palm (*Syagrus romanzoffianum*) is my favorite landscape plant for around the pool. This versatile South American native grows to a modest twenty-five feet, provides scattered shade, drops very little litter, and tolerates partial shade or reflected heat. The straight, gray trunk is an attractive base to the shiny, medium green crown of fronds. Areas near a pool or building usually have a slightly warmer microclimate, making them appropriate for the queen palm. Sensitive to temperatures below 25°, this palm's foliage is damaged if low temperatures are prolonged or repeated, making it inappropriate for areas that frequently have winter temperatures in the mid-teens. It is susceptible to spider mites, root knot nematodes, and bud rot.

Pindo palm (*Butia capitata*) reaches a height of 10–20 feet and develops a stout trunk with cascading gray-green fronds. It is hardy to 15°, making it a better choice in areas with lower winter temperatures. Originally from Brazil and Argentina, the pindo palm provides a tropical feel to the garden, and is appropriate in containers, at poolside, and in transition zones, where its distinctly colored foliage blends nicely with desert natives. Because poor drainage and alkaline soils cause this plant to become chlorotic, it requires an application of chelated iron twice a year. It is also susceptible to root knot nematodes and bud rot.

For the patio or other protected areas, a potted Costa Rican parlor palm (*Chamaedorea costaricana*) makes a bold statement. This ten-foot-tall palm with multiple, reed-like trunks, develops a mature crown width of up to six feet. It tolerates low light situations and thrives in warm, shaded areas, but requires more water than other palms and suffers severe damage if exposed to temperatures below 25°. Other than frost sensitivity, the Costa Rican parlor palm is problem-free in the desert.

Fan palms have palmate or hand-shaped fronds, and are native to South America, North America, and the Mediterranean region. The California fan palm (*Washingtonia filifera*) and Mexican fan palm (*W. robusta*) reach 60–100 feet in height, making them appropriate for very large homes and commercial buildings. It is unusual for them to look properly proportioned in most desert gardens, but several other fan palms create the same look at a lower level.

You'll remember the Mexican blue palm (*Brahea armata*) with its waxy silvery-blue leaves from the section on moonlight gardens. This twenty-foot-tall plant with a frond spread of about eight feet looks good in the transition zone with desert-adapted plants, and in the pool yard with tropicals. Hardy to 15°, it's a slow grower that produces fragrant, creamy-white flower clusters in the summer. With no special problems and low water use, the Mexican blue fan palm is an asset to any garden that can accommodate its size and scale.

Similar to the Mexican blue palm is the Guadalupe palm (*B. edulis*). It has medium green fronds that hold their color year-round and flower clusters that are less conspicuous than those of the Mexican blue palm. It works well in containers and is a perfect substitute for the California fan palm when its scale is too large. It tolerates a wide range of soil types and temperatures and prefers deep, infrequent irrigation. There are no significant cultural problems with this plant in the desert Southwest.

Different in shape and form, the Mediterranean fan palm (*Chamaerops humilis*) is the most cold-hardy of all the palms. It is short and slow-growing, reaching a maximum height of fifteen feet after many years. During this time it will produce side shoots and develop into a clumped grouping that is interesting to the eye and striking in the landscape. This resilient plant tolerates nearly any soil type and temperatures as low as 12°. It's great as a specimen plant, in groups, or with taller palms. The effect is appropriate for desert, tropical, or Mediterranean themes.

Two other fan palms that are native to Mexico, Hispaniolan (*Sabal blackburniana*) and Sonoran (*S. uresana*) palmettos are similar in appearance and culture. Tall, evergreen, and slow growing, they tolerate temperatures in the mid teens and adapt well to hot, dry regions. Regular water and fertilizer help promote their glossy, deep green or blue-green appearance.

The last palm I recommend is the windmill palm (*Trachycarpus fortunei*). Small and slow-growing to a maximum height of twenty feet, it develops many fan-shaped leaves that protrude windmill-like from the slender, tapering trunk. Old fronds form a hairy covering at the top of the trunk. Native to China and Burma, it is hardy to 10° and is an excellent choice for poolside, atrium, patio, and transition zone. It is not a good selection for an area where it will receive reflected heat, since it tends to sunburn, and the fronds become tip-burned and tattered in hot, high winds. Otherwise, there are no significant problems in the Southwest.

The stately saguaro

The saguaro (*Carnegiea gigantea*). Nothing says desert Southwest like this signature plant. Native to southern Arizona and northern Mexico, saguaros grow very slowly to a height of over sixty feet and live for up to two hundred and fifty years. Several decades of simple columnar growth lead to the development of one or more arms. In late spring, white flowers tip those arms and attract numerous birds, insects, and bats. Historically, Native Americans have harvested the red fruit that ripens in summer, using it for syrup, jam, and candy. Birds are equally fond of the fruit, eating the flesh, as well as the tiny black seeds hidden inside.

Transplanting saguaros is common in the Southwest, even though success rates are questionable, since they grow and die very slowly. It can take as many as seven years for a saguaro to die after transplanting, but by that time most people assume another cause. Saguaros are protected by law and cannot be removed or moved without a tag issued by the United States Department of Agriculture. Do not accept delivery of a purchased plant lacking an official tag.

If you decide to plant a saguaro in your landscape, pay particular attention to its needs. They are sensitive to sunburn and frost damage with a change in exposure, so place transplants in the ground with the same side facing north that was facing that direction at the nursery. Saguaros require rocky or loose soil with excellent drainage. If a berm exists in your landscape, plant the saguaro near the top to avoid excess water during monsoon or winter rains. To plant a saguaro, set it into a wide, shallow hole and bury the cactus no deeper than it was before. It may be necessary to prop it up until new roots develop. If it's more than a couple of feet tall, professionals with appropriate equipment should plant it. Supplemental irrigation is only necessary during times of extreme drought, when watering a wide area around the base of the plant is beneficial.

The main health problem associated with saguaros is bacterial necrosis. This develops as a darkening and softening of tissues, followed by splitting. When this splitting occurs, a dark, thick, foul-smelling liquid oozes from the wound and spreads the infection to other areas of the plant. Removal of the infected tissue is the only practical method of control. Use a sharp tool and dig out all of the rotting material. The walls of the cleaned-out pocket should be smooth and disease free. Thoroughly wash the wound and tools with a ten-percent bleach solution. The plant will heal over the exposed area, creating hard scar tissue that provides protection.

WATER: A CONSTANT DESERT ISSUE

Because we live in the desert, water use is a significant and perpetual issue. With increasingly hot weather and monsoon season a month away, conservation is most important. Continue checking your landscape plants and decrease the number of days between irrigations only when they require more water. Surprisingly, summer loss of landscape material usually results from overwatering, not lack of water.

The most frequently overwatered landscape feature is the lawn. This is also the source of the most common summer disease problem—fungus. Dark sections, gray areas, or silver spots on turf usually are caused by fungal disease. Overwatering is the primary cause. To eradicate the diseases, apply Daconil or Bayleton according to package directions. To prevent reinfection, adjust your watering practices.

In June, turf may require early morning irrigation every other day. It needs 1–1½ inch of water per irrigation. Measure this by placing several empty tuna cans on the grass before you water. Run the cycle and measure the water in each can. If the cans have more than an inch and a half, reduce the time-per-cycle. If the containers have less than the required amount, then increase the irrigation time. If the cans have varying amounts of water, your sprinklers are not delivering evenly and need to be adjusted. Making these changes can save water and prevent disease.

Melons and beans

WEEK
25

If you still have unfilled garden space, plant another series of vegetables. Many of the melons do well in the desert. Follow general guidelines for soil preparation, and plant seeds as directed on packages, which is usually twice the depth of the seed size. If you want to plant watermelon, consider 'Dixie' hybrid, 'Improved Peacock', 'Klondike', 'Sugar Baby', 'Yellow Baby', or 'You Sweet Thing' hybrid. Cantaloupe varieties well suited to the desert include 'Ambrosia', 'Sampson', 'Saticoy' hybrid, and 'Venus'. When provided with plenty of water and room to spread, homegrown melons are a sugary sweet, tasty treat when eaten fresh out of the garden. If you're looking for perfection, pack them in ice an hour or two before dinner. Nothing compares.

Chinese pole beans and yard long beans go into the ground now, ripen in about fifty-five days, and love the summer heat. Requiring upright support at least six feet high, their bright green foliage and colorful blossoms make attractive screens when trained on a trellis, a fence, tepees, or poles. If fertilized every 4–6 weeks, these beans produce heavily, so a twenty-five square foot plot will provide enough beans for most families. The foot-long pods are tasty and visually impressive. I like to snap off the ends, cut them into two-inch pieces, and sauté them with bacon and onions as an accompaniment to grilled chicken or pork, sliced tomatoes, and fresh fruit.

Persistent pests

Some old, familiar pests haunt the garden now, as well as a few summer newcomers. You'll continue to see grape leaf skeletonizers, and must diligently check leaves and spray with Sevin when they appear. Birds also become a nuisance in the vineyard, dining on the ripening fruit. They will consume your entire crop if you don't act quickly. My favorite grape crop protection is knee-high stockings. When slipped over the grape clusters and fastened at the top with green garden tape or a twist-tie, the stockings prevent insect and bird damage, yet allow sunlight and air to circulate. Difficult to detect from a distance, the stockings preserve the vines' attractive appearance while protecting the ripening fruit. After harvesting the ripe grapes in a few weeks' time, rinse the stockings and store them for next year.

Agaves often show signs of distress in June, leading many gardeners to suspect irrigation problems. In most cases, the agave weevil, rather than a lack of water, is the problem. During spring, the snout-nosed weevils emerge from the soil to feed and mate, then the females lay their eggs near the base of the agave. Upon hatching, the larvae, or grubs, burrow into the root zone, eating roots throughout the summer and fall. As summer heat places greater demands on the roots, the damage becomes noticeable. The leaves flop over and darken. Sometimes the entire plant will topple. If not treated now, the grubs continue to chew and may destroy the plant by October or November. Saturate the soil around the plant with a five-percent rotene solution. Three applications, made a month apart, will usually kill the grubs as they migrate to different soil depths in response to changing temperatures. As a precaution, treat the area in the same manner for two or three consecutive months.

Up to ¾ of an inch long, the fuzzy gray or brown leafcutter bees are large when compared to other insects. The adult female cuts perfectly round sections from soft green growth and carries them to a burrow that is subsequently lined with the material. This creates a soft tunnel in which offspring develop. As they gather pollen to serve as food for their growing young, leafcutter bees provide a vital pollinating service in the garden. The damage they

Leafcutter bee on citrus

do is short-term and inconsequential. Eradicating them would be both difficult and detrimental to the ecology of the garden. Absolutely no control is
warranted or recommended.

Cicadas announce their presence in the desert garden with song, producing a high-pitched, whistling sound that reminds me of the noise of electric
wires in the desert wilderness of my childhood. Much like grasshoppers, cicadas
bore holes, chew leaves, and damage plants, and are more difficult to attack
with clippers than grasshoppers because they are quicker to react. By the time
we see them in our trees and hear them in our gardens, cicadas have emerged
from a two-year underground hiatus during which brown nymphs transformed themselves into lovely green adults. Rather than worrying about eradication, I credit them for spending so much time in development, and evading
me so effectively. Besides, by the time I think I can no longer tolerate their shrill
songs, they're gone, into the ground, to begin another generation of gestation
and development.

Palo verde trees host a couple of pests during June, most notably the palo
verde borer. The adult form, a 3–5-inch dark brown beetle, hangs out on
patios and porches, having been attracted by lights. The beetles lay their eggs
beneath landscape plants including citrus, cottonwood, privet, rose, stone
fruits, and Mexican palo verde, and seem to prefer drought or disease-stressed
plants. When the eggs hatch, the grubs feed on plant roots for about three years,
then pupate underground. As the soil warms up in late spring and early summer, the adults emerge. To treat an infested area, saturate the soil around the
base of affected trees and shrubs with a five-percent rotene solution.

Wasps are active this month, especially if your garden includes a pool,
pond, or fountain. Although they frighten us, wasps are not aggressive when
left alone, so give them a wide berth. Like honeybees, they pollinate fruits,
nuts, and vegetables. Although most wasps feed on nectar, some hunt other
insects, making them beneficial to the health of your garden. No control is necessary unless wasps build their nest in high-traffic areas, a common occurrence
since they often choose entryways and patios. If this happens, use insecticides formulated especially for wasp nests, which allow the user to remain
fifteen feet or more from the nest. These strongly propelled aerosol insecticides are effective and inexpensive. If you get stung, apply ice to the wound.

See a doctor if extreme symptoms, such as excessive swelling, numbness, or breathing difficulties develop.

Web worms, or tent caterpillars, are seasonal problems on palo verdes and other trees. The worms create silken tents that enlarge as they grow and increase their feeding area. Not only does the webbing become unsightly, but also the undisturbed caterpillars can defoliate an entire tree within days. To manage the pests, spray the clusters with a strong jet of water to break them open, and then treat with Bt. If the infestation is particularly heavy, use insecticides that include carbaryl, rotene, or Malathion.

A SUMMER PLANTING FRENZY

WEEK 26 In our house, springtime involves projects requiring labor and effort. This is when we build masonry walls, dig trenches, and create raised beds that have been on our wish list for quite some time. Since we mainly work on the landscape during weekends and evenings, it takes a few weeks to complete larger projects, and by the time we've finished, the weather's heated up. The next item on our wish list inevitably involves planting an area of the garden. If the plan calls for non-native plants, or varieties that must adapt to our desert extremes, we put the task off until milder weather returns. We learned the hard way that it takes too much water to maintain less-adaptable plants during intense summer heat. Generally, nurturing new plants through the summer is time-consuming and expensive. Exceptions to this rule include native or desert-adapted plants.

June is a better time for planning than planting, and I usually recommend waiting until September to initiate major landscaping projects. But many people just can't wait. Many families move at the end of the school year and spend several weeks settling into their new homes. Only now are they able to give landscaping their attention. This also is the time of year when folks from the east coast, Midwest, or moderate west coast locales think about planting. Sometimes, impatience strongly motivates, and gardeners can't wait. If you are determined to plant, stick to recommended varieties, and expect to coddle transplants through the heat.

When planting trees now, acacia, desert willow, eucalyptus, mesquite, palo verde and sumac are wise choices. They are native or desert-adapted and won't go into shock when the thermometer climbs above 95°. Dig a hole five times the diameter of the root ball and only as deep as the original container. Center the tree in the hole and refill with the original soil, then water thoroughly and pack the dirt down tightly. Water the tree every other day for a couple of weeks, and then move to every four days for two more weeks. For the remainder of the summer irrigate every 5–7 days, increasing the duration between irrigations as the trees become acclimated. Plan to provide supplemental irrigation for at least two years.

Shrubs that survive when planted in June include Mexican bird of paradise (*not* the tropical sort), dalea, senna, fairy duster, lantana, sage, and verbena. Yellow bells or coral bells are large, semi-deciduous shrubs that tolerate drought and alkaline soils. They flower profusely and attract hummingbirds from early spring to first frost, and make excellent background plants and warm-weather screens. All of these plants provide a basic framework to which you can add more fragile plant material in early fall when temperatures are less extreme. Follow the same planting procedures as for trees, and the same general irrigation schedule. Dalea, senna, and fairy duster will require supplemental irrigation for the first year or two. The others will continue to need infrequent irrigation for the life of the plant.

If you don't like the idea of watering everything forever, include sotol, desert spoon, and red or yellow yucca in your landscape. These quick-to-adapt species look spectacular when interplanted with the more herbaceous material mentioned above. I am especially fond of the contrast between these spiny, flower-shaped plants and chuparosa. Purple trailing lantana adds a finishing touch.

When adding color to flower beds, borders and containers, be prepared to provide regular water and water-soluble fertilizer monthly. It is beneficial to space intensively so that the plants shade one another as well as the surrounding soil. This, in addition to a thick layer of mulch, maintains soil temperature and prevents water evaporation. In shady locations, try coleus, impatiens, and periwinkle. All three are available at garden centers and thrive in our high

159

temperatures when planted out of direct sunlight. They require amended soil and look good at the base of trees, near foundations, or in pots. Planted in the right location and fertilized every two or three weeks, they flower abundantly throughout the summer.

Areas in the garden that receive scattered sunlight, or morning sun and afternoon shade, require different plants to look their best. In these spaces I suggest coreopsis, globe amaranth, lantana, lisianthus, purslane, and annual sage. These plants look especially nice when backed by purple fountain grass or large-leafed basil plants. Small purple basils look great mixed among the other plants too. I also like to mix perennial butterfly bush and autumn sage toward the back for contrast and interest. They can be transplanted to a long-term location in the fall or left in the flowerbeds as the seasons change.

Full-sun flowerbeds and planters look most attractive when planted with material that thrives in those harsh conditions. I like to use golden fleece, Mexican sunflower, sunflower, and zinnia. For variety, chile peppers and eggplants are striking when mixed with these flowers. I have seen beautiful garden arrangements that utilize varieties of giant hyssop and lemon grass as background plants to sun-loving annuals, and thyme and *Santolina rosemarinifolius* look terrific mixed with profusely flowering moss rose in the front of most beds.

To create a perennial bed at this time of year, consider several standout, drought-tolerant plants. Chocolate flower is a bright green plant with yellow blossoms that really do have a chocolate scent. When mass planted or in tight groupings they make a bright, bold statement. *Gazania* is a nice bedding plant, often used to control erosion on steep banks. It looks best as a single species planting and comes in colors ranging from bright yellow and orange to deep purple and white. It spreads by runners and clumping to create a full, low-lying mat. Lantana is great on its own or mixed with other plants. I love the bright blossoms almost as much as the hummingbirds and butterflies do. Plants vary in size and blossom color. Pink, red, orange, yellow, white, lavender, and purple blossoms entice the color-conscious gardener. Small trailing plants and large mounding shrubs are all part of the lantana family, allowing you to use lantana in numerous situations. Do your homework and know what you're buying before you plant them in your garden.

Mexican evening primrose (*Oenothera berlandieri*) looks beautiful when planted en masse or interplanted with other flowering perennials. One of the most stunning rose gardens I've ever seen was underplanted with pink Mexican evening primrose. It also is used to create a lush meadow with great success. Cup flower (*Nierembergia*) maintains a fairly low profile and blooms brightly in purple and white. An excellent plant for borders, edges, and underplantings, it nicely fills in and covers soil. I especially like it planted beneath potted palm trees. In addition to these adaptable plants, palms, cacti, and succulents can be planted during the heat of the summer.

Mexican evening primrose (Pemptjera berlandieri)

Euphorbias

Euphorbiaceae is a plant family containing annuals, perennials, shrubs, and succulents. Most exude a milky sap when cut and have colorful bracts often mistaken for flowers. First identified and utilized as ornamentals nearly two thousand years ago, they were named and classified by the Greeks and Romans, then the English. The milky sap, a latex, was used for poison-tipped arrows and to render fish immobile for easy catching. The sap has long served medicinally as a purgative.

Be mindful of the toxicity of euphorbia sap and use caution when working with the plants. Sensitivity to the toxins varies, as does the degree of toxicity within specific varieties. Particularly vulnerable individuals suffer severe damage to mucous membranes if the sap is ingested or makes its way into eyes, nose, or mouth. Incidents of blindness have been documented when highly sensitive people have touched their eyes after working with euphorbias. Because you cannot be certain of your sensitivity level, nor of the toxins in specific plants, always exercise care while handling any euphorbia. When transplanting or pruning, wear rubber gloves and long sleeves. Avoid touching your face until you have thoroughly washed your hands with plenty of soap, since the milky sap resists water alone. Most of us have only a mild reaction to euphorbia sap, but beware of the potential problem and protect against any possibility of reaction. For these same reasons, avoid euphorbias in landscapes or homes where small children or animals have a history of disturbing or ingesting plant material.

Having offered due caution, I must say that I'm wild about euphorbias in the garden. Their distinctive shapes and forms provide interest and visual contrast. They make excellent potted outdoor specimens, valuable landscape components, and unique houseplants.

E. amygdaloides is a clumping perennial that grows to nearly three feet and does well in desert soil. This purple-foliated variety has chartreuse inflorescences that stand out when planted beneath trees or in lightly shaded rock gardens, and tolerates temperatures down to zero, making it appropriate for nearly all desert gardens.

E. characias is a shrubby evergreen perennial that grows to a full four feet. This drought-tolerant plant displays vivid blue-green leaves on crowded stems. In late winter, clustered lime-green flowers create an eye-catching display that holds its color until early spring. When the seeds ripen and the color fades, prune out the yellowing stalks. New shoots already will be forming for next year's colorful display.

E. epithymoides (*E. polychroma*) are low-growing perennials that reach a maximum height of eighteen inches. Excellent in borders and rock gardens, these plants clump and spread in rounded mounds displaying bright yellow bracts in the spring. The showy plants turn yellow, orange, and red before going dormant with the arrival of cold weather.

E. heterophylla, often called Mexican fire plant, is a three-foot summer annual with bright green leaves. In summer, the upper leaves develop bright red and white blotches. This plant requires little water, loves the heat, and thrives in hot, dry locations with poor soil, making it an excellent candidate for back borders and transitioning to arid zones.

E. lathyris is a biennial plant reputed to repel burrowing rodents , thus it is dubbed mole plant or gopher plant. The sap of this particular variety is quite caustic and can burn the skin. During its first year, in the ground this vivid yellow-green plant increases in size by clumping and mounding. In its second year, it sends up stems that develop yellow flowers at the tips. Flowers develop seeds and the plant dies, but it usually already has its replacements growing at its base, providing long-term color and form.

E. pulcherrima is the traditional poinsettia we all admire during the holiday season. This tall, leggy Mexican native was propagated and hybridized to develop into the full, compact plants we buy. These plants survive outdoors when planted in a frost-free area, or against the south side of the house. They prefer slightly acidic, well-drained soil and produce more bracts if the branches are thinned every summer. To increase the red color, feed with a nitrogen fertilizer every two weeks once the red begins to appear.

E. tirucalli is called milkbush, pencilbush, and pencil tree, and is one of my favorite indoor plants. It can grow to thirty feet, although it usually is much smaller. Single or multiple trunks support tangled light green, pencil-shaped little branches with no obvious leaves. They provide a striking form when placed against light-colored walls or windows. Requiring very little water, this plant prefers bright light and regular feeding. Stems exude a milky sap when cut. This latex sap is difficult to remove when it dries. I am fond of this plant not only because of its interesting form and easy care, but also because it is easy to prune and propagate. I top my plants when they get too tall and replant the pruned section in sterile potting soil. I treat the new cutting just like the mother plant, irrigating and feeding regularly. These cuttings begin to grow in a couple of months, never having lost their vigor or attractive appearance.

163

July

- Protect container plants from sun
- Watch for signs of water stress
- Irrigate in early morning to conserve water and discourage fungus
- Collect rain water
- Dethatch Bermuda grass every 2-3 years
- Deadhead flowers to encourage bloom
- Use strong jet of water to remove cochineal scale from prickly pear
- Fertilize palms and grapes
- Harvest apples, grapes, melons
- Watch for signs of Texas root rot
- Sharpen mower blades
- Remove storm-damaged branches

A Native American vegetable garden

WEEK 27 Native American food crops do very well in backyard gardens and require less water than commonly marketed varieties. Amaranth is an ancient grain whose growth and production have enjoyed resurgence in recent years. Amaranth seeds can be ground into flour, sprouted, used as a green, or cooked whole. It is easy to grow and comes in several varieties, some of which grow wild along Southwest roads and canyons.

Bolita beans, similar to pinto beans, are popular among native New Mexico populations. Although edible when young and green, historically they have been left on the vine until dry, then harvested and stored for later rehydration and preparation. Tepary beans are a high-protein, drought-tolerant crop, domesticated from a wild plant by the Tohono O'odham of Arizona. Like bolita beans, teparies are harvested and stored dry.

Chiltepines are tiny, round, hot chiles that grow on small, dense bushes. These native plants have been domesticated and survive year-round if protected from frost. They reseed prolifically, providing hot, spicy peppers year after year. Other native chiles are frequently sold along roadsides in Arizona and New Mexico. They sprout and grow easily, with minimal attention, and are often grown from locally adapted seeds that have been saved and passed on from generation to generation.

Blue corn, grown by the Pueblo and Hopi Indians, and Papago corn, grown by the Tohono O'odham, are flint corns that are dried and ground into flour for tortillas and other baking, rather than eaten as a fresh vegetable. Mexican June corn originated among tribes in Mexico and is grown during the late spring rather than in summer and fall. It produces larger, sweeter kernels, making it excellent for use in posole, menudo, or green corn tamales.

Devil's claw, or unicorn plant, is a desert native with dark seeds, eaten like sunflower seeds, and tender two-inch fruits that are picked and pickled like okra. If allowed to mature further, they become inedible and their coarse fibers are harvested and used in the creation of textiles. The mature fruits of a white-seeded devil's claw are used as fibers in basket weaving by several Native American tribes.

Striped cushaw squash is one of many native squashes for which seed is readily available. This versatile squash is harvested young and eaten fresh, like zucchini or other summer squash. When left on the vine, the fruit becomes much larger, developing flavor and characteristics similar to pumpkin.

Tomatillo, a Mexican native of the *Solanaceae* family, is easy-to-grow and develops fruit that looks like a small tomato encased in a papery husk. Eaten fresh or cooked, tomatillos are an excellent base for salsas and sauces, and a nice addition to fresh fruit and vegetable dishes.

Seeds for all of these, or similar plants, are available through Native Seeds/ SEARCH in Tucson, Arizona, and Plants of the Southwest in Santa Fe, New Mexico. Both companies have retail outlets that are open to the public as well as thriving catalog businesses. It is worthwhile to peruse their offerings when determining which native crops to grow.

The Hopi, famous for blue corn, diversify their crops by planting two or three small plots in areas where rain either falls or runs. Each plot contains several crops including beans, corn, squash, and watermelon. By planting this way, they ensure that a flash flood destroying an entire section does not limit the diversity of their diet.

Another group, the Akimel O'odham, have traditionally lived along riverbanks. They grow beans, corn, and squash, as well as domesticated varieties of native plants like devil's claw, at the river's edge, taking advantage of natural irrigation. With the river providing a constant source of water, the Akimel's greatest concern is not drought, but flood. Overflow of the river's banks can wipe out entire fields. For this reason, seeds are sown along different sections of the river so that not all will be threatened if the river swells.

The Tohono O'odham have inhabited portions of the Sonoran Desert for hundreds of years, using several methods of plant management to develop and sustain a varied diet. Like other tribes, these native people historically and currently use indigenous plants to sustain their way of life. They use bear grass and devil's claw in both wild and domesticated forms to create the distinctive, multi-colored baskets for which the tribe is known, and yucca fibers in making baskets, cloth, and other household items.

The Tohono O'odham eat wild chia seeds, the sweet-smelling, native salvia plant that freshens interior spaces when broken branches are brought indoors. Cholla bud are harvested green, and eaten fresh and dried. Each bud contains as much calcium as an eight-ounce glass of milk. Creosote is the plant that perfumes the desert after a rain. It is harvested and used medicinally as a salve to soothe and heal sores, as an inhalant to loosen chest congestion, and as a health-promoting tea. Mesquite provides wood for building and burning, as well as seedpods that are ground into a sweet flour to be used in cooking. Like mesquite, ocotillo branches are used in tools, furniture, and dwellings.

Seeds from plantago, a wild grass often referred to as Indian wheat or Indian grass, are a valuable food source, as are the pads and fruit of prickly pear cactus. When in season, the greens from tansy mustard add variety to the menu. Tepary beans, a mainstay of the Tohono O'odham diet, have been domesticated and grown so extensively that the tribe is nicknamed "the bean people."

Because members of the Tohono O'odham tribe have always lived in areas where annual rainfall ranges from less than an inch to only fifteen inches, they long ago learned to access and use whatever rain fell. Ak Chin is an irrigation method based on the philosophy of planting where water is, as well as where it will be. It involves diverting the flow of water after heavy rains so that it is absorbed in planting areas. This is the model for the current xeriscape practice of creating berms and swells in the landscape, directing water into planted areas and preventing runoff and loss.

The Ak Chin method fascinates me and, with monsoon season just around the corner, this is the right time to give it a try. Because no building or irrigation system is required, sunken beds can be dug and improved, and the seeds purchased and planted in a very short time.

To create a sunken bed garden, it is important to know where the runoff goes during and following a heavy rain. Your goal is to dig the beds in a spot where they will collect water that is already running or settling. Bed size should be based on the width of the area in the runoff or settling zone. Make it as big as the water flow will support. You'll be able to step into the bed for harvesting, so width is not restricted. Estimate the crop size that the water can realistically support and let this be your limiting factor. Also consider how much you are willing to irrigate if rain fails to materialize.

Once you determine location and size, mark the bed off and remove eight inches of soil, creating a pit. Use part of that soil to build berms on the "down-river" side of the bed, which will act as a retaining wall, holding the water in. Leave the "up-river" side of the bed open to allow the runoff to flow into the hollows. During very heavy storms, the water flow may be too intense. It may fill the garden beds and push its way around the berms or even cut right through them. Don't panic. This happens to the Tohono O'odham too. You may lose some of your crop, but these cuts are easily repaired.

Native American gardeners compost the planting area with previous crop waste and corral their animals in the same area, allowing them to fertilize and till the soil. Simulate these procedures by tilling the soil in the pit to a depth of eight inches and stirring in a four-inch layer of composted material. This is less than in a typical vegetable bed because the crops require less fertile soil. Mix in the amendments, even out the soil, and plant your seeds according to package directions. Mix seed types in the bed to mimic a traditional multi-crop sunken bed.

Apply a thick layer of organic mulch to the bed to protect the seeds from animals and to maintain a steady soil temperature. The mulch will also retain moisture and prevent evaporation once the rains begin. You can water the seeds now, or wait for monsoon to provide regular afternoon rains that will stimulate germination and encourage growth. If you decide to irrigate, remember that you must continue to provide moisture so that the seeds and seedlings do not dry out. Take note of the number of days each crop requires to fully mature and mark your calendar.

Your garden during monsoon

WEEK 28 There's nothing like summer rain. But, while we welcome the moisture that monsoon brings, we dread the damage inflicted on our trees by the high winds. Trees that have large, dense canopies are most susceptible to wind damage. To reduce the likelihood of damage, remove up to twenty-five percent of the tree's branches to lighten the canopy's weight and create unobstructed spaces through which the wind can rush.

Never trim the ends off of branches and twigs to remove weight. This is a common garden practice that leads to pronounced problems after a few years. Every time a tip is removed in this fashion, the plant is stimulated to produce more growth. There is actually a chemical message sent through the plant saying, "Put on new growth, right here, right now!" As a result, the trimmed spots develop not one new shoot, but two or three, creating bulk and weight in exactly the wrong spots.

Prune out branches that rub on other limbs or have an excessive amount of foliage. Select branches whose removal will not adversely affect the appearance of the tree and cut them off just above the branch collar, where they meet the trunk or a lateral branch.

Once the branches most in need of removal are pruned consider whether or not you have reached the twenty-five percent mark. If so, you are finished, because removing too much of the tree is just as detrimental as leaving it to the wind's mercy. If you have not removed twenty-five percent, stand back and look at the tree's appearance. Remove entire branches whose presence is not significant to the tree's shape and form. This thoughtful pruning will assure your tree's long, healthy life, relatively unhindered by storms and high winds.

If you put off thinning your trees and the first storms hit hard, you may have some limb damage to repair. If this is the case, prune now by cutting back to the branch collar behind the damaged section. A clean lopper or saw cut is less likely to harbor pathogens than the jagged break. After removing all damaged wood, determine if more than twenty-five percent has been taken out. If so, wait until next year to prune for beauty and balance. If less than one-

169

Properly pruned Arizona Mesquite (Prosopis velutina)

fourth of the branches have been removed, view the tree from a distance and determine what else should be pruned to balance the tree and create an attractive form. By all means, keep this experience in mind so that next year you prepare for monsoon rather than react to it.

Monsoon season should also prompt other preparations in the garden. This is a good time to clean out rain gutters and make certain that drainage systems are in proper working order. Use a ladder and common sense when performing this yearly chore. Place the ladder in an area that provides adequate balance and support, and use an assistant. As a bonus for your hard work, the material removed from rain gutters and rooftops is usually decomposing and makes an excellent addition to the compost heap.

Once the rooftop is in good order, check the drainage in your garden. If you have drains installed in the ground, make sure the grates are clear and accessible. The system will not work if a year's worth of silt and gravel have accumulated over the tops of drain sites. If you have masonry walls, with drain holes at their bases, remove debris from in front of these spaces so water will flow as planned. This inspection and corrective action will prevent serious flooding, especially in small, partially enclosed gardens.

Having prepared for the negative possibilities of the summer rainy season, you can now take advantage of the coming rain. This is one of the best times to apply a pre-emergent to control weed growth in your garden. Apply the chemical before a forecasted storm, to be watered in by the rain. Be very careful when applying any pre-emergent. Read the directions and apply it in exactly the prescribed rates, using the suggested methods. These powerful chemicals do their jobs very well and must be carefully controlled. Misuse can seriously affect the landscape and surrounding areas.

In addition to weed control, July is a good time to apply fertilizers if you want the rains to wash them into the soil. I will often apply fertilizer to perennials, flowers, vegetables, and herbs when storms are predicted on consecutive days. I apply fertilizer the day after a soaking storm has saturated the soil and let the next storm water it in. If the "watering-in" storm fails to appear, I use my hose to do the job. This is also a good time to fertilize palm trees. Palms require micronutrients that most other plants don't need, so buy fertilizer designed especially for palm trees, and use the suggested amounts. Since it needs to be watered in, just prior to or during a storm are good times to apply palm fertilizer, and this can be an exhilarating experience as long as lightning isn't threatening. It's refreshing and fun to do a little gardening in the cool comfort of a summer rain.

Protecting plants from the summer sun

At this time of year I keep a close eye on my potted plants, looking for the distinct signs of sunburn. Leaves with yellow patches whose centers turn gray or brown are sun damaged. They are reacting to the sun in the same way our skin does, by displaying the work of damaging rays through color change. If I discover sun damage, I move the pot to a spot that gets fewer hours of afternoon sun. I move my pots around a lot, using them as an interior decorator would use accent pieces in a home. When they require a move for their own health, I try to choose a spot where they will receive the necessary break from the sun and still stand out as an accent piece. Potted plants heavily accent my patios, ramada, and potting shed in the summer. They take on a retreat-like ambiance, and the plants enjoy the additional benefits of shade and a cooler microclimate, thanks to the combined transpiration of their neighbors.

Plants in the landscape may also develop signs of sunscald. The same yellow patches with brown or gray centers appear on larger-leafed species including roses and tropicals. If it is possible to provide additional afternoon shade, do it. Erect shade cloth on the south or west sides of plants using rebar or PVC pipe to hold it up.

If plants in your garden suffer greatly during the summer, make note of the problem in your journal, with additional ideas concerning how to change those microclimates before next summer. It is too hot and too stressful to transplant sun-sensitive species now, but when moderate weather returns either transplant the affected plants to more suitable locations, plant additional landscaping to provide the necessary shade, or erect hardscape to do the same. It is not only hard on plants to be so stressed year after year, but they are unattractive through periods of heat and recovery, making their visual contribution to the garden questionable. All of us plant things in the wrong places. When it is clear that this is the case, correct it.

Some plants may be looking stressed because they are not getting enough water. The appearance of drought-stressed plants is similar to that of sun-stressed plants, but some distinct features allow the gardener to differentiate between the two. Drought-stressed plants yellow and proceed to brown, but they lack the distinctive burnt-looking patches characteristic of sun stressed plants. The first symptom of drought-stress is wilting. This can be mild at first, but increases in severity as inadequate irrigation continues. When plants wilt during the heat of the day, but then perk up at sunset, there is no cause for concern. However, if they wilt and never fully recover, they may need longer or more frequent irrigation.

To determine how to adjust your system, probe the soil immediately following a watering cycle. If the moisture has reached a depth of one foot for annuals and ground covers, two feet for shrubs, or three feet for trees, the length of time is correct. In this case, reduce the number of days between irrigations. If you probe the soil and discover that the water has not reached the necessary depth, increase the length of each irrigation and probe again after the next regular cycle. Continue this process until a single irrigation distributes water to the appropriate depth. If your plants still look drought stressed, then water more frequently while maintaining the predetermined duration of irrigation. Now all you have to do is remember to turn off the system when the rains provide adequate irrigation, and make sure to turn it on again when the rains fail to materialize.

Summer pests and parasites

As if summer storms and extreme heat aren't enough to keep the desert gardener busy, a plethora of pests and parasites continue to plague the landscape. Manually remove persistent cochineal scale from prickly pear pads or spray the affected areas with insecticidal soap. This scale does not normally kill the host plant, but does significant damage to the pads. Remove severely affected pads with a sharp knife or clippers, cutting at the joint where one pad connects to another pad or the stem. This is also a good method to control growth and is most effectively performed when new pads are emerging, although it can be done at any time with no ill effects to the plant.

Green fruit beetles, the scarabs that are sometimes called Japanese beetles, fly around the garden through July and August. Emerging from the soil where they spent their larval stage as giant grubs, the adult beetles often congregate in palm trees and fruit trees. They chew leaves, eat flowers, and sometimes defoliate shrubs. The females burrow into the soil to lay eggs that develop into the larvae, or grubs, which feed on nearby roots. To control them, take a two-pronged approach: Destroy the beetles and destroy the grubs. When you encounter the beetles, handpick them from the plant and drown them in a bucket of soapy water. When you locate the grubs in the soil, smash them. A five-percent rotenone solution effectively treats the soil in areas of heavy infestation.

Leaf-footed plant bugs, easily recognized by their characteristic brown color with yellow stripe and distinctive leaf-shaped protrusion on their back legs, are active in the garden this month. They infest annual leaves and flowers, causing deformed growth and dwarfed buds and shoots. Damaged leaves display the familiar yellow or brown stippling. Prevention can go a long way in controlling leaf-footed plants bugs. Clean out garden debris and leaf litter in early spring to remove over-wintering eggs. When the pests appear, handpick them and put them in a jar of soapy water or spray them with insecticidal soap. The more toxic spraying of Sevin is rarely necessary.

Giant mesquite bugs are 2$\frac{1}{2}$–3-inches long with red and black, banded legs. They feed on sap oozing from mesquite trees and sometimes puncture seedpods. Notwithstanding the furor these translucent-winged insects cause while flying through the neighborhood, they are harmless. They do not affect the health of the mesquites on which they feed, nor do they cause other damage in the garden. They are a food source for birds and lizards, contributing to the local food chain in a significant way.

Several diseases plague oleanders during the summer rainy season. The first is oleander gall, a bacterial disease spread by sucking insects that causes flowers to emerge blackened and deformed, branches to split, and wart-like growths called galls to form. Other than pruning out diseased branches, there is no reliable treatment for oleander gall. Cut to the crown of the plant or the nearest lateral branch, remove all infected wood, and clean tools with a ten-percent bleach solution after every cut to prevent spread of the disease.

The 3–5-inch palo verde borer beetle, often seen crawling near lights on summer evenings, does not bite and is harmless in this form. The damage assigned this species occurs when the grubs of the beetle chew on roots. They chew roots for an average of three years before emerging during springtime as adult beetles. The adults seek out drought-stressed trees and lay their eggs in the soil beneath them to begin the cycle anew. Proper irrigation is the most effective prevention. Where this fails, treat the soil with rotenone beginning in early spring.

The last pest to be on the lookout for is not an insect, but a plant. Dodder is a parasitic plant that looks like yellow or orange string whose color indicates its inherent lack of chlorophyll. Without the ability to photosynthesize and make its own food, dodder taps into other plants and steals what they produce. Weaving itself over host plants and sending suckers into their branches, dodder simultaneously blocks sunlight and saps nutrients. Because there is no fail-safe way to remove dodder from its host, the entire plant, or at least the infested branches, should be removed and placed in garbage cans or burned. The seeds remain viable for a long time, so remove the parasite before it sets seed, and *never* compost it.

Water harvesting

WEEK
29

We're lucky to live in a place where summer rains are part of the natural cycle and we receive half of our annual precipitation as monsoon moisture. The desert drainage system is amazingly effective in moving large volumes of water from the mountains, through the foothills, down canyons, across plains, and into the water table or the ocean. By mimicking these natural patterns, you can control and utilize the flow of water that graces your garden. This process of saving as much rainfall as possible is called water harvesting.

The main goal of water harvesting is to keep all the water that falls on your property right there on your property. You don't want to see this precious commodity running out your gates, over your curbs, or away from your garden. If rain falls on your land, consider it your personal property and make an effort to keep it. Holding onto water begins by examining where the water falls and where it goes afterward.

Observe and record the flow of water during and after a storm. Sketch your lot, including the buildings, hardscape, and landscaping. Include plants, planters, paths, walls, and gates. This simple sketch should contain everything one would see from a bird's-eye view. During a storm, go outside and actively observe and where the water goes. Note the flow patterns on your sketch. Determine and identify which landscape features block, divert, or reclaim the water. Do this while the rain falls and shortly thereafter. If this timing isn't possible, get outside soon after a storm and note what the water has done based on puddles, erosion, and waterways worn into the soil.

Rain gutters on the eaves of the house claim and direct the water that falls on the roof. Placing a barrel, water tank, or cistern at the base of the gutter system stores all of that water, and a spigot or valve at the base of the storage container allows the gardener to siphon it off when needed.

The gutter system also can direct water to less obvious storage areas in the landscape. If you don't want to store the water, but want to utilize it and control its flow, direct the end of the gutters toward an area in the garden that can hold water. This could be a tree well, a lawn, or a depression in the soil lined with rocks for this specific purpose.

If you divert rainfall to a tree well, make certain it's designed to hold the volume of water directed there. The tree well should be several inches deep and at least as wide as the tree's canopy, with a depression on the side where the water will flow in, and a berm or raised edge on the opposite side to prevent the water from flowing out. The water will soak into the soil at a rate of about one foot for every inch of water that settles into the well.

A wise steward plans the landscape around the water runoff pattern in the garden, using berms and swales to direct the water into areas where plants benefit from it. These berms need to be several inches high, with landscape material planted in the adjacent depressions, or swales. To take full advantage of the available moisture, place plants that like quick draining soil near the tops of berms, and plants that tolerate longer periods of "wet feet" in the swales. A series of these berms and swales creates a natural looking, water-wise landscape with interest and character.

Collecting runoff in a catchment area or basin is beneficial because it helps replenish the immediate water table, prevents erosion in other parts of the garden, and may soak in and spread out so that it irrigates nearby plants. Catchment basins are attractive components of the landscape when lined with river rock or similar material and serve a dual role as picnic or patio areas during dry times.

One of the most devastating plant diseases in the desert Southwest is Texas root rot, sometimes called cotton root rot. It occurs throughout the southwestern United States and Mexico, being most prevalent in areas below 5,000 feet. Texas root rot is a disease caused by the soil-borne fungus, *Phymatotrichopsis omnivora*. This fungus is indigenous to our soils and exists in deep, as well as superficial, soil samples. It exists in the soil as hair-like or hyphal structures, called sclerotia, which are protective organs that allow it to reside for long periods of time in soil lacking host material. When the sclerotia come in contact with acceptable host material, strands grow and invade the outer surface of the roots.

Texas root fungus has a very wide host range, negatively affecting over two thousand species by colonizing on the roots and creating a thick web of hyphae, or strands, that penetrates the roots and causes decay. The strands then grow through the soil and infect nearby roots. The fungus does not produce airborne spores like many other fungi, but spreads only by the growth of these strands in the soil.

No current soil test will identify the presence of *P. omnivora* in the soil unless a plant has been infected. Examination of the rotten roots under a microscope will determine if *P. omnivora* is the responsible pathogen. The hyphae of fungus will be present on the roots if Texas root rot is the cause. These strands have straight side branches with two thin crossarms. White, cottony, or spongy spore mats may also develop on the surface of the soil after a rain.

Infected plants usually exhibit characteristic symptoms that indicate Texas root rot without the need for a soil or root examination. The obvious symptom is a sudden, rapid wilting and drying of foliage following summer rains or deep irrigation. Unlike other types of leaf browning, dead leaves cling to the plant with Texas root rot.

There is no reliable cure for Texas root rot. Treatments with soil amendments, including composted manure, soil sulfur, and ammonium sulfate sometimes delay the inevitable. Infection with Texas root fungus is usually fatal. When this is the case, your only recourse is to plant immune or resistant species.

Immune species:
Agave
bird of paradise (*Caesalpinia*)
Dracaena
giant reed (*Arundo donax*)
palms (see Week 24)
pampas grass (*Cortaderia*)
Yucca
Highly resistant trees:
Acacia
aleppo pine (*Pinus halepensis*)
cedar (*Cedrus*)
Citrus
cypress (*Cupressus*)
desert willow (*Chilopsis linearis*)
Eucalyptus
feather bush (*Lysiloma microphylla thornberi*)
mulberry (*Morus*)
palo verde (*Cercidium*)
pomegranate (*Punica granatum*)
sycamore (*Platanus wrightii*)
western hackberry or palo blanco (*Celtis reticulata*)
Highly resistant shrubs:
cacti (*opuntia var.*)
crape myrtle (*Lagerstroemia indicia*)
creosote bush (*Larea tridentate*)
elderberry (*Sambucus*)
honeysuckle (*Lonicera arizonica*)
hop bush (*Dodonaea viscosa*)
juniper (*Juniperus*)
ocotillo (*Fouquieria splendens*)
oleander (*Nerium oleander*)
rosemary (*Rosmarinus officinalis*)
Russian olive (*Elaeagnus augustifolia*)
star jasmine (*Trachelospermum jasminoides*)

Highly susceptible trees:
almond (*Prunus dulcis var. dulcis*)
apple (*Malus*)
apricot (*Prunus armenaica*)
bottle tree (*Brachychiton populneus*)
California pepper (*Schinus molle*)
carob (*Ceratonia siliqua*)
cottonwood (*Populus fremontii*)
elm (*Ulmus*)
fig (*Ficus carica*)
maidenhair tree (*Gingko biloba*)
peach (*Prunus persica*)
plum (*Prunus saliciana* or *P. domestica*)
poplar (*Populus*)

Highly susceptible shrubs:
butterfly bush (*Buddleia davidii*)
castor bean (*Ricinus communis*)
Cotoneaster
flowering quince (*Chaenomeles*)
lilac (*Syringa*)
Photinia
roses
senna (*Cassia*)
silverberry (*Elaeagnus commutata*)
Spirea
Texas ranger (*Leucophyllum*)

Another frequent cause of rapid decline in numerous landscape plants is anthracnose, a fungus that affects many herbaceous and woody plants. Susceptible plants include berries, leafy green vegetables, peppers, tomatoes, passion vines, ash trees, elm trees, maples, oaks, and sycamores. Symptoms vary according to affected species, but generally cause sunken gray, tan, or brown spots on leaves, stems, fruits, and twigs. These spots may enlarge to cover entire leaves and may become watery, with pink or tan mounds in their centers. Ultimately leaves wither and drop, followed by twigs and branches.

Annual plants infected by anthracnose are difficult to save. It is better to pull them up, discard the plants and any litter left in the garden, and plant again. You may want to treat the soil with a copper-based fungicide and composted manure before replanting. Large, perennial plants respond to a treatment or two with a fungicide containing lime sulfur, Bordeaux mixture, or chlorothalonil.

Less frequently, verticillium will infect, among others, sunflowers, roses, melons, tomatoes, maples, cherry trees, peach trees, and olive trees. Scattered branches die and flowers become stunted or non-existent. Leaves turn yellow, and annuals wilt from the bottom up. To manage this disease, grow resistant varieties and remove diseased plant material immediately. In annuals, this means removing the entire plant. In perennials, cut out the affected branches with properly sterilized tools.

You may see another form of fungi growing in your summer garden— mushrooms. The subject of folklore and fairy tales, mushrooms sprout like miniature umbrellas in soil where organics are decomposing. Because they are not detrimental to the health of your plants, mushrooms require no aggressive treatment. They will, however, release spores when their caps open, so pick them from your landscape when they first emerge in order to limit future growth.

On the subject of mushrooms and toadstools—many poisonings occur every year due to ingestion of toxic or unsafe mushrooms. Unless you have developed an expertise in the area of fungi identification, do not consume any mushrooms that come up in your garden.

Several other active fungi cause disease during monsoon season. Lawns are particularly susceptible to fungal infections if they receive too much water through rain or irrigation. If your grass develops silver or gray spots, black rings, spreading brown patches, or dead areas that follow the flow of water, suspect fungus. Treat it with a product containing Daconil or Bayleton.

Dethatching Bermuda grass

Lawns are more susceptible to fungal growth when they need to be de-thatched. Dethatching is the process of removing the build-up of dead grass blades, stolons, roots, and runners from the base of the individual grass plants. This build-up raises the height of the grass, decreases air circulation, and inhibits the penetration of water to the root zone. Most hybrid Bermuda lawns require dethatching every two or three years.

Equipment-leasing companies carry dethatching machines for rent by the hour, half day, or day. These small, gas-powered machines quickly cut through and remove thatch, making short work of an otherwise time consuming task. If this equipment is unavailable to you, a hard-tined rake is effective. By pushing the rake down into the lawn and aggressively pulling it back, you loosen and pull up the thatch. You can then rake it out of the lawn and dispose of it. The job is easier if you mow the grass before beginning. Once you hard-rake the lawn, mow it again to cut and remove any attached runners. I always water and fertilize my lawn after dethatching.

An indoor vegetable garden

WEEK 30 In much of the country, harsh weather chases gardeners indoors for the winter, so many of them retreat to the desert Southwest to avoid the forced hibernation. Predictably, those gardeners hustle back to cooler climes as the desert heats up to avoid temperatures of the opposite extreme. Many of us choose to live and garden in the desert year-round, and have options of our own when the temperatures become unbearably hot. We can stay indoors and grow vegetables in containers.

Indoor gardening challenges the gardener to modify skills that were developed raising crops in outdoor beds, planters, and pots. Most significantly, indoor gardening requires wise plant choices, suitable containers, proper planting media, appropriate location, and adequate light.

Given adequate light, many traditional vegetables grow well indoors. Commercial growers have known this for years and often grow the sold-at-market vegetables in large indoor settings. The key is proper plant selection. Clearly, plants with long vines or excessive size are not well suited to indoor container gardening, although I have a friend who often has productive vines wrapped around her screened sun porch. In the beginning, however, I recommend smaller plant varieties.

Vegetable	Plants per container	Pot size
beets	3–5	8 inch
bell peppers	1 or 2	10 inch
bunching onions	6–10	10 inch
carrots	6–8	10 inch
chard	4–6	10 inch
eggplant	1 or 2	12 inch
kale	2–4	12 inch
leaf lettuces	4–6	10 inch
mustard greens	4–6	10 inch
radishes	6–10	8 inch
summer squash	1 or 2	5 gallon
tomatoes, cherry	1 or 2	5 gallon
tomatoes, roma	1 or 2	5 gallon
turnips	3–5	12 inch

Containers for indoor vegetable gardening must adhere to the standard requirements for growing plants. Each container must be large enough to support fully grown plants. They must hold soil without allowing it to spill or wash away, and must have holes to allow adequate drainage. If the indoor garden is within view of a main part of the house, appearance may be an issue. If the garden will be out of company's view, even black nursery containers are fine, as long as they aren't exposed to a full day of direct sunlight that would heat the soil beyond tolerable temperatures.

The planting medium or potting soil in an indoor vegetable garden must be free of pathogens, insect eggs, and larvae. Indoors, without the benefit of natural airflow and winds, disease and insect control are critical, and starting with clean soil is the key to controlling these problems. Buy or mix new soil to guarantee that it's free of infestation. Any good commercial potting soil will work, or you can make your own by combining equal amounts of peat moss, sand, perlite, and aged steer manure. If the steer manure is too odorous for your location, use well-aged compost.

If you re-use soil in which other plants were grown, sterilize it first. Use your home oven to accomplish this task. Spread a two-inch layer of potting soil on a jelly roll or cake pan with sides to hold the soil. Place the pans in a 200° oven for an hour to kill any pathogens remaining in the soil. Use care when handling the pans of soil because they will be heavy, awkward to hold, and hot. Place the soil in your containers when it is completely cool.

A south-facing sunny window is the best location for an indoor vegetable garden. Sliding glass doors, which transmit more light, are even better. Many Southwest homes have Arizona rooms or screened porches, which are ideal if they receive six or more hours of sunlight. If you are lacking an appropriate location, create one with a combination warm-white/cool-white fluorescent lamp or a grow light. These fixtures provide the necessary types of light for full plant development. If you are growing your plants near a window and they become spindly and pale, or fail to produce flower or fruit, light deprivation is probably the problem. Use the same supplemental light sources to correct it.

Providing adequate light will be your biggest challenge when gardening indoors, but whiteflies, aphids, and fungus gnats also may become a nuisance. Whiteflies and aphids are especially fond of tomatoes and peppers, but will infest anything with new, lush growth. Anticipate their arrival and check your plants daily. Look at the undersides of leaves and on stems, where eggs will be deposited first. At the first sign of insect infestation, remove what you can by gently rubbing the areas with thumb and forefinger and immediately treat with insecticidal soap.

Fungus gnats are not as easily controlled, but do less damage to the plants. You will become aware of their presence when they buzz around your plants and through your home, much like fruit flies. They lay their eggs in the soil and the larvae feed on fungi that naturally occur there. If the gnats become too irritating, saturate the soil with soapy water when you irrigate. If the insecticidal soap doesn't work, use properly diluted Sevin on the soil. Read the directions carefully, especially in reference to food crops and harvesting time following application.

GROWING SPROUTS

For those who want to grow something indoors, but aren't interested in full-on vegetable gardening, growing sprouts is an excellent alternative. Sprouting seeds is an easy way to exercise your mental gardening muscles, while sparing the physical ones. It also provides the cook/gardener with variety in taste, texture, and nutritional value while utilizing little effort or space.

Sprouts make crisp, tasty additions to salads and sandwiches and are attractive garnishes, but you can also add sprouts into your favorite bread recipe, sprinkle them atop soups or stews when ladling individual bowls, add them to pancakes, waffles, and muffins, or use them as a tasty ingredient in stir-fry.

By germinating, the little seedlings have converted their fats and starches into protein, sugars, and vitamins. These young plants are nutritional powerhouses that pack a positive dietary wallop with negligible calories. They are excellent additions to the diet if you're trying to lose a few pounds or simply trying to increase the nutritional value of what you actually consume.

Seeds for sprouting must be intended for consumption as seed or sprout. Purchase them in grocery stores, health food stores, or catalogs specifying this use. Many seeds are treated with chemicals that prevent fungus or other pathogenic growth. These chemicals are not safe for human consumption, and so treated seeds should not be used for sprouting.

Seeds that sprout easily fall into three general categories: grains, legumes, and vegetables. They should be whole, untreated, food-quality seeds.

Grains:	Legumes:	Vegetables:
barley	adzuki beans	pumpkin
corn	alfalfa	radish
oats	lentils	squash
rye	mung beans	turnip
sunflower	soy beans	chard
wheat		

To begin, sterilize a quart size jar. Place 1–2 tablespoons of seeds into the jar and cover the top with mesh or screen. I like to use the yellow net lemon-half covers available in specialty cooking shops. The elasticized edge holds it on the jar perfectly and they can be cleaned and re-used for months. If you are using a piece of mesh or screen, secure it to the jar with a rubber band.

Add water to the jar right through the netting and give it a good swirl for about a minute, then dump the water out. Add enough clean water to cover the seeds, set the jar on the counter, and soak overnight. In the morning, pour off the soak water and thoroughly rinse the seeds again, draining well. Place the jar of rinsed and drained seeds in a spot where they receive bright light, and thoroughly rinse and drain them two or three times a day. This is very important. If you do not rinse the seeds well, they become sour and inedible. When the seeds start to sprout, you will notice the discarded seed hulls. These can be left in the sprouts or removed, depending on taste. You will know the sprouts are ready to eat when they have a small stem and the first two leaves. For most seeds this will take 3–5 days. Your homegrown sprouts, stored in a covered container, will stay fresh in the refrigerator for a week.

General July chores

Even if there isn't a big vegetable garden to tend, many tasks coax the caretaker into the July garden. Despite the fact that it's monsoon season, some supplemental watering is required. It's best to supply this between 4 and 8 a.m. so that the heat of the coming day evaporates any excess moisture. Landscapes, particularly lawns, irrigated in the evening are more susceptible to fungal disease than those watered in the early morning hours. This simple practice will help keep your garden disease-free and attractive.

Another way to keep your garden looking its best is deadheading; the practice of removing spent blossoms from flowering plants. Garden flowers including cosmos, geraniums, marigolds, roses, sages, and zinnias benefit from deadheading in two ways. First, the plants look more attractive when old, faded blossoms aren't clinging to their stems. Second, removing faded flowers directs the plant's energy to the production of additional flower buds rather than the development of seeds, so the garden will offer a floral display for a longer period of time. Use sharp pruning shears rather than pulling the flower heads to ensure removal of the embryo, or seed-producing portion, of the plant.

While in the garden, you may notice many underdeveloped fruits lying under the canopy of your citrus tree. Unless it is excessive and the tree looks dull and wilted, do not worry. Citrus trees produce much more fruit than they can carry to maturity and drop the excess when the elements become more stressful. This phenomenon is typically called June drop, but can persist into, or sometimes begin, in July.

It is time to fertilize grapes again, and several varieties will be ready for harvest. All of the 'Beauties' and 'Perlette' ripen in July. When picking the clusters of grapes, use a sharp knife or pruners and cut the stems just above each cluster. Avoid pulling bunches, since this will cause damage to twigs and branches.

Watermelons and apples also are ripening in the desert garden. My grandfather, who worked on a Texas watermelon farm in his youth, could look at a melon, give it a tap, and know if it was ready to pick. I am not so gifted. It is difficult for most of us to determine when a watermelon is ready to harvest, but there are a few visual cues to help us. Ripe watermelons have yellow spots on their undersides. The vine also gives us clues in the form of tendrils that grow along its length. If the tendrils just above the melon are brown and dry, the melon is ripe. If they are green, wait a few days and check again.

Check apples daily and harvest them when they reach peak ripeness to avoid spoilage on the tree. Aroma and taste are your best clues. A few hot days can degrade ripe apples to the point of being inedible, so check them every day once ripeness is near. 'Anna' and 'Ein Sheimer' apples will be ripe and require care in harvest and storage. 'Anna' apples keep for many weeks if you have a cool, well-ventilated storage space. They are best when individually wrapped and carefully stacked to avoid bruising. Immediately use damaged or bruised fruit.

'Ein Sheimer' apples do not keep well and should be eaten fresh, processed, and canned or frozen as soon as possible. My grandmother traditionally mixed up pie filling and froze it inside gallon size freezer bags that she placed in pie plates. When the filling was completely frozen, she removed the pie plate and had a filling, frozen in the correct shape to be cooked. When she wanted to bake a pie, she pulled the frozen filling out of the freezer bag and put it in a pastry-lined pie plate. This, she topped with a vented crust and popped into the oven. No defrosting was required and those pies were the best I ever tasted.

August

- Last month to plant new Bermuda grass lawns and palms
- Plant beans, corn, pumpkin, squash
- Plant indoor herbs
- Divide and transplant iris
- Treat iron-deficient roses with chelated iron
- Cut back tomatoes/encourage new growth for fall harvest
- Fertilize citrus, flowers, vegetables, and lawns, landscape plants
- Watch for scorpions, spiders, snakes, swarming ants, and termites
- Control weeds stimulated by rain
- Keep pecan trees well-watered
- Cut out branches affected by oleander gall

August

AN INDOOR HERB GARDEN

Herbs have grown on the windowsills of French, Italian, and South American kitchens for generations, adding flavor and aroma to the dishes created there. Easily cultivated in small pots, most herbs require minimal space, need little attention, and reward the gardener with tasty leaves and blossoms in a short period of time. Transplant them from four-inch pots you purchase at your favorite nursery, or experiment with greater choice and diversity, and propagate them from seed. Herbs require bright light, well-draining soil, regular water and fertilizer, and frequent pinching back. With these needs met, they live long and produce abundantly.

Most herbs flourish in eight-inch terra-cotta pots, which provide adequate room for root development without crowding your counter or rack. Because of their porous nature, terra-cotta pots "breathe," allowing excess moisture to evaporate more quickly, which helps prevent root rot. The pots must be placed in a location that provides a full day of bright light. A kitchen counter, shelf, or potter's rack located near a south-facing window is ideal. The plants must be easy to reach so that you can rotate them regularly to compensate for the single-direction light source. Easy access also enables the gardener/cook to harvest conveniently and frequently. As with other indoor growing projects, cool-white/warm-white fluorescent bulbs can be used to augment available light, but many herbs grow just fine without them.

The potting medium for herbs must be fast draining, yet moisture-retaining. I recommend two parts potting soil mixed with one part sand and one part perlite or vermiculite. This mix is light and friable, and encourages rapid root development. It's a good idea to mix a tablespoon of Osmocote in each pot prior to planting it with seeds or small plants.

If you decide to purchase small plants to begin your indoor herb garden, choose them with care. Gently lift each plant from its container and inspect the roots. They should be healthy and white, with no sign of brown, black, or decaying fibers. The soil in the root zone should be moist and insect-free. The roots themselves should be growing along the sides and bottom of the container, with some room for future growth. If the roots have not reached the sides or have grown into less than half the depth of the container, they are underdeveloped and not yet ready to transplant. If they crowd the container, bulging the sides, or growing over the top, the plant is root bound. Look for another. Small plants don't usually overcome early, extreme stress, so choose only the healthiest specimens.

When you get your seedlings home, pot them up as soon as possible. In those small nursery pots they quickly dry out without the frequent attention of full-time employees. To pot each one up, put a pottery shard or stone across the drain hole of a pot and add a large handful of potting mix. Remove the plant from its plastic container and gently rough up the roots with your fingers. Place the plant into the pot and fill around the edges with more potting soil, gently pushing it down to compress any air pockets. When the potting soil is even with the original root ball, set the pot in its saucer and water it thoroughly. If you have adequately watered, a small amount of water will drain into the saucer.

If planting from seed, choose varieties whose characteristics predispose them to pot culture. Standard and dwarf, or miniature, varieties are always good choices. Avoid anything referred to as giant, colossal, or otherwise larger than average. To insure viability, use seeds packed for the current season only. Since herb seeds germinate more quickly when soaked overnight in a small bowl of warm water, do this the night before you plan to plant.

To begin planting, cover the drain hole and fill the pot with potting mix. Water it gently, to moisten the surface. Sprinkle 12–24 seeds on the soil surface and cover them with a thin layer of potting soil. Evenly wet the entire soil surface, using a spray bottle so you don't disturb the seeds. Cover the pot with plastic wrap held in place with a rubber band. The plastic acts like a mini-greenhouse, providing a suitable environment for germination. You will see emerging plants and the development of first leaves in 2–3 weeks.

When the first leaves develop, remove the plastic. Keep a close eye on the young plants, watering them several times a day if necessary, to prevent drying out. As they grow, they develop a second set of leaves, or true leaves. When this happens, thin the plants so that only a few well-spaced seedlings remain. The exceptions to this rule are chives and onions, which thrive in crowded conditions and provide a better harvest when grown thickly and densely.

Herbs that do well in indoor pot culture:
basil (*Ocimum basilicum*)
chervil (*Anthriscus cerefolium*)
chives (*Allium schoenoprasum*)
dill (*Anethum graveolens*)
garlic chives (*Allium tuberosum*)
lemon balm (*Melissa officinalis*)
lemon verbena (*Aloysia triphylla*)
marjoram (*Origanum majorana*)
nasturtium (*Tropaeolum*)
oregano (*Origanum vulgare*)
Parsley
rosemary (*Rosmarinus officinalis*)
sage (*Salvia*)
thyme (*Thymus*)

Lemon verbena, rosemary, and sage are best started from cuttings or transplants. The others germinate quickly from seeds, cuttings, or transplants.

Marjoram, oregano, rosemary, sage, and thyme are Mediterranean in origin and prefer less moisture than the other herbs listed, so do not overwater them. You'll know this is the case if the lower leaves begin to yellow and then turn dark brown or black, then shrivel up. If this happens, cut back on the frequency of irrigation and pour off any water that settles into the saucer.

Fertilize indoor herbs with a one-quarter strength water-soluble fertilizer at every other irrigation. Depending on the heat and humidity in your home, you may need to water as often as every three days or as infrequently as once a week. Pay attention to the plants and soil in the first few weeks to develop the ability to anticipate their needs.

Nasturtiums are the only herb listed whose flowers serve the primary culinary role. Treat them like annual flowers, removing the blossoms when they are in full bloom to encourage the development of more flowers. To harvest leaves or stems from your other herb plants, pinch or cut back tip growth to a point just above the next branch or set of leaves. This approach will encourage full, bushy growth and prevent tall, lanky plants. Harvest chives and garlic chives in sections cut from the base of the plants. Except for chives, garlic chives, marjoram, oregano, and rosemary, whose flowers are as edible as they are attractive, herbs lose intensity of flavor and become bitter when allowed to bloom. To maintain high quality, pinch tips to prevent flowering.

To keep your herb garden in full, year-round production, harvest frequently and fertilize regularly.

When annuals such as basil, dill, nasturtium, and parsley grow slowly and look weak, propagate additional plants to replace them. When chives, garlic chives, lemon balm, marjoram, and oregano produce blossoms, shear them to the base of the plant and give them an additional fertilization. This rejuvenates perennials and encourages new growth.

Pests, especially whiteflies and fungus gnats, sometimes can be a problem with indoor herbs. Treat them with insecticidal soap as quickly as possible to prevent population increases. Regular inspection of leaves and soil will alert you to unwanted insect visitors. By following these guidelines, you will have an indoor herb garden that provides the cook in your household with a constant, fresh supply of the basic culinary herbs.

Composting: Making your own black gold

Mother Nature never went to a garden center and purchased ammonium sulfate. She's always had a perfect plan for increasing soil fertility, and thriving gardens have existed for hundreds of years without the addition of synthetic fertilizers. Like my grandmother, gardeners of old made their own rich, fertile soil by composting. I remember carrying the kitchen scraps out to Grandma's compost heap. It was a simple thing. She had a twelve-foot length of chicken wire rolled into a circle and hooked onto itself. It sat upright in the dirt at the back of her lot. We put not only all of the fruit and vegetable trimmings in the bin, but also fallen leaves, garden debris, wilted flowers, and chicken manure. The chicken manure went in because Grandma had a chicken coop that required regular cleaning. Whatever we raked and shoveled out from under those cages went into the compost heap. She also had a boysenberry patch right next to the heap, and since the boysenberry vines were watered regularly, so was the compost. With this kind of attention and the temperate Southern California climate, Grandma's compost brewed quickly and was regularly added to the vegetable and flowerbeds, or spread in a three-inch layer under the fruit trees.

The composting process is not always as quick here in the desert, but the basics are the same. By layering your kitchen scraps, garden trimmings, and lawn clippings with the dry leaves and weeds you pull from the landscape, you can create your own rich, dark compost. It is beyond compare when used in raised beds, flower and herb gardens, and vegetable plots. You need to water the compost occasionally and must never add meat or fat. I also find it helpful to cut the components into pieces three inches or smaller. I've left them larger and they don't decompose completely. The compost also breaks down more rapidly if you turn the heap every week or two.

Over the years, I've taken many approaches to composting. I have had a chicken wire ring similar to my grandmother's. I've also used a series of bins between which I transferred the compost as I turned it. I've had a heap sitting out in the open near sprinkler overspray and in little containers that I turned by hand. I've even dug small holes in areas I wanted to amend and buried the blended contents of my kitchen compost bucket every time it was full. But for quite some time now, I've satisfactorily used a simple, recycled piece of equipment.

Several years ago I bought a compost bin from the local city government. It is a decommissioned trash dumpster turned upside down with a hinged lid made from the bottom. Several two-inch holes drilled into the sides allow air circulation. I keep it in a fairly shady place, hidden between a wall and a Texas ranger. The shade is beneficial in our arid climate, and the location keeps the unsightly process out of view. I always keep a pile of dry material (palo verde "needles," leaves, and other yard trimmings) next to the bin. Under the kitchen sink I keep a three-pound coffee can in which I save vegetable and fruit trimmings, coffee grounds, tea bags, egg shells, and other non-protein food waste.

When the coffee can is full, I empty it into the compost bin, add a layer of dry material, and then pour in the water used to rinse the can. This practice makes for a fairly even distribution of damp and dry elements; and the compost "cooks" more quickly. I sometimes add my grass clippings, although I usually apply them as mulch under the fruit trees. If we expect a rain shower, I leave the lid open to catch some extra moisture. I also add things like depleted potting soil from transplanting projects, leftover fertilizers, and all of the trimmings from flowers, herbs, and vegetables in the garden. I usually fill and then empty the compost bin every six months.

During the first six years I spent developing my present garden, my homemade compost completely changed the nature of the soil in several sections. It takes time and patience, but homemade compost works magic in our alkaline soils. The finished product also is an excellent fertilizer when used as a side dressing around almost anything growing in your garden. Composting is a worthwhile effort because it is nearly cost-free and very beneficial.

There are a few common concerns regarding compost piles or bins. Many people resist the idea of composting in their own garden for fear of attracting pests. In all the years I have composted, I've never had a single rodent in my bin or pile. They are not interested in decaying plant material. After all, that's what compost is. Rodents would definitely be attracted to the compost if you added meat scraps, bones, dairy, or fats, but these are strictly forbidden in my compost heap.

Another common concern is that a compost bin will exude unpleasant odors. Proper layering and watering keep the decomposition process moving along, and prevent odors. If too much green material is added without a layer of dry, it will not break down quickly. This happens most often with grass clippings. When too many are added without dry, brown material, a thick, sludgy mass, with a distinct, unpleasant odor results.

Many folks also have concerns about insects. Ants and roaches do like compost. For this reason, it is wise to turn it regularly for aeration, layer properly so that it stays hot, and water frequently. Following these guidelines, a few ants wander in, but they won't stay and build a colony. Roaches come and go in the compost world, and are actually beneficial as they help aerate the pile. Nevertheless, I don't want roaches moving into my house, and have always kept the compost bin some distance from the house as a precaution. When I turn or empty the bin I always see the familiar red desert roaches. I just turn the other cheek while turning the heap and try not to get too worked up. They are a natural part of the desert ecosystem and I know I will encounter them if I'm maintaining a healthy, balanced garden.

Tending the vegetable and herb beds

If you're still working outdoors, there are a few veggie-garden tasks that require your attention now. To take advantage of the summer rains and the remaining hot weather, sow another series of seeds. Pole beans, lima beans, corn, cucumbers, black-eyed peas, and winter squash can all be planted now for a late fall harvest. Remember the basics of seed sowing—keep the soil evenly moist to encourage germination and irrigate the newly emerging seedlings twice a day to allow their small vascular systems to take up nutrients and moisture while developing. To protect young, tender shoots from the intense July sun, provide afternoon shade if the bed is not already receiving it.

During July, I often buy several pony packs of heat-loving annual flowers to fill in the holes left from harvesting and removing spent plants from the vegetable garden. This dresses up the bed and offers shade to the lower parts of neighboring plants. By covering exposed soil, it also prevents rapid evaporation. Be sure to carefully inspect nursery plants, since they are notorious for introducing fungal diseases into the garden in the summer. Look for plants whose roots are healthy, white, and free of decay. Leaves should be dark green, with no spots or dry leaf margins. If some plants look healthy but nearby plants are diseased, shop elsewhere. Fungal diseases can be airborne and exposure may have occurred, even though symptoms are not yet evident.

Some plants in the garden provide smaller amounts of produce as they adapt to increasing temperatures. Tomatoes, cucumbers, and sweet peppers may completely quit producing until cooler weather returns. Cut your tomatoes back to one foot in height to rejuvenate them for a second crop that will begin ripening in late September, and continue through first frost.

Eggplant and chile peppers, the heat-lovers of the desert vegetable garden, continue to provide lots of fruits as long as you continue to harvest regularly and fertilize every few weeks. A tip for harvesting: Do not expect your egg-plants and peppers to grow to the size of grocery store specimens (although they sometimes will). Pick them when they are deeply colored and glossy.

If you are disappointed in your vegetable garden's performance, call it a season and clear everything out. Clean up the debris and cover it with four-inch layer of composted manure and a generous sprinkling of soil sulfur. As monsoon rains water the nutrients into the soil, the beds will be reinvigorated and ready for September planting.

Herb beds also disappoint many gardeners in August, particularly if mon-soon has brought lots of rain. The Mediterranean herbs are especially per-snickety about humidity and moisture, frequently falling victim to August "die out," which is caused by fungus that clogs the transporting organs of the plants. We also discover whether or not our herb beds are well draining dur-ing this hot, damp season. If the roots of many herbs continually sit in damp soil, they rot and the plants decline.

Lavender, marjoram, oregano, rosemary, sage, and thyme are susceptible to fungal disease and root rot if they live in poorly drained soil. If your plants look wilted and dry in the presence of moisture and damp soil, suspect root rot or fungal disease. Sometimes fungicide applied to the soil will help, but the problem is actually cultural, so improving the drainage is the real answer. Sand and organic material added to the bed improves drainage and increases the likelihood of herb success. This is difficult to do around existing plants. If they are doing poorly, consider taking them out and starting the bed again. Perhaps some of the plants can be potted up and saved, but usually they are infected by disease and should be replaced.

The butterfly garden

WEEK
32

I can sit at my kitchen table and watch dozens of butterflies pass through my garden and across my field of vision, floating from nec-tar plant to nectar plant, swooping with and against the wind as they feed on the sweet offerings of blossoms planted specifically for their nourish-ment. The butterflies lay their eggs on the foliage of other landscape plants whose primary purpose in this place is to entice and nurture their species.

This activity guarantees the return of next year's butterfly population, and their parade of colors and fanciful flight.

To attract and sustain a steady flow of the elusive creatures, the garden must provide shelter, water, and food sources for the mature butterfly as well as its larval stage, the caterpillar. The caterpillar is a creature that gardeners view with mixed emotions. The fact that they grow up to be beautiful butterflies makes them welcome, but knowing that large numbers can defoliate entire plants has the opposite effect. A thoughtful plan creates balance in the garden and includes a variety of plants so that one or two are not singled out and destroyed. A well-planned garden allows for the beauty and survival of plants and *Lepidoptera*, the insect group to which butterflies belong.

To effectively plan a butterfly garden, it is necessary to understand their life cycle. The female butterfly lays eggs on or near a plant that supplies food to the larva. In just a few days, the eggs hatch and the little caterpillars hungrily emerge. They immediately begin eating and growing, consuming larger amounts of the food plant as they increase in size. For 2–4 weeks the caterpillars grow rapidly, shedding their outer "skin" (actually their exoskeleton) as many as five times to accommodate their increased size.

When fully grown, the caterpillars crawl to a sheltered place to pupate, shedding their skin one last time. This final shedding forms pupae cases or chrysalides. Over a period of two weeks, the caterpillars liquefy and are transformed into their adult form, ultimately emerging as butterflies. Here in the Southwest there are more than two hundred and fifty butterfly species representing six native families. These families are called *Hesperiidae, Libytheidae, Lycaenidae, Nymphalidae, Papilionidae* and *Pieridae*.

Hesperiidae, or skippers, are small to medium butterflies whose wingspans range from less than an inch to over three inches. They vary in color from brown, black, or white, to orange. Some experts consider them moths rather than true butterflies. Skipper caterpillars eat Bermuda grass, blue gramma grass, and locust tree leaves. In summer they flit over Bermuda grass lawns in large numbers, especially after a rain or irrigation.

Libytheidae, or snouts, have a wingspan of one and a half inches and are brown, orange, and white. In the larval stage, they dine exclusively on hackberry leaves. Hackberries also entice cardinals and other birds with bright orange berries that ripen from early fall through winter. Quail and other desert birds utilize hackberries as nesting sites, since their dense foliage and sharp thorns provide protection. With bright green foliage and an attractive mounding form, these desert natives make excellent landscape plants despite the thorns on some varieties.

Lycaenidae is the family name for the blues and hairstreaks. These one-inch butterflies come in a range of colors including blue, brown, gray, lavender, and orange. Their caterpillars feed on acacia, senna, dalea, fairy duster, and mesquite, all of which are hardy, colorful additions to the desert landscape. These butterflies are abundant in the desert from early spring to late fall, with a few tough types continuing to grace our gardens through winter.

The brushfoots, or *Nymphalidae*, get their interesting name from their smaller-than-normal front legs that force the butterflies to use only four legs. The angle of their stance is distinctive when they land on a flower or plant. The group includes some of the most beautiful, eye-catching butterflies in the desert, including the buckeye, crescent, fritillary, monarch, painted lady, and queen. They can have a wingspan from a diminutive one inch to a large and commanding four inches. They vary in color combinations that include black, brown, orange, and tan. Larval foods for this group include *Asclepias* (otherwise known as milkweed and including butterfly weed), hackberry, lippia, passion flower, and veronica.

The dearly loved swallowtails belong to the family *Papilionidae*. These large butterflies have wingspans of 3–5 inches, making them standouts in the garden. Their distinctive black and yellow coloring and tail-like projections make them some of the most recognizable desert insects. The swallowtails lay their eggs on or near citrus trees, dill (both wild and cultivated), and the vining Dutchman's pipe. Their well-camouflaged caterpillars, which look like bird droppings, can defoliate young citrus trees, but do only minor damage to mature specimens.

Our last family, *Pieridae*, includes sulphurs and whites. These butterflies range in size from 1–4 inches and come in varying shades of peach, orange, white, and yellow. Acacia, senna, dalea, hop bush, and feather tree will attract these pretty butterflies to your garden. This is the most commonly seen family of butterflies, often migrating in large groups that cause quite a stir along highways and in large open fields.

In addition to larval food sources, the butterfly garden must contain nectar-producing plants for the adults. The following list includes the names, both botanical and common, of plants whose nectar attracts and sustains butterflies in the desert garden.

Arizona, velvet mesquite (*Prosopsis velutina*)
baja fairy duster (*Calliandra californica*)
bamboo muhly (*Muhlenbergia varieties*)
bee bush (*Aloysia gratissima*)
butterfly bush (*Buddleia davidii*)
butterfly mist (*Ageratum corymbosum*)
catclaw acacia (*Acacia greggii*)
chaste tree (*Vitex agnus-castus*)
Dalea varieties
desert hackberry (*Celtis pallida*)
dill (*Anethum graveolens*)
dogweed (*Thyrrophylla [Dyssodia] pentachaeta*)
feather bush (*Lysiloma microphylla thornberi*)
fern acacia (*Acacia angustissima*)
Lantana varieties
passionflower (*Passiflora incarnata*)
pine-leaf milkweed (*Asclepias varieties*)
red bird of paradise (*Caesalpinia pulcherrima*)
senna (*Cassia*)
verbena (*Glandularia [Verbena]*)

CREOSOTE

The most intoxicating and familiar aroma during a desert rainstorm is that of the creosote bush (*Larrea tridentate*). Creosote is one of the most common desert natives, growing to a maximum height of 4–8 feet. It is open and straggly, showing off dark, gracefully twisted branches beneath a canopy of small, oily, light green leaves. It is that oily secretion that gives the desert its distinct odor.

Creosote bushes can be very difficult to propagate. If you want to plant one in your garden, your best bet is to purchase a small seedling in a plastic, "long-Tom" starter pot that allows for taproot development. When planting, carefully place the seedling in loosened, native soil that will drain well. Take extreme care not to disturb the roots and place the seedling in a hole dug out of the loosened soil. Slit the sides and bottom of the pot and hold it together while putting the root ball into the soil, removing the plastic pot from inside the hole when the plant is in place. Replace the native soil, firmly pat it down, and water well. Irrigate the plant every few days until it is established. It will not need supplemental irrigation after a few months, and will grace your garden with bright color and intoxicating aroma for years to come.

Iris

WEEK **33** Near my house there lives a man who knows everything there is to know about cultivating irises, a spectacular family of plants whose species number 200–300. While most of what he does is fairly "by the book," when you visit his place, he'll often say, "Well, I know that's how they say you're supposed to do it, but…" And for the price of listening carefully, the potential for greater success in the iris bed is yours.

I make several visits to this colorful garden every spring to buy cut flowers, listen to stories, and soak up the casual, yet elegant, beauty of the place. I've not yet learned enough from this gentleman, so I hope I have many more springs in which to share his company. It's not that he hasn't tried to pass on a lot of information, it's just that there's so much to know about irises. Conversely, there is so little one needs to know in order to grow them in the desert Southwest.

Scores of color combinations, forms, heights, blossoms, and bloom times characterize different varieties of this large group. There are American, Dutch, English, German, Japanese, Siberian, and Spanish irises. Some are bearded; some are not. Some grow from bulbs, some from rhizomes. Some are native to the mountains, some to meadows, and others to the arid regions of northern Africa. And all are advertised and sold in the pages of dozens of catalogs. With so many variables to consider, and so many types from which to choose, getting started with irises can be daunting. That is why we begin thinking about fall-planted, spring-blooming irises in August. Now is the time to learn, choose, and order.

The German, bearded irises are the easiest to grow in the low deserts of the Southwest. Available in many heights and sizes, they grow from rhizomes, which are thick, modified stems. Their sword-like leaves overlap each other, forming flat planes of fanned foliage. Tall bearded irises bloom in mid-spring on branching stems that reach 2½–4 feet in height. They come in standard, ruffled, and fringed forms, in all colors but red and green. Excellent border plants, tall bearded irises are also nice in the cutting garden and look fabulous when planted en masse.

German, bearded iris
(Iris sp.)

Miniature tall bearded irises (sometimes called table irises because of their cutting quality and size) and border bearded irises grow 15–18 inches tall and produce proportionately smaller flowers in the same color ranges as their tall counterparts. Intermediate bearded irises attain this same height, but bear flowers that are larger, about 3–5 inches across. They flower earlier than tall bearded irises and later than dwarfs, so a garden that contains all three will be in flower for several consecutive weeks. The intermediates sometimes have a second bloom in the fall, making them doubly enticing.

Standard dwarf bearded irises are shorter. They can reach a maximum height of fifteen inches, with some stems only eight inches tall. These profuse bloomers like our desert winter chill, so if you live in town and have a significantly warmer microclimate, you may not get the great performance as in cooler areas. Miniature dwarf bearded irises reach only eight inches in height and have larger flowers. They are the earliest bloomers in the bearded group, putting up flowers as many as six weeks before the tall varieties. They are very hardy, require winter chill, and multiply quickly. They also need more frequent irrigation than the others, perhaps because of their smaller root systems. Growing them in the front of a bed makes this easy to achieve.

Dutch and Spanish irises also grow in the desert Southwest, but require winter mulching to protect their sometimes frost-tender bulbs. Differing from sword-like fans of leaves of the bearded iris, the foliage of Dutch and Spanish irises is thin and reedy. Individual plants are narrow and upright with blossoms in shades of blue, brown, mauve, orange, white, yellow, and bicolor combinations. In March and April, Dutch irises produce 3–4-inch flowers on stems that are nearly two feet tall. Spanish irises have slightly smaller blossoms and bloom about two weeks after the Dutch varieties.

Dutch and Spanish irises grow from bulbs rather than rhizomes and must be "lifted" each year. Plant them in September or October and mulch in early November for winter protection. They will produce blooms in March and April. During the months of May and June, the foliage "ripens" and then dries out. In July or August, when the foliage is completely dry, carefully dig up the bulbs. Inspect them for disease or damage and store the healthy ones in a cool, dry place until September or October, when they go back into the ground to begin again.

Many gardeners get good results from English, Japanese, Louisiana, Pacific Coast, and Siberian irises, even though they are not as well adapted to our desert climate and soil as the German bearded, Dutch, and Spanish types. One of the main reasons is summer watering. The irises that easily grow here prefer sparse summer moisture. They prefer to dry out in the summer, roots and all; and overwatering at this time can cause rot or encourage early regeneration and nematode infestation. This feature makes them an excellent xeriscape candidate. Other irises like to be in wet soil all the time, and still others need hard winter freezes. These requirements are a challenge in the desert Southwest.

All irises require full sun or afternoon shade, good drainage, and like well-amended soil. Once you choose your location, prepare the soil by deeply digging in a six-inch layer of organic material, which can include compost, peat moss, well-aged manure, or other soil conditioners. Add ammonium phosphate at a rate of four pounds per hundred square feet and water heavily to wash in the fertilizer and settle the soil.

When the soil is dry enough to work, plan and shape the layout of the beds so that irrigation will reach all of the plants, but excess water brought by storms or overwatering will drain off. Test your bed by running the irrigation, letting it sit for a few days and running it again. Correct water flow and drainage problems before planting your rhizomes and bulbs.

Plant your bulbs and rhizomes when daytime temperatures stay below 100°, usually at the end of September. Bulbs go into the soil so that their tops are barely covered. Plant rhizomes horizontally and close to the surface, with only an inch of soil covering them. Space the plants a foot apart and pack the soil tightly. Water immediately and then once every week to ten days. New green growth will emerge in November, but will not grow vigorously until December or January.

When robust growth is apparent, increase watering to every five days and fertilize every two weeks with a water-soluble balanced fertilizer. Flower stalks appear in March, with the most profuse bloom in mid-April. Fertilize the plants every other week throughout this time. When blooming stops, cut the foliage back to 6–8 inches and fertilize one last time to encourage the development of new vegetative buds on the sides of the rhizomes. These develop into next year's. During the summer months, water infrequently if rains fail to materialize.

Dig and divide bearded irises when clumps become crowded or fail to produce blooms. This is usually every two or three years. They can be lifted from late July through September and kept out of the ground for several months if stored in a cool, dry place with good air circulation. *Do not refrigerate them!*

When you dig up the rhizomes, remove the entire clump. Brush away the soil, hold the rhizome in one hand, and trim the healthy leaves to about six inches. Cut the outer rhizomes off and discard the old bloom stalk and all rhizomes lacking leaves. Trim the leaves on each remaining rhizome in an inverted "V," and either store or replant in the newly loosened and amended bed.

A few problems can crop up in the desert iris bed. If individual leaves seem wet or greasy and the plant falls over, suspect bacterial soft rot. A rotten potato odor is usually the first obvious symptom, when the rhizome is rotting but the leaves are not yet affected. To treat this disease, lift the plants and use a sharp knife to cut away the diseased tissue and some surrounding healthy tissue to guarantee complete removal of the disease. Disinfect the knife between cuts to avoid spreading the disease. Drench the plant and the soil with a ten-percent bleach solution and replant the healthy portions of the plant.

When the leaves of irises emerge deformed and the plant remains short, suspect aphid damage or a zinc deficiency. This condition, known as pineappling, also inhibits blossoms, or causes blooms to open at ground level. To treat, cut out the deformed portion of the plant, leaving the rhizome in the ground. Control aphids by regularly treating with insecticidal soap. If no aphids were present or you are uncertain, apply zinc to the soil according to package directions.

Irises do not escape the voracious appetites of grubs. Brown leaf tips followed by a complete drying of the plant indicate grub damage. On closer inspection, the rhizome may be devoid of roots or obviously chewed. When tips begin to brown, gently dig in search of grubs and, if you find any, treat the soil with pyrethrum or rotenone.

Grasshoppers, snails, and slugs can be a problem in the iris bed and are best controlled by handpicking. You will usually see the culprits when you notice the damage they wrought, which includes holes in the leaves and flower parts. Insecticides are not effective in controlling these creatures and they are rather easy to catch or squish.

Swarming ants and termites

Following warm weather rains, the early morning desert horizon swirls with brown, hazy clouds of swarming ants and termites. The wet soil is a signal for them to move up and out, prompting them to migrate to new locations and create new colonies in higher, drier ground. For this special time of year they sprout temporary wings that get them where they want to go and which are quickly shed. In the process, they push up mounds in patios, garden beds, and landscapes.

The gardener can control the creators of little dirt hillocks all around the garden by applying insecticide around the mound openings. If there is a concern about whether the flying creatures are ants or the more detrimental termites, identification and discrimination are rather simple. Ants have segmented bodies and straight antennae. Termites have non-segmented bodies and antennae that resemble miniature strings of dark pearls.

On close inspection, most gardeners discover that they are looking at ants, not termites. This is generally a relief, since termites are native to our soils and have earned terrible reputations based on the number of wooden structures they damage or destroy. If a termite infestation is suspected, seek professional control to avoid greater problems.

Palo verde trees

WEEK
34

When commencing work on my current garden, I planted trees as quickly as possible, knowing that the scattered or afternoon shade they created would provide a more tolerable environment for other plants I wanted to include in the landscape. I wanted to maintain the dignity of the desert, and since we moved near a national forest, native plants in their original splendor were within walking distance of our front door. It was both helpful and educational to wander through the nearby desert and foothill areas, learning what naturally lived there, unassisted by irrigation, fertilization, and temperature protection.

I loved the look of the desert and appreciated the importance of maintaining native and desert-adapted landscapes. I wanted to create a lush, oasis-like environment on my own property, but didn't want to waste water doing so. I also wanted to plant trees that belonged in the desert rather than importing things that would not be at home in the extremes that exist here. It didn't take long to decide that palo verde had a place in my plan. With several different trees in the palo verde family, I had to decide which variety best suited my landscape needs.

Palo verdes fall under by two genus names, *Cercidium* and *Parkinsonia*, both of which belong to the pea family *Fabaceae* (*Leguminosae*).

Blue palo verde (*C. floridum*) is one of the first desert plants to bloom in the spring, producing waves of bright yellow blossoms splashed in broad strokes across the native landscape. From the highway, travelers through the low desert enjoy the impressionistic scene that blue palo verde evokes. Up close, the small blossoms perfume the air with a light, sweet fragrance that attracts bees and other pollinators.

Reaching a mature height of twenty feet, with a canopy only slightly wider, blue palo verde is a small tree. Its distinctive bluish-green bark is smooth and its leaves are small and compounded with round leaflets that it sheds during extreme temperatures. This shedding response allows blue palo verde to be hardy to about 15°, and tolerate summer heat near 120°, if adequately irrigated and in general good health.

Blue palo verde is tolerant of most soils, but prefers good drainage. Minimally, it requires a monthly, deep irrigation, but accepts even more, making it a good candidate for lawn settings. When choosing a location for a blue palo verde, consider the significant amount of flower and pod litter this tree produces.

The roots of drought-stressed blue palo verde are the favorite food of the larvae, or grubs, of the palo verde beetle. To avoid this problem in your landscape, keep the tree as healthy as possible through proper irrigation and the removal of parasitic mistletoe when it develops. Additional grooming includes pruning out clumping, multi-shoot growth, called witch's broom, and raising the height of lower branches to create a tree from a plant that wants to be a giant shrub.

Like most fast-growing trees, blue palo verde reaches its maximum height in just a few years, and is short-lived. The average lifespan of a well-maintained specimen is 20–40 years, significantly shorter than olives, oaks, and other hardwood trees, but not unusual for fast-growing desert natives.

Little-leaf palo verde or foothills palo verde (*C. microphylllum*) is smaller than the blue palo verde, attaining a mature size of only about fifteen feet. It is more tolerant, thriving in very poor soils and adapting well to drought and winter cold by dropping all of its leaves and small twiggy branches. It produces a profusion of perfumed pale-yellow blossoms in March and April, followed by pods that contain the typical pea-like seeds.

Little-leaf palo verde requires very little water once established, surviving on average rainfall alone. When planted in a well-drained location, it requires supplemental irrigation for the first year and then does fine on its own. Its yellow-green bark and rugged, scraggly shape make this tree an excellent choice for a naturalized area in the garden, or the arid zone in a xeriscape plan. Be cautious about location as the branch tips end in sharp spikes, discounting its use along walkways or near play areas.

Wherever you decide to plant a little-leaf palo verde, beware of the litter it continuously produces. Winter cold prompts leaf and twig drop; spring ushers in blossoms that fade and fall; in early summer pods begin to shed; and late summer leaf and twig drop occurs in response to high temperatures. Despite the litter, little-leaf palo verde is a welcome addition to the landscape because birds nest amid the close-growing branches and several desert animals eat the flowers and seeds.

One of the most attractive native desert trees, Sonoran palo verde (*C. praecox*), also called palo brea, makes a stunning impression as a specimen plant in the desert landscape. This tree has a smooth, lime-green trunk that supports a lush canopy of bluish-green leaves reaching twenty feet high and twenty-five feet across. Hidden in the branches, numerous half-inch spikes make for treacherous pruning, and require great care by the gardener. Consider the microclimate when planting this handsome tree because Sonoran palo verde is less tolerant of cold, incurring extreme damage when temperatures dip below 20°. Its attractive form, lacy foliage, and bright yellow flowers make it a good choice as an accent plant in most landscapes.

Sonoran palo verde is less messy than its relatives, but nevertheless is inappropriate for poolside. It provides nesting sights and shelter for many desert birds and looks its best when clustered with other desert natives, such as daleas or fairy dusters.

Mexican palo verde (*P. aculeate*) is also called Jerusalem thorn. As its nickname suggests, its branches are covered with small, sharp thorns that require extra caution near traffic areas and when pruning. This species is less shrubby than its relatives and prone to single trunk, erect growth. Its yellow-green bark becomes brown and rough as it matures to its full height of twenty feet.

The Mexican palo verde produces long leaves with midribs lined by tiny leaflets. These midribs fall throughout the year, creating a pine needle-like mat under the tree. They make good compost material, but wreak havoc in the pool filter. In the spring and summer, the entire tree wears a crown of fragrant, yellow flowers, which attract large numbers of birds and bees. This flush of bloom precedes six-inch seedpods that dry and fall off during summer and fall. It is the rare month when the ground under the canopy of Mexican palo verde is free from debris. Still, they create valuable scattered shade and can be underplanted with a large variety of drought-tolerant plants. They often are used in street and lawn plantings, in both desert and tropical settings, and are an excellent choice in the transition and arid zones because they require no supplemental irrigation after the first year.

Like other palo verde trees, Mexican palo verde is susceptible to infestation by the palo verde beetle and the removal of mistletoe is sometimes necessary. The tree is hardy to 18° in its youth, and tolerates lower temperatures as it matures. Its stately natural shape is a welcome addition to the landscape. Mexican palo verde thrives in high heat, tolerates nearly all soil types, prefers good drainage, but will grow in caliche or clay-laden soils.

Late August activities

We've reached the end of the month and there are still several tasks to be completed in the desert garden. First and foremost is fertilizing. Citrus requires the last application of fertilizer for the calendar year. This application will promote growth and allow the plants to store energy for continued leaf and fruit production. This is also true of deciduous perennials and ornamentals, so now is a good time to provide nourishment to get them through the fall and winter. If you wait much longer, the first frost in November will burn tender, new growth. If applied now, that tender growth has a chance to toughen up before winter.

I also fertilize my lawn with ammonium phosphate at this time and amend the flower and vegetable beds if I haven't already done so. Signs that plants need fertilizer include pale green foliage, decreased flower and fruit size or production, lack of vigor, or failure to grow. Any balanced fertilizer will treat these symptoms and return your plants to peak health. Always water both before and after every fertilizer application to avoid root damage.

Late August is also a good time to inspect potted plants for root rot. At this time of year, plants that prefer well-drained soil often get too much moisture because of high humidity and rain, in addition to regular irrigation. If foliage seems dry when the soil never dries out, root rot is the culprit. Change your watering habits to allow the soil to drain. This may mean less water applied more frequently. Many plants require a change in irrigation when humidity levels are high.

Scented geraniums are among the plants commonly affected by increased humidity. They don't tolerate moist conditions and often suffer from root rot or other fungal diseases during monsoon. They brown out, lose leaves, die back, and generally decline. To prevent this, locate scented geraniums in a place with good air circulation, adequate sunlight, and appropriate irrigation. Apply fungicide to these plants if you cannot get symptoms under control. This usually does the trick, but renders the blossoms and leaves unacceptable for culinary purposes for several weeks.

In particularly wet years, cacti and succulents develop fungal disease. If this happens, remove the diseased portions, sterilizing both the cut section of the plant and your tools with a ten-percent bleach solution after each cut. This will prevent the spread of disease and disinfect the wound. If the plants are small and overwhelmed by disease, remove them and plant a more tolerant species.

It's also important to stay on top of weed control during the rainy season. Continue to remove weeds when they are young and have not set seed to prevent future weed development and reduce the need for removal. Hoe summer annuals since they will not grow back from the root, but remove perennial weeds, root and all, or treat with Round-up or Finale.

Your last August task is a fun one. Pull out your mail order catalogs and decide what you want to plant in your cool-season garden beds. Choose and order flower, herb, and vegetable seeds that will produce the winter bounty you most anticipate.

September

- Prepare vegetable and annual flower beds for fall planting
- Refrigerate bulbs for four to six weeks and prepare beds
- Divide and transplant iris
- Fertilize tomatoes and peppers
- Fertilize landscape plants
- Place Christmas cactus and poinsettia in total darkness 12–16 hrs/day
- Plant cool-weather herbs
- Plant landscape plants
- Plant desert-adapted and native trees
- Sow wildflower seeds
- Battle whiteflies with insecticidal soap
- Remove and discard split and cracking citrus
- Prune palms

September

BEAUTIFUL BULBS FOR THE DESERT

WEEK 35 What is it about flower producing bulbs that so fascinates the gardener? No matter what part of the world we're from, flowering bulbs provide special interest to most of us. I've never met an avid gardener who hadn't experimented with bulbs of one sort or another, and I've met many people whose gardening experiences include the planting of scores of bulbs every year. Of course, these folks usually achieved that particular accomplishment at a location outside the desert Southwest. If we lived where soil was acidic and rainfall abundant, we could naturalize bulbs, planting them by the hundreds, even thousands, to effortlessly create seas of springtime blossoms.

A few determined individuals have managed such an extensive display in the desert, but most of us realize the inherent challenges and scale down our attempts. We may not be able to attain the abundant splendor found in East Coast or European gardens, but with proper selection and preparation, we can create beds brimming with adaptable spring blooming bulbs.

In their natural habitats, bulbs grow in rich, acidic soil whose main component is decomposing leaf litter. The successful gardener understands and recreates this environment to encourage growth and development. Most important in improving an area of the garden dedicated to bulbs is the addition of organic material, such as peat moss, aged manure, and compost.

Loosen eight inches of soil, and then add soil sulfur, ammonium phosphate, and six inches of organic material. If the soil is heavy with clay or caliche, add 2–3 inches of sand to aid drainage. Till the bed to evenly distribute the amendments, then smooth the surface, and water deeply. If you've had trouble with grubs or other soil-borne insects, apply insecticide to eradicate the problem before planting.

Fall-planted bulbs do best when put in the ground when daytime temperatures remain below 90°. Before and after putting the bulbs in the ground, water thoroughly. Make sure the moisture penetrates beneath the level of the bulbs, and then apply a layer of mulch. It is not necessary to water again until the first leaves have pushed up through the soil. Then, full-sun beds require water about once a week, and shade plantings every two or three weeks.

Fertilize your bulbs every six weeks with a low-nitrogen fertilizer to avoid excessive foliage growth at the expense of the bloom. Fertilizers developed specifically for bulbs provide the best results, contributing to good blossom size and color. The soil may require regular treatments of insecticide to keep soil-borne insects from damaging the bulbs. Control aphids and other foliage-eating insects with insecticidal soap.

Consider which bulbs are pleasing to you and how you want to arrange them in the bed. A plot plan or map of the bed is a good guide, helping you to properly purchase and plant, since each variety has its own planting specifications and spacing needs. In addition to the iris, which is known to perform well in the desert, several other bulbous plants can be rewarding. Learn about the various bulbs and create your plan based on the information below and the location you have chosen.

Lily-of-the-Nile (*Agapanthus*) is a reliable April to June bloomer, producing eighteen-inch stems topped with drooping clusters of flowers in shades of blue, lavender, or white. Beautiful as a poolside planting, lily-of-the-Nile is also an excellent border plant in the perennial bed, the bulb garden, or planted en masse. Depending on microclimate and variety, lily-of-the-Nile is either evergreen or deciduous, and can be planted in a wide range of exposures, from full sun to the minimum three hours of sun a day. Plant the bulbs a foot apart at a depth that is twice the thickness of the bulbs. Divide lily-of-the-Nile every five years.

Ornamental onion (*Allium*) has enjoyed increased popularity in recent years. These hardy, sun-loving plants send up leafless stems ranging 1–5 feet in height, topped with a sphere of small flowers. They are a distinct presence in the garden because of their brilliant colors, including blue, pink, red, rose, violet, white, and yellow, and their familiar onion aroma when bruised or cut. Increasing rapidly, ornmental onions require division every three years, since they fail to produce blooms when overcrowded.

The wisest bulb purchase for the desert gardener has to be amaryllis (*Amaryllis belladona*), also called belladonna lily. This vibrant plant comes in varying shades of orange, pink, red, and white, is very hardy, and does as well in a pot as in a bed. Unlike other bulbs, amaryllis must be planted so that its tip peaks through the soil. Beyond this important consideration, it is truly an easy-care plant, never requiring lifting or division and producing impressive April and May blooms for years.

Calla lily (*Zantedeschia aethiopica*) is not nearly as carefree as many other bulbs, but is beautiful and popular among desert gardeners. These flowering plants require partial to full shade, bi-weekly fertilizing, and heavy watering from early fall through the March and April bloom period. Callas come in many shades, including black, pink, white, and yellow, but the white are decidedly more productive in the desert. They reach heights ranging from 18–36 inches when in bloom, and should be planted 4–6 inches deep, and a foot apart. They look nice in rows, as foundation plantings, in pots, and mixed variety beds.

Native to the tropics and subtropics, *Canna* adores heat and sunlight. Cannas also add a tropical look to their surroundings, making them excellent candidates for poolside and patio plantings. They have large, brilliant green and bronze leaves that resemble banana leaves. Their blossoms range in color from apricot and peach to bold gold, yellow, and red. They flower all summer and into the fall, usually right up to first frost, are as attractive in pots as in mass plantings, and make excellent background plants, reaching 2–6 feet in height. Plant them eighteen inches apart at a depth of 3–5 inches in an area where the blossoms can be enjoyed in the garden because they do not hold up well when cut.

Cape lily (*Crinum*) is closely related to amaryllis. The cape lily, also known as veld lily, has a longer stalk, which sometimes reaches four feet, and longer, more slender flowers. Unlike amaryllis, the long-lasting crinum blossoms are highly fragrant and make a striking picture when surrounded by clumps of sword-shaped leaves. Plant cape lily four inches deep and two feet apart in partial shade. They produce blooms in shades of pink, red, and white from mid-May through fall, making them one of the longer-blooming bulbs. Possessing individual interest, crinums look good when planted singly or in groups, beds, or pots. Divide and replant them every few years.

The Dutch crocus (*Crocus vernus*) is one of the most popular flowering bulbs. With thin, grassy leaves and cup-shaped flowers on stem-like tubes, the 4–6-inch crocuses are a recognizable symbol of spring. These toxic plants adapt to sun or partial shade and work well in rock gardens, tropical settings, under trees, or in beds, borders, and pots. Plant them two inches deep and as closely as you like. The sight of many, closely planted crocus blooming from late December to early March is hard to beat.

Daffodil (*Narcissus*) is by far the most valuable spring-flowering bulb in the desert Southwest. This partial-shade lover blooms in white and yellow, with some orange to red bi-color varieties. They are most permanent, increasing in number and drifting across the garden, if allowed to do so. Unlike many other bulbs, daffodils are not attractive to rodents and are completely unaffected by extremes in heat and cold. Fun to observe throughout the day, daffodils turn their faces toward the sun, just like sunflowers. They are at home under trees or large shrubs, in rock gardens, near patios, in perennial beds, or in pots. Plant daffodils 4–8 inches deep and 4–8 inches apart. They bloom from January through May, depending on variety. Allow foliage to completely brown and dry before removing it, and divide the bulbs every four years.

Natives of South Africa, fragrant *Freesia* varies in color from blue, lavender, purple, pink, and rose to orange, yellow, and white. These plants bloom in March and look best in masses, two inches deep and two inches apart. The flowers dry out after blooming, dropping seed to self-sow and should be divided every three or four years. Plants that come up from seed often revert to the original cream with purple and yellow blossoms.

While not impossible to grow in the desert, hyacinth (*Hyacinthus orientalis*) requires a very dedicated gardener. These plants must be refrigerated for four weeks every September and then planted (or replanted) six inches deep and six inches apart in full shade in October. Highly fragrant hyacinths are an attractive indoor choice as well, planted in groups of five or seven in eight-inch pots. Blooming from February to April, they send up multi-flowered blue, pink, red, purple, or white stalks. After the blooms fade, continue to water regularly until the foliage also dies back. At this time stop watering, then lift and refrigerate the bulbs in September.

Star of Bethlehem, pregnant onion, and false sea onion are common names for the popular and easy-to-grow lily *Ornithogalum*. Plant any time in the fall, in masses, beds or pots, in partial shade to full sun. This white-blooming bulbous plant possesses a striking form and long, grass-like foliage, with long-lasting cut flowers. It reaches a height of about one foot and blooms April through May, usually dying back when temperatures dip below freezing in late fall.

The tulip (*Tulipa*) probably is the most consistently recognized and identified bulbous plant. It is attractive and tempting to purchase and, if mature enough, blooms that first year. It is important to buy the highest-grade tulip bulbs available, because smaller, younger bulbs may not flower for several years. In the desert that spells disaster, because tulips don't acclimate well to our arid, alkaline conditions, and it's unusual for them to bloom after their first year in the ground. In fact, they behave like annuals in most gardens, although lifting and refrigerating them for several weeks every fall may produce good results.

Watsonia, in white and scarlet, is an excellent addition to the bulb garden, requiring little to moderate water. From the iris family, this plant resembles gladiolus but is more tubular, with smaller blossoms on taller stalks. Planted four inches deep and a foot apart, they produce foliage in the fall, then bloom in March or April, reaching a height of 1–3 feet. Divide the overcrowded clumps in the summer, following bloom.

Grown for its culinary use rather than its floral display, garlic goes into the ground now, too. Plant this *Allium* in the flowerbed, vegetable plot, pots, or barrels by dividing heads and planting single cloves two inches deep, with the root section down. Each clove will develop tender, green, grassy foliage and add form to the garden. In late spring, following the production of attractive white flowers, the foliage will dry out. When it is completely dry, harvest and store the bulbs in a cool dry place for use in the kitchen.

ROSE REJUVENATION

As temperatures creep down, roses perk up. Given a little bit of tender loving care, they produce an admirable floral display through the early fall. Light pruning is the first step toward rose garden rejuvenation. Sharpen your hand pruners and get ready to do some cutting back. The first task is to remove any damaged, diseased, or dead wood. These canes should be removed at least two inches below the damage. If the bulk of the cane is in poor health, cut it all the way back to the base of the plant. Clean your pruners after every cut to avoid spreading disease.

After removing diseased wood, check the base of the plant and remove shoots or canes developing from the rootstock. Rootstock growth emerges from below the graft point, which on rose bushes looks like a knuckle at the base of the plant. If not removed, the root stock growth will overtake the desirable, grafted plant. The resulting bush is lanky, with whip-like branches rather than sturdy, upright canes.

After you have removed all of the dead or damaged wood and rootstock canes, prune for new growth. The cuts you make now will stimulate the growth from which blossoms will develop. Cut back by one-third any canes that are the diameter of a pencil or larger. Be sure to cut at an angle, just above an outside bud, making the highest point of the angled cut on the same side of the cane as the bud. This method allows moisture to run down the cane on the side opposite the bud.

Once pruning is complete, remove leaf litter and twigs from the ground around the rose bushes and water thoroughly. Follow this irrigation with an application of a balanced fertilizer to stimulate the bushes to produce more large buds. Water again to wash salts out of the root zone and carry the fertilizer where it is accessible. I usually begin fertilizing every other week now, until the weather gets too cold and the plants stop producing blossoms.

In about two weeks you'll notice significant improvement in your rose garden's appearance. New leaves will be larger and bright green. The canes themselves will be green and rosy and free from brown, dry blotches. Soon, blossoms begin to appear. Regularly removing blossoms and keeping bushes deadheaded stimulates flower production and increases the blooming period.

As in the spring, new growth sends out a dinner invitation to aphids. Check your plants regularly and keep an eye open for green and black aphids. If aphids begin to infest your garden, use insecticidal soap immediately to limit their damage. Another option is the application of a systemic insecticide that keeps all insect pests at bay. If you choose this approach, the roses cannot be used in any culinary application.

Winter vegetable beds

WEEK
36
Tomato plants burst forth with flourishing, bright green foliage that conceals thumbnail-sized fruit. Pepper plants have shed their sun-damaged summer leaves and stand tall with brilliantly colored, glossy leaves that provide shade to the large crop of shiny peppers. Chiles are still producing, and the plants seem to be "bulking-up," thanks to the less demanding weather. All of this productive activity in the beds that I want to till, amend, and plant anew.

Every year I look at the plants that are still providing a good deal of produce and debate over which to leave for an elongated warm season and which to pull and toss into the compost heap. I almost always yank the eggplants because my family has had their fill by now, and I don't feel like engaging in further culinary cleverness. But since I love their fruit so much, tomatoes and peppers usually get a reprieve.

Once decisions are made and plants are removed, I till the available bedding space, mixing in a layer of compost and a generous sprinkling of ammonium phosphate. After breaking up clumps and smoothing the surface out, I water the beds and let them rest for a week before adding seed and seedlings.

At the back of my winter vegetable garden, I like to trellis sugar snap peas or sweet pea flowers. They climb up the trellis and add their lovely and fragrant flowers to the bed. Other peas for the desert winter garden include Burpee's Burpeanna Early, Blue Bantam, and Mammoth Melting Sugar, and Little Sweetie from Stokes. Call your local Extension Office to learn about the specific varieties they currently recommend.

My family eats a salad or wilted greens every evening, so I use a large part of the garden beds for greens, including a mesclun mix marketed by either Burpee or Shepherd's, and arugula. Additional lettuces that do well in the Southwest include oak leaf, buttercrunch, and Stoke's 'Mesa 659-M-I'. Other greens with which desert gardeners have success are spinach, bok-choi, and Swiss chard. Although a little more difficult to germinate and quick to bolt in a hot spell, chicory, endive, and escarole are worth trying.

In addition to the greens, many other vegetables grow well in the desert winter garden. All of the brassicas do best if planted now. Consider buying seedlings rather than seeds for this family that includes broccoli, brussels sprouts, cauli-

215

flower, kohlrabi, and rapini, since they're difficult to start from seed. Because most families rarely want more than four or five of each plant in their garden, pony packs provide a good number of seedlings as well as a head start.

I sow my first planting of beets, carrots, radishes, and turnips now, followed by additional sowing every two weeks. I buy these seeds from catalogs and from local nurseries and hardware stores. I have had success with even the most inexpensive current season root crop seeds. If kept evenly moist through germination, and adequately watered in properly amended soil, it is almost impossible not to experience success with these vegetables. I also plant them in flowerbeds to show off their attractive, lacy foliage.

Bush beans are another crop that almost guarantees success. With old reliables such as Greencrop, Tendercrop, and Tendergreen still available, you can plant time-tested varieties that have produced bountiful crops for years. I also like to try unusual beans, like Nickel, a mini filet that is an improved form of the classic European miniature beans; Roc d'Or, a slender, yellow bean with a buttery flavor; or Verandon, an *haricots verts* that lives up to its French/epicurean reputation as a tender, tasty little thing. All of these beans, available from Shepherd's Seeds, can be eaten raw, briefly cooked, or blanched and frozen for later use. I have even had some delicious pickled bush beans that make me want to plant just a few more bushes.

Onions also go into the ground this time of year. If you want to grow large, bulb onions that are harvested and partially dried, consider Granex 33, New Mexico Yellow Grano, Texas Gran, and Yellow Granex. If you are unable to locate any of these specific varieties, look for other onions labeled "short day." Bunching onions, sometimes erroneously referred to as green onions or scallions, are harvested and eaten when fresh and green. Varieties that do well here and are easy to find include Beltsville, Southport, White Lisbon, and Papago onions.

In recent years seed companies have developed their own unique mixes. These include not only unusual greens and lettuce mixes, but also Asian salad and stir-fry mixes. These easy-to-grow crops that cost $5–7 a pound in a gourmet produce section, are inexpensive to grow, germinate well, and mature quickly. Most people enjoy their spicy, fresh flavor, but if you're displeased with the final product, you'll still have time to sow a different crop after harvesting the initial one.

Fruit rather than vegetable, strawberries do best in the desert when planted now for an early spring harvest. They require very fertile, loamy soil and a fair amount of water. Plant each crown or individual plant on a slightly raised mound and water from below since overhead watering encourages fungal growth on the foliage and the fruit. The plants must be protected from freeze, so most gardeners lay plastic row covers or old sheeting over the plants when frost threatens, removing it as the sun rises each day. In addition, strawberries need frequent fertilization. A fertilizer high in phosphorous provides fuel for lots of blossoms and fruit.

You'll experience the greatest success and productivity with your winter vegetable garden if you record location, planting dates, and specific varieties in your garden journal. This serves as a reminder of what was actually planted and when to expect maturity, and is helpful when determining what to plant again. After the initial planting, water the beds often enough to maintain surface moisture until the seeds have sprouted. Once germination has occurred and plants are growing, reduce your watering schedule to once every day or two. After a week reduce it even further, watching for signs of drought stress. Your winter garden watering goal should be one irrigation every five or six days.

In addition to frequent irrigation, a regular application of fertilizer high in both nitrogen and phosphorous will increase the garden's yield. If your garden produces puny beans or your carrots take a long time to mature, add more nutrients to the soil. Because annual plants grow rapidly, the necessary elements in the soil are quickly utilized and must be replenished. Monthly fertilization guarantees that the plants have all the nutrients necessary to produce at their peak. Mark your calendar every four weeks from now through February to remind you to apply fertilizer throughout the growing season.

REVISITING THE HERB GARDEN

As a desert dweller, I'm always sad to see humidity levels drop as monsoon leaves for the year. As an herb gardener, I'm glad when monsoon is over and the dry desert air returns. Many desert-adapted herbs are of Mediterranean origin and dislike high heat and humidity. As the thick, moist air settles in and refuses to move, some of my herbs just give up. Even after years of growing herbs in my garden, I still lose something by summer's end, a disappointing fact that I still aim to change.

One year I lost all but one of my lavender plants. They had been in for more than two years, which is quite an accomplishment for lavender in the desert soil. Suddenly they began to brown out and wilt, and within two weeks they were gone. Nothing but fragrant dry twigs remained. Another summer laid claim to the sage plants, which didn't wait until August to perform a mass exodus. They began to die, one-by-one, in early July and continued to fade away until none remained. An entire sage bed laid bare by fungus and root rot.

One year the Greek oregano given to me by a Greek friend succumbed to fungus after living in the same location for years. I was so disappointed! I loved that plant because it represented the octogenarian who shared it with me, and all the things he had seen and done. That oregano was far beyond being a culinary herb. Why did it suddenly die? What was the cause? What was different? As usual, clear thinking and a little investigation offered up the answers.

Subtle changes in the landscape make a big difference to some plants. My Greek oregano lived and grew like a weed in the corner of a well-drained, highly amended raised bed. It was far enough from the soaker hose to remain relatively dry. The opposite end of that same bed was home base for a beautiful flowering vine that grew up and over the ramada, cascading through the woodwork with fragrant clusters of lavender-pink blossoms. Every year the vine grew quite a bit, impressing us with its vigor and luxuriant bloom. Over time it shaded much of the surrounding area. Unfortunately, the shade enveloped the oregano. There was no longer enough direct sunlight to satisfy its needs and dry up excess moisture. The immediate environment, or microclimate, changed, and the oregano could not adapt.

After I remove all diseased plant material from my herb beds, I till the soil and add a small amount of compost. I test the drainage to make sure I don't lose my new plants to root rot. If fungus was present in the bed, I treat the soil with a copper-based fungicide and let it rest for a couple of weeks. While I wait, I plant my perennial and annual additions to the herb garden.

Perennial herbs flourish when planted in the fall. They grow a bit on top, but do their real work underground, developing strong, healthy roots to support rapid growth in the spring. Many botanical gardens and parks hold fall plant sales that include perennial herbs. Along with a good local nursery, they are reliable sources for healthy plants. Bee balm, chives, lavender, marjoram, Mexican tarragon, oregano, rosemary, sage, French tarragon, and thyme are all basics in the perennial herb bed.

As with vegetables, cool-season annual herbs go in the ground now. I am most fond of borage, calendula, cilantro or coriander, dill, fennel, parsley, Queen Anne's lace, violas, and violets. I usually plant more than one type of each species so that I can compare their landscaping and culinary virtues. In my garden, fern leaf dill is an exceptional performer year after year, but I still plant other types. Bronze fennel is beautiful when planted alongside annual flowers, and cilantro is the best filler for the flowerbed. It creates the illusion of an arrangement in a giant vase. Tall Italian parsley is a flat-leaf variety that grows and grows no matter how many outer leaves I remove, and its lacy appearance nicely accents delphiniums under-planted with violas.

I plant many of these species just outside my back windows so that I can enjoy the display. Others go in beds with winter vegetables so they can take advantage of the irrigation system. I also have a few in pots scattered throughout the garden. Regardless of where you plant your herbs, a few hours devoted to selecting and planting perennial and annual species will lead to a bountiful kitchen garden that is as attractive as it is useful.

BACK TO LANDSCAPING

This is the best time to put many landscape plants in the ground since they will spend the next few months developing strong root systems that will better nourish spring growth. In many cases, fall planting is better than spring planting since the roots have time to develop without coping with summer heat. Now is a great time to add native or hardy desert-adapted trees, shrubs, and groundcovers to the landscape.

If adding trees to the landscape now, consider acacia, desert willow, eucalyptus, mesquite, palo verde, and xylosma. All adapt quickly, require minimal water, do well in alkaline soils, and tolerate our weather. They are appropriate for xeriscapes as well as more lush environments.

Shrubs and groundcovers that are hardy enough to tolerate winter chills and make it through to spring without significant damage include autumn sage, crape myrtle, dalea, fairy duster, gaura, myoporum, sugar bush, Texas olive, Texas ranger, and verbena.

Avoid planting any tropical or subtropical plants; wait until after the last frost date next March to plant them. Bougainvillea, senna, citrus, cycads, euphorbia, hibiscus, palm, and tender sage all adapt to our desert climate, but may not survive the winter if planted now. If you're not sure whether or not a particular species will survive now, ask your nurseryman or check the label for hardiness. Remember that many plants tolerate extreme cold once established, but will die if exposed to freezing temperatures within a few months.

In addition to adding plants to the landscape, this is a great time of year to add landscape rock, paths, raised beds, concrete features, and other hardscape. The weather is cool enough to make heavy outdoor work comfortable, yet not so cold as to discourage long hours in the garden. We usually look forward to doing one big project each fall/winter, and appreciate the moderate temperatures in which to do it.

POOLSIDE PLANTINGS

Since it will soon be too cold to use the swimming pool, it's a good time to begin landscape work in that part of the garden. Many plants look particularly nice when planted around a pool, adding interest to both the landscape material and the water feature. I recommend several trees for poolside, since they produce little litter.

Shoestring acacia, an open, weeping, evergreen tree, adapts to all soil types and tolerates poor drainage and "wet feet." The scattered shade it creates is perfect for poolside since dense shade prevents pool water from achieving and maintaining heat in the summer. Xylosma is a small, graceful evergreen tree or shrub whose growth and shape are easily controlled. With leaves the same shade and sheen as citrus trees, it looks lush, requires minimal irrigation, and tolerates pool water fairly well. Other poolside favorites include the slow-growing Texas mountain laurel, Mexican ebony, and Texas ebony. All three need little water or maintenance and contribute a lush, cool green to their surroundings. But be aware of the painfully sharp thorns on Texas ebony.

When trying to create the illusion of a mountain lake, nothing beats traditional evergreens. Desert adapted and drought tolerant varieties of cedar, cypress, juniper, and pine contribute to the feeling of cool retreat and produce very little litter. A poolside setting with a few of these species feels like a vacation getaway just outside your back door.

It is important to consider pool maintenance as well as beauty when selecting poolside plantings. Shrubs and vines that look particularly nice without creating excessive litter include jasmine, juniper, fortnight lily, Lady Bank's rose, lantana, lavender, rosemary, and hardy sages.

Other perennials that nicely accent the lush poolside landscape are lily-of-the-Nile, agave, aloe, canna, cypress, hesperaloe, Jerusalem sage, santolina, and yucca. All these plants have interesting texture and form, making them good choices when viewed from a distance or up close. Although citrus trees and palms are among the best choices for poolside plantings, plant them in April to avoid frost damage. Do everything in the landscape job except planting tender plants, and all you'll have to do in the spring is pop them into the prepared ground to create your own bit of paradise.

A few excellent landscape plants are not appropriate near the pool. Many acacias and all of the mesquites drop blossoms and leaf litter that stain pool surfaces and shed small leaves that require extra filtering. Some homeowners build pools in lush mesquite bosques only to discover that they must run their pool filters continuously to prevent staining. This becomes expensive and stresses equipment.

Bougainvillea looks fabulous around water, but causes litter and staining. During warm weather, it continuously sheds brightly colored bracts, causing litter all summer long. The same scenario occurs when bottlebrush, Mexican bird of paradise, and fairy duster are too near the water. By considering plant characteristics as well as wind patterns and other weather facts, you can plan and plant an oasis in the desert pool yard that provides maximum pleasure with minimum work.

Edible landscape plants

Most gardeners plant things to serve more than one purpose and fill more than one role. The edible landscape does just that, addressing beauty, theme, and function. Edible landscapes are as varied as the gardeners who create them. One of the most common approaches to edible landscaping includes planting fruits and vegetables as anchors in the garden, filling in with more commonly used landscape material. This approach was beautifully implemented in the front yard of an old home I recently saw while walking through a residential section of a fairly large city. In this neighborhood, houses stood close to the street on smaller-than-average lots, had tiny lawns, a tree or two, several accent plants, and a concrete path to the door. On a street where nearly all homeowners followed the norm, a uniquely designed frontyard stood out in the crowd. On closer inspection, this traffic-stopping landscape proved functional as well as attractive.

Useful, beautiful plants replaced the lawn, and the concrete walk took on a charming new life, broken up and stacked to retain berms and mounds of amended soil that had been added to the terrain. Paths laid with chipped wood led visitors on a pleasant walk through the gardens and toward the front door. A sprinkler system that previously threw gallons of water into the air while irrigating the lawn was refitted with soaker hoses, mini-sprinklers, and bubblers that applied the right amount of water in the right locations. Each of the beds, a series of raised or dug-out, free-form shapes, contained plants with similar needs and requirements, and soil and irrigation were designed to address specific plant needs.

The late-spring garden, at first glance a field of flowers and greenery, was a source of culinary delight, intensively planted with beans, chiles, cucumbers, eggplants, peppers, pumpkins, squash, and tomatoes. These crops replaced cool weather beets, lettuce, radishes, snow peas, spinach, Swiss chard, and turnips. Flowering kale and cabbages accented corners and edges of several beds, soon to be replaced with more heat tolerant plants. Annual flowers including calendula, globe amaranth, marigold, nasturtium, red sage, snapdragon, viola, and young zinnia grew in large numbers around the vegetables, along with a dozens of daffodils. A variety of basils and parsley grew in pots on the porch.

The beds containing irises, drought-tolerant herbs, and flowers had sandy soil to provide drainage. Several varieties of chives, marjoram, oregano, rosemary, sage, and thyme filled minimally watered sections of the garden that got scattered afternoon shade. Because they were raised, these sections of the garden drained quickly during storms and the water flowed to tree wells and sunken beds where the gardener had planted species that didn't mind "wet feet."

Grapevines clung to an arbor and the chainlink fencing that separated the lots, while several lavender plants grew in unirrigated locations receiving "trickle down" from nearby beds, and the lacy foliage of asparagus softened the edges of the porch. Another section of the garden harbored four rose bushes underplanted with chives, garlic, garlic chives, and society garlic, bordered by catnip or catmint. Because of the repellent properties of the under-plantings, those roses rarely entertained aphids or thrips.

Apple trees replaced the ash trees that still grew in nearly every other front yard, providing fruit, summer shade, and full sun in winter. One tree stood in front of the living room window, another outside the breakfast nook where an eager child could open the windows on a warm summer day and pluck his afternoon snack off the tree that graced the house with cool shade.

Several things about this landscape made it work. Ornamental grasses, agaves, and succulents added color, form, and texture to the beds of edibles. Large pots strategically dotted the landscape, filling holes and creating atmosphere. Their contents, including 'Meyer' lemon and bay laurel, suggested that they lived in pots to allow movement with the seasons, and protection from extreme heat or cold. Very few plants with a propensity toward self-sowing grew here, preventing the wild, overgrown appearance often plaguing this sort of garden. It was a picture of controlled abundance.

As attractive as that garden was, it is not for everybody. A landscape composed primarily of annual flowers and vegetables is rather high-maintenance, requiring daily insect inspections and weed patrols. Care must be given to plant selection so that nothing overtakes its neighbor and everything remains tight and compact. This landscape scheme also demands significant time and money since many of the beds must be amended and replanted two or three times a year. The owner of this type of garden spends hours researching varieties, ordering seeds, and propagating them to create a well-balanced look.

If all of this preparation sounds like too much work, consider the opposite end of the edible garden spectrum. As we learned from the Native American farmers, many native plants are edible. They thrive in our alkaline soils and extreme temperatures and adapt to the challenges. They are easy to transplant, simple to grow, and require very little maintenance or water. With a few instructions and recipes, a desert gardener can grow a variety of food crops in a native landscape.

Several desert natives produce edible fruits in the spring and summer. Desert mahonia, desert hackberry, wolfberry, and skunkbush sumac all bear small orange or red berries that can be eaten raw or boiled in a small amount of water, strained and eaten as a sauce or spread. They vary in sweetness, depending on variety and local climate. If too tart, cook and sweeten them with mesquite honey.

During the winter and spring, chuparosa, a small desert shrub, produces attractive orange flowers with a surprisingly familiar cucumber taste. The blossoms make a nice addition to green salads or relish trays, and can be eaten out of hand. Soaptree yucca also produces spring blooms whose petals are edible. Remove them from the flower head and eat them like a vegetable, either fresh or cooked in a small amount of water.

The native gray-thorn is cousin to the commonly planted Chinese jujube tree. Both plants produce small, purplish fruits with large seeds whose taste is reminiscent of ripe apples. They are tasty when eaten fresh and can be cooked and strained to make a slightly sweet sauce. They are delicious cooked in simple syrup and candied, tasting like ripe dates.

Prickly pears and saguaros have been a source of sweets in the Tohono O'odham diet for generations. Fruit develops on the cacti in the spring, ripening by mid-summer. Collect the dark red ovals when they are swollen and beginning to split. Cut the fruit in half and scoop out the pulp. To separate the small black seeds from the pulp, mix with a small amount of water and simmer for about twenty minutes, then strain. Use the resulting juice as a beverage, in jelly making, as a thick, sweet syrup. Dry the seeds in a low oven or in the sun and eat them as a nutty treat.

Several varieties of cholla cactus produce flower buds that are gathered when still tightly closed. Using tongs, pick the firm buds while standing upwind to avoid the hair-like glochids that may blow off the plant. Rinse the buds in running water and boil them for fifteen minutes. Using clean tweezers, remove any remaining spines, then serve the buds as a vegetable or marinate them for an antipasto or pickle. To preserve them for later use, place the cooked buds in the sun for about five days until they are well dried, or dry them in a low oven or food dehydrator. Rehydrate the dry buds by simmering them in water or broth until tender.

Mesquite trees produce seedpods that are ground into sweet, tasty flour. Heat the collected beans in a 180° oven for about an hour. Break the cooled beans into two-inch pieces and fill a blender container one-quarter full. Grind for thirty seconds, or until the pods are completely milled, then sift the flour to remove seeds and seed coats. Keep the flour in an airtight container in the freezer, using it to replace all or part of the flour in your favorite recipes. Store the course material left after straining in a glass jar to steep as a sweet, distinctly flavored tea.

Mormon tea, or joint-fir, is another desert native commonly brewed into a flavorful piney tea. The common named developed when the Mormons brewed *Ephedra* as a substitute for coffee or tea. Herbalists use the same tea as a decongestant, tonic, diuretic, and cold medication. Any time of year, the flowers and stems of this plant can be collected, dried, and stored for later use. To make the traditional drink, simply boil the dried plant in water.

The most widely consumed and adaptable desert plants are the prickly pears. Collect young pads in the spring when they are less than five inches in diameter and their spines are still soft and leaf-like. Using tongs, pick and hold them. Remove the spines and glochids by scraping a vegetable peeler in the opposite direction from which they grow. Also remove the outer edge of the pad and the joint end. Rinse and dice the pads, then boil them in a large amount of water for ten minutes, drain, and rinse. Eaten as a vegetable, the diced pads, or *nopales*, make a tasty addition to stews, soups, scrambled eggs, and burritos, and they nicely substitute for green bell peppers, asparagus, or green beans.

Poisonous plants

Sometimes gardening enthusiasts are compelled to taste and try every blossom in their garden once they begin growing edibles. This is not only unwise but also downright dangerous. Many beautiful flowers should never be eaten and can cause mild to serious illness. Although it is not all-inclusive, the following list identifies poisonous plants that are frequently found in the landscape or garden. Use caution when working with these plants, and never use their blossoms in or near food. If you have a plant not listed here, do some research before considering it for culinary use. Botanical names that are identical to common names are not listed.

aconite (*Aconitum sp.*)
amaryllis (*Hippeastrum*)
Anemone
Anthurium
azalea (*Rhododendron sp.*)
bird of paradise (*Strelitzia reginae*)
black locust (*Robinia pseudoacacia*)
bleeding heart (*Dicentra spectabilis*)
bloodroot (*Sanguinaria canadensis*)
boxwood (*Buxus sp.*)
burning bush (*Euonymus sp.*)
Caladium
calla lily (*Zantedeschia*)
Carolina jessamine (*Gelsemium sempervirens*)
Carolina laurel cherry (*Prunus caroliniana*)
castor bean (*Ricinus communis*)
chinaberry (*Melia azedarach*)
creeping buttercup (*Ranunculus repens* 'Pleniflorus')
daffodil (*Narcissus sp.*)
deadly nightshade (*Atropa belladonna*)
Dieffenbachia
evening primrose (*Oenothera sp.*)
false hellebore (*Veratrum viride*)
four o'clock (*Mirabilis jalapa*)
foxglove (*Digitalis purpurea*)
heavenly bamboo (*Nandina domestica*)
hyacinth (*Hyacinthus orientalis*)
Hydrangea
Iris

ivy (*Hedera helix*)

Jerusalem cherry (*Solanum pseudocapsicum*)

jonquil (*Narcissus jonquilla*)

lantana (*Lantana camara* and *L. montevidensis*)

larkspur (*Delphinium scaposum*)

Lobelia

morning glory (*Ipomoea tricolor*)

Nicotiana

oleander (*Nerium oleander*)

periwinkle (*Vinca sp.*)

petunia (*Petunia hybrida*)

Philodendron

Pittosporum

poinsettia (*Euphorbia pulcherrima*)

privet (*Ligustrum*)

sacred datura (*Datura wrightii* or *D. metaloides*)

Schefflera

spurge (*Euphorbia sp.*)

sweet pea (*Lathyrus sp.*)

tansy (*Tanacetum vulgare*)

Texas mountain laurel (*Sophora secundiflora*)

Wisteria

yellow oleander (*Thevetia peruviana*)

WILDLIFE IN THE GARDEN

| WEEK |
| 38 |

One of my fondest garden memories is my early morning, close encounter with a large bobcat. My rational mind told me it was the dog, but I quickly knew that was not the case. I didn't trust my own assessment of the situation and called my son to have a look.

I pointed to the image and asked him what he thought. Not the least bit surprised by the animal's presence, he replied, "It's a bobcat, Mom. What else could it be?" We stood and watched him drink from the pool and survey the garden before casually, slowly sauntering through the wrought iron fence. To be that close to something wild and regal was an experience we'll never forget.

The topic of wildlife in the garden stimulates strongly held, often opposing reactions. For every gardener yearning to create a wildlife habitat in which to observe and enjoy nature's creatures, another wants to plant and develop gardens excluding local critters and their effect on the landscape. Interestingly, the information necessary for each to achieve his goal is the same: understand the animals' needs.

All wildlife need the same things: food, water, shelter, and space. If you want to attract animals to your garden, you must know and provide the environmental elements that best meet their requirements. Conversely, if you want to prevent wildlife from taking up residence on your land, the same information helps to eliminate the attraction. Knowledge of the animals in your locale and their individual needs leads to happy coexistence.

Birds flock to most gardens in small numbers because the existing landscape provides some basic needs. To encourage larger numbers of specific species, stock your garden with their particular food or habitat preferences. A clean, reliable water source is key. Pools, ponds, fountains, and waterfalls are best because they contain running water that doesn't sit and become stagnant. If you have a birdbath, empty and refill it regularly to avoid the spread of disease that accompanies an unsanitary water source.

Aside from water, food sources, especially insects, invite native birds including flickers, flycatchers, gnatcatchers, martins, mockingbirds, poor-wills, verdins, shrikes, woodpeckers, and wrens into the garden. Grubs, the pupae stage of beetles, are particularly delectable to thrashers, who do an excellent job of controlling them in my garden. Encouraging the natural food chain increases the bird population, as well as the number of lizards and toads, and eliminates the need for excessive pesticide use.

Plants that offer delicious seeds and flowers naturally augment the diets of various birds. Berry-producing plants, like mahonia and pyracantha, are especially bountiful, as are plants and grasses that drop seeds after flowering. Even plants that we consider pests, like mistletoe, fit into the natural scheme, since the berries of this parasitic plant are the favorite food of the phainopepla, or black phoebe, a beautiful black bird that resembles the cardinal.

Lure cardinals and pyrrhuloxia into the garden with native berry-producing plants, sunflowers, or feeders containing black sunflower seed. Feeders should either house a very hard seed block made specifically for cardinals, or should be constructed to discourage use by doves, sparrows, or starlings. There are many "dove-proof" feeders on the market that will allow you to enjoy the beauty of unusual species without attracting too many nuisance birds.

To encourage quail in your garden, make seed-producers and low, scratchy plants a part of the plan. Quail especially love desert hackberry and the petals of pansies and petunias. Once you've attracted quail pairs, encourage nesting by providing low, dense shrubs as protective sites. The presence of nesting quail nearly guarantees that a roadrunner is not far behind. Usually dining on insects, snakes, and lizards, the roadrunner considers baby quails a delicacy and is often observed following behind a line of trailing quail, casually, swiftly, gulping down the stragglers.

Roadrunners develop a certain level of domesticity, approaching windows and doors to display the day's catch before gobbling it up. A friend of mine could set her watch by the morning appearance of a large, male roadrunner. Every day, at exactly the same time, he came right up to the sliding glass door and showed her the snake, lizard, horned toad, or mouse in his beak, before retreating to the back of the patio to consume the day's meal.

Once these smaller species are regularly visiting your garden, the larger, predatory creatures follow. It's a thrill to look out the dining room window and see a great horned owl perched on the edge of the ramada. When this hap-

Greater roadrunner (Geococcyx californicus)

pened at our house, we weren't certain if he was after baby birds, little mice cavorting near the woodpile, or the neighbor's cat cavorting after them. He was magnificent, and I am grateful for whatever it was that lured him into view. Hawks, kestrels, and various owls live and hunt in areas that support wildlife. If small creatures are in your garden, large birds will follow.

Large birds aren't the only predators attracted to a well-populated plot of land. In the desert Southwest, big cats and coyotes sometimes wander into the garden. These large, wild creatures rarely damage landscaping, but can be dangerous for domesticated animals. If you have pets or livestock, be aware of the potential danger and prepare for it. Even if you have never had such an encounter, provide protection for the animals in your care.

Doves, ground squirrels, mice, pigeons, pocket gophers, rats, sparrows, and starlings are all considered nuisance animals and pests by most gardeners, and controlling them can be difficult. The removal of water and food sources is key to eliminating large populations of unwanted wildlife. Loose birdseed is the most frequent lure for these visitors, followed by easily accessible dog, cat, or livestock food. Replace bulk birdseed with hard blocks or large seeds to reduce the number of nuisance birds and still attract desirable species with thicker, heavier beaks. To drive rodents away, disturb their holes several times a day and they will usually relocate. Of course, the new location may be elsewhere in your garden, so be prepared.

Other methods of control include digging barriers a foot into the ground to prevent burrowing, tightly covering garbage cans and feed containers, limiting weed growth, and reducing brush and litter. Some gardeners resort to fumigants or rodenticides to control pests. I do not recommend this approach and urge caution if you decide to utilize such extreme measures.

Fumigants are toxic gasses, usually sold in cartridges that are forced into the hole of burrowing rodents. They are most effective in moist soil since water prevents the gas from diffusing. This method is often ineffective because the target animals quickly close off the targeted tunnels and retreat to other sections of their underground network of passageways.

Rodenticides are either anticoagulants or acute toxins. Anticoagulants are incorporated into grains that are ingested by the animals. They take several days to kill because the doses are small enough to work over time while not making the animal feel too sick, encouraging it to continue eating the bait. Acute toxins are strong and do not require multiple doses. The problem with both methods is control. How do you guarantee that no other creature consumes the poison? How do you guarantee that no predator or pet consumes the carcass of the dead or dying creature, thus falling victim to secondary poisoning?

Generally, anything green, growing and available attracts rabbits. Because everything in your garden becomes alluring, denied access is the best rabbit deterrent. Completely enclosing the planted area, including barriers in the ground to a depth of twelve inches, will keep the rabbits out.

If fully enclosing your garden is not possible, landscape with plants that are "rabbit-resistant." While a hungry, thirsty rabbit will eat almost anything, resistant species are less attractive than most. Consider landscaping exposed areas with them to reduce the friction between you and the desert natives.

Rabbit-resistant plants

Aloe
Asparagus
cape plumbago (*Plumbago auriculata*)
Chrysanthemum
creosote bush (*Larrea tridentate*)
Cuphea
emu bush (*Eremophila*)
Eucalyptus
French lavender (*Lavendula dentata*)
gopher plant or mole plant (*Euphorbia lathyris*)
heavenly bamboo (*Nandina domestica*)
indigo bush (*Dalea pulchra*)
Iris
Lantana
lavender cotton (*Santolina chamaecyparissus*)
marigold (*Tagetes*)
Mexican evening primrose (*Oenothera berlandieri*)
mint (*Mentha*)
pineapple guava (*Feijoa sellowiana*)
rosemary (*Rosmarinus officinalis*)
sage varieties (*Salvia var.*)
scented geranium (*Pelargonium sp.*)

silk oak (*Grevillea robusta*)

Texas mountain laurel (*Sophora secundiflora*)

verbena *(Glandularia[Verbena])*

The hummingbird garden

The sight of tiny, iridescent hummingbirds flitting through the garden at warp speed demands immediate attention. I have strategically landscaped areas near windows so that I can attract and admire the "hummers." Near my bedroom window, two cape honeysuckles feed the crew from spring through fall, with a brief summer hiatus covered by annual red sage. Even in mid-winter, the protected Cleveland sage puts up its characteristic "puff-ball" blooms that satisfy the sugary needs of these sprightly little birds.

Windows line the back of my house, providing views from the dining room, kitchen, breakfast nook, and family room. From each window I enjoy an unobstructed view of indigo spires, and pink, blue, and Mexican sages, warm-weather basil, trumpet vine, several agastaches, zinnias, and other annuals. The hummingbirds flock to these nectar-producing plants. Some are migratory, spending a portion of each year in my part of the world; the remainder live here year-round, adapting to and enjoying the local climate.

To attract hummingbirds, provide nectar plants or sugar solution in feeders. To make your own feeder solution, combine one part sugar with four parts water and boil the mixture for a minute or two. After it cools completely, pour it into hummingbird feeders and hang them in the garden. Sometimes the heavily trafficked feeders require daily refills.

I no longer put out feeders, relying instead on plants to do the attracting. I changed my approach after observing beak damage on many birds at my feeders. I learned this was caused by pathogens growing in the feeders and hated the idea that my carelessness contributed to fungal disease and bacterial infections. The feeders require a thorough cleaning and sterilization every other day in order to be safe. That soon became a lot of work, so I abandoned them altogether and planned this garden with hummers in mind, alleviating the need for artificial attractants. I also learned that many of the hummer-attracting plants invited orioles, thus doubling my bird-watching pleasure.

We in the Southwest are lucky to live in prime hummingbird country. At the equator there are over one hundred and sixty hummingbird species, and declines the farther north one travels. The same is true with an east/west perspective. There are fifteen species of hummingbirds in the West and only one in the East. We are smack in the middle of that region that supports the largest number of species.

To naturally attract hummingbirds to your garden, choose as many plants as possible from the following list and add them to your landscape. Consider the needs of the plant, the location, and your ability to view the birds in action. Once attracted to your garden, the small wonders will return season after season to delight and entertain you.

Color plants

bee balm (*Monarda*)
Begonia
blazing star (*Mentzilia*)
bleeding heart (*Dicentra spectabilis*)
butterfly weed (*Asclepias tuberosa*)
Canna
cardinal flower (*Lobelia cardinalis*)
carpet bugle (*Ajuga reptans*)
century plant (*Agave Americana*)
columbine (*Aquilegia sp.*)
Dahlia
fire pink (*Silene virginica*)
flowering tobacco (*Nicotiana alata*)
four o'clock (*Mirabilis jalapa*)
foxglove (*Digitalis sp.*)
gayfeather (*Liatris sp.*)
Gladiolus
hollyhock (*Alcea rosea*)
hyssop (*Hyssopus oficinalis*)
hummingbird flower (*Zauschneria*)
Impatiens
Lantana
larkspur (*Delphinium scaposum*)
lily (*Lilium sp.*)
lupine (*Lupinus sp.*)

monkey flower (*Mimulus sp.*)
nasturtium (*Tropaeolum*)
paintbrush (*Castilleja*)
Penstemon
petunia (*Petunia hybrida*)
Phlox
pincushion flower (*Scabiosa*)
red-hot poker (*Kniphofia uvaria*)
sage (*Salvia sp.*)
scented geranium (*Pelargonium sp.*)
spider flower (*Cleome hasslerana*)
sweet William (*Dianthus barbatus*)
verbena (*Glandularia [Verbena]*)
Yucca
Zinnia

Shrubs and vines
Abelia
azalea (*Rhododendron sp.*)
butterfly bush (*Buddleia davidii*)
cape honeysuckle (*Tecomaria capensis*)
Hibiscus
honeysuckle (*Lonicera sp.*)
jasmine (*Jasminum sp.*)
morning glory (*Ipomoea sp.*)
pink trumpet vine (*Podranea ricasoliana*)
scarlet runner bean (*Phaseolus coccineus*)
trumpet creeper (*Campsis radicans*)
trumpet honeysuckle (*Lonicera sempervirens*)
yellow or coral bells (*Tecoma stans var.*)

Trees
chaste tree (*Vitex agnus-castus*)
chinaberry (*Melia azedarach*)
Eucalyptus

foothill palo verde (*Cercidium microphyllum*)

hawthorn (*Crataegus sp.*)

horse chestnut (*Aesculus*)

locust (*Robinia*)

orange tree (*Citrus sinensis*)

silk oak (*Grevillea robusta*)

tree tobacco (*Nicotiana glauca*)

MESQUITE

WEEK **39**

I love mesquite trees (*Prosopis*). When driving by a natural mesquite bosque, I heave a sigh, let go of the tension, and take in the beauty around me. The unique, twisted trunks, widespread branches, and vivid green leaves soften the desert scene and soothe the eye. I think they also soothe the soul. Silhouetted against the sky—blue at midday or rosy-hued at sunset—each tree displays its unique personality.

Native to North and South America, mesquites for centuries have provided shade, shelter, and fuel, as well as basket and building materials. They've also been a source of food, providing bark and pods for animals, including livestock; pods for flour making; seeds for birds and rodents; and nectar-producing flowers for butterflies and honeybees. Few plants are as generous.

Mesquite trees adapt to a wide variety of difficult conditions, tolerating poor soil as well as varying degrees of drainage and exposure. Many varieties protect themselves by producing sharp thorns in their youth that remain until the tree is large enough to survive nibbling wildlife. These thorns, and a tendency toward rapid, uncontrolled growth, give mesquites a poor reputation. In the more humid regions of Texas, mesquites behave like noxious weeds, reseeding and propagating freely, then succumbing to Texas root rot. In drier climates, however, root rot is not a problem.

The rampant growth, when managed by proper planting and irrigation techniques, is not a significant concern. Many homeowners apply too little water too frequently, thus encouraging quick top-growth and inadequate root development. Trees with a large canopy and underdeveloped roots tend to blow over in heavy winds. Instead, mesquites should be planted in loosened, well-drained soil and irrigated infrequently to a depth of three feet.

Native mesquites possess long taproots that provide access to the water table as deep as one hundred and fifty feet. They also have a broad network of shallow, supportive, lateral roots that provide balance and keep the trees upright during storms. When living in an area with abundant underground water, mesquites grow to thirty feet or more. If the water table suddenly recedes, which frequently occurs in rapidly developing areas, the trees may die. More resilient than many species, mesquites recuperate from this severe stress if supplemental water is provided in time.

Mesquites produce sweet-smelling yellow flowers in the spring, followed by seed-producing pods that drop to the ground through summer and autumn. Providing summer shade and allowing the winter sun to shine through, they're a great choice near the house or patio. Their dark, textured bark creates a vivid contrast against green lacy leaflets, a combination that makes a bold visual statement, both tropical and desert in tone.

Argentine mesquite (*Prosopis alba*) is the fastest growing of the species, reaching a significant size in five years. It grows in a more upright manner than most mesquites, reducing the need for serious training, and has a dense crown of blue-green foliage. Nearly evergreen, it will shed some leaflets in winter, but reserves its main leaf drop for early spring, when new growth appears.

Chilean mesquite (*P. chilensis*) the hybrid most commonly sold in nurseries, grows rapidly upright to a height and width of 25–40 feet. Its scattered, fern-like foliage is evergreen, but drops during a sudden cold snap, and damage occurs when temperatures dip below 10°. This symmetrical tree produces just a few seedpods in attractive clusters that curve and seem to spin when they dry, making them useful in floral arrangements. Before using them as decor, place the dry pods in the freezer for a couple of hours to kill any insects that might be dining on the encased seeds.

Honey mesquite (*P. glandulosa*) is also called Texas mesquite. Native to that state, as well as Kansas, New Mexico, and Mexico, honey mesquite recently naturalized in Arizona. The large, bright green leaves on this beautiful tree hang from small branches in a manner reminiscent of California pepper. It is completely deciduous, making it appropriate near west-facing windows. Honey mesquite requires more water than others of its genus, and will remain small and shrubby if not adequately irrigated. While this tree's long thorns may seem like a negative attribute, they do provide a protected habitat to small animals and birds, making this variety a reliable attractant.

Screwbean mesquite (*P. pubescens*) is one of my favorite trees, and one for which I must find a spot in my garden. This petite, multi-trunked tree reaches a height and spread of only about fifteen feet, with fern-like leaves, spring and summer blossoms, and interesting coiled pods. The fascinating screwbeans are as attractive in a bowl on the dining room table as they are hanging on the tree. Their unusual appearance lends itself to a variety of decorator applications, making this tree a must for the garden crafter. Screwbean mesquite prefers well-drained soil and full sun, tolerating temperatures as low as 0° with no adverse reactions.

Velvet mesquite (*Prosopis velutina*) is the sophisticate of the family, looking much like an impressionist painting when viewed from a distance. The young growth, bright green and covered with fine hairs, develops into four-inch, gray-green "fronds" with 16–40 leaflets. This delicate foliage and shaggy bark camouflage one-inch thorns emerging at the leaf bases. Exercise caution at pruning time, since velvet mesquite prefers to be a large shrub and needs help developing its tree identity. In spring, this tree puts on a thick display of fragrant, three-inch yellow catkins, followed by five-inch tan and red streaked pods. Deciduous, velvet mesquite tolerates temperatures to 5°.

Regardless of the variety you plant in your garden, mesquites add personality and character to the landscape. They are appropriate anywhere except poolside, where the tiny leaflets settle and stain the plaster. If your goal is to create a desert scene, a tropical paradise, or a lush getaway space, mesquites definitely fill the bill.

SENNAS AND JOJOBAS

I find sennas, also known as cassias, to be a most interesting family because of their multinational roots. Various sennas are native to eastern Africa, Argentina, Australia, Brazil, Mexico, South America, the tropics, and the southwestern United States. The fact that sennas have multiplied and populated so many regions of the world is a testament to their versatility and adaptability, characteristics that make them exceptional landscape plants.

The usually evergreen sennas bloom in brilliant hues of yellow and gold, and range in size from the typical three-foot shrub to twenty-five-foot trees. Many of these varieties grow in the desert, making the genus a possibility for nearly every landscape situation. Sennas grow in any soil type, prefer good drainage, and need little or no supplemental irrigation or fertilization. Light, occasional pruning is their only maintenance requirement. If you can identify a space you want to fill, there is probably a senna that will fill it.

Spiny senna (*Senna armata, syn. Cassia armata*) grows natively in the sandy soil of Southwestern washes and plains 500–3000 feet in elevation. It reaches a mature height of only four feet and a width of six feet, with two-inch-long leaves made up of several thick leaflets clustered on thornless, sharp-tipped branches. This senna produces insignificant half-inch yellow blooms beginning in March, and once established, tolerates temperatures down to 15° and survives on rainwater alone. From a distance, it resembles ephedra, or Mormon tea.

The much smaller bauhin senna (*S. bauhinioides syn. C. bauhinioides*) reaches a diminutive one square foot at maturity. What it lacks in stature it makes up for in interest with its velvety green leaves and one-inch blossoms that continue from April through August, then again from September through late October. Bauhin senna dies back to the ground if winter temperatures drop below 20°, but the root is hardy to below 0°. It grows natively in the gravely soils of Mexico and the desert Southwest at elevations between 2000–5500 feet. Bauhin senna prefers full sun, well-drained soil and light bi-weekly summer irrigation.

The bright green, ferny leaves of two-flowered senna (*S. biflora syn. C. biflora*) reveal its native distribution, which includes moister regions of Chihuahua and Sonora, Mexico, as well as tropical America. Temperatures below 15° damage it, with root hardiness to below 0°. Since it flowers from October through April, two-flowered senna requires a protected location, preferably near a building from which winter blossoms can be enjoyed. Two-flowered senna's inch-long, bright yellow flowers occur in pairs, providing the source for its name. Plant this desert beauty in perennial beds or with evergreen shrubs, in either full sun or partial shade, and water every other week.

Desert senna (*S. covesii syn. C. covesii*) is a good choice near walkways and patios, as an accent plant in natural landscapes, or in large numbers to make a bold statement. Its compound leaves and bright yellow flowers are interesting and attractive to both people and pollinators, and it is tolerant of most soils, preferring full sun. With a little supplemental water in the summer, the April through October blossoms develop more profusely and live longer. This small, woolly-leafed plant is hardy to the low twenties, and pops up all over the garden if located near a water source.

Lindheimer senna (*S. lindheimeriana syn. C. lindheimeriana*) resembles desert senna, but is darker green and larger, attaining a mature size of three feet high by two feet wide. Its dark green, velvety leaves are six inches long and hold clusters of one-inch bright yellow flowers from June to September. Well-drained soil and a little summer irrigation encourage rapid growth and abundant flowering. Dying back to the ground when the temperature reaches 20°, Lindheimer senna quickly recovers in the spring, rapidly filling its small space in the garden. Because its leaves are so nice to touch, this plant is especially appropriate along walkways and near patios.

From a distance, many people mistake shrubby senna (*S. wislizenii syn. C. wislizenii*) for a creosote bush, since it grows to a similar height and width, has the same general form, and produces a flower of similar color about the same time of year. The leaves of shrubby senna are lighter green and more oval than creosote, however, and they drop when temperatures dip below freezing, allowing the interesting dark bark to show through. It adapts to most soil types, prefers full sun but will tolerate shade, and grows denser with a little summertime irrigation. I think they look nice when planted along with evergreens to provide contrast in color and texture.

Jojoba (*Simmondsia chinensis*) is a 6–10-foot evergreen shrub that is native to the washes of southern California, Arizona, Baja California, and Sonora, Mexico. It prefers full sun, but will tolerate partial shade. Initially, provide regular irrigation to establish the dark green, leathery-leafed plants, followed by infrequent, deep irrigations to maintain growth and fruit production. The yellow-green flowers develop from December to July, followed by one-inch fruits on the female plants that resemble unripe dates. Both male and female plants are necessary for fruit production, an enterprise that has met with some commercial success.

Native Americans ate the fruits raw or boiled, and settlers to the region later dried and ground the fruit into course flour that was mixed with egg yolks,

239

sugar, and milk to create a tasty hot drink. None of these uses led to its commercialization, however. It was the high oil content of the fruit that led commercial farmers to plant jojoba by the thousands in Southern California deserts, in an effort to produce a cheap, renewable substitute for whale oil. Only slightly successful, these farmers developed alternative uses for the oil in cosmetics and cleaning products, and some farms still produce moderate crops.

For the home gardener, the oil in the fruits is of little importance, since its landscape value lies in its tough, hardy nature and undemanding reliability. Jojoba's dense foliage makes a solid screen and windbreak, while its texture and color make it attractive planted near homes, walkways, or outdoor entertainment areas. Devoid of spines, it is a good plant for children's play areas, bike paths, and parks. Since jojoba needs little water, is hardy to 15°, and requires no regular upkeep, it is frequently used in medians and roadsides. If you have a stretch of parkway to plant, interplant jojoba with native trees for an always attractive, fuss-free, and durable landscape.

STILL MORE PESTS

As we approach the end of September, your gardening activities transition from a warm season focus to cool weather preparedness. Start to water less, replace heat-loving annual color with cold-tolerant species, plant cool-season vegetable crops, and winterize your beds with mulch. As your gardening activities change, so do the pests. The many critters that plagued the garden through the long hot summer are soon to be replaced by their cold-loving counterparts.

Grasshoppers will make their last parade through the garden. They ultimately deposit eggs in the leaf litter under shrubs and trees. By clearing out areas where leaves pile up, you reduce the number of grasshoppers in the garden next spring and summer. Add this material to your compost bin, and as it heats up the eggs will die and the leaves will deteriorate into rich, dark humus that adds nutrients to the soil.

Salt marsh caterpillars and sphinx caterpillars are still present in the garden, particularly if temperatures remain high. Although their numbers will soon diminish, they can cause significant damage in the meantime. Look for these hornworms in the vegetable garden as well as on perennials, and hand-pick them to prevent further damage, since the traditional caterpillar insecticide, Bt, is ineffective on the larger worms.

Orange dog caterpillars are at their peak now, chewing away at the foliage of citrus trees since emerging from the little eggs left behind in previous weeks by the magnificent swallowtail butterflies. If the trees are very young, remove the caterpillars when you see them. More mature trees can handle the mild defoliation and you will benefit from continued swallowtail populations in upcoming years.

Green aphid populations are diminishing, while gray aphid numbers are increasing. Use insecticidal soap and rely on natural enemies as much as possible. If you can avoid using toxins for this common pest, a natural balance can usually be struck, and it never becomes a serious problem. The number of lacewings, ladybugs, lizards, and hummingbirds that aphids attract impresses me. However, I diligently monitor the rose garden and vegetable beds because in these two places the aphid population sometimes gets ahead of the beneficials. Insecticidal soap always does the trick.

Whiteflies know no seasonal limitations in my garden, and I have some infestation at all times. Still, protected locations are ideal whitefly environments, and in my garden the plants of choice are always in pots. I use insecticidal soap, dipping the whole crown of the plants into a bucket whenever possible. If the plant or pot is too large for this approach, I saturate the plants with the soapy liquid to get rid of the little pests.

As temperatures begin to fall and cool-weather crops go into the ground, cabbage loopers and armyworms may enter the garden scene and demand your attention. You will see the former looping along, inchworm fashion, on vegetables and annual flowers. In my garden, they are particularly fond of petunias and snap dragons. Handpick them if possible, or liberally spray the plants with Bt or Sevin. Army worms are the little caterpillars that march along in groups, heading straight for the fresh, green seedlings emerging in your garden beds. Control them, too, with Bt or Sevin after reading directions regarding edibles.

October

- Plant seasonal annual color
- Plant cool-season vegetables
- Plant perennials, cacti, agave, winter-hardy trees, shrubs, and vines
- Plant herbs
- Plant strawberries
- Plant prepared bulbs in amended beds
- Sow wildflower seeds
- Harvest pomegranates
- Overseed Bermuda grass
- Reduce irrigation frequency
- Remove citrus fruit damaged by birds
- Remove and discard diseased plants
- Dry gourds in cool, dry location
- Mulch for winter protection

October

'Dig-less' vegetable gardening

WEEK 40 Many people want to begin gardening before they've firmly established a landscape plan, or designed and built their garden beds. For these people, temporary garden beds allow a full planting without building raised beds, double digging, or amending native soil.

A variety of material works well when building temporary raised beds. One of the most successful temporary gardens I've seen belonged to a friend who owned livestock and wanted to dabble in gardening near her corrals. She bought extra bales of straw on her regular trip to the feed store and used them as the outer walls of her raised bed, butting them together to make a small rectangle. She then filled the interior space with potting soil, added fertilizer, and stirred it all together. Finally, she laid irrigation lines, diverted from her animal's watering system, right on top of the soil. This was especially effective for a couple of reasons. The soil settled after the initial watering, and rather than add more, this smart gardener allowed the soil line to remain several inches below the top of the straw bales. When weather threatened, depending on the season, she laid either shade cloth or sheeting over the top of the beds to protect her plants. The only drawback was that plants on the edges received extra shade, increasing their maturation time.

This same design lent itself to effective cold frames when panes of clear acrylic were placed over the tops of the bales. The acrylic intensified the sun's heat during the day, and retained that heat at night. Since she tended the animals several times a day, it was convenient to raise or remove the lightweight acrylic to vent the beds on particularly warm days. With this simple arrangement and the addition of soil each season, she successfully raised warm-weather herbs and flowers throughout the winter and continued to use the beds for several years. They looked right at home in the barnyard, and allowed her to grow several crops before her permanent garden was completed. When she was ready to move into her "real" garden, she used the straw-bale beds as compost bins, adding yard waste and muck from stalls. In the end, this little bit of land produced much.

In an equally interesting approach to "dig-less" gardening, another friend leveled some land in her side yard and set out heavy, black plastic garbage bags. After poking drainage holes in the bottom of each bag, she added about two feet of commercially prepared potting soil and soil amendments, effectively turning each bag into a relatively sturdy vegetable bed. Of course, size limited the number of plants grown in each bag; but this approach enabled her to grow several varieties of lettuce, carrots, radishes, turnips, and herbs.

Because it was a small garden in a small space, and the little beds were somewhat delicate, she carefully watered the bags by hand rather than using an irrigation system. But the simplicity of the system makes the garbage bag approach easy to implement in almost any landscape, especially in small, in-town gardens.

Many "quick and dirty" gardeners have used an adaptation of this technique for years: Buy a large bag of potting soil, preferably one that already contains fertilizer. Lay it in the desired, full-sun location, and cut away the face of the bag, being careful to leave enough support around the edges to contain the soil within. Poke holes at the bottom of the bag to allow excess water to drain away, and then plant the seeds of your choice, making sure they require no more than the available depth. Some possibilities include round radishes, turnips, small carrots, lettuces, chamomile, cilantro, parsley, and short varieties of dill. Water regularly, using a gentle sprinkling can, or a hose with a shower attachment. Wait for sprouts, thin, water more, and harvest.

While on a trip through a hot, dry area of southern California, I saw still another "dig-less" garden using materials that would otherwise have been considered garbage. Old tires, of fairly large diameter, stood in three-high stacks completely surrounding the front lawn of this creative gardener's landscape. From these mini-towers grew an abundance of florals and edibles. I don't know what was used as soil, but it obviously was rich enough to support a wide variety of flowers and vegetables. This little garden looked like it could produce enough for a small family, with some to spare. The "beds" were easily accessible and protected from rodents that traditionally plagued gardens in this neighborhood.

What could have been a rather unattractive approach to gardening was made lovely by the use of trailing varieties that cascaded over the sides of the tires, camouflaging them with foliage and blossoms. Varieties intermingled, creating a densely planted container garden within each stack. It looked like a new rendition of the old kitchen gardens, where flowers, herbs, and vegetables grew up together.

Of course, the most common method of "dig-less" gardening involves the use of large containers. Several intensively planted pots provide a patio or apartment gardener with enough herbs and vegetables to supplement the household menu. To increase the yield and makes the potted garden more productive, water with diluted, water-soluble fertilizer.

A gardener with a little more experience can begin with seeds and grow more interesting varieties. A novice can use any of these methods, planted with seedlings from the local nursery and experience gardening success. Of course, radishes and carrots are easy to grow from seed, and should be planted by even first-timers. A unique sense of accomplishment accompanies that first harvest; the salad made from homegrown greens. This practice of growing ones own food, regardless of the operation's scale, is fulfilling and rewarding in ways physical, emotional, and spiritual.

Those black nursery pots

I don't use black nursery pots to contain specimen plants in my garden. The garden should be beautiful and inviting, and black nursery pots don't fulfill either of these requirements. I stick to terra cotta and stone containers, or I put the plants right into the ground and raised beds. But I am contemplating an exception to this rule, after having seen a productive winter garden utilizing those very containers.

I enjoy the friendship of a fellow gardener, retired after a long, travel-filled career. This gentleman always yearned to garden, but wasn't home long enough to give it a good effort. Upon retirement, he took advantage of every day at home and completely devoted himself to his garden. We are very different sorts of gardeners, he and I. I look at gardening as an opportunity to decorate and beautify, experiment, and produce. He is strictly into production. He often asks me, "If you can't eat it, why grow it?"

This utilitarian perspective drives him to use his land with almost scientific precision as he builds raised beds with standard-sized material to avoid waste, and visits commercial nurseries to copy their practices and order irrigation supplies. This is where the black nursery pots come in.

The back of this man's lot looks like a commercial nursery. He has several two-by-two rows of closely placed five- and fifteen-gallon black nursery pots. Each pot is watered by a modified drip irrigation system that lies atop the ground, between pots, and applies an appropriate amount of water to each plant. He never dug irrigation trenches, nor buried miles of PVC. A timer, which he resets with variations in the weather, controls the entire irrigation system. He turns it off when his pots lie fallow.

His incredible garden produces unusual varieties of intensely planted vegetables and herbs grown from seed ordered by mail. He also grows heirloom varieties, increasing their yield by altering the immediate microclimate to better match their native environments. And he fertilizes with a tea made of organic components that he applies with a watering can every two weeks.

My friend is a "snowbird," meaning he leaves the desert Southwest when it starts to heat up. Because he has no warm-weather garden to consider, he worries little about the heat that builds up in black pots. When they're too hot to use, he's not here to use them. But during cool seasons, the pots create and hold heat not unlike hot beds and greenhouses, and he finds that they increase his yield and reduce growing time. Strategically placed frost protection allows him to grow tender vegetables almost continuously. Because those seeds need heat to germinate, he starts them indoors and moves them out when they are ready. The summer squash that he actually grew in early winter was impressive.

FALL AND WINTER COLOR

It's a treat to feel the subtle changes in the weather, and I usually respond by replanting my color beds and pots for the cool season. After the long, hot summer and early fall, I'm happy to say goodbye to what remains of summer color plants and replace them with fresh, new seedlings. If I had the time a few weeks ago, I propagated from seeds and have little plants ready to go. But this is not usually the case. More often than not, I plant seeds directly into the ground and buy seedlings from a local nursery.

Varieties that do well in our desert cool season are quite different from the summer choices. Although I have over-wintered many summer plants, I stick to cold-tolerant material when I'm planting now. If summer flowers still have a lot of life in them, as is often the case with zinnias, I leave them for the time being. Cool-weather flowers can be planted as late as February and still have time to put on a colorful floral display before the weather becomes too warm.

As a border plant or low filler in pots and beds, nothing beats *Alyssum*. Ranging 2–6 inches in height, alyssum comes in white and purple varieties. I plant it more intensively than suggested to create thick, dense mats of color beneath other flowering annuals.

Bells-of-Ireland (*Moluccella laevis*), two-foot tall winter annuals that contrast nicely with alyssum, produce bell-like, green flowers in groups of six from the plant's base to the tip of its spikes. The unusually colored flowers demand attention in the garden and make excellent bouquets. They also dry well, making them a versatile plant. Refrigerate the seeds for a week or two before planting bells-of-Ireland and fertilize every two weeks with a complete fertilizer for continuous bloom.

Calendula (*Calendula officinalis*) is one of my favorite winter annuals. I love the beautiful yellow to orange blossoms whose petals I use in salads and as a garnish, and I enjoy tea made from the dried blossoms. This herbal workhorse develops blossoms on sturdy stems that look nice in cut flower arrangements and provide spots of vivid color against brilliant green foliage in the garden. I've had luck planting them in full morning sun with dappled afternoon shade. My winter flowerbeds are not complete until the calendula bloom.

Sweet and spicy pink (*Dianthus*) behaves as a perennial in many parts of my garden, beginning to bloom again now after having taken a few weeks off. In full afternoon sun, these clumping plants maintain lovely apple-green foliage when fertilized regularly. Their flowers, which come in lavender, pink, purple, red, and white, stay fresh in a vase for many days and sturdy on the plant for many more. For the carnation lover, pink is a nice desert substitute to put in the ground now.

Although technically herbs, cilantro (*Coriandrum sativum*) and dill (*anethum graveolens*) always find their way into my color pots and floral arrangements. I plant lots of cilantro and both the tall and shorter, fern-leaf varieties of dill. I sow fresh seed between other seedlings to create the same effect in the garden that florists create with baby's breath. The contrast between lacy cilantro and dill and sturdier flowers is striking. Their white umbrella-shaped blossoms add even more interest later in the season.

Dusty miller (*Artemesia stellerana*) is an excellent plant for dry sections of the flower garden. Its silver-gray foliage and gold, clustered blossoms create an interesting contrast. Many people mix this drought-tolerant plant in their flowerbeds, and it does just fine with the additional irrigation. I reserve this plant for garden spaces where irrigation is insufficient for other varieties. It beautifully plays this fill-in role, adding interest, color, and texture to locations that would otherwise remain barren.

There are few things more attractive in the winter than a corner bed symmetrically planted with flowering kale (*Brassica oleracea*). The contrast created by the triangle-shaped bed and the round, mounding kales standing in straight lines is striking, and the developing heads, variegated purples, greens, and creams create additional interest. I like these plants unaccompanied by other varieties, but if you must use another plant in the bed, line the edges with alyssum or curled parsley, and let the kale steal the show.

Johnny-jump-ups, violas, and pansies—all varieties of *Viola*—look up from the garden with their lovely faces and beg for adoration. Striking combinations of blue, purple, yellow, and white contribute to their beauty as these vivid all-time favorites emerge from deep green foliage. They've reigned supreme in color gardens for decades, and are favored in my house because of their versatility. We love to see them spread in the garden and relish making tiny little arrangements in particularly small, glass vases. We carefully select perfect blossoms to press and dry for future projects, and to coat with simple syrup and sugar as a garnish for sweet treats.

To make a bold statement in the back of the bed, consider larkspur (*Consolida ambigua*). Also called annual delphiniums, these plants grow sturdy and upright and set densely packed flower spikes in blue, pink, rose, salmon, red, and white. They require full sun and moderate water in well-drained soil, and are heat resistant, which is nice when we get those occasional mid-80° days in the middle of winter.

Another plant with a similar flowering habit is baby snapdragon (*Linaria maroccana*). This short, wispy plant prefers partial shade and looks best planted in large numbers, close together. Flowers develop in shades of blue, cream, gold, mauve, orange, pink, purple, red, rose, yellow, and violet.

My winter vegetable bed is never without a row or two of nasturtiums (*Tropaeolum*) cascading over the sides of the raised edge. I always plant both the single and double varieties and have great luck with seeds purchased from Burpee and Shepherd's Garden Seeds, as well as those purchased from my local hardware store. Mail-order plants get bigger and produce larger, more profuse blooms, but the others do in a pinch. These trailing plants add color and charm to my raised beds and spicy character to salads and vegetable dishes, with their distinct peppery flavor that I combine with arugula for real bite.

A large bed of petunias planted outside my kitchen window provides constant, reliable color and fragrance. These easy plants flower for months on end, and come in candy colors of purple, red, and white. Some are solid. Some are striped. All bloom prolifically with minimal water and infrequent fertilization. Increase both, and you'll have the most abundant flowerbed ever.

Iceland poppies (*Papaver nudicaule*), with their tissue-thin, crinkly petals are both delicate and tough. They withstand rain, wind, sleet, and hail, losing their current blossoms, but immediately sending up new stems. A couple of tricks encourage success with these brilliantly colored annuals. I have planted them from seed, but now rely on nursery six-packs. The seeds are tiny and difficult to place precisely, and because of their size, irrigation usually moves them to a new location. Besides, the nursery packs are easier to work with. Plant the seedlings on eight-inch centers in a somewhat protected area, then water, fertilize, and deadhead frequently. Keep the bed damp and provide nutrients every couple of weeks. Remove spent blossoms and their stems daily. By following these steps, you stimulate the plants to flower continuously until the heat of late spring puts an end to their productivity.

Snapdragons (*Antirrhinum majus*), stock (*Matthiola incana*), and statice (*Limonium*) are standards in the cool-season flower garden. I usually put them in now and enjoy them through spring. With regular irrigation and bi-weekly fertilization, these three plants produce an abundance of flowers that make beautiful cut arrangements. Snapdragons are available in almost every color and grow in spikes on narrow-leafed upright branches. Stock, usually lavender or white, is the bloom that gives florist shops their distinct aroma. One or two of these fragrant stems can perfume an entire room. This quality alone is enough to merit their inclusion in the garden. Statice is an excellent filler plant, adding color and texture to the garden bed as well as cut arrangements.

At last we reach the sweet peas (*Lathyrus*). Second only to stock in fragrance, sweet peas shriek "old fashioned" and evoke one of my favorite childhood memories. I remember how my mother would attach string from the eaves of the house down to a board on the ground and would plant a single sweet pea seed at the base of each string. In just a couple of weeks the little seedlings would emerge, sending up tendrils to grasp at the support. Over the next few months, they would climb those strings, creating a wall of greenery in front of my brothers' bedroom window. When the fragrant blossoms opened, so did that window, and the sweet scent wafted through the house, accentuating the bouquets we cut and brought into the kitchen.

Whenever I smell sweet peas, I fondly see my mother stretching that string. I don't stretch string on my house. The eaves are too far up. Instead, I have a trellis at the back of a raised bed on which I grow my heirloom seeds. They cling and climb just as I remember, and produce delicately colored blossoms that smell just as sweet. Growing them provides a link to a happy time in my early life and, hopefully, creates similar memories for my children.

What to plant in October

WEEK
41

After many years as a desert dweller, I've become comfortable with the gardening calendar and routine, and it would be hard for me to move to a place where weather prevented me from planting in the fall. I love to garden at this time of year. Because the extremely high heat has passed and the plants are back in action, I relish the opportunities to bring in large floral bouquets. I enjoy successive planting in the vegetable beds to insure nonstop harvest through the winter and spring, and I like to add to the landscape during this more temperate season.

Many planting possibilities present themselves now, including the vegetable beds, where you can add additional rows of beets, radishes, and turnips every two weeks to provide continuous harvest once the original sowing matures. Some lettuces are "cut and come again" varieties, which means as you harvest the outer leaves, the plants develop new growth. Successive planting is not necessary when these grow in the garden, but if you've planted varieties that require you to harvest the entire plant, additional seed sowing will lengthen your production time. Several other types of seeds to plant now include carrots, chard, kale, kohlrabi, onions, parsley, parsnips, scallions, and spinach. If you prefer a head start, plant seedlings of broccoli, brussels sprouts, cabbage, chard, kale, kohlrabi, or spinach.

Other vegetable choices include peas and fava beans, which you can plant through November since the seeds germinate in cool soil. These plants provide a dual service in the fall and winter garden, as they fix nitrogen in the soil in addition to producing delicious fruit over a long period of time. In overly simplified terms, these members of the legume family collect nitrogen from the atmosphere and deposit it into the soil. Since nitrogen is a vital plant nutrient, this action increases soil fertility, making it richer and more nutritious for spring planting. Many farmers plant nitrogen-fixing plants as a cover crop, or "green fertilizer." When not planning a crop for a section of the winter garden, I plant favas or peas to enrich the soil.

Fava beans, also called broad beans or horse beans, are not beans at all, but a type of vetch. They acquired the name horse beans after years of cultivation for animal feed. These pod-producing plants grow to a bushy four feet, maturing in one hundred and twenty days. Plant the large seeds an inch deep, on eighteen-inch centers. Since fava beans are insect pollinated, interplant them with dill or annual flowers to attract pollinators. Harvest the pods when they are immature and prepare them as you would sugar snap peas. Shell the mature pods and prepare them, either fresh or dried, like lima beans. Some Mediterranean recipes call for drying the beans and grinding them into flour that replaces the more conventional cornmeal or wheat flour.

Peas of any sort are rarely prepared in our kitchen because we eat them fresh and raw. We are notorious for picking and eating as we go along, consuming the entire batch before we make it to the house. Sometimes, though, a small basket of peas hits the kitchen table and we manage to rinse them off and toss them into a green salad, or a bowl, to be eaten on their own. I like them best with a little vinaigrette. Someday I will dedicate more garden space to peas so that we can enjoy them in all the recipes that I continue to collect. Until then, they are the reward for the day's harvester.

Aside from the vegetable garden, this time of year lends itself to the planting of hardy perennials. Several perennials that do well when planted now are yarrow, Jupiter's beard, chocolate flower, coreopsis, pink, Mt. Lemmon marigold, penstemon varieties, cape plumbago, and Cleveland sage. All of these plants establish their root systems through fall and winter, and then burst forth with fresh, new growth in the spring.

I usually purchase and plant deciduous fruit trees in January when they are available bare-root, since they are cheaper than the potted trees that are available year-round. Sometimes, though, retailers wanting to clear out their inventory have incredible deals that cannot be rejected. Many of my gardener friends now prefer to plant their fruit trees at this time of year to take advantage of the good price and the already developed root system. If you decide to plant deciduous fruit trees now, make sure that the bargain is really a bargain. Many of the plants left in the nurseries are varieties not recommended for the desert. That is why they are still there. Check the label of each tree you purchase to ensure that the variety is appropriate for our unique climate. If it is not labeled, or isn't one of the varieties recommended below, don't buy it.

Recommended varieties include:
Apple: Anna, Ein Shemer, Golden Dorsett
Apricot: Castlebrite, Gold Kist, Katy
Peach: August Pride, Babcock, Desert Gold, Earligrande, Flordaprince,
   Midpride, Royal Gold, Tropic Snow, Sweet Ventura
Plum: Santa Rosa, Satsuma
Pomegranate: Wonderful
Quince: Orange, Pineapple, Smyrna

Dig your holes only as deep as the root ball and five times as wide. Place the tree in the center of the hole, being careful not to disturb the root ball, and replace the original soil patting it down firmly with shovel or foot. Create a watering well around the base of the tree and fill it with water. When this water has drained, add additional soil to bring the level up to the point that existed in the container, then fill the well again. Water the tree every three days for two weeks, then once a week until it goes dormant. While dormant, water once every three or four weeks and wait until January to prune.

You can also plant winter-hardy trees, shrubs, and vines now. The best way to guarantee that what you are interested in planting will survive the extreme winter cold is to learn the temperature tolerance of the particular plants so that you know what temperature causes dormancy, and what temperature causes death. Without an established root system, a newly added plant will not perform optimally and should be allowed a few degrees leeway. If, for example, the plant description says "hardy to 15°," I wouldn't plant it until spring since temperatures normally drop below 18° in my location. The struggle to establish itself, when combined with very low temperatures, puts too much strain on a new root system, so it is better to wait until the coldest part of the year has passed.

To expand the native garden, consider adding some cacti or succulents to the landscape. It is often easier to do this in the fall, because we can easily envision the upcoming frost, which is the limiting factor for many of these plants. Springtime warmth reminds us of the impending summer heat and washes away memories of below-freezing temperatures. We often fail to consider one end of the weather spectrum when preparing for the other. Now, however, we know the freeze will come. This is significant since many cacti and succulents are frost sensitive, requiring protection in the winter. This dictates planting in pots so that the specimen can be moved when weather threatens, or carefully choosing a location in a microclimate that provides adequate protection.

I plant agaves this time of year. I always have friends whose mature plants have developed pups and need to be divided. This is the ideal time to do that. I gently dig up the small upstart, taking care not to damage the roots of the mother plant. Choosing a sight with afternoon shade, I loosen a large area and then dig a small hole in the middle of that. The plant goes in, followed by the native soil and a thorough watering. Unless the plant shows signs of withering, I water once every two or three weeks through the winter. In the spring, when the agave is better established, I water only in times of drought.

Preparations for cooler weather

People who've never lived in the desert consider it a place of high heat and limited moisture, but these perceptions represent only half the story. We also deal with torrential summer rains that fall on poorly draining soils, and below-freezing winter temperatures. The desert demands much of the gardener and is not a place for the weak-willed. Attention must be paid. There are several tasks to be done before the sudden and surprising change of seasons arrives and cold blasts down on the garden.

One of the first things I do in October is lay a thick layer of mulch around all my plants, except citrus, since mulching citrus trees encourages *Phytopthera*, or foot rot. The mulch conserves moisture by reducing evaporation and protects plant roots by maintaining soil warmth. It also dresses up the garden like a coat of white wash on a picket fence.

By the time I have laid the mulch, temperatures have dropped sufficiently to allow me to cut back on irrigation. I usually increase the time between waterings by a day or two, continuing this practice through the fall and winter, as temperatures decline. By adjusting the automatic timer during the cool season, I use less than half the water the garden requires when it is warmer. Many people, intimidated by their automatic sprinkling systems, never change them. The newer systems are much less complicated than they used to be and are easier to adjust. You'll save a lot of that precious natural resource and greatly reduce the water bill. If you have a system that is controlled by an old, difficult-to-adjust timer, consider replacing it with one that you understand. Through reduced water bills, you'll save more than the cost of the new timer in the first year, making the effort and investment worthwhile.

If you have cold frames, get the covers out of storage and clean them for upcoming use. Greenhouse owners should prepare for the most productive season. Make sure the venting system is in order and the irrigation still works, and then consider what you will bring in from house and garden and what you will propagate and grow. You can begin all of these activities now, as well as starting tomatoes, peppers, and eggplants in this wonderful, artificial environment.

A GREEN WINTER LAWN

Many homeowners plant Bermuda grass and allow it to go dormant in the winter, considering this more natural and fuss-free. An equal number want a green and attractive lawn year-round, and are willing to commit the necessary time to prepare the turf, fertilize, and water through the winter. To keep your lawn green through the winter, overseed with perennial rye seed while the ground temperatures are still warm enough to facilitate rapid seed germination. If you wait until November, it will take much longer for the little green blades to rise above the browning Bermuda.

The first step in preparing your lawn is verticutting. This process lightly cuts through the thatch and runners of the Bermuda, allowing seed and water to penetrate its thick mat. I use a hard-tined rake to verticut my lawn, pushing the teeth down into the turf and pulling gently. This takes some time, but is quite effective. Machines are available through equipment rental companies that perform the same task in much less time. After verticutting the lawn, mow it very closely. Sometimes the thatch is too thick, requiring an initial mowing at a slightly lower-than-normal height, followed by a second mowing on the lowest setting.

The lawn is now ready to be seeded. Perennial rye, although nearly twice as expensive as annual rye, is recommended because of its darker green color, sturdier blade, and tolerance for lower temperatures. It also consumes less water than the annual variety, thus saving the extra money you spent buying the seed. I also think it holds on longer in the spring, making the Bermuda's transition out of dormancy less noticeable.

Spread the perennial rye seed and apply ammonium phosphate at a rate of one-half pound per hundred square feet. This will give the grass a boost when it germinates. Cover the seed with a thin layer of mulch or sand to retain moisture. Do not use manure, since it is often too hot or salt-laden, and may burn the emerging plants. Manure is also a frequent source of weed seeds; another reason to avoid its use at this time.

To keep the seeds moist, water the newly planted lawn for five minutes, 3–5 times a day during the first ten days. Reduce the frequency of irrigation once the seedlings have emerged, watering often enough to keep the lawn healthy and green. After the tender, new lawn has developed, mow it to a height of two inches, every 7–10 days and fertilize it monthly with a high-phosphate or winter lawn fertilizer. When temperatures warm up in February, switch to a high nitrogen fertilizer, such as ammonium sulfate.

Two issues in land development make erosion control necessary. When homes are built on hilltops, steep grades, or near natural waterways, the terrain dictates drainage and runoff. Landscaping within those parameters often leads to plans using plant material to control that drainage. Other homes have been built close together, on artificially compacted lots that stack their way up a hill, leaving each homeowner with a steep side yard that degrades with heavy rain or irrigation when not properly covered or planted to retain the soil. Challenging planting sites are usually more difficult to water efficiently, and require good drip systems or well-built basins. Each of these scenarios calls for plants that develop root systems capable of holding the soil in place.

Landscaping concerns always begin with the upper story, or trees. While no specific trees inherently retain dirt, I suggest native or desert-adapted trees that require less water and thrive in our soil. These species establish more quickly, which translates into rapid root development and more stable soil. Not having to irrigate heavily over a long period of time also gives you a big advantage when you plant natives rather than more exotic trees that will always need extra water and care. It is also wise to plant trees needing little pruning and long-term management since fragile or steep locations are compromised by foot traffic.

Some good trees for erosion control in the desert include acacias, Chinese pistache, desert willow, mesquite, palo brea, palo verdes, *Rhus lancea,* and *Rhus ovata*. All of these trees require regular irrigation for the first two years and can then survive on normal rainfall. They need little or no fertilizer and pruning and, when properly planted, are not damaged by winds. Since this list includes evergreen, semi-deciduous, and deciduous species, at least one will be appropriate for almost any landscape style or need.

After selecting and planting trees, consider adding shrubs to fill in the understory. Several shrubs grow well in the desert and help to retain soil and prevent erosion. *Cistus*, or rockrose, is an evergreen shrub native to the Mediterranean that grows to a height and spread of 2–6 feet, depending on variety. In spring, this gray-green plant produces bright pink, purple, red, or white flowers. Often used as a dry-bank cover, the sun-loving, drought-tolerant rockrose grows fast in even the driest, most alkaline soil when given minimal water. It is at home in rock gardens, along paths, and in naturalized landscapes.

Cotoneaster, a member of the family *Rosaceae*, is evergreen, semi-evergreen, or deciduous, depending upon variety. Although not all cotoneaster plants are appropriate for the desert Southwest, several grow beautifully in our alkaline soils and extreme temperatures. Types and sizes range from groundcovers to tall shrubs, all of which grow vigorously with little or no care. They produce numerous white or pink spring blossoms that look like small roses, followed by fall and winter berries that are useful in dry arrangements and look striking when left on the plants. Cotoneasters prefer poor soil and infrequent irrigation and need only an occasional pruning to enhance their naturally arching shape.

California buckwheat, saffron buckwheat, and wild buckwheat—all *Erio-gonum* varieties—are natives of the western United States and grow best in loose, gravely soil. They tolerate alkaline soils, high temperatures, and wind, while requiring small amounts of water. These clumping shrubs have dark gray-green leaves, grow to a height of three feet and produce pink, white, or yellow flowers from May to October. The flowers, often dried and used in arrangements, turn red and tan when left on the plant and allowed to develop into seedpods. These seedpods drop and flutter in the wind, frequently producing volunteer seedlings that transplant well. This habit makes the buckwheat family particularly useful on a naturalized hillside.

Another family of Mediterranean plants useful for erosion control is *Juniperus*. Woody, evergreen juniper shrubs vary in texture to include both needles and scaly foliage. They are susceptible to root rot, and require careful irrigation to avoid constantly damp soil and the accompanying fungal growth. In the summer, junipers prefer scattered or afternoon shade and sometimes require copper sprays to control twig blight in July and August. Another common problem associated with junipers is aphid or spider mite infestations, which are easily controlled with insecticidal soap. When buying junipers, be aware of your microclimate's winter temperatures so that you select appropriate plants from more than one hundred available varieties.

The popular and versatile lantana, in its many sizes and colors, develops roots that effectively control erosion, as does creeping mahonia (*Mahonia repens*). Mahonia is easy to grow in lean, dry soil and requires average amounts of water. It looks good all year, with evergreen holly-like leaves and yellow spring flowers that develop into blue-black or red berry-like fruits. Birds love the fruit and also do a good job of controlling the only common pest, a small looper caterpillar. You can also apply Bt if an infestation becomes severe.

Another holly-like plant that is exceptional for erosion control is the evergreen hollyleaf redberry (*Rhamnus*). This Arizona and California hillside native grows 3–15 feet at maturity, depending on available water and location. An established plant requires little-to-no supplemental irrigation, no fertilization, and is attractive when allowed to grow in its natural form or when pruned or shaped. Developing small, inconspicuous flowers in the spring, hollyleaf redberry is often grown for its berry-like fruit that attracts many birds to the garden.

Rosemary (*Rosmarinus officianlis*) is also a favorite plant for hillsides and other areas that are susceptible to erosion. Rosemary is ruggedly attractive, imparting a Mediterranean feel to any garden. Good drainage is vital for these sturdy plants that can tolerate high heat, direct sunlight, stiff winds, and poor soil. You can control growth by pinching tips back or cutting old growth back to a side branch or the base of the plant. Useful as a culinary or medicinal herb, rosemary serves many purposes when planted in the desert garden. The small clusters of blue, pink, or white flowers set against glossy gray-green leaves attract bees, butterflies, and hummingbirds. It is an excellent and useful filler plant, providing aromatic foliage for years.

If you still have more ground to cover after planting trees and shrubs, or if you just want to carpet the area with growth, consider ground covers. By virtue of their growth habits, ground covers shade themselves and spread densely enough to prevent evaporation. Three particular ground covers effectively control erosion in steep, arid locations. They are crown vetch, ice plant, and *Myoporum parvifolium*.

Crown vetch (*Coronilla varia*) if a member of the legume family, related to beans, clovers, and peas, making it beneficial when planted beneath other landscape material as it fixes nitrogen in the soil. It spreads rather aggressively by creeping roots and rhizomes that develop stems as tall as two feet, and its small, oval leaflets grow on long leaves that bear lavender or pink flowers in the spring that develop into bundles of brown seed pods that readily reseed the area. A perennial, crown vetch goes dormant in the winter and looks dry and tangled until spring, when it should be sheared back, fertilized, and deeply watered to stimulate rapid new growth. Once established, crown vetch is difficult to get rid of, so be sure you really like it before getting it started.

Ice plant (*Malephora*) is a succulent that has been planted along steep embankments adjacent to Southern California freeways for decades. This dense, blue-green plant tolerates heat, wind, car exhaust, and infrequent irrigation, even when planted in the poorest soils. It grows to a height of eight inches and spreads several feet in every direction, developing new roots as it creeps along the soil. It takes hold on particularly steep slopes making it easier to establish than other plants. It is hardy, tolerating high heat and freezing temperatures, and requires little irrigation once established. Depending on variety, ice plant produces pink, red-yellow, or yellow flowers. The greatest challenge when planting ice plant is protecting it from rabbits until it is established.

Myoporum parvifolium is an evergreen ground cover that spreads to an astounding nine feet wide. It develops showy white flowers in the spring and summer and weathers winter rather well, hardly changing in appearance. Plants start out rather sparse, but become dense and matted in as little as six months, rooting and spreading wherever branches touch moist soil. Myoporum requires regular, sparse water to look its best and is highly susceptible to fungus if over-watered. Breaking under the weight of traffic, it is not intended to be walked on but will recover quickly if this occurs. There are several varieties available, including a dwarf with little leaves called 'Burgundy Carpet', which has red stems and burgundy new growth. 'Pink' variety blooms light pink rather than the traditional white, and 'Putah Creek' is a more vigorous, hardy cultivar. All adapt well to the desert garden.

POMEGRANATE

When I was a little girl I eagerly anticipated Halloween for all of the usual reasons. We wore our costumes to school and our parents put together an annual carnival that translated into hours of friends, food, and fun. It was exciting to assume a different identity and wander the streets as a completely different character, enjoying camaraderie and chaos. Only the bucket of candy that was all mine by evening's end surpassed the thrill of trick-or-treating.

As fabulous as all of this was, the highlight of each Halloween was a visit to the back patio of a particularly interesting home. I adored going through the large wooden gate that normally blocked my view and prevented my entrance into this delightful garden. The brick patio had a matching built-in grill and counter, creating an outdoor kitchen that seemed exotic to me. With furniture in the center and lush plants all around, this patio was like a tropical dream. I remember thinking these people must be pretty special to have such a haven outside their back door.

Every time I stepped foot inside that haven, I breathed in the smell of hot chocolate and apple cider, both of which these generous neighbors heated on their outdoor stove and offered to the wandering crowds. Along with the hot drinks on those cool nights, our friends offered apples and another sort of treasure. I even bartered with my brothers and sister in order to have more

Pomegranate
(Punica gramatum)

than just one. What was worth begging and trading away handfuls of candy? You guessed it: Pomegranates!

The pomegranate (*Punica granatum*) originated in Asia, but has been cultivated in the Mediterranean for hundreds of years. We can thank Spanish explorers for bringing this legendary plant to Mexico and other parts of the Southwest. The crimson juice from pulpy seeds that are embedded inside the tight, pithy compartments of the mature fruit has been valued as an aphrodisiac and health enhancer by many cultures. The full, round shape of the fruit actually resembles the belly of a woman in whose womb the treasure matures. The time and effort involved in extracting the delicious, sweet nectar from this protective vessel makes it all the more appreciated. I treasure the full bowls that decorate my house in the fall and provide precious seeds and juice for several weeks of every year.

Usually a large shrub, the pomegranate grows to an average height and spread of ten feet in the desert. Its twiggy branches make an interesting silhouette during the winter months and explode with brilliant bronze foliage every spring. As they mature, the leaves develop a bright green, glossy sheen that carries them through the summer, when bold red flowers transform into globes of bronze-green fruit. The fruits increase in size and deepen in color until they reach their dark red peak in early to mid October. Even with the fruit removed, the tree continues to attract admirers as the foliage transforms yet again into a golden cloak that is shed at first frost.

The variety I recommend is called 'Wonderful'. This tough plant requires little irrigation once established and tolerates poor soils, hot winds, high temperatures, and cold weather. It is resistant to Texas root rot and other fungal diseases, and tolerates complete neglect. I fertilize my tree once a year, just before bud break, and am rewarded with a fine fruit crop every fall.

With their natural cascading shape, pomegranates make exceptional specimen plants and can be espaliered, planted in groups, or sheared into a hedge. They were even planted as windbreaks surrounding commercial citrus groves at one time. They tolerate any amount of water, but prefer occasional deep soakings, not unlike citrus trees. In areas that receive more than ten inches of annual rainfall, established pomegranate trees do not require additional irrigation. The only watering advice I offer is to maintain an even schedule of application while fruit is maturing in order to avoid splitting.

There are a few disease problems associated with pomegranates, although I have yet to encounter them in my garden. Internal black rot is an infection that begins in the blossoms, or enters the fruit through splits or injuries, and causes a thin, black line of decay through the fruit. This line continues to develop into a mass of decaying, black material with an unpleasant odor. Removal of all damaged fruit is the only control.

Maturing fruits are susceptible to splitting and this tendency is more pronounced in sunburned or ripe fruit. To prevent this from happening, avoid sudden fluctuations of moisture and harvest mature fruit before it becomes overripe. Another disease that sometimes plagues pomegranates is dry rot, caused by parasitic yeast that enters the fruit through punctures caused by insects. The leaf-footed plant bug is the most common insect pest and should be controlled by handpicking or the use of insecticidal soap or Sevin. The only persistent problem I have had with my pomegranate tree is bird damage. Every year I lose about twenty-five percent of my fruit crop because birds puncture the outer skin and decay ensues. I make no efforts to control this in my garden, maintaining that there is enough fruit for the birds and for me. Mylar strips, bird netting, caging, or other deterrents would be effective in reducing, but probably not eliminating, the problem in your garden.

When we harvest our fruit, we eat some out of hand and juice the others, using a citrus juicer to extract the liquids, and then straining it through triple layers of cheesecloth to remove any remnants of the bitter white pith. This clear, sweet juice is the basis for exceptional jellies and syrups, and makes a unique and delicious drink when added to orange juice. It is also the base for grenadine syrup.

Each year I dry a portion of the harvest by keeping the fruits in large, airy baskets for several weeks. I then use the dried fruits to decorate wreaths, trees, and window valances. They are beautiful when stacked in rustic wood or pottery bowls and lend interest to seasonal centerpieces and table decor. Smaller specimens add texture and contrast to bowls or baskets of potpourri. I like to fill large, clear glass apothecary jars with dried pomegranates and pinecones, and have even lined them up along the center of my dining table, adding a touch of fall interest to the room.

WEEK 43 Like so many things botanical, my love of wildflowers was propagated and nurtured by my grandmother. During my childhood she lived on a large lot abutting an open field that provided bounteous natural beauty, including my favorite wildflowers—alyssum, native sunflowers, and poppies. Along with native grasses, the abundant flowers provided a wealth of materials for nosegays and bouquets.

I smile when I recall the enthusiasm and appreciation with which Gram always accepted the handfuls of often-stemless blossoms. As she placed the blooms in cups and glasses from her kitchen cupboard, she taught several important lessons. She encouraged us to give and receive graciously, appreciate the simple things in life, and enjoy nature's beauty. My children have been blessed with similar experiences, and I look forward to the time when my grandchildren and I exchange kindred moments of generosity and acceptance.

Because our homes are not always adjacent to a field of flowers, and collecting them from parks and other public lands is illegal, we desert dwellers must often create our own wildflower meadows. Thanks to increasing interest in native flowers of the Southwest, this is easier now than ever before. Botanical gardens, catalog companies, nurseries, and parks all sell wildflower seeds. Coupled with basic knowledge and proper preparation, these seeds can mark the beginning of several generations' memories.

Not all wildflowers grow in all locations, and they can actually be some of the most difficult plants to start. To increase the likelihood of success it is most important to know the soil and environmental conditions that exist in your garden so you can either plant appropriate species or alter the site to accommodate the plants you want. Wildflowers grow and bloom in a wide range of specific microclimates, so knowing what you have and what you want is vital.

Once you've identified the garden location, properly preparing the seedbed encourages a high rate of germination. Like other plants grown from seeds, wildflowers sprout and grow more reliably in loosened, crumbly soil. This environment creates tiny nooks and crannies in which the seeds nestle and remain moist until they sprout. The little spaces allow both sunlight and protection, and prevent the seeds from blowing away.

263

Using a spade or a rototiller, loosen the soil in your wildflower garden to a depth of eight inches. Cover the area with three inches of composted material to increase fertility and water retention, and then till again. If the ground is mostly clay, you should also mix in a three-inch layer of sand to improve drainage. Smooth and level the soil, then water the bed two or three times over a two-week period, removing any weeds that emerge. Next, gently rake in ammonium phosphate at a rate of one-half pound per hundred square feet, and water again. The bed is now ready for planting.

At this time it is particularly helpful to take note of the native plants growing in your area. With a few exceptions, such as creosote, plants that come up on their own, and others with similar needs, are easily grown from seed. Collect seed from nearby natives, or from the plants of generous neighbors, and plant them in your garden when they go to seed. You can also identify the particular species you have seen in the wild and order that variety from a good wildflower seed source. The book I use most often to identify wildflowers is *Wildflowers of the Desert Southwest*, by Meg Quinn. This book, published by Rio Nuevo Publishers, contains exceptional photographs and reliable species-specific information on eighty-six species found in the Sonoran, Chihuahuan, Mojave, and Great Basin deserts.

Regional wildflower mixes are widely available and nice for the first-time wildflower gardener, but a word of caution is necessary. These mixes are often general, and include species not adapted to every region of the Southwest, so no matter how well you prepare your site, some of them will not germinate or grow well. Another common complaint about these mixes is the high percentage of weed seeds in the less expensive ones. To avoid pitfalls, only buy seeds marketed by a reputable company, or learn which specific plants will do best in your area and make your own mix from individual seed packets.

Wildflowers that grow well in most regions of the desert Southwest:
Ajo or desert lily (*Hesperocallis undulata*)
baby blue eyes (*Nemophila menziesii*)
blackfoot daisy (*Melampodium leucanthum*)
bladder pod (*Lesquerella gordonii*)
blue flax (*Linum perenne lewissii*)
California poppy (*Eschscholzia californica*)

chia (*Salvia columbariae*)

common sunflower (*Helianthus annuus*)

desert bluebells (*Phacelia campanularia*)

desert lupine (*Lupinus sparsiflorus*)

desert marigold (*Baileya multiradiata*)

desert paintbrush (*Castilleja chromosa*)

desert zinnia (*Zinnia acerosa*)

dogweed (*Thymophylla [Dyssodia] pentachaeta*)

firecracker penstemon (*Penstemon eatonii*)

Goodding or desert verbena (*Glandularia [Verbena] gooddingii*)

larkspur (*Delphinium scaposum*)

Mexican goldpoppy (*Eschcholzia mexicana*)

Palmer's penstemon (*Penstemon palmerii*)

Parry's penstemon (*Penstemon parryii*)

royal beard tongue (*Penstemon spectabilis*)

summer poppy or Arizona poppy (*Kallstroemia grandiflora*)

Remember that not all seeds will come up at the same time of year, or even in the same year, so have patience and be observant as the wildflower garden emerges and matures. This is another time when your garden journal can be helpful and encouraging as you log names and dates when specific varieties emerge, flower, and go to seed.

You can perform a few tricks to increase seed germination rates, the first of which is quite simple. Put your seeds in a quart jar, along with a cup or two of damp sand, put the lid on the jar, and vigorously shake it for five minutes. This scarifies, or roughens up, the outer seed coats and increases the germination speed and rate. An alternative is to soak the seeds in hot water to soften the outer coat. I like the sand approach, because wildflower seeds are often quite small, and mixing them with sand enables me to have a little more control when I scatter them.

To plant the seeds, broadcast the sand/seed mix evenly over the prepared bed. Using a hoe or the back of a shovel, tamp down the soil surface to force the seeds into the ground, then cover with a quarter-inch layer of sand or compost for moisture retention. Gently sprinkle the bed with water so that you add the necessary moisture without disturbing the newly planted seeds. To develop and maintain a dense, healthy stand of wildflowers, water the area regularly and keep the seed bed evenly moist. This is a step that many gardeners skip, thinking that wildflower seeds require no irrigation. You may need to irrigate as often as two or three times a day to get the plants started.

Once the seedlings emerge, continue to provide frequent light waterings until you see no new sprouting. During a hot, dry, or windy fall season you may need to water every other day. If temperatures are lower and you receive occasional rains, water less often. Your goal is to keep the soil moist until all of your plants have emerged, then reduce watering to about once a week through March, when the plants will have passed their blooming peak.

When plants begin to poke through the soil, birds and rodents will begin to visit your garden. Remember my sunflower house experience? The same thing often happens with wildflower plantings. Be prepared by covering the bed with bird netting, chicken wire, or fiber cloth that is held several inches above ground level. One effective method of protection is to set two-by-six boards upright around the perimeter of the wildflower bed. Keep the materials in place until the seedlings have several sets of leaves and are no longer as attractive to most wildlife.

When you remove the protective covering, also remove any weeds that have emerged along with your wildflowers. This is a challenge, since it demands that you know the difference between weed seedlings and wildflower seedlings, but doing it will keep your bed more attractive and reduce competition for water and nutrients. To encourage vigorous growth and abundant flowering, apply a water-soluble fertilizer every three weeks during the growing season.

Gardeners who have created exceptional wildflower displays usually reseed the area for two or three consecutive years. This builds up the number of seeds in the soil and improves the odds that the bed will reestablish itself year after year. It is also important to allow the plants to go to seed before cleaning the area up if you want to develop a superior wildflower garden. This step, one that is difficult for the gardener who likes things well structured and perpetually tidy, is necessary to maintain a long-term wildflower meadow.

Once your meadow is established, you will be rewarded in several ways. You will have a colorful floral display that requires only a moderate amount of water. The beautiful blossoms will invite many visitors to your garden, including butterflies, bees, and hummingbirds that are naturally attracted to wildflowers and will arrive in large numbers when your plants are in bloom. People are also enamored with wildflower meadows and will visit and enjoy your display if given the chance.

Ripening citrus

In addition to calamondins, limes, and lemons, which can bear ripe fruit year-round, many other citrus fruits are starting to "color up" during this time of year. During October, oranges, blood oranges, and grapefruits seem to change color daily, as bright yellows and oranges appear on skins where deep greens once existed. We will soon be enjoying the delicious fruit and juice grown in our own gardens.

As grapefruits, oranges, mandarins, and tangerines ripen, eat them straight off the tree rather than harvest the entire crop at once. On the tree, they'll stay fresh and increase in sugar content for many weeks without deteriorating. Grapefruits are the most amazing, remaining firm and gaining sweetness through May. How do you know if the fruit is ripe enough to eat? Pick one and taste it. If the color is good, it's worth a try. In the case of Valencia oranges, a tinge of green remains on ripe fruits.

Unfortunately, we are not the only ones fascinated and excited by ripening citrus. At this time of year, woodpeckers and other desert birds wreak havoc on the ripening fruit. They puncture the skin and drink the sweet juice, leaving the damaged fruit to be further consumed by insects. Many gardeners discover the damage after insects have entered the fruit to eat or reproduce, and assume that they are the primary problem. Of course this is not the case. The opportunistic creatures simply took advantage of the birds' work.

I don't know any preventative measures that effectively keep the birds at bay. Deterrents that provide some positive results, such as reflective tape and plastic owls, have only short-term effects. The birds quickly discover the lack of real danger and ignore our attempts to discourage their presence. Short of building a cage completely surrounding your tree you will have to accept the fact that the birds will damage part of your harvest. Once the birds have done their damage, the insects move in, attracted by the exposed, sweet fruit juices.

To reduce insect problems, remove the damaged fruit as soon as you notice it, and pick up and discard fruit that has fallen to the ground.

October in the desert is notorious for fierce, drying winds, so keep an eye on your trees and irrigate when they look parched or dry. Signs of drought stress include a loss of sheen in the leaves, curling leaves, brown or gray foliage, leaf drop, and general droopiness. If you notice any of these symptoms, irrigate deeply, making sure the water reaches a three-foot depth. This encourages the tree to devote its energy to developing fruit, rather than merely surviving.

Because of rapid changes in fall weather, cracking fruit is another thing to watch for this month. Fruit splits open if the weather changes rapidly or if the tree has gotten too dry before being irrigated. If you find that some of your crop has split, remove it from the tree and discard it. It will not improve or recover, and should be removed so that it doesn't sap the tree of additional energy or attract insect pests. If changes in weather were not responsible for the damage, consider your irrigation practices and make adjustments.

EUCALYPTUS

As fall winds blow across the desert, stirring up dust clouds and drying the landscape, many homeowners consider planting a windbreak. One of the most frequently considered trees for this purpose is the eucalyptus. Certain varieties of this popular tree have been planted around vineyards and orchards for decades, providing protection, and creating rows and screens familiar to long-time Southwest residents.

Of course, eucalyptus trees are important in the desert landscape for reasons other than their value as an effective windbreak. They are excellent shade trees and, unlike our smaller native trees, they are attractive and appropriately scaled when planted in large, open areas. Having originated in arid lands, they are drought-tolerant, desert-adapted, and accept alkaline soils. If you have a large lot that can accommodate the eventual size of a mature eucalyptus, consider this attractive family.

Over five hundred kinds of eucalyptus grow in their native Australia and Tasmania, and species have grown in many other parts of the world for hundreds of years. Over eighty varieties were planted in Southern California during the late 1800s, and more than twenty are still commonly planted there. In recent years, interest in drought-tolerant Australian natives has increased in the desert Southwest, resulting in the importation and propagation of even more species. Expect to see a greater number of interesting eucalyptus trees on the market in the next few years.

Eucalyptus trees are tolerant of almost any soil type, but do best with good drainage. To develop a healthy, supportive root system and encourage rapid establishment, they require deep irrigation while young. Once established, they require no more than the annual ten to twelve inches of rainfall. If you live in an area where annual rainfall amounts are lower, or in times of drought, even established trees require supplemental irrigation.

One of the greatest disadvantages of eucalyptus is their tendency to break, or drop large branches, in high winds. This is caused by excessive, rapid growth, the risk of which can be reduced by watering deeply and regularly, but not too often. A monthly irrigation is usually adequate. Some species also shed leaves, flowers, seedpods, and bark, and are not appropriate near pools or in gardens where tidiness is a must.

Eucalyptus trees have greedy, aggressive root systems that grow toward any source of water and gobble it up. They are often found under concrete slabs where a plumbing leak has occurred. The trees do not cause the leaks, but complicate matters when their roots invade and increase in size as they absorb the excess moisture. I recommend planting eucalyptus in large, open areas rather than near buildings, where their admirable qualities can be appreciated and their disadvantages are not a problem.

All eucalyptus share a distinct aroma that makes them easy to identify, but their differences can be amazing. Some eucalyptus trees are shrubby and short; some attain a height of a hundred feet. Some have long, narrow leaves and others have rounded leaves that grow shish-kebab style, as if skewered by their branches. Still others have distinctly circular leaves that hang in attractive clusters. Color, shape, size, and flowering habits vary from species to species, making the eucalyptus family one of great diversity and interest. Here are just a few of my favorite eucalyptus trees.

Red gum (*Eucalyptus camaldulensis*) attains a mature height of one hundred twenty feet with weeping branches covered by long, thin, dark green leaves. Its trunk is an attractive mosaic of browns, grays and tans, caused by the annual shedding of bark. Appropriate only for large lots, Red gum makes an excellent windbreak when planted fifteen feet apart. Temperatures below 15° damage it.

White ironbark (*E. leucoxylon*) grows to a maximum height of 20–50 feet, making it more adaptable to smaller sites. Its young leaves are round and grayish; mature leaves become oblong, slender, and curved. The bark resembles a jigsaw puzzle as patches of older, white bark flake away to reveal pink inner bark. Depending on variety, white ironbark produces beautiful pink or purple flowers. Hardy to 15°, this is excellent as a specimen plant or grown in groups to create a grove or screen.

The common coolibah tree (*E. microtheca*) is one of the hardiest eucalyptus varieties, tolerating temperatures from 5° to over 110°. This tree grows much more slowly than other eucalyptus, reaching a height of forty feet in twenty years. This slower growth rate decreases the likelihood of wind damage and makes this tree appropriate in smaller gardens and near buildings. Trunks are smooth and gray and leaves are light green with a gray tinge. Small flowers hang in clusters, giving this tree a pepper-like appearance.

Silver dollar gum (*E. polyanthemos*) is one of the most attractive and popular trees in its family. Hardy to 15°, this tree grows moderately fast to a height of forty feet and is covered with beautiful round, silvery leaves that are often used in dried arrangements. The trunk is covered with red bark that sheds in strips, creating an attractive, mottled texture and appearance. The silver dollar gum grows in any location with good drainage, and requires minimal water. A group of three, five, or seven at the back of a large lot makes a beautiful, small "forest."

Rose mallee (*E. rhodantha*) is a hybrid that is hardy to 8° and grows to a petite ten feet. Its slender gray stems skewer through long, bluish leaves, and are attractive in fresh or dried flower arrangements. This is one of my favorite eucalyptus trees because of the striking fringy, red, three-inch flowers that cover the tree almost year-round. Rose mallee can be trained to espalier, pruned to remain a shrub, or grown as an attractive small tree. It requires well-drained, sandy soil, moderate irrigation, and part to full sun. This versatile tree is lovely along walking paths, near drives, patios, or courtyards, and planted as a specimen plant or focal point.

It is not necessary to prune palms to insure their continued good health, but most gardeners like the tidier appearance of palm trees without the old, brown fronds. If you fall into this group, now is the right time to do that removal. The extreme heat of summer is leaving us, taking its scalding rays with it. Potentially damaging, low winter temperatures are far enough away that the palm trees can become acclimated before they arrive.

All palms produce new growth from the terminal bud at the top of the palm crown. Always avoid this growth point since damage to it will mean the demise of the tree. New fronds develop and emerge from the terminal bud as older fronds turn brown and begin to dry. It is at this stage that the fronds should be removed, since they are still slightly green and pliable, not completely dry and hard.

To remove fronds from most palms, use a sharp linoleum knife or razor and make a shallow, horizontal cut along the base of the frond, then bend it back. The frond will usually pull away and break along the cut. Using a sharp pair of hand pruners, cut the remaining fibers to completely remove it. Avoid removing too many fronds, or going too high on the trunk, because this exposes tender tissue and may cause scarring. Removing too many fronds not only interferes with the plant's growth processes, but also causes constriction or splitting of the trunk, leading to permanent damage.

A date palm cannot be pruned with a linoleum knife because it is too dense and woody. Tree trimmers often use a power saw or axe to remove old leaves once a year. Neatly trim the leaves back to an even length from the trunk to avoid a scraggly look. As with all tasks requiring power equipment, wear gloves and goggles to prevent injuries.

Sharp tools are the key to success when pruning palms. Use care and go slowly. Stand back and look at the tree after the removal of each frond, assessing appearance and shape before removing more. It is better to prune too little than to trim away too much. If you are not sure, stop and go back to the task in a few days. Living with the new form for a short while will allow you to decide if you've pruned enough.

November

- Rake autumn leaves, add to compost pile
- Repair irrigation system
- Harvest citrus
- Plant winter color plants
- Plant prepared bulbs in amended beds
- Prepare for first frost around Thanksgiving
- Fertilize vegetable beds
- Watch for cabbage loopers in vegetable bed
- Reduce irrigation frequency as temperatures drop
- Harvest pecans
- Force bulbs indoors for winter blooms

November

Amaryllis

WEEK 44 Aside from the poinsettia and an evergreen tree, amaryllis is the most popular holiday plant in the United States. Nearly four million amaryllis bulbs are imported from Holland every year, a number that has increased rapidly as breeders have created a wider range of colors and plant sizes. These easy-to-grow flowers come to us ready to plant and grow. There is no worry about chilling hours or months of darkness. When you buy them, plant them. They will grow.

Amaryllis belladonna, a South African native, is a single species in the genus *Amaryllis* and is not widely grown. *Hippeastrum*, native to the tropics and sub-tropics, is the genus that provides us with the many species that we frequently admire and grow. Named varieties bloom in shades of orange, peach, pink, red, salmon, white, and yellow, as well as striped and variegated forms. The sturdy two-foot stems set among broad, spear-shaped leaves, support two or more flowers that can be as large as nine inches in diameter.

I have a lovely coral-colored amaryllis in my garden that was given to me several years ago by a generous gardening friend. She divided her mother's amaryllis plant, started a few of the small bulbs for herself, and gave me one, too. It was described to me as a "wild amaryllis." My wild amaryllis didn't bloom that first year, but did develop thick, healthy foliage that was attractive on its own. I put the small pot in my perennial bed and left it alone.

A year later, I was pleased and surprised to see a stem emerging from the bright green foliage. I watched it intently and soon was treated to the most attractive medium-sized blossom, closely followed by two more. Surprisingly, another blossom emerged just a few weeks later. That was several years ago, and my wild amaryllis continues to offer up several blossoms every year, sometimes weeks or even months apart. Grown in a fairly protected area, it has foliage almost continuously. I have never given it bulb food, but regularly provide nutrients from compost and a water-soluble fertilizer. It is one of the most rewarding little plants I have.

The attractive reliability of that one wild amaryllis instigated an interest in the genus that borders on obsession. I can think of scores of centerpiece, table-top, and windowsill arrangements for potted amaryllis. I am considering the dedication of an entire bed to their outdoor propagation. When I receive bulb catalogs in the mail, I tend to fold down the corner of every page that contains an amaryllis. I can't even go into Home Depot this time of year without search-ing for the annual shipment of boxed amaryllis bulbs that arrives in time for holiday blossoms.

To begin your amaryllis collection, select the largest bulb you can find. I open the boxes in which they are sold and compare their contents to find the largest, most blemish-free bulbs in the lot. This assures me that I am getting the most mature plants available. Because amaryllis bulbs prefer cramped quar-ters, each one is planted in a relatively small pot. Leave only about an inch of space between the bulb and the inside edge of the pot. When planted in a pot that is too large, the bulbs sometimes fail to produce flowers.

Amaryllis also are attractive when planted in a larger container, creating a miniature bed. I particularly like the look of three or five plants situated in an oblong terra cotta planter. This makes a striking arrangement for the kitchen counter or fireplace mantle. I also like the idea of creating a small garden in the pot by planting rye grass seed or thyme around the bulb. One pot planted this way makes a strong statement when sitting alone.

A good growing medium is one that provides support to the top-heavy plants and allows for quick drainage. An even mix of sand, peat moss, potting soil, and vermiculite is a good one. The addition of a time-released fertilizer is beneficial when the plant begins to grow. Some people also like to add charcoal, to improve drainage and prevent the growth of unwanted pathogens. I am not convinced that this is helpful. Instead, I rely on good watering.

When you've chosen your pots and have prepared the potting medium, cover the drainage hole with a pottery shard or screen and fill the pot so that one-third of the bulb will sit above the soil line. Place the bulb in the pot and gently push it down so that it sits firm and level. Fill with potting mix, leaving an inch or so below the rim of the pot for watering. Use your fingers to push the soil down to remove any air pockets in which fungus or bacteria could develop.

Water the pot thoroughly so that the water saturates the soil and runs out the bottom, and then place it in a location where the temperature will stay above 65°. Do not water the plant again for three weeks, or until you see signs of growth, whichever comes first. From this time on, water the plant when the soil feels dry to the touch. Insert a bamboo stake in the soil to tie the stalk to if it is a particularly tall variety. Avoid damaging the bulb by putting the stake away from its center. When the bulb blooms, move it out of direct sunlight so that the flower will last longer.

As the blooms begin to wither, cut the stalks down to the soil line. Once flowering is through, enjoy the attractive green foliage by providing regular water, fertilizer, and bright light. You can either treat it like a houseplant or put it outdoors in a location that provides scattered or indirect sunlight so that the leaves do not sunburn. Continue to water and fertilize until mid July. Keep in mind that the plant's current health will dictate the quality of blooms next year.

It seems funny that a holiday bloom requires our attention in July, but such is the case. From mid-July through October, the bulb must remain dry. You can either leave it outdoors or bring it into a cool, dark place for this period of time. I encourage you to experiment with your own plants because I have had success with both approaches. At the end of October, trim any foliage to an inch or two and water thoroughly. Do not water again until signs of growth are evident.

When considering which variety of amaryllis to plant, think about its ultimate location. If you want the blossoms to decorate your holiday table, choose a deep red variety such as Orange Sovereign, Pamela, Red Charm, Scarlet Baby, or Sensation. Other red Amaryllis include Hercules, with its white striped centers and Amigo, a shorter variety that sends up three or four blossoms on each stem.

If you prefer a bloom that resembles the stargazer lily, with creamy white petals edged in pink or red, you will like Apple Blossom, Carnival, Clown, Double Record, and the incredible Picotee. Las Vegas presents the opposite

275

effect, with carmine red petals centered with broad white bands, like a light glowing from its core. Hermitage is very similar as its lighter red petals surround creamy white centers.

If you are planning a holiday celebration that centers on Hanukkah or a silver or gold decor, nothing is more appropriate than Jewel, with its pure white double petals and a sweet fragrance that is almost unheard of in the amaryllis family. Another exceptional choice along this theme is Wedding Dance, a pure white, star-shaped flower that stands tall on fifteen-inch stems.

If you're hooked on double-flowered varieties, consider some newcomers to the amaryllis market, thanks to recent breeding achievements. Aphrodite bears a large double blossom reminiscent of the stargazer look-alikes. Its creamy white center boldly contrasts lavender-pink ruffled edges. Lady Jane is pure white, accenting the complex form of the bloom itself. I think this is the perfect centerpiece for the wedding table, or any other formal, evening event. Double Record richly combines salmons, pinks, and reds to create a bouquet effect at the top of foot-long stems with thick, deep green leaves. Each of these three are fabulous on their own or arranged in clusters.

Desert Dawn is another late December bloomer that stands out in the crowd with salmon to apricot flowers that are borne on fifteen-inch stems. It is particularly appropriate if your holiday decorations lean toward the deep jewel tones associated with an old English or French decor. A long table, illuminated by candlelight, covered with a brocade or damask cloth, and centered with a row Desert Dawn will make a lasting impression on your holiday guests and set the tone for an elegant evening.

Forcing bulbs

Amaryllis isn't the only bulb that has caught my fancy. When in college, I received a pot of purple hyacinth (*Hyacinthus*) that had been forced to bloom in the middle of winter. When I first got them, just a few insignificant but interesting leaf tips peaked out from the top of the soil, promising something more to come. The anticipation was delicious. I carefully watched the amazing metamorphosis as the leaves increased in size daily. After several days, a round, straight stem shot up, followed by another, then another. The pot was soon crowded with several stems standing tall beneath tightly closed clusters of flower heads.

When the flowers finally opened, I realized their full value as they perfumed not only my room, but also the entire upstairs with a strong, sweet scent that shouted "*hyacinth!*" Those flowers remained brilliant and attractive for a couple of weeks. That gift was a sensory delight that left a strong impression— beautiful, long-lived blossoms, incomparable fragrance, and attractive foliage. Ever since, I can neither see nor smell a hyacinth without fond memories of that time so long ago.

I am not the only one with intense memories associated with indoor blooming bulbs. Many of my friends have had similar experiences with crocus and varieties in the *Narcissus* family—including narcissus and paperwhite—and trumpet daffodils. They all have lovely stories of how and why. Some of them derive so much pleasure from the process and the results that they continue to force bulbs every year. One winter, a gardening friend of mine covered her counters and tabletops with glasses and containers of blooms that she had forced, giving her home a springtime appearance months before spring had arrived.

To force bulbs for indoor winter blooms, you must begin with proper bulb selection. Bulbs should be large, heavy for their size, and completely blemish-free. If ordering from a catalog, opt for the slightly more expensive number-one bulbs, since they're older and produce a large, significant blossom. The smaller, less expensive bulbs are usually younger and may not bloom for two or three years, so make your selections carefully. If they are available, select bulbs produced specifically for forcing.

Bulbs that are easily forced include crocus, daffodils, Dutch iris, grape hyacinths, hyacinths, jonquils, narcissus, paperwhites, and tulips. Pre-chilled, ready-to-plant bulbs are sometimes available through catalog companies, florists, and other bulb suppliers. Some suppliers either do not provide this necessary cold treatment or fail to state whether or not it has taken place. If you are uncertain as to whether or not your bulbs have been pre-chilled, assume that they haven't and proceed.

All of the bulbs we normally force are native to environments that include low winter temperatures. They use that cold, dormant time for the development of strong root systems and flower bud formation. As far as the plant is concerned, this "down time" is more important than the period of active growth and bloom. Plant your bulbs in the container in which you will display them and put the whole thing into the refrigerator to simulate cold weather.

To plant your bulbs, select containers that are wide at the top and somewhat shallow. Cover the drain hole with a pottery shard or a piece of screen to prevent the soil from washing out. Use a well-drained growing medium, such as equal parts of peat moss, vermiculite, and perlite. It is a good idea to add a time-released fertilizer, like Osmocote, to the soil so that it will be available when the plants are actively growing. Fill the pots half full and set the bulbs atop the soil.

I like to crowd the bulbs, setting them shoulder-to-shoulder and making sure they're level. This creates a full, lush look when they bloom. I start in the middle of the pot and work my way out, facing the flat side of the bulb next to the pot's edge when I get to the outermost bulbs. Putting this flat side out helps the stalks stand tall rather than lean out when they are mature. I then cover the bulbs with soil so that their tips are just level with, or slightly protruding from, the soil surface, water them gently, and place the entire pot inside a plastic bag. I seal the bag, clearly label its contents, then put the container into the refrigerator where it will stay for two or three months, depending on the variety. Most packaging recommends a specific chilling time.

An exception to this approach is hyacinth bulbs. Hyacinths grow beautifully in clear or colored glass containers whose shape was developed specifically to hold a blooming hyacinth bulb. If I plan to display my hyacinths in a hyacinth glass, I refrigerate the bulbs in the package in which I bought them. When I remove them from the refrigerator, I fill a hyacinth glass with water and set the bulb in the glass, making sure that the emerging roots are touching the water. I keep the water level fresh and high by emptying and refilling the glass every other day, so that the roots are always wet. Once a week I fill the glass with a weak solution of a water-soluble fertilizer.

I mark my calendar so that I don't remove the bulbs from the refrigerator too soon. If you plant more than one container, it is a good idea to remove the pots from the refrigerator on a staggered schedule so that you have a succession of blooms for several weeks. It is not detrimental to leave them in the refrigerator a few weeks longer than necessary.

Once the containers have been removed from the refrigerator, take them out of the plastic bag, water them well, and place them in a cool (40–50°), low-light location for a week. This allows them to acclimate before you put them in a well-lit room where the temperature never drops below 60°. Water them regularly, keeping the soil moist but never wet. They also benefit from the application of a water-soluble bulb or all-purpose fertilizer every other week through blossoming.

When the flowers fade, gradually reduce watering so that you provide just enough moisture to keep the foliage green. At this time I usually move the pots to a protected area in a flowerbed where the pot is inconspicuous and the foliage adds color and texture. Most forced bulbs will not flower the following season, so I either discard them or plant them in the ground, knowing that they may never again produce an incredible blossom. With this mindset, I never feel disappointed and sometimes enjoy a pleasant surprise.

PRESSING FLOWERS AND FOLIAGE

WEEK 45 My daughters and I often collect leaves and flower heads to press and use on homemade cards, gift-wrap, and baked goods. We always plant Johnny-jump-ups, violets, and pansies for this purpose, and harvest and press them regularly to insure abundant flowering. We also have successfully pressed wild grasses, non-succulent foliage, and the individual petals of most edible flowers. We now have a flower press, but used parchment paper and heavy books for years. It is still a happy surprise to flip through a reference book and find a pressed flower, placed and long forgotten, to remind us of the happy times when we enjoyed this activity together.

When collecting botanical material for pressing, choose flowers, leaves, and petals that are relatively thin. A pansy is thin; a rosebud is not. If the material is too thick, it neither dries nicely nor lends itself to use on paper and baked goods. Pressed-in materials that are too thick also tend to mold and mildew before they dry. Choose specimens that are blemish-free, with no evidence of insect damage or disease. I collect flowers and leaves in the morning when they are quite fresh and not yet reacting to sun and wind. If they are moist with dew, I let them air dry before pressing them.

To press the plants, cut and fold parchment paper like a greeting card, so it is large enough to hold the blossom or leaf inside. I use parchment because the flowers are less likely to stick to it, and buy the squares sold as tamale wrappers in the Mexican food section of the grocery store. Set the parchment on a page of a large, open book and lay the plant on one side of the fold. Situate the petals or leaves in a pleasing arrangement, avoiding overlap. When drying whole flowers, use your finger to gently flatten the thick center so that it will dry more quickly. Fold the paper over, as if you were closing a card and carefully close that page of the book. I put many pressings in each book, working from one end to the other, leaving several pages in between so that I never disturb the material that I have already arranged.

Keep the book flat and stack several other books on top of it to apply even, constant pressure. Check the pressed material after two weeks. In the desert this is usually enough time for botanicals to dry. If the plants are still damp, close the book and check it again in another week. When the plants are dry and ready to remove, I leave them in their individual parchment paper folders and store them flat, in a little wooden box. You can keep them in any container that will allow them to lie flat and undisturbed.

When ready to use my pressed flowers and leaves, I carefully remove them from the parchment using small tweezers and a gentle touch. When glued on white or cream acid-free paper, covered with glass and framed, they are an excellent alternative to botanical prints. To create unique stationary, I glue them to cards and papers using a small amount of Elmer's Glue-All. Adhered to 3x5-inch cards that are folded in half, they make beautiful place cards for the dinner table. I've encased them between two panes of glass held together by copper tape for trays and window hangings, and used clear contact paper to create bookmarks and other durable and long-lived items.

PREPARING FOR FIRST FROST

WEEK 46 | It is mid-November and the first frost of the season is just around the corner, usually arriving on a chilly night near Thanksgiving. Although we gardeners cannot change the weather, we can make changes in our gardens that will enable our plants to better withstand freezing winter temperatures. The first task is to move container plants to protected locations for the remainder of the winter.

Succulents and exotic cacti need special care when the temperatures dip. Many of these plants are native to tropical or subtropical regions and cannot tolerate freezing temperatures. If they are in pots, a wise choice for exotics, move them to a protected location. If they are in the ground, cover them with fabric or newspaper every evening, removing the material in the morning so that the plants can benefit from the day's warmth. Very large specimens are difficult to cover and call for another approach. Using a ladder if necessary, cover the tips and branch ends of large, frost-tender species with a doubled or tripled paper bag. Loosely secure the bag with twine so that the plant remains undamaged, but the bag will not blow off in the wind. This usually prevents frostbite on those tender tips.

Another easy technique to combat a freeze is deep watering the day before temperatures are forecasted to drop below 32°. Wet soil holds more heat than dry soil, and well-hydrated plants fend the cold off better than dry ones. This quick treatment is especially beneficial for citrus. One more method of protecting young citrus from the cold involves wrapping the exposed trunk with burlap, newspaper, craft paper, or cardboard. Warm air is trapped between the layers of paper, and thus insulates the tender trunk wood from the cold. This is usually only necessary for the first couple of years, after which most citrus trees will have developed thicker trunks, heavier bark, and skirting branches that will protect it.

During the cold, winter months, citrus trees that have been in the ground fewer than four years benefit from additional attention. To provide and retain heat during the night, string Christmas lights through the branches, or hang a 60-watt light bulb in the center of the tree and cover the entire canopy with fabric, supported so that it does not touch the foliage. Use PVC pipes, tree poles, or boards to prop the fabric up. Remove the fabric and turn the lights off every morning, then repeat the process each night that a freeze is predicted. When my citrus trees were young, I sewed old sheets together to make a large-enough covering. This was very effective, and made the process quick and easy.

In the garden beds, commercially available "Walls of Water" protect warm-weather plants from the cold, and extend their season. Rather than invest in these moderately expensive devices, you can carefully dig up your eggplant, pepper, and tomato plants, and transplant them in five-gallon buckets that can be kept in a warmer location through the winter. If properly protected, they'll continue to produce into next spring and summer. I've had tomato plants produce for an uninterrupted eighteen months, which was an exciting experience. But in most cases, I pull out the frost-tender plants, replant with a winter crop, and call it a season.

If you have vegetable or bedding plants that aren't hardy enough to make it through the projected cold temperatures, cover the beds with fabric rather than plastic, which actually intensifies the cold. Drape the fabric over the plants on evenings when you anticipate a freeze and remove it every morning. Keep the plants well-watered and properly fertilized so that they are as healthy as possible. If you have not already done so, lay a thick layer of mulch around the plants to retain moisture and heat. Be sure to keep the mulch several inches away from plant stems to avoid disease.

Young landscape plants, even those that can withstand the cold when mature, may need frost protection their first winter. In this case, cover the plants with old sheeting, blankets, or quilts, or a commercially available cold-cover cloth. The key to this approach is putting the material on just before sunset and promptly removing it the next morning so that the plant and soil can benefit from the day's sunshine. *Do not* leave the plants covered day and night, all winter long.

If you have swimming pool equipment that is exposed to the cold, you may want to set your timer to come on at 4 a.m. This is generally the coldest time of night and running the filter may prevent water from freezing in the lines. Of course, this is only necessary in the coldest parts of the desert, or during particularly cold winters. Other water features have specific care needs during freezing temperatures. Talk to the manufacturer or retailer if you are uncertain of what care, if any, is required.

Wrap exposed water or irrigation pipes in newspaper or some other form of insulation to prevent freeze and rupture. This is especially important if you've added additional spigots or hose bibs away from buildings. Without the reflected heat of a nearby structure, these fixtures are more vulnerable to temperature fluctuations. Prepare for the inevitable changes in the weather by paying attention to daily weather reports and the elements of your garden and providing the necessary protection.

By now you should be harvesting your first planting of radishes and some leafy greens, including young spinach, arugula, and lettuce. Of course, you should also plant more seed to fill the spaces left behind, as well as those rows you initially left for successive planting. The seeds you are still able to plant in the vegetable garden include beets, carrots, collards, endive, kale, kohlrabi, leeks, lettuce, mustard, onions (bunching and dry bulb), parsnips, peas, radishes, rutabagas, spinach, and turnips. You can also plant bok choy, broccoli, brussels sprouts, cabbage, and cauliflower seedlings. Lastly, slip garlic and elephant garlic cloves, as well as onion sets, into the ground now to develop into spring-harvested, mature bulbs.

Continue to irrigate regularly and fertilize your garden beds every four weeks to ensure a bountiful harvest. When working in the garden, regularly inspect your plants to detect and treat potential problems. Most problems are predictable and treatable, if not preventable. Beets are susceptible to curly top virus. Upward-curling, brittle leaves are the most obvious symptom of this disease, which is spread by leafhoppers and is difficult to control. To avoid it in your garden, plant resistant varieties. It is also possible to buy seeds that are resistant to downy mildew, leaf spot, and root rot.

Bok choy, broccoli, brussels sprouts, cabbage, and cauliflower are all susceptible to bacterial soft rot and black rot. Symptoms include yellow, wilted foliage with small, water-soaked spots that rapidly enlarge, causing the plant to become soft and stinky. Sound garden practices usually prevent this disease from developing. Well-drained soil and good air circulation are important. Remove all garden debris before tilling and planting the bed. Inspect seedlings before purchase and avoid overcrowding when planting them. If you notice signs of disease, immediately remove infected plants to keep it from spreading to nearby plants.

Another fungus common to the brassicas is club root, which causes misshapen roots with swellings or knots, yellow, wilting leaves, slow-growth and eventual plant death. Once it is discovered in your garden, you must rotate crops and plant only varieties that are not affected. Insects that often congregate on these same plants include aphids, cabbage loopers, cabbage worms, and harlequin bugs. Handpicking and insecticidal soaps are your best defense.

283

Carrots are sometimes infested by carrot rust flies, which lay their eggs in the soil or young foliage. The young larvae then emerge and bore into the carrot flesh, creating brown tracks on the outside. This infestation is usually minor and requires no treatment, but it is nice to know what is causing the damage. Sometimes carrots develop split roots, suggesting either an excess of nitrogen in the soil, or inconsistent watering, resulting in periods of prolonged drying between irrigation.

Bacterial soft rot and bacterial leaf spot are also a problem for the lettuces, usually caused by overhead watering or overcrowding. You will know of their presence when your lettuce leaves become soft, slimy, and smelly. To manage the disease, plant resistant varieties, remove plants if they become infected, thin the bed to improve air circulation, and water from below rather than from above.

Peas are susceptible to fusarium wilt, whose symptoms include yellowing lower leaves, often on one side of the plant, stunted growth, wilting and eventual death. The interior of a cut stem will be orange or red, indicating the presence of this fungus that destroys the plant's ability to conduct water. Remove and destroy infected plants immediately and plant resistant varieties.

Radishes are sometimes damaged by cabbage root maggots, which leave brown holes and streaks in the root. They sometimes chew on the foliage, causing the plants to wilt, yellow and die. The damage they do to the radish itself is purely aesthetic, but can be so severe that it essentially destroys the vegetable. Floating row covers prevent the flying adults from laying eggs and crop rotation helps control them in the soil. Removing debris from the soil before planting also provides control.

Spinach leaves may be damaged by leaf miners, the larvae of a small fly that burrow through the flesh, leaving tunnel-like marks on the leaf surface. Pick off the infected leaves and keep weeds out of the garden area to prevent re-infestation. Small reddish-brown wireworms feed on the roots of turnips. They almost always are present in poorly drained soil, serving as indicators of the larger problem. If you discover wireworms in your garden soil, improve drainage, and rotate crops to prevent future damage.

Many other things can go wrong in the vegetable bed, but most gardeners never encounter them. If you are adding organic material every season to create fertility and good drainage, watering properly and fertilizing regularly, you will have very few problems. If your garden plot becomes plagued with problems, suspect poor husbandry and give the soil some time to recover. I suggest adding organic material and planting a nitrogen-fixing cover crop like fava beans through the winter. In the spring, harvest the beans, remove all garden debris, and cover it with tightly secured clear plastic. The soil temperature will soar over the summer, killing pathogens, and readying the bed for the addition of organics, a good tilling, and new plantings next September.

SHARING THE BOUNTY

WEEK 47

As citrus fruit ripens and cool weather crops mature, many gardeners harvest more than they can eat or share with friends and family. If this is the case in your household, consider donating your surplus to an organization whose goal is to feed the hungry or needy. Churches often serve meals to the homeless and community food banks make staples and donated foods available to those in need. Nearly every community has at least one group that accepts food donations from the public to distribute to others.

Make some calls and find out who can use the fruit and vegetables that you have grown in abundance. Harvest and deliver the produce to the appropriate location at a pre-arranged time to ensure careful handling and distribution. As you pick the fruit and vegetables, place them in grocery bags or boxes to avoid bruising or crushing. Citrus fruit can become quite heavy; so pack bags lightly enough that an average person can easily carry them.

In some communities, the food bank will even send a volunteer to your home to pick the fruit, relieving you of that duty, preventing waste, and providing healthy, fresh fruit to those who may not otherwise have any.

SWEET POTATO HOUSEPLANTS

One of the highlights of fall is the abundance of yams and sweet potatoes stacked tall in produce bins at the local grocery store. I usually buy a whole box of sweet potatoes when they become available in large quantities at low prices. They keep well, if stored in a cool, dry place with good air circulation. Unlike regular potatoes, their quality is not compromised by exposure to light, so I keep them on a large platter in the dining room or in a wire basket in the corner of the kitchen. They say "*autumn!*" They say "*bounty!*" They say "*delicious!*"

While enjoying the sweet potato season, I am always reminded of my great-grandma and her houseplants. She had one in the corner of her kitchen/dinette and another in the living room. The plants were green and lush, resembling philodendron or pothos, with longer stems. From time to time one would die and she would have to replace it. It was on one such occasion that I learned yet another magical lesson about plants and food and growth and life.

Although it seemed so to the young me, my great-grandma was not the first woman to bring the outdoors in by way of houseplants, and she was not the first to grow sweet potatoes for that purpose. In Victorian homes, the sweet potato was the most common indoor plant, requiring little care and moderate sunlight.

All you need is a firm, healthy sweet potato or yam and a glass jar filled with water. Choose a jar or vase that is narrow enough to hold the tuber in its opening without the need for toothpicks poked into the flesh for support. I have grown avocados from pits by putting those toothpicks in, but find that the punctures become sites of infection in a sweet potato.

If the jar is the right size, the sweet potato will sit snugly in the jar's mouth, with half above the rim and half below the rim. The jar must be deep enough to hold a fair amount of water, with at least a couple inches between the bottom of the sweet potato and the bottom of the jar. It might even be helpful to take the jar or vase you intend to use to the grocery store when choosing your potato.

Once you have an appropriate container, fill it with water and insert the sweet potato. Allow any excess water to drain out, then set it in a sunny, indoor location. I put mine in my south-facing kitchen window where the low autumn sun can warm the water and encourage root development. Take care not to disturb new growth. In as little as two weeks, small red/green nodules will appear, and leaves and roots will begin to form. Keep the water fresh, changing it regularly as the plant develops into a full, green specimen. If properly cared for, it will continue to grow and fill-in all winter long.

In the spring, remove the tuber from the water-filled container and cut the rooted shoots into separate plants that can be planted in pots filled with potting soil. Soak the soil with a water-soluble fertilizer and place the pot in a brightly lit location. Keep the soil damp, not wet, and fertilize every two weeks. If you are particularly adventurous, you can plant the young plants outdoors after the last frost date. If planted in fast-draining soil in full morning sun, and watered regularly, your well-fertilized plants may reward you next fall with a sweet potato harvest after first frost.

BIRD FEEDERS AND BAT HOUSES

I have eight bird feeders in my garden right now, situated in the succulent garden, on the baker's rack, among the scented geraniums, and hanging from trees. They all were made by friends or family members and have sentimental value. They are attractive, adding color, charm, and interest to each "room" they decorate.

Most communities have feed stores whose employees can suggest food preferences for the particular species you would like to attract. These stores are also an excellent source for feeders that allow particular species to feed while deterring unwanted types. This is an important consideration since you could end up attracting scores of doves, pigeons, or rodents into the garden rather than the songbird you were hoping to watch and photograph. A well-informed gardener can easily avoid a problem situation.

I adamantly oppose bat houses partly because they are known to be quite effective in attracting bats, and that is a problem in the desert Southwest. Several years ago, a number of magazines and television shows ran features on bats and the essential roles they play in the ecosystem. These informative narratives encouraged people to preserve bat nesting locations and to create additional sights when possible. It seems that natural bat nesting sights are being destroyed to make way for development, as well as people's sensitivities. This has led to a decline in bat populations.

To encourage growth in bat numbers, companies developed bat houses that are, unlike many birdhouses, actually attractive to mating and nesting bats. In many parts of the country, these bat houses have directly affected local bat populations, creating new nesting sites and increased numbers. Most of these success stories take place in milder climates, where summers are significantly cooler than ours. In the desert, the story does not have the same happy ending.

Many of those "proven successful" bat houses were purchased and properly erected in the Southwest by people interested in wildlife preservation, bat-lovers, folks hoping for natural insect control, and gardeners who anticipated a free source of guano for the garden. To their delight, the bat house worked, attracting bats that began to set up housekeeping and multiply. The experiments went quite well until summer heat descended upon the desert.

The bat houses, built so well that they almost always attracted inhabitants, were not designed to provide protection from high temperatures. Outdoor temperatures rose above 100° and the interior temperature of the bat houses soared even higher. They became miniature ovens, literally roasting their inhabitants. Very few bats survive their first summer in a desert bat house. Unless you can erect your bat house in a location that will offer protection from the summer sun and heat, do not consider one.

Harvesting pecans

WEEK 48

A few years ago, I met a young woman whose family owned several acres of pecan trees (*Carya illinoensis*) planted in soil that, just decades before, rested below a flowing river. The trees' vigor and health attested to the fact that this low-lying land was an excellent location for a pecan orchard. Growing tall and stately, the trees created a lush, green forest surrounding her family's home. I only learned this information because it was November when we first met and her hands provided undeniable evidence that she had been harvesting pecans.

Unlike other fruit and nuts that are picked off the tree before becoming overripe, pecans will be shriveled or bitter if they are picked from the tree too early. Pecans are harvested in the fall, usually after a cold snap or first frost, after they ripen completely and fall off the tree. Once collected from the ground, pecans must be shucked. The familiar glossy, oblong shell we see in our local produce bins hides beneath a thin green-brown shuck that, when peeled away from ripe pecans, reveals the nut we know. If you have never seen a "fresh from the tree" pecan, it's a bit of a surprise.

As evidenced by my young friend, the peeling, or shucking, process stains the hands doing the work. After just a few minutes of this work, fingertips turn gray-brown or black, and it takes several days for the stains to completely disappear. Cuticles and fingernails develop a yellow-brown cast that remains even longer. To avoid this, wear thin latex, plastic, or cotton gloves to protect your fingers and fingernails.

After they have dried, pecans can be bagged in their shells and stored in a cool, dry place for near-future use. They can also be shelled for immediate use or longer-term storage. Avoid breaking the nutmeats during the shelling process since pecan halves stay fresh longer than pecan pieces. Store them in large glass jars or in doubled plastic freezer bags. Shelled pecans keep well in the refrigerator for up to four months. For longer storage, keep them in the freezer.

Home gardeners are often disheartened when they shuck and shell their pecans. Sometimes, rather than plump, healthy nut meats, they discover dry, shriveled, or black nuts. The trees may have been drought-stressed during the summer or early fall, or the grower failed to apply supplemental zinc earlier in the year. In either case, avoid making the same mistakes in the upcoming year so that you can enjoy a better quality crop of nuts.

THE ASPARAGUS BED

Right around the time of first frost, the asparagus bed is depleted of its energy and looks like a ferny little weed patch. The tall fronds are dry and brown and new growth has ceased to emerge. It is time to put the bed to rest for the winter. To do this, sharpen your hand pruners and cut the entire bed back to the ground. Some people recommend leaving four inches of growth. While I don't think this will do any harm, I also think it does no good, and makes the bed unsightly and difficult to mulch.

With the foliage completely removed, cover the entire bed with a four-inch layer of mulch. Don't use anything with manure in it, since the manure may prematurely stimulate new growth. Water the bed thoroughly, and then leave it alone until spring. Your asparagus will develop more roots and new shoots as it lies quietly under that protective layer of mulch, preparing for even greater production next spring and summer.

BOTANICAL WREATHS

Over the years, I've experimented with many homegrown and natural materials to make a large number of wreaths for both holiday and year-round decor. November is the time of year when many of the materials that naturally lend themselves to wreath making are ripening and drying "on the vine," awaiting a gardener/crafter to come along and make use of them. With just a few store-bought items and lots of gathered materials, you can create lovely botanical wreaths for decorating and gift giving.

A few carefully chosen supplies will make your botanical wreath project easy and fun. You will need a wreath base, scissors, hand pruners, florist wire, florist tape, toothpicks, a hot glue gun, and glue sticks. To keep your wreath vivid and intact, you will need dry floral preserver, hairspray, or clear paint to spray on the completed project. It also helps to have a willingness to experiment, a sense of humor, patience, and a devoted assistant.

Before you begin, create a workspace that is large enough for you to lay your materials out and work on them, too. Choose a well-lit spot where you can comfortably reach all of your supplies, with access to electricity for the glue gun. If everything is conveniently located, the project will be a pleasure rather than a chore. I use my dining room table, and consider it out of commission for a week or so once I've covered it with newspaper and gathered my materials.

The first consideration in wreath making is the basic material with which the wreath will be built. When I am planning such a project, I take my clippers and brown paper grocery bags as I head out on a scavenger hunt. I clip and collect whatever looks like it will hold together and dry nicely. I focus on a variety of characteristics during my search, including base plants and fillers, as well as material for color and texture. With these things in mind, it is easy to collect several bags of material in a very short time.

I use several common plants as base material. Eucalyptus leaves and branches—clipped, clustered, and wired together—are popular choices. I have also achieved great results with foliage and branches from *Dalea* species, glycerin soaked citrus leaves, sage leaves and flowers, native grasses, cypress branch tips, juniper boughs, and pine needle clusters.

Look through magazines to get additional ideas regarding colors and textures that might work for you. Wander through your garden, collecting clippings. Cut small branches, clusters of leaves, blossoms, and pods that look interesting. Choose anything that catches your eye. Let them dry for a few days to determine whether or not they will hold together and dry nicely. If so, use them. Experiment and create your own unique designs.

In addition to base material, you will need to add filler, color, and texture. This is where the fun begins. Wild grass clusters and seeds make excellent filler material, contributing a baby's breath-like effect. Other fillers include herb clusters like bay leaves, marjoram, thyme, oregano, lavender stems and flowers, sage leaves, and rosemary sprigs. I also like to use seed pods, especially those from Texas mountain laurel, Texas ebony, mesquite trees, crape myrtle, chaste tree, Mexican bird of paradise, and carob trees. Collect and experiment.

Color is always important when creating botanical wreaths. There are many flowers and blossoms that retain their shape and color when dried. Add them while they are still fresh and allow them to dry in the arrangement. Carefully situate the entire wreath so that the blooms are properly positioned, since they will dry exactly as you leave them. You can also dry the material prior to adding it to the arrangement. Roses, hung upside down, dry nicely and remain sturdy enough to work with. Two sages—Mexican bush sage (*Salvia leucantha*) and Cleveland sage (*Salvia clevelandii*)—hold their shape and color if cut at their peak, before they have begun to lose their petals. Lavender flowers, globe amaranth blossoms, zinnias, phlomis blossoms, strawflowers, and dried sunflowers stay colorful and add texture. I've been very successful adding dried, pressed flowers to wreaths, especially pansies and violets.

Botanical wreath

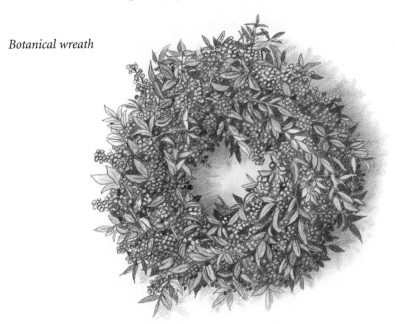

Dried fruits add interest and character to botanical wreaths. Dried apples and apple slices add a country touch to arrangements. Citrus fruits, thinly sliced, salted and dried in a 250° oven provide color and texture. I've used dried pomegranates and chiles for exceptional color.

Through experimentation, I learned that some materials are not appropriate for dried botanical creations. Mesquite and palo verde branches, leaves, and flowers do not remain intact when dried. Texas ranger falls apart, as do the honeysuckles, Mt. Lemmon marigold, acacias, and autumn sage. While they dry nicely, fading to a gray-green color, the spines on Texas ebony, ironwood, and catclaw acacia branches make them too difficult to work with and dangerous to hang.

After collecting your plant material and deciding how you want to put it together, determine which type of base you will use. I've successfully used grapevine and straw wreath bases, both of which are available at craft and discount stores. By virtue of their appearance and methods of attachment, they lend themselves to different types of wreaths. If you want a wreath that is open and airy, with a more rustic or natural appearance, start with a grapevine circle. These lightweight, easy-to-hang wreath bases come in several sizes, so consider the location for which you are making the wreath and select the size that best fills the space.

Straw wreaths are excellent bases for full, solid wreaths made of one main material, such as citrus leaves, evergreen sprigs, or grasses. They demand complete coverage with small segments of material, so that none of the base shows through, and lend themselves to more traditional wreaths that end up being larger, heavier, and more formal in appearance. I particularly like them when completely covered with bay leaves, in fish-scale fashion, then wrapped with a silk ribbon.

In addition to using commercially available wreath forms, I've made my own from grapevines, Lady Bank's rose canes, Carolina jessamine, coral bells branches, and other soft, pliable growth. As long as you can twist it and wrap it into a pleasing form, it can be used as a base. Use it immediately, or create the form and allow it to dry until you are ready to embellish it with other material. I've stripped the branches of all their foliage and made wreaths with the foliage intact. Both methods contribute their own brand of interest and charm. I especially like grapevine wreaths created with the tendrils and leaves attached. They lend a feel of country living that is hard to match.

Regardless of which base you choose, or what materials you've collected, the secret to creating a professional looking wreath is properly securing the plants in small, uniform clusters. Beginning with your base material, gather a small bunch and wire the bottoms together. Cut off excess stems at an angle, making a quill-like tip. Glue, or wire, this directly to a grapevine wreath, or wire it to a toothpick and insert it into a straw form. Continue to create and add these small clusters directly adjacent to the one previously applied, working your way around the wreath while carefully filling all of the space. When you have finished, inspect your work for gaps or heavy spots, filling in or cutting back to create a balanced, uniform look.

After applying your base material, create clusters of filler to add interest and texture to the wreath. Before attaching anything, lay it out on the wreath and stand back. Look carefully at what you've added, and move or remove things until the total effect is pleasing to your eye. Have confidence in yourself, take your time, and only attach what you love.

Once you decide where to add filler and texture, wire the stems and attach them within the base clusters, using additional wire or hot glue. I usually use both methods of attachment, depending on the place of attachment and the material used. If there are no stems, create them with wire and floral tape by threading the wire through an inconspicuous section of the plant material, then wrapping it with floral tape for strength. When this step is complete, use the same techniques to add colorful flowers, blossoms, fruit, and pods as you complete the design.

When your project is complete, attach a wire hanger to the back. Then spray it with dried floral preservative, hairspray, or clear spray paint to retain shape and color. Hang it out of direct sunlight and away from the shoulders and elbows of passersby. If kept free of dust and insects, most dried botanical arrangements retain their fresh appearance for four or five years.

It's also a good idea to refresh arrangements every couple of years with the addition of bright, new material to replace components that haven't aged well. It's possible to stretch the life of a wreath by annually replacing different portions with materials that add new interest and accent your decor. A few simple changes can update and brighten a wreath, making it seem like a completely new creation.

December

- Transplant onion seedlings
- Harvest citrus
- Plant bare-root roses and deciduous fruit trees
- Plant cool-season vegetables
- Compost leaf litter and garden debris
- Watch for pantry pests and garden insects as they move indoors
- Protect frost-tender plants
- Fertilize your overseeded Bermuda lawn once monthly
- Reduce lawn irrigation if fungus develops
- Mow dry lawn to minimize spread of disease
- Watch for pine blight

December

GIFTS FOR THE GARDENER

WEEK 49 I could fill a shop with wonderful things, both practical and whimsical, that would make any gardener happy. At the top of my list is a pair of rubber gardening clogs, in the $19–50 price range. I keep a bright red pair just outside my back door, to slip on as I run to the kitchen garden or out to the compost bin.

A good pair of gloves is also a welcome sight when the wrapping paper is removed and the box is opened. I prefer two particular types. My favorites are soft and supple, made of sheepskin that adapts to the shape of my hands, becoming increasingly comfortable with wear. The natural lanolin softens the skin, leaving my hands smoother than before I put them on. Tough and resilient, they last a lifetime if properly cared for. The only negative aspect of these gloves is their inability to hold up to water. If they get too wet, they stiffen and shrink, rendering them useless.

The other gloves that I love are made of washable leather and imported from France. I have seen them in several catalogs and specialty stores. Made of strengthened cowhide that has been stitched with nylon thread, they stay soft, even when they get wet. I've used them in mud and even concrete, and they retained their integrity. They come in a variety of sizes and bright colors, making them easy to spot when you take them off and lay them down in the garden.

Another important piece of desert gardening apparel is a hat. Panama straw hats are an excellent choice as the woven material allows airflow while keeping the burning rays of the sun at bay. Another nice hat is often called the

Australian outback hat. Both of these hats have a leather cord to keep the hat in place during windy weather, a real plus during the spring and fall, but most especially during monsoon season.

Well-made hand tools are another thoughtful gift for the gardener on your list. Most of my gardening friends prefer wood-handled tools whose heads are held in place with sturdy metal brads or screws. These don't break easily, unlike some of the discount store tools, and last for years if kept out of the sun and rain. Although wood handles are nice, I prefer solid, cast-aluminum tools. They fit nicely in my hand, won't weather or give splinters, and last a lifetime. I've seen these in catalogs and nurseries, as well as the local Wal-Mart, where they are reasonably priced and often sold in sets.

A good gardener can never have too many watering cans. I prefer galvanized metal cans that are rugged enough to stay outdoors and endure the elements. Functional and well-made, they also possess an inherent beauty and character unmatchable by anything made of rubber or plastic. They usually have a solid brass rose and brass banding, making them even more attractive.

Bulbs for forcing, or better yet potted bulbs already forced, make great gifts. Match the container to your gardener's decor to make it even more personal. To take this thoughtfulness even further, send a monthly potted bulb through White Flower Farms, or regular cut bouquets from Martha By Mail. A floral gift that continues to give is especially appreciated.

Terra cotta or ceramic pots, whether filled or empty, make nice gifts, as does garden statuary. I'm usually given one or the other for Mother's Day. Another fabulous idea is gazing balls of glass or polished metal. Available through catalogs, garden centers, and specialty shops, these brightly colored orbs evoke mystery and interest in the garden they grace.

For help when harvesting or collecting flowers for a bouquet, consider giving an attractive basket. Shepherd's Seeds has some lovely split-ash market baskets that are made in America and come with a lifetime guarantee. They are not only beautiful, but also rugged. Shepherd's also sells a very practical, heavy-duty harvest basket. Made in Germany of steel wire that's corrugated, these baskets should last generations. Because the wire is galvanized, they're immune to weather and allow you to rinse your fruit and vegetables right in the basket before carrying them into the house.

Considering the abundance that can be harvested from a well-tended vegetable bed, a good recipe book, describing a variety of ways to prepare fresh produce makes a terrific gift. Two exceptional titles are *Recipes from a Kitchen Garden* and *More Recipes from a Kitchen Garden*, both written by Renee Shepherd and Fran Raboff, and published by Ten Speed Press. They include hundreds of delicious and healthy recipes made from garden-fresh ingredients. I've tried several other garden cookbooks, but always come back to these tried and true favorites.

Indoor holiday plant care

For centuries, people have decorated their homes at the most celebrated times with plants, foliage, and flowers. This tradition allows us to feel connected to the world around us, especially the natural world. The plants that we bring into our homes add fragrance and color, and elicit feelings of good will.

Greens that frequently are used to create mantle pieces, wreaths, and garlands include bay leaves, boxwood, cedar, cypress, eucalyptus, olive, and pine. All of these either dry beautifully or remain green and supple for up to three weeks, making them perfect for holiday decorating. Pinecones, pods, and fresh fruit make attractive accents and carry out the natural theme.

To make a garland, tightly wire thin, pliable, woody branches to a length of twine or cording. On top of this base, add wired bunches of evergreen material, much like you did to make a wreath. Begin at one end of the base and work slowly toward the other end, frequently checking for and filling in gaps. This fresh garland, and any fresh wreaths you make, requires only a light misting of water every day. If lights are part of the decoration, skip the misting, and be prepared for the greens to dry out more rapidly.

Many gardeners buy potted trees to be used as landscape plants after the holiday season. If this is your intention, plan your purchase so that the tree remains indoors for only 1–2 weeks. A longer indoor stay will compromise its health. Keep the tree in its nursery container and water it every day with warm tap water. Do not fertilize or add anything else to the water. Limit the number of lights and the length of time they are on to avoid drying the needles and branches. When your holiday festivities are over, dig a hole as deep as the root ball and several times as wide, take the tree out, and plant it immediately. Water it thoroughly, keeping the roots moist until it is established.

Aside from the Christmas tree, the poinsettia is the most frequently purchased holiday plant, but this was not always the case. In the early 1900s Paul Ecke and his family began propagating and growing fields of poinsettias that originally grew in Mexico and then grew wild on the southern California hillsides. They initially sold them as cut flowers while Ecke traveled around the country with samples in a suitcase, increasing interest in the plant and building his business. The family began hybridizing the interesting plants with bright red flowers, growing the more sensitive cultivars indoors and selling them as container plants.

As they continued to experiment with poinsettias, the Ecke family developed over thirty varieties of plants in a wide array of colors including peach, pink, yellow, white, and marbled specimens. Their family business supplies about ninety percent of the world's poinsettias, annually shipping millions of plants and cuttings to growers, wholesalers and retailers.

To select the freshest poinsettia, look for the yellow or green round clusters, called cyathia, which are grouped at the tip of stems inside the red bracts. As diminutive as they may be, these are the true poinsettia flowers. They should be tightly grouped together rather than open or drooping, and the red bracts should be fully colored, not tinged with green. These factors indicate that the plant is fresh and ready to be marketed.

At home, keep the plant at 65–75°, away from heat sources, direct sunlight and drafts. It requires 6–8 hours of bright light each day and should only be watered when the soil feels dry to the touch. Thoroughly moisten the soil and avoid letting water sit in the saucer since this can cause root rot, fungal disease, or leaf yellowing and loss. If properly cared for, your poinsettia will add color to your home well into the spring.

In the desert Southwest, the Christmas cactus (*Schlumbergera bridgesii*) and crab cactus (*Zygocactus truncates*) are old favorites during the holidays. These spineless cacti grow up to three feet across and are made up of many scalloped, segmented branches that can hold hundreds of three-inch, rosy-red flowers at Christmas time. Native to the tropics, these cacti thrive in highly organic, amended soil and require bright, indirect light, frequent water, and regular feeding. Apply a water-soluble fertilizer once a week to keep them healthy and blooming. Cacti purchased at this time of year have received a dark, cooling treatment that stimulates bloom. To encourage December bloom next year, you must keep your plant in the dark for twelve hours during November, and expose it to cool night air.

Catalogs for January perusal

There are literally hundreds of mail order companies who carry gardening supplies and seeds. Most of these companies aim to please and work hard to assure customer satisfaction. Many of them, however, have literature and seeds that are inappropriate for the desert Southwest. Others have not been as reliable as I would like. Although I have used many others, a few of my favorite catalog companies are listed below.

W. Atlee Burpee
Warminster, PA 18974
(800)-888-1447
www.burpee.com

Gardener's Supply Company
128 Intervale Road
Burlington, VT 05401
(800)-863-1700
www.gardeners.com

High Country Gardens
2902 Rufina Street
Santa Fe, NM 87505-2929
(800)-925-9387
www.highcountrygardens.com

Johnny's Select Seeds
299 Foss Hill Road
Albion, ME 04910
(207)-437-4301
www.johnnyseeds.com

Native Seeds/SEARCH
526 N. Fourth Avenue
Tucson, AZ 85705
(520)-622-5561
www.nativeseeds.org

Seeds of Change
P.O Box 15700
Santa Fe, New Mexico 87592
(888)-762-7333, www.seedsofchange.com

Shepherd's Garden Seeds
30 Irene Street
Torrington, CT 06790-6658
(860)-482-3638
www.shepherdseeds.com

White Flower Farm
P.O. Box 50
Litchfield, CT 06759-0050
(800)-503-9624
www.whiteflowerfarm.com

Gifts from your garden

WEEK 50 — Every holiday season I consider and appreciate the people that make my life rich and interesting, and want to show my appreciation in a way that reflects my feelings, as well as my personality. Naturally, many of the gifts I give to these important people are, at least in part, home-made and from the garden.

For years I've combined my love of clear glass and herbs to create and share several items that are perfect for gift giving. The first is simple, yet greatly appreciated by those who love to cook but don't garden. I collect and save small and medium glass jars of interesting or unusual shape. At holiday time, I fill the jars with herbs from my garden that have been dried and crushed, or rubbed, into usable kitchen spices. One of my friends loves oregano, so I fill a small jar with dried leaves from the plant my Greek friend gave me years ago.

A length of raffia wrapped around the lid with a hand lettered, leaf-shaped parchment tag an attractive and practical gift. If I'm lucky, I'll receive an invitation to dinner to enjoy a meal made with this savory herb.

The same technique works with any of the herbs that you normally harvest from the herb garden and dry for storage. Bay leaves, culinary sage, juniper berries, lavender, marjoram, peppermint, parsley, and rosemary are just a handful of the herbs that I've shared with friends. It's also nice to put several different herbs into small jars and offer them up as a set in a basket or rack that will match the kitchen decor of the recipient. Small talavera jars, a traditional Mexican pottery, make attractive containers that most desert dwellers would appreciate.

To my friends who love to cook with fire and spice, I have given small jars of hot red peppers from my summer garden. After picking these little gems, I dry them whole and store them in glass jars or paper bags in a cool, dark cupboard. To give them as gifts, I crush or grind the chiles and package them in attractive jars. If making chili powder, I combine several types of chilies and grind them in a small electric coffee grinder until they are rather fine. For crushed red pepper or pepper flakes, I either use a mortar and pestle, or put them in a doubled freezer bag and roll them with a rolling pin. These freshly ground chiles have a flavor that is more intense than their store-bought counterparts.

Sometimes I make herb blends by combining several herbs in a big bowl, mixing them thoroughly, then packaging the mixture in attractive containers with a list of ingredients and directions for use. The easiest of these to create is an Italian mix. To make six 1-cup gifts, with a little left over for my own pantry, I mix two cups each of dried basil, oregano, and rosemary. I then add one-fourth cup fennel seeds if I have them, sometimes even buying them at the store. Next, I break six bay leaves into very small pieces and stir this into the blend, along with two tablespoons freshly ground pepper and four tablespoons sea salt. To add a little zip, I sometimes crush one dried red pepper and stir that in too. This delicious blend, packaged in small glass jars or cellophane bags, makes an excellent gift when given with unusual pasta or a bottle of red wine.

Another way to share the flavors of your herb garden is through herbed vinegars. I usually buy good quality vinegars and experiment with whatever herbs I have on hand. My favorite vinegars for these projects are red-wine vinegar, unflavored rice vinegar, and champagne vinegar. They each have distinct flavors that blend nicely with herbs and spices to make unusual accents for salads and vegetables.

To make herb vinegars, sterilize attractive glass jars or bottles by running them through the hottest cycle on the dishwasher, or by boiling them in a large kettle on the stove. When the bottles are cool enough to handle, add sprigs of freshly gathered herbs that have been rinsed and cleaned to remove any brown or dry leaves. Use long wooden skewers to place the herbs in narrow-necked bottles. Sometimes I even thread peeled garlic cloves or hot peppers on these the skewers and add them to the bottles for extra flavor.

Once the herbs have been placed in the bottles, add room temperature vinegar and seal the jar with a screw-on lid or cork. I used to bring the vinegar to a boil, then pour it into the jars, but the heat of the boiling liquid leached the color from the herbs, leaving a dull and faded appearance. After doing a little research, I learned that the vinegar itself was mildly antiseptic and did not require the addition of heat to ensure a sterile end product. I buy bags of various sized corks in the canning section of my local hardware store. They are also available at craft and home-brewing stores.

The herbs I most often add to vinegars include dark opal basil, lemon basil, purple ruffles basil, Siam queen, and sweet basil. I also use calendula flowers, chives and chive blossoms, garlic chives and blossoms, lavender flowers, marjoram, oregano, rosemary, sage and sage flowers, scented geranium leaves and blooms, French tarragon, and Mexican tarragon. I combine them as much for appearance as for flavor, since this is a gift that will sit on the counter for the next several months, adding beauty to the kitchen and flavor to the menu. Below are some suggested combinations to get you started.

Red wine vinegar, fresh tarragon

Red wine vinegar, whole dry red pepper, peeled garlic cloves, green basil sprigs

Rice vinegar, red or pink rose petals, rose geranium leaves

Rice vinegar, bay leaves, whole cloves, peppercorns, garlic cloves, sage sprigs, and sage blossoms

Rice vinegar, purple basil, green basil, basil blossoms

Champagne vinegar, peppermint leaves, violas, or Johnny-jump-ups

Champagne vinegar, orange mint, dried orange peel, citrus blossoms
if available

Champagne or Rice vinegar, lemon balm, lemon verbena, lemon
thyme, calendula blossoms

Any vinegar, garlic chives, chives, chive blossoms

I also like to give baskets filled with condiments and canned goods that I "put up" when the ingredients were at their peak. These baskets include a variety of things, depending on what was bountiful in the garden. Some favorites are plum jam or jelly, roasted red peppers packed in olive oil, zucchini pickles, orange marmalade, Indian lemon pickle, and my husband's favorite, pepper hash. Canned and stored throughout the year, these items are quick to throw in a basket, wrap in cellophane, and carry as a holiday or hostess gift.

In addition to the herb and vegetable gardens, many of my holiday gifts begin on the citrus trees. Most of my friends and acquaintances buy all of their winter fruit in the grocery store and are thrilled with a basket or bucket filled with freshly picked citrus. I try to choose containers to please each recipient, including pottery, woven baskets, galvanized metal containers, and colorful mixing bowls. I fill them with fresh blood oranges, grapefruits, kumquats, lemons, and oranges. To the person who only eats picked-and-shipped fruit, homegrown produce is a special treat.

If I have an abundance of ripe lemons at holiday time, I make several batches of lemon curd to share with friends. It is easy to make and stays fresh in the refrigerator for up to three weeks. Although there are many good recipes out there, I've developed one that is absolutely my favorite.

Lemon curd
3 eggs
pinch of salt
2 cups sugar
1/2 cup lemon juice
2 tsp. lemon zest, finely chopped
1/4 cup unsalted butter, cold and cut into 8 pieces

In the top of a double boiler, over low to medium heat, beat eggs lightly. Add salt, lemon juice, and zest. Blend well. Stir until mixture is quite warm and slightly thickened. Add butter, one chunk at a time, stirring until completely melted. Stirring constantly, cook for an additional 10–15 minutes, or until thickened and smooth. Pour into sterilized glass jars and cool at room temperature. When completely cooled, place in refrigerator where it will remain fresh for up to three weeks. Serve with toast, scones, cheesecake, or sponge cake. Makes a nice filling for tarts and layer cakes.

Dried herbs in muslin bags make nice sachets for drawers, closets, and baths. Friends appreciate a small packet of these easy-to-make gifts, wrapped in twine with directions for use. I buy several yards of good-quality muslin when it is on sale and make bags in varying sizes, depending on their intended use. Three-inch squares are nice for lingerie drawers; five-inch bags hold enough to nicely scent bath water; and eight-inch bags with a small loop to attach to a hanger are adequate to perfume a closet. For these purposes, I stitch three sides of each bag, turn it right side out and iron it flat, then I add the dried herbs and hand-stitch the open side. When the filling has been added, I wrap the bag closed with raffia or ribbon.

Herbs that add fragrance to drawers and closets, while also repelling moths and silverfish, include lavender, lemon balm, lemon thyme, lemon verbena, rosemary, and vitex or chaste tree. Dried botanicals that make a nice bath sachet include lavender, lemon herbs, mints, rose petals, scented geranium leaves, and vitex. They can be used singly, or in any pleasing combination, and also make a relaxing bath soak when mixed with Epsom salts.

To give someone a real treat, make several bags filled with rosemary and bay leaves, bundle them with twine and instructions to drop one in a pot of boiling water and steep for five minutes, then carefully remove the pot from the stove. For a cleansing facial, lean over the pot with a towel over your head to capture the steam. This feels wonderful, and clears up sinus congestion too.

There are so many gifts to give from the garden and from the heart. Look in your own pots and garden beds, and think of ways to combine those ingredients to create something special for the people on your holiday gift list.

I'm a gardener at heart, a gardener in my soul, and even I forget to go out into the garden when life gets really busy. How can that be? I can't explain it, but I admit that it happens. And it happens a lot in December, when the holiday hustle and bustle cranks up to warp speed and I must remind myself to go out and put my hands in the dirt.

Many gardeners think they can't plant anything from seed in December but, lucky for us, this isn't true in the desert Southwest, and there are quite a few flower seeds that will do just fine now. All of the following flowers will germinate in our winter weather if kept moist.

baby's breath (*Gypsophila paniculata*)
carnation (*Dianthus caryophyllus*)
cottage pink (*Dianthus plumaris*)
cup flower (*Nierembergia*)
English daisy (*Bellis perennis*)
evening primrose (*Oenothera*)
floss flower (*Ageratum houstonianum*)
forget-me-not (*Myosotis arvensis*)
glory lily (*Gloriosa*)
Lobelia
Mexican goldpoppy (*Eschscholtzia mexicana*)
nasturtium (*Tropaeolum*)
nemesia (*Nemesia strumosa*)
snapdragon (*Antirrhinum majus*)
spring star flower (*Ipheion uniflorum*)
stock (*Matthiola incana*)
sweet alyssum (*Lobularia maritima*)
sweet pea (*Lathyrus odoratus*)

305
ॐ

Prepare your bed by loosening the soil and adding four inches of organic material, like compost or well-aged manure. Work the amendments into the bed until they are completely blended. Smooth the bed out and run your irrigation system to check it and help settle the soil. Sprinkle the surface with ammonium phosphate or ammonium nitrate at a rate of one pound per hundred square feet, and then water again. Let the bed sit for a week, then plant your seeds according to package directions.

Begin by planting the tallest varieties in the back, then move forward, row by row or section by section, until you plant the shortest plants in front. If you're unsure of mature plant height, check the seed packet for this information. I usually stack my packets according to plant height, with the tallest on top, so I can work directly from the stack without having to re-check plant specs. This not only makes planting easier, but also ensures that everything will be visible when the plants mature.

Once the bed is planted, water it so that it is moistened to a depth of three inches. Check the bed every day by putting your finger in the soil as deep as your first knuckle. If the soil is dry, water it again because it's important to keep the seeds moist until they germinate. Once the sprouts emerge, cut back on water, applying it every few days, depending on weather. As with any seed-planting projects, thin the seedlings when they've developed their first set of true leaves to provide enough space to each plant. Don't hesitate to thin later if necessary, since overcrowding can lead to stunted growth and disease.

Winter lawn care

Your Bermuda grass should be completely dormant after having experienced a few freezing nights. If you did not overseed it, your only winter concern will be weed control. Remove them when you first notice them. They will only cause more problems if you let them stay. Broadleaf weed killer applied to the entire lawn is not effective at this time because it must be watered in and, if your lawn is dormant, you should not be irrigating. This approach is only warranted during dormancy when you have more weeds than lawn. If you have a few weeds sprouting up, it's easiest to use a screwdriver and pluck each one out by its roots, or judiciously apply herbicide to each plant, taking care not to spray the surrounding grass. Either method works, as long as the weeding is done.

If your lawn is overseeded, it requires a regular schedule of care and maintenance. Annual and perennial rye lawns need weekly mowing to a height of two inches. If your lawnmower is set lower for the hybrid Bermuda grass, raise the blades until spring, when the rye dies back and the Bermuda emerges from dormancy. Irrigation is also a consideration. Depending on rainfall, drying winds, and temperatures, your winter lawn should be watered once every 5–10 days. I know this is a wide range, but I start my cycle at five days, and if the lawn looks good, I stretch the watering out by a day or two. It quickly becomes obvious when the lawn needs to be irrigated sooner, and I set the duration back by a day or two, leaving it until spring. By adjusting the cycle to the lawn's needs, I avoid higher water bills and fungal disease.

If your lawn has brown patches, lots of toadstools, black streaks, or large sections that seem to die back, you probably have a fungal disease. Fungus, especially in the winter, is caused by excessive moisture. The first thing you must do to control the spread of disease is adjust your irrigation schedule. Reduce your watering frequency whenever possible, then treat the entire lawn with a fungicide. I recommend Daconil or Bayleton, but your local garden center or nursery will have something appropriate for your area. Follow instructions carefully, including the schedule for repeated applications to assure the product's effectiveness.

The last bit of care necessary for winter lawns is regular fertilization. Every month, apply a nitrogen-based fertilizer to keep it green and healthy. A product made specifically for winter lawns is best, but some gardeners prefer to use ammonium phosphate or ammonium nitrate. Avoid using ammonium sulfate until spring, since it will not work in winter's cold temperatures. These simple steps will help your lawn look green and lush through the winter and into the spring, when the Bermuda greens up to carry it through the warmer season.

Winter weed control

WEEK
51

Half of the desert's annual precipitation falls during the winter months. This moisture, combined with relatively high daytime temperatures, encourages winter weed growth, particularly if a warm spell follows a rainy period. I wander through my garden nearly every day, and make a point of pulling the few weeds that spring up. By being regularly attentive and picking young tender weeds before they've gone to seed, I rarely have a huge job to tackle. If the weeds do get ahead of me, I apply Round-up when they are still small.

Another approach to winter weed control is the use of a pre-emergent herbicide. When applied and watered in, a pre-emergent controls weeds by preventing seed germination. Many gardeners apply a pre-emergent two or three times a year and rarely deal with weeds. I don't use this method because I often like the seedlings that naturalize in my garden, and prefer to decide what can and cannot remain.

It's also important to keep an eye on the weeds in the vegetable and annual beds, as well as in the lawn. Because they are well watered and contain nice, friable soil, beds are easy to weed. When harvesting your produce or deadheading the flowers, pull out any weeds that are competing for water and nutrients. A simple, consistent routine keeps everything in check. Lawns may need an application of a "weed and feed" product, if weeds begin to take over in thin winter rye. If you did not overseed, carefully remove or spray weeds that spring up in the dormant Bermuda. Don't let them get the upper hand.

COLD FRAMES, HOT BEDS, AND GREENHOUSES

Many desert gardeners feel like they're fighting the elements, with little time for reprieve. It's a battle to keep things growing through the hot summer months, then we enjoy a wonderful fall growing season that is often cut short by freezing temperatures. This narrow window of opportunity has prompted the use of cold frames and hot beds to extend the season and allow gardeners to grow flowers, vegetables, and herbs throughout the winter.

A cold frame is useful for early sowing of spring and summer annuals, protecting tender plants in the winter, rooting cuttings, and growing plants out of season. The simple construction of four short walls and a clear glass or acrylic cover allows you to control temperature, humidity, and light to make an environment favorable for plants. It works by trapping, holding, and re-radiating the sun's rays, and also protects its contents from cold, drying winds, thus preventing evaporation and wind-chill issues.

Cold frame kits are available from garden supply companies or can be built from common materials. In its basic form, a cold frame is a four-sided, solid structure with a hinged lid that allows the sun's rays to shine through. The lid must be raised and lowered, depending on the interior temperature, so a thermometer is a helpful component. It is a good idea to raise the lid to vent the cold frame when the interior temperature rises above 85°, but be sure to close the lid as evening approaches to retain the day's heat. To use the cold frame in summer, coat the glass or acrylic with whitewash to reflect heat and lower the interior temperature.

I have a friend who uses cold frames to successfully grow basil, salad greens, and edible flowers throughout the year, supplying several up-scale restaurants with the locally grown, organic produce for which they are known. Hers are the most basic four-sided raised beds with hinged, frame-glass tops that she props open with sticks when venting is necessary. Her inexpensive and low-tech arrangement provides surprisingly profitable results.

A hot bed is nothing more than a cold frame with heating cables in the bottom. These cables increase the soil temperature from below, speeding germination and growth rates during cold weather. They're available from garden supply companies and come with complete instructions for installation and use. These instructions often include plans for basic cold frames too.

I have another friend who wanted to dabble in hydroponics and tropical plants, so he invested in a greenhouse. His greenhouse attaches to the south side of his home, taking advantage of the sun in winter and some shade during summer. It has a concrete floor, a clear acrylic roof, and sides with base vents. The frame consists of aluminum poles and rafters, and he added a window-mounted evaporative cooler for summer use. He never buys produce or flowers, relying on home production of high quality, organically grown varieties, and considers the rather substantial cost an investment in both his hobby and his health.

A greenhouse is a significant investment that consumes a fair amount of garden space and requires constant monitoring and upkeep. Its advantages are also significant. A greenhouse provides a place where seeds and cuttings can be propagated and seedlings protected, and allows you to grow any crop at almost any time, including tomatoes, peppers, squash, and cucumbers during the winter and salad greens and peas in the summer. The structure itself eliminates the need to protect the garden from birds, rodents, other wildlife, and most insects. Lastly, weeds are rarely a problem in a greenhouse environment.

Whether you buy a kit, a plan, or build your own design, consider several factors when erecting a greenhouse. In order to fully benefit from available sunlight, the structure must have good clearance from trees to the south, southeast, and southwest. The ridgeline of the roof should run north and south to increase the amount of light in the early morning and late afternoon. Most greenhouse owners prefer a rectangular greenhouse to an igloo-shaped structure for optimum usable space. It is best to have a concrete floor to deter burrowing rodents, insects, and disease but, if this isn't possible, bricks laid in sand are a good alternative. Another option, although less desirable, is a three-inch layer of pea gravel. Avoid a dirt or wooden floor since both encourage insect problems. A heat source is necessary, whether solar, electric or gas. If you intend to use the greenhouse during the warmer months, an evaporative cooler must also cool it.

I have not made the greenhouse investment because I keep myself plenty busy using more conventional home-gardening techniques. But I must admit, when I visit my friends who have made the commitment and use their greenhouses to full advantage, I get a bit envious.

PINES IN THE DESERT LANDSCAPE

WEEK 52 · Nothing evokes a sense of cool retreat like a stand of pine trees. The deep greens, attractive pinecones, and statuesque forms are visually comforting. In the desert, this transformation enables some newcomers to acclimate to our foreign and challenging environment. But as tempting as these trees are, they should only be considered if you have a large enough space to accommodate their mature size and a willingness to commit to long-term irrigation.

Pine trees tolerate lawn watering and benefit from regular mulching. The needles must be raked up and pinecones collected. Aphids and spider mites are sometimes a problem, but both can be treated with insecticidal soap, pyrethrum, or a systemic insecticide. Pines occasionally suffer from twig blight, most often when irrigation has been sparse or sporadic. When regularly watered, pine trees are generally problem-free.

Aleppo pine (*Pinus halepensis*) is probably the best pine tree for the desert. Like other landscape plants, it needs about two years in the ground before it's firmly established and begins a period of rapid growth to 30–50 feet in height at maturity. Aleppo pines usually are gray-green, produce light-brown three-inch cones, and four-inch needles in bundles of two. As they mature, Aleppo pines drop their lower branches, resulting in trees with no branches below ten or fifteen feet. This natural canopy creates excellent underplanting opportunities and provides a shaded outdoor space.

Avoid aleppo pine blight. A common problem in arid regions, this blight is indicated by brown tips and twigs. Remedy the problem with regular irrigation, mulching, and twice-yearly manure applications. It is important to supply supplemental irrigation during times of extreme heat or drought for the life of the tree. This is an excellent time of year to plant a pine and, hardy to 13°, aleppo is an exceptional choice. It is interesting to note that the Greeks and Europeans cut and decorated Aleppo pine trees during their winter celebrations, making it the first evergreen used as a Christmas tree.

Another pine choice for the desert Southwest is the Canary Island pine (*P. canariensis*). This Canary Island native is a rapid grower. If properly cared for, it will grow to a mature height of 50–80 feet, while maintaining a fairly narrow girth. Juvenile foliage is light green and resembles that of a spruce, often leading to its misidentification. Upon maturity, the Canary Island pine has deep, blue-green, twelve-inch needles that grow in bundles of three and create a soft, airy appearance. Canary Island pinecones, which are a deep, glossy brown, grow 4–9 inches long and are particularly attractive. This tree is appropriate for lawns and locations too narrow for other pines, but must be planted in protected areas, since it is damaged by temperatures below 20° and killed at 10°.

If you have a large garden, consider Coulter pine (*P. coulteri*). Native to the dry, rocky slopes of Southern California mountain ranges, this tree is resistant to heat, aridity, and wind and is hardy to 0°, making it quite adaptable to the desert. Unlike traditional pine trees, the Coulter pine matures with a wide, open form, reminiscent of an oak tree. It requires room to spread and would be too large for small gardens. It develops huge thirteen-inch pinecones that hang on the heavy branches for several years and are coveted by crafters for holiday decor. The deep green, 5–14-inch needles grow in clusters of three, adding to the dense, cool feeling of the tree.

Quite similar to, and often mistaken for, an Aleppo pine, the eldarica (*P. eldarica*), is another fine landscape choice. It is faster growing than many other pines, attaining its maximum height of 30–80 feet in ten years. Given occasional deep irrigations, eldarica pine thrives in heat, drought, wind, and poor soils and is hardy to zero degrees, making it the most tolerant of the desert-adapted pine trees. An excellent choice for a potted Christmas tree to be moved into the landscape after the holidays, eldarica's eight-inch dark green needles grow in twos and produce a vivid color in the garden. The three-inch oval cones produced as the tree matures are lovely for holiday wreaths and bowls.

The Mediterranean region of the world lends us many landscape plants, including the Italian stone pine (*P. pinea*). This pine historically grew in large numbers in and around the city of Rome, and is often depicted in Renaissance paintings. In its youth, it is full and bushy, developing into a thick-trunked, umbrella-shaped tree by mid-life. In maturity, it becomes a stately, broad, flat-topped tree whose silhouette against the sunset-sky is unmistakable. Attaining a mature height of 40–80 feet, the Italian stone pine produces bright green 5–8-inch needles in groups of two, and 4–6-inch glossy brown cones. Hardy to 0°, this tree tolerates heat and aridity once established, requires regular irrigation for the first several years, and will always benefit from occasional, deep applications of water.

The last pine tree that has proven itself in the desert Southwest is the Torrey pine (*P. torreyana*). This fast-growing tree reaches a mature height of 40–60 feet in fifteen years, is gray-green to dark green, and has a broad, open silhouette. It produces long, 8–15-inch needles in dense clusters of five, and numerous 4–6-inch dark brown cones. Although native to the California coast, the Torrey pine is well adapted to the desert, tolerating aridity, hot, dry winds, and alkaline soil. It is hardy to 12°.

There are several other pines that deserve mention as fair performers in the desert: Mexican stone pine *(P. cembroides)*, Coulter pine *(P. coulteri)*, digger pine *(P. sabiniana)*, and Japanese black pine *(P. thunbergii)*. Each of these trees grows well in the desert, but suffers damage from high summer temperatures. If you live in an area where the young and juvenile trees receive protection from the afternoon summer sun, you could consider these varieties. They generally take more water but tolerate lower temperatures, making them even more attractive for gardeners living in slightly higher elevations or cooler microclimates.

If you are planning to buy a live tree to decorate for the holidays, then plant in the landscape, consider one of the above varieties. Each has unique and appealing characteristics that add interest and tone to the landscape. Choose a healthy, bright green specimen, keep it cool and well-watered until you plant it, and choose its location carefully. Given proper care, it will live a good, long life.

INTERPLANTING THE ROSE BED

Many rosarians are purists in the sense that they do not like anything else planted in their rose gardens. Fearing competition for water, sunlight, and nutrients, they want nothing to interfere with optimum rose development and production. I admit that I like the appearance of a formal, stately rose garden, too, but I also find that certain landscapes benefit from a more casual touch, and roses are adaptable enough to fit into this scheme of things. It is more a matter of considering the rose's full potential rather than viewing it from a single perspective. Aside from creating magnificent single-species gardens, roses are excellent components in other beds and borders.

313
∾

Interplanting the rose garden

If your idea of a perennial bed includes roses, or if you want some of these beautiful blossoms from your cutting garden, there are a few things to consider before planting. It is imperative that you remember the elements necessary to good rose production. They require lots of sunshine, abundant water, and regular fertilization. The soil must be well-drained and good air circulation is vital. Avoid overcrowding since it encourages the development of fungal disease.

Plants that make good rose companions share or adapt to their needs. They must thrive with above-average amounts of water and fertilizer and lots of sun. Most desert-adapted or drought-tolerant annuals and perennials aren't good choices, since they need significantly less water. Penstemons, *Monarda* variants such as bee balm and horsemint, and most sages will develop root rot in a rose garden environment. Rose companions should not be hosts to thrips and spider mites, since these are common rose pests, eliminating commonly considered plants like calendula and marigolds.

Despite all this, many plants do surprisingly well when interplanted with rose bushes. Catmint and catnip are traditional rose companions planted in English rose gardens for decades. Their soft, gray-green foliage contrasts nicely with the more rigid rose leaves and stems, softening the overall look. Both *Nepeta* variants produce lavender, white, or blue flowers in spring and summer. Shear them back after blooming to keep the plants from becoming rangy and to encourage additional flowers.

Sweet William (*Dianthus barbatus*) adds to the charm of a rose garden. If one of your goals is to create a fragrance, or sensory garden, this genus must be included. Sweet William forms attractive evergreen mats and produces either single or double carnation-like flowers that are intensely fragrant. My favorites are reminiscent of cinnamon and cloves and—surprise!—roses. They grow to a height of 10–20 inches, depending on variety, make excellent cut flowers, and provide attractive greenery to the garden and arrangements. Deadheading is a must, otherwise the flowers fade, turn brown, and remain atop the plants, giving them a dead or dying appearance.

Dusty miller (*Artemisia stellerana*) with its silver foliage and yellow blossoms, creates a lovely contrast planted around the border of the rose garden, and is particularly stunning if your rose garden has river rock or native stone edging. This dense, hardy perennial grows to a height and width of two-and-one-half feet, loves heat, tolerates cold, and grows like a weed. Its foliage makes attractive filler in cut arrangements and is said to repel insects. It is a real winner in a perennial bed.

Another silver-foliated plant deserving mention as a companion plant, lamb's ears (*Stachys byzantina*) is often considered the best plant to exist alongside a rose bed. Its soft gray foliage and lavender flower spikes contrast nicely with the deep green foliage of most rose bushes. Attaining a maximum size of only eighteen inches, lamb's ears accents rather than overwhelms the garden.

Toadflax or baby snapdragon *(Linaria maroccana)* produces lavender or violet-blue flowers that contrast nicely with roses. Even more attractive is the blue-green foliage whose narrow, erect growth nicely fills spaces between other bushes. This summer blooming perennial is best planted in large numbers, since individual plants are narrow and sparse.

As a border plant, filler for potted roses, or underplanting, nothing beats dwarf cup flower (*Nierembergia hippomanica violacea*). This mounding plant has stiff, lacy looking foliage that is covered with blue or violet cup-shaped flowers all summer long. To induce additional blossoms, shear the plant back, fertilize, and wait for the next display. They grow up and around the bases of rose bushes, creating an arranged look in the garden bed. 'Purple Robe' is a readily available, desert-adapted variety of *Nierembergia*.

Some surprising rose companions include trailing rosemary (*Rosmarinus officinalis*), electric-blue sage (*S. chamaedryoides*), and mealy cup sage (*S. farinacea*). Normally considered drought-tolerant, these three plants adapt well to the lush rose environment without the normal fungus and root rot concerns. Rosemary adds texture and character to the bed while the sages contribute interesting foliage and purple and blue flowers that boldly accent the rose garden.

Another herb that serves well in the rose garden is *Santolina rosmarinifolius*. The silver-gray and lime-green plants make attractive border plants for the rose or perennial gardens, tolerating either dry edges or thorough irrigation. The evergreen foliage grows in attractive mounds and adds a distinctly pleasant fragrance to the garden. Although it may die back in a hard freeze, santolina comes back from the roots, developing finely divided, dense leaves in spring and button-like yellow flowers in summer.

The last plant that I strongly recommend for the desert rose garden is thyme (*Thymus vulgaris*). Available in many varieties, including mother-of-thyme and lemon, common, woolly, and silver thyme, these plant adds texture, interest, and aroma to the front edge or border of any perennial bed. They tolerate minimal water or abundant irrigation, as long as they are planted in well-drained soil. Thyme withstands full afternoon sun in the middle of summer and also does well in partial shade. It hugs the ground, creating a mat-like effect that provides an attractive transition from the edge of a bed into the body of the plant material. In addition, its culinary uses make it a plant no gardener should be without.

If you are considering planting a few roses, putting in a perennial bed, or accenting an existing rose garden, these plants add interest, beauty, and versatility, while softening the formality of a traditional rose garden.

Cleaning up for the New Year

As we move into winter and approach the New Year, it's nice to get off to a good start. In the garden, this means cleaning up remnants of previous seasons to ensure plant health and vitality in the seasons to come. As cold winds rush through our landscapes, deciduous trees and shrubs drop leaves, plants enter dormancy, and tender annuals decline. Left behind is an abundance of yellow, red, and brown debris that was charming in the fall, but losing its luster as the days go by.

To keep insects from overpopulating your spring garden, act now. Many pests—including plant bugs, leafhoppers, and grasshoppers—over-winter in weeds and leaf litter. Eggs laid in this material in the winter and hatch when warm, spring temperatures return. By removing the decaying leaf material now, you will also remove future generations of pests. Add the leaves to the compost pile, where the heat of decomposition will kill most eggs. If you do not compost, properly dispose your yard waste so that you do not create a pest haven elsewhere.

Prune deciduous trees and shrubs if branches are crossing or damage requires attention. Cut and stack the wood you remove so that it dries and seasons over the next year, when it will be ready to warm your home on cold winter nights, or crackle in the belly of a traditional Mexican chiminea.

Don't cut back the frost damage on tender plants like citrus, bougainvillea, or lantana until the first week of April when the threat of frost has passed. If you make this mistake, future low temperatures will further damage and possibly kill the plant. Leaving the brown and sometimes unsightly foliage adds a layer of insulating protection from additional frost.

If you haven't already done so, apply a layer of mulch to protect roots from cold temperatures, retain soil warmth, and discourage water evaporation. Mulch also beautifies the garden, providing a uniform look to beds and planted areas. As it decomposes, it adds to the structure and nutrient value of the soil, providing long term benefits to the garden. This is one of the best investments you can make in your garden and landscape.

If your garden includes paths or landscaped areas covered by gravel or rock, replenish it if necessary. Most landscapers suggest that landscape rock be amended or added to every few years. As time goes by, patches become thin and underlying soil is exposed. Add additional rocks to maintain the desired effect. Now is the best time to inspect and act on these garden jobs. Cool, winter temperatures provide the most comfortable work conditions when shoveling and moving heavy landscape materials in the desert. Do as much of this work now as you possibly can, and save less demanding tasks for the warmer months.

As you survey your flawless garden, reflect on your diligent efforts over the past year. Ponder your successes, and the lessons you learned from your failures. What will you do again in the coming year? What do you vow never to repeat?

Open your garden journal one last time this year and write the answers to these and other significant questions. Look back on what has transpired and on what you have gained, and consider how those experiences will contribute to the upcoming year in the garden. Because the garden—with all her characters, plots, themes, and routines—will continue to perform, and it is your task, as its steward, to direct that dynamic and wonderful production.

Botanical Nomenclature

With a cursory knowledge of the proper names for plants, you can gain an understanding of appearance, native habitat, and even fragrance. Another good reason to learn botanical names is that common names vary greatly.

You don't need to speak Latin to understand the plant-naming system, because botanical Latin is not a real language. It is a combination of Latin terms put together in the mid-1700s by a Swedish naturalist named Carl von Linne. Linnaeus, as he called himself, gave all names proper Latin endings, although the words themselves might originate from any language. Most botanical names refer to where the plants were first discovered or the person who discovered them.

In the system Linnaeus created, every plant gets two names. The first name, a noun, is capitalized and establishes the plant's genus, or general group. The second name, a lower-case adjective, describes the noun and refers to the species. This binomial, or two-word, system replaced plant identification that required detailed, written descriptions. The system has been elaborated to sometimes include a third name that denotes subspecies or variety.

In addition to the proper botanical names, many plant labels carry cultivar information. A cultivar is a plant produced through human intervention, by hybridization or selection. Cultivar names are capitalized, in single quotes, and follow the genus and species identification. Generally, botanical names provide additional information to the reader, although some horticulturalists have named plants for less clarifying reasons. Nevertheless, a basic glossary of botanical terms gives a more thorough understanding of most plants.

As you look at the terms below, notice alternate endings in parentheses. In accordance with the grammatical rules of Latin, endings vary based on the gender of the noun they describe, but carry the same original meaning. Use the following information the next time you go to the nursery and see how well the botanical name fits the physical appearance of the plant.

Natural habitat

alpestris (-e): from lower mountains below the timberline, nearly alpine

alpinus (-a, -um): from high mountains above the timber line; alpine

aquaticus (-a, -um): aquatic; appropriate for a water garden

arenarius (-a, -um): native to sandy soil

arizonica: from Arizona

californica: from California

campestris (-e): from fields, plains or flat, open land

pratensis (-e): originally grew in meadows

maritimus (-a, -um): native to the seashore

mexicana: from Mexico

paludosus, palustris (-e): from bogs or marshes; likes "wet feet"

saxatilis (-e): native to rocky soil

sylvaticus (-a, -um): native to forested areas, woodlands

texanus: from Texas

umbrosus (-a, -um): from shady places

Growth pattern and size

columnaris (-e): column-shaped, upright

fastigiatus (- a, -um): upright and narrow

globularis (-e): shaped like a ball

grandiflorus: large flowered

grandifolius: large-leafed

hystrix: bristly or spiny

procumbens: growing prostrate, flat on the ground

repens: a creeping plant, spreading by runners

schidigera: bearing spines

serratus: saw-toothed or serrated

stans: erect or standing uptight

vulgaris, vulgatus: common

Season of principal interest

aestivalis (-e): summer

autumnalis (-e): autumn or fall

hyemalis (-e): winter

vernalis (-e): spring

Flower or leaf color

albus (-a, um): white

argenteus (-a, um): silver

atropurpureus (-a, -um): dark purple

atrorubens: dark red

atroviolaceus (-a, -um): dark violet

atrovirens: dark green

aurantiacus (-a, -um): orange

aureus (-a, -um): golden

azureus (-a, -um): sky blue

brunneus (-a, -um): dark brown

caeruleus (-a, -um): medium blue

canus (-a, -um): off-white, ashen

cardinalis: cardinal red

carneus (-a, -um): flesh colored

cerasinus (-a, -um): cherry red

cinereus (-a, -um): gray

cyaneus (-a, -um): dark blue

flavus (-a, -um): light yellow

hyacnithinus (-a, -um): deep purplish-blue

luteus (a, -um): bright yellow

purpureus (-a, -um): purple

roseus (-a, -um): pink or rose-colored

ruber (rubra, rubrum): red

semperverens: evergreen

variegatus (a, -um): variegated, splashed with various colors

virisis (-e): green

Fragrances, flavors, and warnings

amarus (-a, -um): bitter

aromaticus (-a, um): aromatic, pleasantly fragrant

capsicus (-a, -um): hot, biting to taste

causticus (-a, -um): burning to taste

deliciosus (-a, -um): fine flavored, pleasing

dulcis: sweet to taste

foetidus (-a, -um): offensive odor, stinky

fragrans: fragrant

inodorus (-a, -um): having no scent

odoratus (-a, -um): sweet-smelling

pungens: pungent

toxicarius (-a, -um): toxic, poisonous

venenatus (-a, -um): poisonous

vomitorius (-a, -um): induces vomiting, emetic

Plant Index

Agave *(Agavaceae)*
Agave, 61, 83, 105, 141, 145, 155, 177, 221, 223, 253
  century plant (*Agave Americana*), 233, 105
  octopus (*Agave vilmoriniana*), 105
  Queen Victoria (*Agave victoriaereginae*), 105
desert spoon, sotol (*Dasylirion wheeleri*), 145, 159
Dracaena, 177
Hesperaloe parviflora, 221
Yucca, 143, 145, 159, 177, 221, 234
  soaptree (*yucca elata*), 224

Bulbs and corms
flowers, 49, 200, 209-213
  amaryllis, belladonna lily (*Amaryllis belladona*), 109, 211, 275
  amaryllis (*Hippeastrum*), 226, 273-276
  calla lily (*Zantedeschia aethiopica*), 211, 226
  Canna, 49, 211, 221, 233
  cape lily, veld lily (*Crinum*), 211-212
  Crocus, 277
    Dutch crocus (*Crocus vernus*), 212
  fortnight lily (*Dietes*), 221
  Freesia, 212
  Gladiolus, 233
  grape hyacinth (*Muscari*), 277
  hyacinth (*Hyacinthus orientalis*), 212-213, 226, 276, 278
  Iris, 198-203, *illus.* 199, 226, 231, 277
  lily (*Lilium sp.*), 234
  lily-of-the-Nile (*Agapanthus*), 109, 210, 221
  Narcissus, 277
    daffodil (*Narcissus*), 212, 226, 277
    jonquil (*Narcissus jonquilla*), 227, 277
  ornamental onion (*Allium*), 210-211

rain lily (*Zephyranthes atamasco*), 143
  spring star flower (*Ipheion uniflorum*), 305
  Star of Bethlehem, pregnant onion (*Ornithogalum*), 213
  tulip (*Tulipa*), 213, 277
  Watsonia, 109, 213
culinary
  garlic, 213, 223, 283, 302
  onions, 48, 216, 251, 283

Cacti
Christmas cactus (*Schlumbergera bridgesii*), 298
crab cactus (*Zygocactus truncates*), 298
old man (*Cephalocereus senilis*), 105
Opuntia
  cholla (*Opuntia sp.*) varieties, 84, 146, 167, 177, 224-225
  prickly pear (*Opuntia sp.*) varieties, 84, 146, 177, 224-225
saguaro (*Carnegiea gigantean*), 153-154, 224

Euphorbia *(Euphorbiaceae)*
Euphorbia sp., 61, 84, 141, 161-163, 220
Euphorbia amygdaloides, 162
Euphorbia characias, 162
Euphorbia epithymoides (*Euphorbia polychroma*), 162
gopher plant, mole plant (*Euphorbia lathyris*) 163, 231
Mexican fire plant (*Euphorbia heterophylla*), 162
milkbush, pencil tree, pencilbush, (*Euphorbia tirucalli*), 163
poinsettia (*Euphorbia pulcherrima*), 13, 163, 227, 298
spurge (*Euphorbia sp.*), 227

Flowers, annual
African daisy (*Arctotis, Dimorphoteca,* or *Osteospermum*), 110
Anemone, 226
Anthurium, 226

baby blue eyes (*Nemophila menziesii*), 264
baby snapdragon, toadflax (*Linaria maroccana*), 249, 315
baby's breath (*Gypsophila paniculata*), 305
Bells-of-Ireland (*Moluccella laevis*), 247
bladder pod (*Lesquerella gordonii*), 264
blazing star (*Mentzilia*), 233
calendula (*Calendula officinalis*), 222, 247, 314
carpet bugle (*Ajuga reptans*), 233
chia (*Salvia columbariae*) (see Sage [*Saliva*], herbs)
cockscomb, Chinese woolflower (*Celosia sp.*)
  Celosia argentea, 100
  Celosia cristata, 100
creeping zinnia (*Sanvitalia procumbens*), 109
desert bluebells (*Phacelia campanularia*), 265
English daisy (*Bellis perennis*), 305
floss flower (*Ageratum houstoni anum*), 305
forget-me-not (*Myosotis arvensis*), 305
foxglove (*Digitalis purpurea*), 59, 226, 233
Gaillardia, 101, 108
glory lily (*Gloriosa*), 305
Helichrysum, 105
Impatiens, 159, 233
Jerusalem sage (*Phlomis sp.*)
  Phlomis fruticosa, 135, 291
  Phlomis russeliana, 136, 291
larkspur (*Consolida ambigua*), 248
larkspur (*Delphinium scaposum*), 59, 227, 234, 265
Lobelia, 227, 305
  cardinal flower (*Lobelia cardinalis*) 233
  Lobelia laxiflora, 109
marigold (*Tagetes sp.*), 102-103, 110, 184, 222, 231, 314
  African (*Tagetes erecta*), 103
  French (*Tagetes patula*), 103

320
  ∾

Mexican tarragon (*Tagetes lucida*) (see Herbs)

Mt. Lemmon (*Tagetes lemmonii*) (see Shrubs)

nasturtium (*Tropaeolum*), 110, 189, 222, 234. 249, 305

nemesia (*Nemesia strumosa*), 305

Nicotiana (perennial grown as annual), 110, 227

flowering tobacco (*Nicotiana alata*), 233

paintbrush (*Castilleja sp.*), 234

desert paintbrush (*Castilleja chromosa*), 265

Penstemon, 109, 115-117, 234, 314

cardinal (*Penstemon cardinalis*), 115

firecracker (*Penstemon eatonii*), 116, 265

Palmer's (*Penstemon palmerii*), 116, 265

Parry's (*Penstemon parryii*), 116, 265

Penstemon barbatus, 117

Penstemon pinifolious, 117

royal beard tongue (*Penstemon spectabilis*), 117, 265

scarlet bugler (*Penstemon centranthifolius*), 115-116

periwinkle (*Vinca*), 159, 227

petunia (*Petunia hybrida*), 59, 227, 234, 249

Phlox, 234

pincushion flower (*Scabiosa caucasica*), 109, 234

pink (*Dianthus sp.*), 59, 110, 247

carnation (*Dianthus caryophyllus*), 305

cottage pink (*Dianthus plumaris*), 305

sweet William (*Dianthus barbatus*), 234, 314

poppy (*Eschscholzia sp.*)

California (*Eschscholzia californica*), 264

Mexican goldpoppy (*Eschcholzia mexicana*), 265, 305

poppy (*Kallstroemia*)

Arizona, summer (*Kallstroemia grandiflora*), 265

poppy (*Papaver*), 59, 89

Iceland (*Papaver nudicaule*), 249

Portulaca

moss rose (*Portulaca grandiflora*), 103, 160

purslane (*Portulaca oleracea*), 110

primrose (*Primula*), 59, 76

primrose, evening (*Oenothera*) (see Ground covers)

red-hot poker (*Kniphofia uvaria*), 234

snapdragon (*Antirrhinum majus*), 249, 305

spider flower (*Cleome hasslerana*), 234

statice (*Limonium*), 249

stock (*Mathiola incana*), 59, 249

sunflower, common (*Helianthus annuus*), illus. 72, 72-75, 100, 160, 265, 291

Viola, 59, 219, 248, 279

Johnny-jump-up (*Viola tricolor*), 248, 279, 303

pansy (*Viola tricolor hortensis*), 59, 248, 279, 291

violet (*Viola odorata*), 219, 248, 279, 291

Zinnia, 103, 109-110, 160 184, 222, 234, 247, 291

desert (*Zinnia acerosa*), 265

prarie (*Zinnia grandiflora*) (see ground covers)

Flowers, perennial

aconite (*Aconitum*), 226

Alyssum, 110

Artemesia, 109

dusty miller (*Artemisia stellerana*), 314-315

French tarragon (*Artemisia dracunculus*) (see Herbs, perennial)

asparagus fern (*Asparagus setaceus*), 143

Begonia, 89, 233

bloodroot (*Sanguinaria canadensis*), 226

blue flax (*Linum perenne lewissii*), 264

Chrysanthemum, 89, 231

coleus (*Coleus hybridus*), 159

columbine (*Aquilegia sp.*), 233

Coreopsis, 100, 109-110, 160, 252

Cosmos, 101, 110, 184

chocolate cosmos (*Cosmos atrosanguineus*), 160, 252

creeping buttercup (*Ranunculus repens* 'Pleniflorus'), 226

cup flower (*Nierembergia sp.*), 160, 305

dwarf cup flower (*Nierembergia hippomanica violacea*), 315

Cuphea, 231

Dahlia, 233

desert lily, Ajo lily (*Hesperocallis undulata*), 264

false hellebore (*Beratrum viride*), 226

fire pink (*Silene virginica*), 233

four o'clock (*Mirabilis jalapa*), 226, 233

gayfeather (*Liatris sp.*), 109, 233

giant hyssop (*Agastache*), 108, 143

globe amaranth (*Gomphrena*), 101, 160, 165, 291

Hibiscus, 143, 220

hollyhock (*Alcea rosea*), 108, 233

Jupiter's beard (*Centranthus ruber*), 108, 252

lamb's ears (*Stachys byzantina*), 105, 315

Lantana (see Ground covers)

Lisianthus, 160

lupine (*Lupinus sp.*), 233

desert lupine (*Lupinus sparsiflorus*), 265

mallow, tall (*Malva sylvestris*), 108

matilija poppy (*Romneya coulteri*), 108

Mexican hat (*Ratibida columnifera*), 109

milkweed (*Asclepias sp.*)

desert (*Asclepias subulata*), 89

butterfly weed (*Asclepias tuberosa*), 233

pine-leaf (*Asclepias linaria*), 197

monkey flower (*Mimulus sp.*), 234

poinsettia (*Euphorbia pulcherrima*) (see Euphorbia)

sacred datura (*Datura wrightii*, *Datura metaloides*), illus. 102, 227

scented geranium (*Pelargonium sp.*), 184, 110, 141, 207, 231, 302, 304

sweet alyssum (*Lobularia maritima*), 60, 305

tiger flower (*Tigrida*), 49

yarrow (*Achillea*), 105, 108, 152

321

ᕭ

Foliage plants
bowstring hemp (*Sansevieria*), 83
Caladium, 226
creeping Charlie (*Pilea nummu-lariifolia*), 141
Dieffenbachia, 226
Philodendron, 227
Shefflera, 227

Fruit
cantaloupe, 97, 155
citrus (see Trees, citrus)
grapes (see Vines)
pome fruit (see Trees, deciduous fruit)
stone fruit (see Trees, deciduous fruit)
strawberries, 217
tomatoes (see Vegetables)
watermelon, 97, 155, 185

Grains
amaranth, 165
corn, 97
    blue, 165
    Mexican June, 165
    Papago, 165
Indian grass, Indian wheat (*Plantago*), 167

Grasses
grass, clumping, 146
grass, perennial
    bamboo muhly (*Muhlen-bergia dumosa*), 108,
    fountain grass (*Pennisetum setaceum*), 108
    giant reed (*Arundo donax*), 177
    pampas grass (*Cortaderia*), 177

Ground covers
blackfoot daisy (*Melampodium leucanthum*), 55, 109, 264
Crown vetch (*Coronilla varia*), 258
desert marigold (*Baileya multi-radiata*), 55, 109, 265
dogweed (*Thymophylla [Dyssodia] pentachaeta*), 197, 265
evening primrose (*Oenothera sp.*), 55, 110, 160, 226, 231, 305
flax (*Linum var.*), 109
golden fleece (*Thymophylla [Dyssodia] tenuiloba*), 55, 160
Gazania, 55, 143, 160
germander (*Teucrium*), 55

hummingbird flower (*Zausch-neria californica*), 55, 109, 233
ice plant (Malephora) (see Succulents)
Lantana, 55, 76, 93, 143, 160, 197, 221, 227, 231, 233, 257, 317
Myoporum, 55, 220
    Myoporum parvifolium, 259
rosemary (*Rosemarinus offici-nalis*) (see Herbs)
spurge (*Euphorbia, sp.*) (see Euphorbia)
tansy (*Tanacetum vulgare*), 167, 227
Texas betony (*Stachys coccinea*), 55
thyme (*Thymus vulgaris*) (see Herbs)
verbena (*Glandularia [Verbena] sp.*), 55, 109, 143, 197, 220, 232, 234
    Goodding, desert (*Glandularia [Verbena] gooddingii*), 265
zinnia, prairie (*Zinnia grandi-flora*), 55, 160, 184

Herbs, annual
basil (*Ocimum*), 39, 50-51, 127, *illus. 127*, 160, 189, 222, 302-303
    varieties, 51, 127-128, 302
salad burnett (*Poterium san-guisorba*), 129
summer savory (*Satureja hor-tensis*), 128

Herbs, perennial
Allium
    chives (*Allium schoenoprasum*), 108, 130, 189, 219, 223, 302-303
    garlic chives (*Allium tubero-sum*), 189, 223, 302-303
Anthriscus
    chervil (*Anthriscus cerefolium*), 189
    Queen Anne's lace (*Anthriscus sylvestris*), 219
bay laurel (*Laurus nobilis*) (see Trees, desert and desert-adapted)
bee balm (*Monarda*), 108, 129-130, 219, 233, 314
borage (*Borago officinalis*), 219
calendula (*Calendula officinalis*), 219, 302-303
cilantro, coriander, (*Coriandrum sativum*) 108, 219, 248

dill (*Anethum graveolens*), 108, 189, 197, 219, 248
fennel (*Foeniculum vulgare*), 108, 219
garlic (see Bulbs and corms)
hyssop (*Hyssopus officinalis*), 131, 160, 233
lavender (*Lavandula*) varieties, 105, 131, 194, 218-19, 221, 231, 291, 301-302, 304
lemon balm (*Melissa officinalis*), 131-132, 189, 303-304
lemon grass (*Cymbopogon*), 132, 160, 304
lemon verbena (*Aloysia triphylla*), 132, 303, 304
mint (*Mentha*) varieties, 132-133, 140, 231, 303-304
nasturtium (*Tropaeolum*) (see Flowers, annual)
Nepeta
    catmint (*Nepeta faassenii*), 223, 314
    catnip (*Nepeta cataria*), 130, 223, 314
Origanum
    marjoram (*Origanum majo-rana*), 133, 189, 194, 219, 223, 291, 301-302
    oregano (*Origanum vulgare*), 104, 133, 189, 194, 218-19, 223, 291, 302
Parsley, 189, 219, 222, 251, 301
rosemary (*Rosemarinus offici-nalis*), 55, 134, 177, 189, 194, 219, 221, 223, 231, 258, 291, 301-302, 315
sage (see Sage (*Salvia*), herbs)
Santolina, 104, 160, 221
    lavender cotton (*Santolina chamaecyparissus*) 231
    Santolina rosmarinifolius, 315
tarragon
    Mexican (*Tagetes lucida*), 103, 219, 302
    French (*Artemisia dracun-culus*), 103, 219, 302
thyme (*Thymus sp.*)
    common (*Thymus vulgaris*), 55, 60, 104, 109, 134-135, 160, 189, 194, 219, 223, 291, 316
    lemon (*Thymus citriodorus*), 303-304

Legumes
beans, 31, 97, 155, 193, 142, 216
    bolita, 165
    fava, 251
    mesquite, 225
    tepary, 165, 167
crown vetch (see Ground covers)
peas, 31, 142, 215, 222, 251

Sage (*Salvia*), decorative 54,
    54, 93, 109, 121-122, 143,
    159-160, 184, 221-222, 231
autumn (*Salvia greggii*), 122, 143
clary (*Salvia sclarea*), 108, 122
Cleveland (*Salvia clevelandi*),
    122, 252, 291
electric blue (*Salvia chamaedry-
    oides*), 122, 315
little leaf (*Salvia microphylla*), 122
mealy cup (*Salvia farinacea*),
    122, 143, 315
Mexican bush (*Salvia leucantha*),
    122, 143, 291
purple (*Salvia leucophylla*), 122
Salvia x superba, 122
scarlet, blood (*Salvia coccinea*), 122

Sage (*Salvia*), herbs 104, 121,
    134, 184, 189, 194, 219, 220, 223,
    231, 234, 290-291, 301-302, 314
culinary (*Salvia officinalis*)
    varieties, 121, 301
chia (*Salvia columbariae*), 167, 265
clary (*Salvia sclarea*), 108, 122
dwarf (*Salvia pachyphylla*), 134
pineapple (*Salvia elegans* 'Pine-
    apple Sage'), 121

Shrubs
Abelia, 234
Artemisia, 105
azalea (*Rhododendron sp.*), 226, 234
bay laurel (*Laurus nobilis*) (see
    Trees, desert and desert-
    adapted)
bee bush (*Aloysia gratissima*), 197
bird of paradise (*Caesalpinia sp.*)
    bush (*Caesalpinia gilliesii*), 54,
    177
    Mexican (*Caesalpinia mexi-
        cana*), 54, 143, 159, 177,
        221, 291
    red (*Caesalpinia pulcherrima*),
        197
bird of paradise (*Strelitzia regi-
    nae*), 143, 226

bleeding heart (*Dicentra spect-
    abilis*), 226, 233
bottlebrush (*Callistemon*), 221
boxwood (*Buxus sp.*), 226, 297
butterfly bush (*Buddleia davidii*),
    160, 178, 197, 234
butterfly mist (*Ageratum corym-
    bosum*), 197
burning bush (*Euonymus sp.*), 226
Camellia, 143
cape plumbago (*Plumbago auric-
    ulata*), 231, 252
castor bean (*Ricinus communis*),
    178, 226
chuparosa (*Justicia californica*),
    159, 224
crape myrtle (*Lagerstroemia
    indica*), 143, 177, 220, 291
Cordia, 54
Cotoneaster, 178, 257
creosote (*Larrea tridentate*), 54,
    167, 177, 197-198, 231
Dalea, 55, 197, 220, 290
    black (*Dalea frutescens*), 105
    indigo bush (*Dalea pulchra*),
        105, 231
    trailing indigo bush (*Dalea
        greggii*), 105
deadly nightshade, (*Atropa bel-
    ladonna*), 226
desert hackberry (*Celtis pallida*),
    197, 224
dwarf pomegranate (*Punica
    granatum* 'Chico')
elderberry (*Sambucus*), 177
emu bush (*Eremophila*), 231
fairy duster (*Calliandra sp.*)
    baja fairy duster (*Calliandra
        californica*), 197
    fairy duster, false mesquite
        (*Calliandra eriphylla*), 54,
        159, 220, 221
flowering quince (*Chaenomeles*),
    178
Gardenia, 143
gaura (*Gaura lindheimeri*), 108,
    220
heavenly bamboo (*Nandina
    domestica*), 226, 231
hollyleaf redberry (*Rhamnus*), 258
hop bush (*Dodonaea viscosa*), 54,
    177
Hydrangea, 226
Jerusalem cherry (*Solanum
    pseudocapsicum*), 227

jojoba (*Simmondsia chinensis*),
    54, 239-240
lilac (*Syringa*), 178
Mahonia
    creeping (*Mahonia repens*), 257
    desert (*Mahonia fremontii*), 224
Mormon tea (*Ephedra*), 225
Mt. Lemmon marigold (*Tagetes
    lemmonii*), 54, 137, 232
myrtle (*Myrtus*), 143
ocotillo (*Fouquieria splendens*),
    54, 167, 177
oleander (*Nerium oleander*), 89,
    143, 177, 227
Photinia, 178
pineapple guava (*Feijoa sell-
    owiana*), 231
Pittosporum, 143, 227
privet (*Ligustrum*), 157, 227
rockrose (*Cistus*), 256
rose (*Rosea*), 20-24, 57-58, 157,
    178, 184, 223, 291, 313-314,
    illus. 313
Ruellia, 54
Russian olive (*Elaeagnus augusti-
    folia*), 177, 297
Russian sage (*Perovskia*), 143
sage (see Sage (*Salvia*), decorative)
senna (*Cassia sp.*), 54, 159, 178,
    197, 220, 237-239
    bauhin (*Senna bauhinioides
        sy. Cassia bauhiioides*), 238
    desert (*Senna covesii sy.
        Cassia covesii*), 239
    Lindheimer (*Senna lind
        heimeriana sy. Cassia
        indheimeriana*), 239
    shrubby (*Senna wislizenii sy.
        Cassia wislizenii*), 239
    spiny (*Senna armata sy. Cassia
        armata*), 238
    two-flowered (*Senna biflora
        sy. Cassia biflora*), 238
silverberry (*Elaeagnus commu-
    tata*), 178
Spirea, 178
sumac (*Rhus sp.*)
    sugar bush (*Rhus ovata*), 54,
        220, 256
    skunkbush sumac (*Rhus trilo-
        bata*), 224
Texas mountain laurel, mescal
    bean (*Sophora secundiflora*), 55,
    75-77, 221, 227, 232, 291
Texas olive (*Cordia boissieri*), 220

323
~

Texas ranger, Texas sage (*Leucophyllum*), 55, 220
wild buckwheat (*Eriogonum sp.*)
  California (*Eriogonum fasciculatum*), 257
  saffron (*Eriogonum crocatum*), 257
wolfberry (*Symphoricarpus occidentalis*), 224
yellow or coral bells (*Tecoma stans*), 55, 159, 234, 292
yellow oleander (*Thevetia peruviana*), 227

Succulents 11, 81-85, 141, 223, 253
Aloe, 145-146, 221, 231
Dutch wings (*Gasteria*), 83
Hen and chicks (*Echeveria elegans*), 104
ice plant (*Malephora*), 259
Kalanchoe, 83
Senecio mandraliscae, 104-105
Senecio serpens, 104-105
stonecrop (*Sedum*), 83

Trees, citrus 18, 64-71, 93, 120, 177, 220, 267, 285, 290, 303, 317
calamondin (*Citrofortunella mitis*), 65, 70, 143, 267
'Bears' lime (*Citrus aurantiifolia* 'Bears'), 65-66, 140, 267
grapefruit (*Citrus paradisi*), 65, 67, 267
kumquat (*Fortunella margarita*), 65, 69, 143
lemon (*Citrus limon*), 65-66, 143, 267
limequat (*Fortunella margarita x Citrus aurantifolia*), 65, 67
'Meyer' lemon (*Citrus sinensis x Citrus limon*), 65, 69, 223
Mexican lime (*Citrus aurantiifolia*), 65-66
orange (*Citrus sinensis*), 68-69, 89, 235, 267
pummelo (*Citrus grandis*), 65, 67
tangelo (*Citrus paradisi x Citrus reticulata*), 65, 67
tangerine, Mandarin orange (*Citrus reticulata*), 65, 69, 267

Trees, deciduous fruit
apple (*Malus*), 19, 178, 185, 223, 252
apricot (*Prunus armenaica*), 19, 178, 252
cherry, Carolina laurel (*Prunus caroliniana*), 226
fig (*Ficus carica*), 19, 45-46, 178
peach (*Prunus persica*), 19, 143, 178, 252
pear (*Pyrus communis*), 19
plum (*Prunus saliciana* or *Prunus domestica*), 19, 89, 178, 252
pomegranate (*Punica granatum*), 19, 177, 252, 259-262, *illus. 260*
Quince, 19, 252
Ziziphus
  Chinese jujube (*Ziziphus jujuba*), 224
  gray-thorn, Southwestern jujube (*Ziziphus lycioides*), 224

Trees, desert and desert-adapted
Acacia, 54, 158, 177, 219, 220, 221, 256
  catclaw (*Acacia greggii*), 197
  fern (*Acacia angustissima*), 197
almond (*Prunus dulcis var. dulcis*), 178
bay laurel (*Laurus nobilis*), 129, 143, 223, 291-292, 297, 301, 304
bottle tree (*Brachychiton populneus*), 178
California pepper (*Schinus molle*), 178
carob (*Ceratonia siliqua*), 178, 291
chaste tree (*Vitex agnus-castus*), 54, 197, 235, 291, 304
chinaberry (*Melia azedarach*), 226, 234
Chinese pistache (*Pistache chinensis*), 256
cottonwood (*Populus fremontii*), 157, 178
desert ironwood (*Olneya tesota*), 54
desert willow (*Chilopsis linearis*), 54, 158, 177, 219, 256
Eucalyptus, 54, 105-106, 158, 177, 219, 231, 234, 268-270, 290, 297
  blue gum (*Eucalyptus globulus*), 106
  coolibah tree (*Eucalyptus microtheca*), 270
  dwarf blue gum (*Eucalyptus globulus* 'Compacta'), 106
  ghost gum (*Eucalyptus papuana*), 106

Kruse's mallee (*Eucalyptus kruseana*), 106
large-fruited yellow gum (*Eucalyptus leucoxylon megalocarpa* 'Rosea'), 106
red gum (*Eucalyptus camaldulensis*), 269-270
red-flowered mallee (*Eucalyptus erythronema*), 106
rose mallee (*Eucalyptus rhodantha*), 270
silver dollar gum (*Eucalyptus polyanthemos*), 106, 270
silver mountain gum (*Eucalyptus pulverulenta*), 106
silver-topped gimlet (*Eucalyptus campaspe*), 106
white ironbark (*Eucalyptus leucoxylon*), 106, 270
evergreen elm (*Ulmus parviolia* 'Sempervirens'), 54, 177
feather bush (*Lysiloma microphylla thornberi*), 54, 177, 197
hawthorn (*Crataegus sp.*), 235
horse chestnut (*Aesculus*), 235
Japanese maple (*Acer palmatum*), 143
locust (*Robinia sp.*), 235
  black locust (*Robinia pseudoacacia*), 226
maidenhair tree (*Gingko biloba*), 178
mesquite (*Prosopis sp.*), 54, 158, 167, 219, 221, 235-237, 256, 291
  Argentine (*Prosopis alba*), 236
  Arizona, velvet (*Prosopis velutina*), *illus. 169*, 197, 226, 237
  Chilean (*Prosopis chilensis*), 236
  honey (*Prosopis glandulosa*), 225, 236-237
  screwbean (*Prosopis pubescens*), 237
mulberry (*Morus*), 177
palo brea (see palo verde, Sonoran)
palo verde (*Cercidium* and *Parkinsonia sp.*), 54, 158, 177, 256
  blue (*Cercidium floridium*), 204
  foothill, little-leaf (*Cercidium microphyllum*), 205, 235
  Mexican (*Parkinsonia aculeata*), 157, 203, 206
  Sonoran, palo brea (*Cercidium praecox*), 205, 256
pecan (*Carya illinoensis*), 77-79, 298-299

324

Podocarpus, 143
poplar (*Populus*), 178
silk oak (*Grevillea robusta*), 232, 235
sumac (*Rhus sp.*), 158
   Rhus lancea, 256
sycamore (*Platanus wrightii*), 177
Texas ebony (*Pithecellobium flexicaule*), 54, 221, 291
tree tobacco (*Nicotiana glauca*), 235
western hackberry, palo blanco (*Celtis reticulata*), 177
Xylosma, 219, 220

Trees, evergreen
cedar (*Cedrus*), 177, 297
false cypress (*Chamaecyparis*), 89, 290, 297
Italian cypress (*Cupressus sempervirens*), 89, 143, 177, 221, 290, 297
juniper (*Juniperus*), 177, 221, 257, 290, 301
pine (*Pinus sp.*), 221, 290, 297, 310-313
   aleppo (*Pinus halepensis*), 177, 310-311
   Canary Island (*Pinus canariensis*), 311-312
   Coulter (*Pinus coulteri*), 312
   eldarica (*Pinus eldarica*), 311-312
   Italian stone pine (*Pinus pinea*), 312-313
   Torrey (*Pinus torreyana*), 313

Trees, palm
fan
   California (*Washingtonia filifera*), 151-152
   Guadalupe (*Brahea edulis*), 152
   Hispaniolan (*Sabal blackburniana*), 152
   Mediterranean (*Chamaerops humilis*), 152
   Mexican blue (*Brahea armata*), 105, 152
   Mexican (*Washingtonia robusta*), 152
   Sonoran (*Sabal uresana*), 152
   windmill (*Trachycarpus fortunei*), 152-153
feather
   Canary Island date (*Phoenix canariensis*), 151
   Costa Rican parlor (*Chamaedorea costarcana*), 151
   date (*Phoenix dactylifera*), 151
   queen (*Syagrus romanzoffianum*), 151
   pindo (*Butia capitata*), 151

Vegetables
arugula, 32, 95, 215
asparagus, 32-33, 223, 231, 289
beets, 31, 89, 181, 216, 222, 250, 283
bell peppers, 181, 254
black-eyed peas, 193
bok-choi, 215, 283
broccoli, 32, 216, 251, 283
broccoli-rabe, 32
brussels sprouts, 32, 216, 251, 283
cabbage, 32, 222, 251, 283
carrots, 31, 108, 181, 216, 244, 251, 283
cauliflower, 216, 283
chard, 181, 251
chicory, 215
collard greens, 283
corn (see Grains)
cucumbers, 97, 148, 193, 222
eggplant, 96-97, 160, 181, 193-194, 222, 254
endive, 215, 283
escarole, 215
kale, 59, 181, 222, 248, 251, 283
kohlrabi, 108, 216, 251, 283
leeks, 283
lettuce, 31, 95, 181, 215, 222, 244, 283
mesclun mix, 215
mustard greens, 181, 283
okra, 97
onions
   bunching varieties, 48, 181, 216, 251
   bulb varieties (see Bulbs and corms)
parsnips, 251
peas (see Legumes)
peppers
   chile, 125-126, 160, 165-166, 193-194, 215, 222, 301
   hot, 97, 301
   sweet, 96, 193, 215, 222, 254
pumpkins, 97, 222
radishes, 31, 181, 216, 222, 244, 250
rapini, 32, 216
roquette, 32
spinach, 31, 89, 215, 222, 251, 283
squash, 97, 166, 181, 193, 222
sweet potatoes, 285-287
Swiss chard, 108, 181, 215, 222
tomatillos, 166
tomatoes, 108, 123-124, 142, 181, 193, 215, 222, 254
   blossom drop, 123
   fungal disease, 123-124
   insect pests and treatment, 124-125
   shade cloth, 148
   varieties, recommended, 96
turnips, 31, 181, 216, 222, 244, 250, 283
zucchini, 142

Vines
bougainvillea (*Bougainvillea spectabilis*), 55, 93, 143, 220, 221, 317
cape honeysuckle (*Tecomaria capensis*), 234
Carolina jessamine (*Gelsemium sempervirens*), 55, 226, 292
cat's claw (*Macfadyena unguiscati*), 55
common trumpet creeper (*Campsis radicans*), 55
coral vine (*Antigonon leptopus*), 55
grape (*Vitus*), 27-28, 46-47, 58, 185, 223
honeysuckle (*Lonicera sp.*), 177, 234
   trumpet honeysuckle (*Lonicera sempervirens*), 234
ivy (*Hedera helix*), 143, 227
jasmine (*Jasminum sp.*), 221, 234
Lady Bank's rose (*Rosa banksiae*), 55, 221, 292
morning glory (*Ipomoea tricolor*), 227, 234
   moonflower (*Ipomoea alba*), 73
nasturium (*Tropaeolum*) (see Flowers, annual)
orchid vine (*Mascagnia*), 55
passionflower (*Passiflora incarnata*), 55, 197
pink trumpet vine (*Podranea ricasoliana*), 55, 234
Pyracantha, 55
star jasmine (*Trachelospermum jasminoides*), 55, 177
sweet pea (*Lathyrus sp.*), 227, 250, 305
yellow morning glory (*Merremia tuberosa*), 55
Wisteria, 227

325
∾

Subject Index

A

annual flowers
  fertilizing, 26-27, 170
  planting beds, 24-26, 193-194,
    263-264
  cool season, 5, 60-63, 246-250,
    305
  warm season, 99-104
arbor, 28, 57
arborvitae, 89
arid zone (see xeriscaping)

B

bare-root planting
  fruit trees, 18-20
  grapevines, 46
  roses, 20-22
bats, 297-298
bird netting, 119-120, 155, 266
birds, attracting, 228-230, 287
  hummingbirds, 232-235, 267
  plants, recommended,
    234-235
botanical wreaths, 289-293, *illus.*
  291
butterflies, 195-196
  swallowtails, 70, 138, 196, 241
butterflies, attracting, 194-197,
  267
  plants, recommended, 197

C

cacti, propagating, 81-85, 253
canning, 303
catalogs, mail order, 1, 207,
  299-300
Christmas trees, live, 12, 297-298
cold frames, 40, 83, 243, 254,
  308-309
compost, 25-26, 93, 95, 99, 107,
  111,120, 168, 182, 190-193,
  201, 206, 209, 215, 218, 240,
  264, 274, 305, 316
container gardening
  indoor, 180-184, 187-190,
    285-287
  herbs, recommended, 189
  sprouts, recommended, 183

vegetables, recommended,
  181, 285
outdoor, 139-143, 159, 245-246
  plants, recommended, 143
cottage garden, 107- 110
  plants, recommended,
    108-109
cookbooks, 98
cycads, 220

D

'dig-less' gardening, 243-246
diseases, plant
  fungi
    Aleppo pine blight, 311
    alternaria leaf spot, early
      blight (tomatoes) 123
    anthracnose, 123, 178-179
    bacterial leaf spot (beets,
      lettuce), 283-284
    bacterial necrosis (saguaro),
      154
    club root (brassicas), 283
    gray mold (tomatoes), 123
    gummosis (citrus), 70
    lawn, 179, 184
    mildew, downy (beets), 283
    mildew, powdery (roses), 34
    mushrooms, 179
    oleander gall, 173
    phytopthera, late blight
      (tomatoes), 123
    rot
      bacterial soft (iris, brassi-
        cas), 202, 283-284
      black (brassicas), 283
      blossom-end rot (toma-
        toes), 123-124
      foot (citrus), 70, 254
      root, 283, 314
      Texas root, 176-178, 207,
        235
        immune species, 177
        resistant species, 177-178
        susceptible species, 178
    wilts
      fusarium wilt (tomatoes,
        peas), 123, 284
      verticillium wilt (toma-
        toes), 123

viruses
  Citrus Tristeza (CTV), 69
  curly top (beets), 283
diseases, human, 99
dodder, 174
dormant spray, 20
double digging, 22
drought stress, 171-172, 268

E

El Niño (climate change), 17
erosion control, 160, 256

F

fertilizer, types
  ammonium phosphate, 23,
    25-26, 57, 201, 207, 306
  ammonium sulfate, 45, 58, 190
  blood meal, 26, 45, 58, 98
  bone meal, 23, 25
  cottonseed meal, 98
  Osmocote, 16, 141, 188
  phosphorus, 25
fertilizing
  flowers, annual, 26-27, 170
  lawns, 58, 207, 255, 307
  roses, 20, 22, 43, 57-58, 170
  seeds, 41, 189
  trees
    citrus, 45-46, 71, 120, 206
    deciduous fruit, 47, 120
    palms, 150, 170-171
  vegetables, 25-27, 33, 95, 98,
    170, 245
flowers, annual, cultivation and
  care
  fertilizing, 26-27, 170
  planting beds, 24-26, 99-100,
    159, 265-266
  winter planting, 41-42
flowers, drying, 149
flowers, pressing, 279-280
frost damage, 93, 317
frost protection
  cacti, 281
  citrus, 11, 44, 281
  irrigation system, 282
  landscape plants, 282

326

succulents, 281
vegetables, 63, 282
fruit, drying, 148-149, 292
fruit leather, 149
fungicides
  Bayleton (triadimefon), 34, 179
  Daconil (chlorothalonil), 179
  thiophanate methyl, 34
  travertine, 34
  triflumizole, 34
fungi (see diseases, plant)

G

garlands, 297
gourds, 111-113
grass (see lawn)
greenhouses, 59, 83, 246, 254,
  309-310
ground covers
  container gardening, recom-
    mended, 143
  low-water-use, recommended,
    55
"grow" lights, 40

H

hardscape, 56-57
herbicides (Round-up, Finale),
  35, 58, 207
herb blends, preparing, 301
herb vinegars, preparing, 301-303
herbs, dried, 304
hot beds, 246, 309
houseplants
  cultivation and care, 14
  pest control, 16
  pruning, 15

I

indoor gardening (see container
  gardening)
insecticidal soap, 16, 35, 79, 86, 89,
  124-125, 139, 190, 241, 257, 310
insecticides, 16, 35, 89, 95, 214
  avermectin, 95
  Bacillus thuriengensis (Bt), 71,
    77, 124, 139, 241, 258
  boric acid, 95
  dimethoate, 90
  Disyston, 91
  Kelthane (dicofol), 91
  Malathion, 35, 90
  Neem (Azadirachtin), 124-125
  Nosema locustae, 139
  Orthene (acephate), 35, 91

Pentac, 91
pyrethrum, 35, 89-90, 125,
  202, 310
rotenone, 35, 90, 202
sabadilla, 90
Sevin (carbaryl), 79, 139, 155,
  241
sulfur dust, 125
insects, beneficial, 87-88
insects, pests
  agave weevils, 156
  ants, 94-95, 192, 203
    harvester, 94
    leafcutter, 94-95
  aphids, 182, 202, 214-215, 223,
    257, 284
    arborvitae, 89
    cotton (melon), 89
    gray, 34, 70, 79, 89, 241
    green, 241
    oleander, 89
    rose, 89
    rusty plum, 89
  armyworms, 124, 241
  bees, leafcutter, 139, *illus. 156,*
    156-157
  beetles
    Colorado potato, 124
    flea, 124
    green fruit, 173
    Japanese, 173
    palo verde borer, 157, 174
  bugs
    giant mesquite, 173
    harlequin, 283
    leaf-footed plant, 173, 316
    spittlebugs, 137-138
    stinkbugs, 125
  cabbage loopers, 241, 284
  cabbage worms, 284
  carrot rust flies, 284
  cicadas, 157
  cochineal scale, 172
  fungus gnats, 18, 182-183, 190
  grape leaf skeletonizers, 138, 155
  grasshoppers, 139, 202, 240, 316
  grubs, 202
  hornworms (caterpillars),
    124-125, 138, 240-241
  leaf miners, 284
  leafhoppers, 90, 139, 316
  maggots, cabbage root, 284
  mites, 125
  roaches, 192
  spider mites, 91, 138-139, 257,
    314
  termites, 203

thrips, 20, 223, 314
wasps, 157
web worms, 158
whiteflies, 90, 125, 182, 190, 241
wireworms, 284
interplanting, rose gardens,
  313-316
iron chlorosis, 45
irrigation, 10-12, 44-45, 107,
  147, 172
  Ak Chin (Native American)
    method, 167-168
  annual flowers, 25-26
  asparagus, 33
  citrus, 10, 11, 268
  color beds, 10
  cottage garden, 107- 110
  deciduous fruit trees, 19-20
  desert-adapted plants, 11
  evergreens, 10
  exotics, 10
  grapes, 47
  herbs, 10
  lawn, 10, 52-53, 58, 154, 179,
    184, 255, 306-307
  native plants, 11, 224
  palm trees, 10, 150
  pine trees, 311
  roses, 58
  succulents, 11
  vegetables, 10, 25-26, 184, 217
irrigation system
  freeze protection, 282
  installation and care, 36-37, 107
  time and amount, 53

J

journal, garden, 4-5, 217, 317

L

La Niña (climate change), 17
lawns, 254-255, 306-307
  dethatching, 180, 255
  fertilizing, 58, 207, 255, 307
  fungal infection, 179, 184, 307
  irrigating, 10, 52-53, 154, 184,
    255, 307
  proper mowing height, 255
lemon curd, 303-304
low-water-use plants, recommended, 53-55
  ground covers, 55
  shrubs, 54
  trees, 54
  vines, 55

327

M

mail order catalogs (see catalogs, mail order)
manure, 25-26, 33, 85, 98-99, 111, 121, 137, 177, 179, 191, 194, 201, 209, 311
mini oasis (see xeriscaping)
monsoon, 168-171, 174
mulch, 26-27, 56, 120, 168, 240, 254, 311, 317

N

Native Americans, 25, 165-168, 224, 239
    Akimel O'odham, 167
    Hopi, 165-166
    Pueblo, 165
    Tohono O'odham, 165, 167-168
NZN (see zinc)

P

perennial flowers
    container gardening plants, recommended, 143
pesticides (see insecticides)
planning future landscape projects, 60-61
plant stress
    drought, 171-172, 268
    sun, 171
planting, successive, 283-285
planting beds
    annual flowers and vegetables, 24-27, 33, 95, 98, 159, 170, 193-194, 244-245, 305-306
    herbs, 194, 217-219, 244-245
    raised beds, 24-25, 57, 243-245
    wildflowers, 265-266, 305-306
poisonous plants, 225-227
potted plants (see container gardening)
potting up houseplants, 15
pruning, 5-10, 168-170
    proper technique
        flowers, deadheading, 184-185
        fruit trees, 7-10, *illus. 8*
        grapevines, 27-28, *illus. 28,* 58, 185, 292
        houseplants, 15
        palm trees, 271
        pecan trees, 79
        roses, 42-43, *illus. 42,* 213-214
        Texas mountain laurel, 77

topiary, 113-114
trees and shrubs, 5, 7, *illus. 8,* 79, 80, 93, 271, 317

R

rabbits, controlling, 231, 259
    resistant plants, recommended, 231-232
ramada, 56-57, 229
Roadrunner, greater, 229, *illus. 229*
rodents, controlling, 230
roses, care
    bed preparation, 22
    deadheading, 58, 184, 214
    fertilizing, 20, 22, 43, 57-58, 170
    floribundas, recommended, 21
    hybrid teas, recommended, 21-22
    pruning, 42-43, *illus. 42*
    winter care, 42

S

seed starting, 39
    sprouting medium, 40, 187-188
    fertilizing, 41, 189
    hardening off, 41
shade cloth, 97, 147-148, 171
shrubs
    container gardening, 143
    low-water-use, recommended, 54-55
    pruning, 93, 317
    topiary, 113-114
slugs and snails, 202
soil
    caliche, 23, 76
    clay, 23, 76
    hardpan, 23
    mixes, 136-137
    probe, 11, 53, 172
    solorization, 149
    sulfur, 25
sprouts, 182-184
succulents, propagating, 81-85, 253
sulfur spray, 34
sun damage
    sun stress, 171
    sunscald, 147
    wilt, 147, 172
swimming pools, 220-221

T

tools, gardening, 30
    lawnmower, 30, 306
    pruning sheers, 6, 30

tools, proper care, 29-30
    disinfecting, 9, 15, 42, 111, 154, 173, 202, 207
    sharpening, 30, 42, 214, 289
topiary, 113-114
transitional zone (see xeriscaping)
trees, citrus, cultivation and care
    damage, 43
    fertilizing, 45-46, 71, 120, 206
    fruit drop, 148, 185
    fungus, 70
    irrigating, 120, 148, 268
    planting, 64, 70
    pruning, 7-10, *illus. 8*
    rootstock, 66
    soil, importance of drainage, 65
    temperture range, 65
trees, deciduous fruit, cultivation and care
    fertilizing, 47, 120
    irrigating, 120
    mulching, 120, 317
    planting, 19, 252
    thinning, 80-81
trees, low-water-use, recommended, 54
trees, palm, cultivation and care
    fertilizing, 150, 170-171
    irrigating, 150
    pruning, 271
turf (see lawns)

V

vegetables, planting beds, 24-26, 31, 122, 193-194, 215, 222
vegetables, fertilizing, 25-27, 33, 95, 98, 170, 245
vines, low-water-use, recommended, 55

W

water harvesting, 174-176
weeds, 35, 170, 207, 223, 306-308
wildflowers, 263-267
wildlife, 227-232
wind
    damage, 168-169
    drying effects, 17, 267
wrought iron, 57

X

xeriscaping, 51-56

Z

zinc, 88-89, 202

328